Resource Management

Richard Mc Dougall
Adrian Cockcroft
Evert Hoogendoorn
Enrique Vargas
Tom Bialaski

Sun Microsystems Press
A Prentice Hall Title

© 1999 Sun Microsystems, Inc.—
Printed in the United States of America.
901 San Antonio Road
Palo Alto, California 94303 U.S.A.

All rights reserved. This product or document is protected by copyright and distributed under licenses restricting its use, copying, distribution, and decompilation. No part of this product or document may be reproduced in any form by any means without prior written authorization of Sun and its licensors, if any. Third-party software, including font technology, is copyrighted and licensed from Sun suppliers.

Parts of the product may be derived from Berkeley BSD systems, licensed from the University of California. UNIX is a registered trademark in the U.S. and other countries, exclusively licensed through X/Open Company, Ltd.

Sun, Sun Microsystems, the Sun logo, AnswerBook, Java, the Java Coffee Cup, and Solaris are trademarks or registered trademarks of Sun Microsystems, Inc. in the U.S. and certain other countries. Oracle is a registerd trademark of Oracle Corporation. Load Sharing Facility (LSF) is a registered trademark of Platform Computing Corporation. All other product names mentioned herein are the trademarks of their respective owners. All SPARC trademarks are used under license and are trademarks or registered trademarks of SPARC International, Inc. in the U.S. and other countries. Products bearing SPARC trademarks are based upon an architecture developed by Sun Microsystems, Inc.

The OPEN LOOK and Sun™ Graphical User Interface was developed by Sun Microsystems, Inc. for its users and licensees. Sun acknowledges the pioneering efforts of Xerox in researching and developing the concept of visual or graphical user interfaces for the computer industry. Sun holds a non-exclusive license from Xerox to the Xerox Graphical User Interface, which license also covers Sun's licensees who implement OPEN LOOK GUIs and otherwise comply with Sun's written license agreements.

RESTRICTED RIGHTS: Use, duplication, or disclosure by the U.S. Government is subject to restrictions of FAR 52.227-14(g)(2)(6/87) and FAR 52.227-19(6/87), or DFAR 252.227-7015(b)(6/95) and DFAR 227.7202-3(a).

DOCUMENTATION IS PROVIDED "AS IS" AND ALL EXPRESS OR IMPLIED CONDITIONS, REPRESENTATIONS, AND WARRANTIES, INCLUDING ANY IMPLIED WARRANTY OF MERCHANTABILITY, FITNESS FOR A PARTICULAR PURPOSE, OR NON-INFRINGEMENT, ARE DISCLAIMED, EXCEPT TO THE EXTENT THAT SUCH DISCLAIMERS ARE HELD TO BE LEGALLY INVALID.

The publisher offers discounts on this book when ordered in bulk quantities. For more information, contact: Corporate Sales Department, Phone: 800-382-3419; Fax: 201-236-7141; E-mail: corpsales@prenhall.com; or write: Prentice Hall PTR, Corp. Sales Dept., One Lake Street, Upper Saddle River, NJ 07458.

Editorial/production superviser: *Faye Gemmellaro*
Cover design director: *Jerry Votta*
Cover designer: *Kavish & Kavish Digital Publishing & Design*
Manufacturing manager: *Alexis R. Heydt*
Marketing manager: *Bryan Gambrel*
Acquisitions editor: *Gregory G. Doench*
Sun Microsystems Press:
Marketing manager: *Michael Llwyd Alread*
Publisher: *Rachel Borden*

10 9 8 7 6 5 4 3 2

ISBN 0-13-025855-5

Sun Microsystems Press
A Prentice Hall Title

Contents

Acknowledgments xxi

Preface xxiii
Sun BluePrints Program   xxiii
Who Should Use This Book   xxiv
How This Book Is Organized   xxiv
Related Books   xxv
What Typographic Changes Mean   xxvi
Shell Prompts in Command Examples   xxvii

Part I.   Architecture

1. **Introduction   1**
   Business Problems   1
   Scope   2

2. **Service Level Management   3**
   Service Level Definitions
      and Interactions   3
      System Level Requirements   4
      Sizing Estimates   4
      Service Level Agreements   5

Real User Experiences 5

Service Level Measurements 5

Policies and Controls 6

Resource Management Control Loop 7

A Simple Approach to Control Theory 8

Viewpoints of Resource Management 9

Diverse Methods 9

The System-Centric Viewpoint 10

The Cluster-Centric Viewpoint 11

The Network-Centric Viewpoint 12

Storage-Centric Viewpoint 13

Database-Centric Viewpoint 15

Application-Centric Viewpoint 15

Integrated Methods 16

The Consolidation Process 17

3. **Policies and Controls 19**

Policy Types 19

Controls 22

Standardized Policy Definitions 23

Subsystem Policies and Controls 25

User-Level Controls 25

Application-Level Controls 26

CPU Power-Level Controls 26

Disk I/O Policies 27

Disk Space 27

Virtual Memory 27

Relationship Between Virtual Memory and Swap Space 29

Physical Memory 30

Network Interfaces and Network Services 34

4. **Workload Management** 35

Workload Analysis Tools 35

Sun Enterprise SyMON 2.0 Software 36

Workload Analysis Products 49

Customized Process Monitors 50

Internet Service Provider Workloads 55

Proxy Web Cache Workload 56

Virtual Web Hosting 60

Managing Web Servers with SRM Software 61

Commercial Workloads 65

Workload Consolidation 65

Database Workloads 71

Database Consolidation 74

Databases in a Resource Managed Environment 77

Database Resource Management Compatibility 78

Resource Manager of the Oracle Database 80

Resource Manager of the Informix Database 85

Batch Workloads 85

Resources Used by Batch Workloads 86

5. **Workload Measurements** 87

The SE Toolkit 87

Measurement Levels 88

The Application Resource Measurement Standard 89

SAP R/3 Measurements 89

Internet Server Measurements 90

　　　　　Configuring and Monitoring a Proxy Cache   90

　　　　　Internet Servers Summary   93

　　Process Information   94

　　　　　Data Access Permissions   97

　　　　　Microstate Accounting   97

　　Accounting   100

　　　　　Solaris Resource Manager Accounting   102

　　　　　Network Accounting Using NetFlow   103

　　Storage Measurements   104

　　　　　Disk Workloads   104

　　　　　Output Formats and Options for `iostat`   105

　　　　　Understanding I/O Measurements   109

　　Network Measurements   116

　　　　　Network Throughput   116

　　　　　Ethernet Statistics   116

　　　　　Protocol Statistics   118

Part II.   Products

6.   Solaris Operating Environment   121

　　When to Use Basic Solaris Features   121

　　　　　Relationship to Other Resource Control Features   121

　　Processor Partitioning   122

　　　　　Processor Sets   123

　　　　　Published Dual TPC-C and TPC-D Results   126

　　　　　How Process Partitioning Works   127

　　Limits   128

　　Disk Quotas   130

　　Configurable Kernel Limits   132

7. **Solaris Resource Manager Software**   135

   When to Use SRM Software   135

       Relationship to Other Solaris Resource Control Features   136

   Solaris Resource Manager Functions   138

       Solaris Resource Manager Policies   138

       Controls Available with SRM Software   140

       Measurement   143

       System Resource Accounting Information   144

   Workload Configuration   145

       Mapping the Workload to the lnode Hierarchy   145

       A Simple Flat Hierarchy   145

   Decay Factors and Parameters   164

       Decay Algorithms   165

       Setting Decay and Scheduler Parameters   176

   Performance and Scalability Factors   185

       Hierarchy Tree Depth   185

       Kernel Memory   185

   Monitoring SRM Software   185

   System Resource Accounting Information   186

       Billing Issues   186

       Extracting Accounting Data   187

8. **Dynamic System Domains and Dynamic Reconfiguration**   193

   Dynamic System Domains   193

       When to Use Dynamic System Domains   194

       DSD Implementation Examples   197

   Resource Management Controls   199

       Managing Resources with Starfire DR   200

Starfire DR-Detach and DR-Attach Timing Reference   201

DR with and without DSDs   202

Clustered DSDs   206

Starfire Architecture   208

Starfire DR Architecture   211

Starfire DR-Detach Details   212

Starfire DR-Attach Details   216

DR I/O Device Driver Requirements   220

9. Solaris Bandwidth Manager Software   223

The Need for Bandwidth Management   223

    Examples of When to Use Bandwidth Management   224

    End-to-End Quality of Service   225

How Bandwidth Allocation Works   227

    Borrowing Bandwidth   228

    Flows   229

    Type of Service Packet Marking   230

    HTTP Support   232

When to Use Solaris Bandwidth Manager   233

    Relationship to Other Resource Management Products   233

Where to Deploy Solaris Bandwidth Manager   234

    Server Mode   234

    IP-Transparent Mode   235

Solaris Bandwidth Manager Architecture   237

    Java Dynamic Management Kit   238

    The Administration Tool   239

    The Policy Agent   240

LDAP Directory Integration   241

Directory Enabled Networks   242

Monitoring, Accounting, and Billing   243

    Statistics   244

    Monitoring Statistics   244

    Interface with Accounting and Billing   244

Customizing and Extending Solaris Bandwidth Manager Software   247

10. Load Sharing Facility Software   249

When to Use LSF   249

    Good Workload Candidates for LSF Software   250

    Commercial Applications   251

Relationship to Other Solaris Resource Control Features   251

    Base Solaris Software   252

    Solaris Resource Manager Software   253

    Dynamic System Domains   253

    Dynamic Reconfiguration   253

    Other Third-Party Batch Management Systems   254

LSF Resource Management Viewpoint   254

    LSF Cluster Viewpoint   254

LSF Functions   255

    Establishing Policies   255

    Resource Controls   257

    Monitoring Resource Usage   262

    Exceptions and Alarms   263

    Job Starters   264

Analyzing Workloads   265

LSF Workload Configuration   265

    Setting Correct Permissions   267

High Availability Features   268

Parallel Jobs with Sun HPC   269

    Parallel Job Support in LSF Software   269

Other Similar Products   271

11. The Jiro Initiative   273

The Storage Management Problem   273

Storage Solution Requirements   274

The Jiro Solution   275

Jiro and Resource Management Possibilities   276

Jiro Architecture   276

    Object Model   277

The Java Community Process   278

Momentum Behind Jiro   279

12. Sun Enterprise SyMON 2.0 Software   281

When to Use SyMON Software   281

    SyMON Software Availability and Support   281

SyMON Software Architecture   282

Resource Monitoring with SyMON Software   283

    The SyMON Health Monitor   283

    Handling Alarms in SyMON Software   287

    Process Monitoring with SyMON Software   292

    Browsing Configuration Information   292

13. IBM Workload Manager for OS/390   297

Mainframe Data Center Resource Management   297

Workload Manager Overview   298

    WLM Modes of Operation   298

Defining Service Policies within WLM   299

WLM Components   301

WLM Control Architecture   302

    Gathering Metrics   303

    The Performance Index   303

    Component and Server Topology   304

    Policy Adjustment   304

Typical Uses for WLM   307

Glossary   309

Index   327

Figures

FIGURE 2-1	Service Level Management Interactions	4
FIGURE 2-2	Resource Management Control Loop	7
FIGURE 2-3	Example Control Loop	8
FIGURE 2-4	Storage Area Network	14
FIGURE 2-5	Integrated Methodology by Viewpoint	16
FIGURE 3-1	Example Policy Architecture	24
FIGURE 3-2	Determining Solaris Process Limits	25
FIGURE 3-3	Three Levels of Virtual Memory Limits	29
FIGURE 3-4	Swap Usage Only Accounts for Shared Segments Once	30
FIGURE 3-5	Memory Allocation with `netscape` and `gimp`	31
FIGURE 3-6	Memory Allocation with `netscape` and `dtmail`	32
FIGURE 3-7	Memory Allocation with Priority Paging Enabled	33
FIGURE 4-1	Sun Enterprise SyMON 2.0 Main Console Window	36
FIGURE 4-2	Sun Enterprise SyMON 2.0 Load Solaris Process Details Module	37
FIGURE 4-3	Process Details Module Parameters	38
FIGURE 4-4	Sun Enterprise SyMON 2.0 Process Details Window	39
FIGURE 4-5	Selecting the Process Monitoring Option	40
FIGURE 4-6	Process Monitor Parameters Setup	41
FIGURE 4-7	Unconfigured Process Monitoring Display	42

FIGURE 4-8	Adding a Row to the Process Monitor	43
FIGURE 4-9	Setting Up Process Details for a Row	44
FIGURE 4-10	Complex Pattern Specification for a Row	45
FIGURE 4-11	Initial Process Monitoring Display	46
FIGURE 4-12	Optimized Layout Process Monitoring Display	47
FIGURE 4-13	Process Monitoring Alarm Configuration	48
FIGURE 4-14	Workload Graph Example	49
FIGURE 4-15	Output from the `pea.se` Command	51
FIGURE 4-16	Output from the `-DWIDE pea.se` Command	52
FIGURE 4-17	Example Output from pw.se	53
FIGURE 4-18	Sample `pw.se` Configuration Script	54
FIGURE 4-19	Example Output from Configured pw.se	54
FIGURE 4-20	Sample Process Monitoring Rule	55
FIGURE 4-21	Direct Web Service without Proxy Cache	57
FIGURE 4-22	Indirect Web Service	58
FIGURE 4-23	Resource Management of a Consolidated Web Server	62
FIGURE 4-24	Resource Management of a Single Web Server	63
FIGURE 4-25	Solaris Web Server Parameter File	64
FIGURE 4-26	Practical Example with a Database Server and a Decision Support Process	72
FIGURE 4-27	Transaction Flow and Resource Management Product Assignment	72
FIGURE 4-28	Consolidation of Two Databases with Solaris Resource Manager	75
FIGURE 4-29	Oracle8i Resource Manager	80
FIGURE 4-30	Using Processor Sets or Domains to Allow Oracle8i Resource Manager	84
FIGURE 5-1	Log-to-Log Plot of Response Time Versus Size	92
FIGURE 5-2	Perspective Log-Log Plot of Response Time Versus Size Distribution	93
FIGURE 5-3	Process Information Used as Input by the `ps` Command	94
FIGURE 5-4	Additional Microstate-Based Process Information	95
FIGURE 5-5	Summary of Microstate Process Data Reported by `msacct.se`	97

FIGURE 5-6	Combined Process Information from SE Toolkit Process Class	98
FIGURE 5-7	Accounting Data Format	102
FIGURE 5-8	`iostat -x` Output	105
FIGURE 5-9	Simple Old Disk Model	109
FIGURE 5-10	Two-Stage Disk Model Used by Solaris 2	110
FIGURE 5-11	Kernel Disk Information Statistics Data Structure	111
FIGURE 5-12	SE-Based Rewrite of `iostat` to Show Service Time Correctly	114
FIGURE 5-13	Complex I/O Device Queue Model	115
FIGURE 6-1	Example Systemwide Resource Limits Shown by `sysdef`	128
FIGURE 6-2	Per Shell Current and Hard Limits	128
FIGURE 6-3	Setting for System V shared Memory Size Limit	132
FIGURE 6-4	Setting for Maximum User Process Count Limit	133
FIGURE 6-5	Monitoring Process Count Settings	133
FIGURE 7-1	Accounting Based on the Workload Hierarchy	144
FIGURE 7-2	A Simple Flat Solaris Resource Manager Hierarchy	145
FIGURE 7-3	Creating Online and Batch Shares with Solaris Resource Manager Software	151
FIGURE 7-4	Consolidation of Two Databases with Solaris Resource Manager Software	152
FIGURE 7-5	OLTP Application Using SRM to Separate Batch and Interactive Users	153
FIGURE 7-6	Managing Resources on a Consolidated Web Server	156
FIGURE 7-7	Fine Grained Resource Management of a Single Web Server	157
FIGURE 7-8	Solaris Web Server Parameter File	158
FIGURE 7-9	A Hierarchy Allowing Policies by Executable Name	159
FIGURE 7-10	Simple Combination of Solaris Resource Manager and Processor Sets	161
FIGURE 7-11	Complex Combination of Solaris Resource Manager and Processor Sets	162
FIGURE 7-12	Something to Avoid: Users Spanning Multiple Processor Sets	163
FIGURE 7-13	Effect of Decay Time on Allocation Fairness	166
FIGURE 7-14	Two Levels of Scheduling in SRM	167
FIGURE 7-15	Effect of Decay on Process Priority	167

FIGURE 7-16	Process Priority Decay with Two Different `nice` Values	169
FIGURE 7-17	Process Priority Increase and Decay	170
FIGURE 7-18	Comparison of Usage Decay and Priority Decay	171
FIGURE 7-19	CPU Allocation with Controlled Instantaneous Use	172
FIGURE 7-20	CPU Allocation with Decay to Include Usage History	173
FIGURE 7-21	Throughput of a User Starting Affected by Decay	175
FIGURE 7-22	Effect of Maximum User Share Clamping (default maxushare=2)	181
FIGURE 7-23	Effect of Setting `maxushare` to 10	182
FIGURE 7-24	The Effect of the `maxushare` with Group Scheduler Enabled	183
FIGURE 7-25	Life Cycle of Usage Data	187
FIGURE 7-26	A Sample Hierarchy	188
FIGURE 8-1	DSDs Implementation Examples	197
FIGURE 8-2	The SSP Hostview `drview` Application	205
FIGURE 8-3	The SSP `dr` Monitor Application	205
FIGURE 8-4	DSD Clustering Options	207
FIGURE 8-5	The SSP Network Connection	208
FIGURE 8-6	DSD Representation by SSP's Hostview GUI Application	210
FIGURE 8-7	Solaris 7 5/99 Starfire DR Software Architecture	211
FIGURE 8-8	DR-Detaching a Single System Board from a DSD	216
FIGURE 8-9	DR-Attaching a System Board to a DSD	219
FIGURE 8-10	I/O Device Tree Representation	221
FIGURE 9-1	Hierarchical Class Definitions	227
FIGURE 9-2	Bandwidth Allocation	228
FIGURE 9-3	IP Type of Service Byte	231
FIGURE 9-4	DS Header Field	231
FIGURE 9-5	Server Mode	235
FIGURE 9-6	IP-Transparent Mode	236
FIGURE 9-7	Solaris Bandwidth Manager Architecture	238

FIGURE 9-8	Policy Agent Components 240
FIGURE 9-9	Graphical Depiction of Statistical Information 243
FIGURE 9-10	Solaris Bandwidth Manager Converts Accounting Information to ASCII 245
FIGURE 9-11	Solaris Bandwidth Manager Working with NetFlow FlowCollector 246
FIGURE 9-12	Solaris Bandwidth Manager Using Local Application 247
FIGURE 10-1	LSF Scheduler Components 263
FIGURE 10-2	LSF Cluster Configuration 266
FIGURE 10-3	LSF Failover Features 268
FIGURE 10-4	Job Execution Flow of a Parallel Application 270
FIGURE 11-1	Jiro Architecture 277
FIGURE 12-1	SyMON Software Architecture 282
FIGURE 12-2	The SyMON Software Console 284
FIGURE 12-3	Load Health Monitor Module 285
FIGURE 12-4	Host Details Window 286
FIGURE 12-5	The SyMON Software Domain Console 287
FIGURE 12-6	Domain Status Details Window 288
FIGURE 12-7	Alarm Details Window 289
FIGURE 12-8	Acknowledged Alarms 290
FIGURE 12-9	Refreshed Domain Status Details Window 291
FIGURE 12-10	The SyMON Software Domain Console with No Alarms 291
FIGURE 12-11	Detailed Configuration Window 292
FIGURE 12-12	Logical View of Hardware Configuration Tree 293
FIGURE 12-13	Physical View of Rear of System 294
FIGURE 12-14	Board Level Physical View 295

Tables

TABLE P-1	Typographic Conventions	xxvi
TABLE P-2	Shell Prompts	xxvii
TABLE 4-1	NFS Workload Resources	66
TABLE 4-2	Database Resource Management Vendor Support	78
TABLE 4-3	Company XYZ Resource Plan	81
TABLE 4-4	Order Entry Subplan	82
TABLE 4-5	Company XYZ Resource Plan	82
TABLE 7-1	Solaris Resource Manager Functions	138
TABLE 7-2	SRM Scheduler Parameters	176
TABLE 7-3	Identifiers to the `limreport` Command	190
TABLE 7-4	Operators to the `limreport` Command	191
TABLE 8-1	Dynamic Reconfiguration Functionality Matrix	199
TABLE 9-1	Example of Borrowing Bandwidth	229
TABLE 10-1	Internal Load Indices Collected by the LSF Software	259
TABLE 10-2	Static Resources Reported by the LSF Software	261

Acknowledgments

Any large work is achieved with the help of many who work behind the scenes. This book could not be what it is today without the extraordinary efforts and dedication of all who are mentioned here.

Special thanks to Charles Alexander for providing the inspiration, vision, and opportunity for the Sun BluePrints Program. A very special thanks to Mark Connelly and Anne Schowe for supporting it.

Thanks to those who took the time to review and comment on the text: Brad Carlile, Kevin Colwell, Ian Griffin, Neil Gunther, Keng-Tai Ko, Jeannie Johnstone-Kobert, Sandra Lee, Jean-Christophe Martin, Jeff McMeekin, Rajiv Parikh, Ravi Pendekanti, Eric Pilmore, Paul Strong for the WLM chapter (he could almost be listed as an author), Martin Tuori (of Platform Computing Corporation), Amanda West, Brian Wong, and Alison Wyld.

Thank you to the folks at Oracle Corporation, especially Mark Smith, who together with Sumanta Chatterjee and Ann Rhee, spent an enormous amount of time to ensure that the Oracle material is accurate and reflects our combined vision. Thanks to Ganesh Ramamurthy, Allan Packer, Tony Li, and other members of Sun's database engineering team for the time and effort put into testing databases with Solaris Resource Manager.

Thanks to Barb Jugo, whose tireless coordination pulled the Sun BluePrints Program together and made it all happen. Thanks to Alice Kemp, James Langdell, and Shuroma Herekar for their publications and editorial expertise. Thanks to Gabe Camarillo and Jennifer Chan for illustrating the book. Thanks to Stan Stringfellow for his work on the glossary. Thanks to Kavish & Kavish for their above-and-beyond effort in the cover artwork.

Finally, a personal thanks to our families for enduring many months of our distraction at home while we focused on this book, working late hours and weekends. Thanks especially to Evert Hoogendoorn's wife, Michele, and their daughter, Alice, who decided to be born during the holiday break. Thanks to Richard Mc Dougall's wife, Traci, for all the encouragement to write, and for keeping him sane. Thanks to Enrique Vargas's wife, Michelle, who provided an audience for his SE-TV rehearsals as well as other valued assistance, and to his daughters Saralynn and Christine for their patience and understanding.

The Resource Management BluePrint Team:

Richard Mc Dougall,

Adrian Cockcroft,

Enrique Vargas,

Evert Hoodendoorn,

Tom Bialaski.

Preface

This book is one of an on-going series of books collectively known as the Sun BluePrints™ Program. The Sun BluePrints Program is managed by the Enterprise Engineering Group. This group provides a framework to identify, develop, and distribute best practices information that applies across Sun products for the data center. This *Resource Management BluePrint* describes the best practices for combinations of products to manage resources.

Sun BluePrints Program

The mission of the Sun BluePrints Program is to empower Sun customers with the technical knowledge required to implement reliable, available, extensible, and secure information systems within the data center using Sun products. The Sun BluePrints Program is managed by the Enterprise Engineering Group. This group provides a framework to identify, develop, and distribute best practices information that applies across the Sun product line. Technical subject matter experts in various areas contribute to the program and focus on the scope and usefulness of the information.

The Enterprise Engineering Group is the primary provider of the technical content of the Sun BluePrints Program that includes books, guides, and online articles. Through these vehicles, Sun can provide guidance, installation and implementation experiences, real-life scenarios, and late-breaking technical information.

The bimonthly electronic magazine, Sun BluePrints OnLine, is located on the Web at `http://www.sun.com/blueprints`. To be notified about updates to the Sun BluePrints Program, please register yourself on this site.

Who Should Use This Book

This book is for experienced system administrators familiar with UNIX® and the Solaris™ operating environment.

How This Book Is Organized

This book is divided into two major sections.

Part I, "Architecture," describes the overall architecture of resource management solutions. It introduces policy definition and resource control and describes a selection of workloads and common methods of measurement. It contains the following chapters:

Chapter 1 "Introduction, "Introduction," introduces the business problems that resource management addresses and explains the scope of this book.

Chapter 2 "Service Level Management, "Methodology," defines the overall methodology of service level management so that the resource management component can be put into a wider context. It also describes and compares several different approaches to resource management.

Chapter 3 "Policies and Controls, "Policy and Controls," examines a range of policy and control types and ways to implement them, then looks at each subsystem in turn to see what resources can be managed.

Chapter 4 "Workload Management, "Workload Management," describes several scenarios to illustrate the diversity of real life situations and the different tools that are appropriate.

Chapter 5 "Workload Measurements, "Workload Measurements," discusses the measurement sources that are important for resource management and the detailed meaning of some of the available measurements.

Part II, "Products," describes the products available for resource management and explains how they work alone and together. It contains the following chapters:

Chapter 6 "Solaris Operating Environment "Solaris Operating Environment," discusses the Solaris operating environment, focusing on several standard capabilities that are useful for resource management.

Chapter 7 "Solaris Resource Manager Software "Solaris Resource Manager Software," discusses the Solaris Resource Manager (SRM) software, which provides the ability to allocate and control major system resources.

Chapter 8 "Dynamic System Domains and Dynamic Reconfiguration, "Dynamic Systems Domains and Dynamic Reconfiguration," discusses the Dynamic Systems Domains and Dynamic Reconfiguration within the framework of resource management.

Chapter 9 "Solaris Bandwidth Manager Software, "Solaris Bandwidth Manager Software," explains how to use this product as part of a resource control framework.

Chapter 10 "Load Sharing Facility Software, "Load Sharing Facility Software," explains how to deploy LSF as a resource management tool and how it interoperates with other Solaris resource management controls.

Chapter 11 "The Jiro Initiative, "Jiro and Resource Management," describes this product in detail and explains how to use it as part of a resource control framework.

Chapter 12 "Sun Enterprise SyMON 2.0 Software, "Sun Enterprise SyMON 2.0 Software," describes when and how to use this product for monitoring resources.

Chapter 13 "IBM Workload Manager for OS/390, "IBM Workload Manager," provides an overview of what is possible with extensive use of resource management and serves as a guide to help design long term resource management goals for application developers.

Glossary is a list of words and phrases found in this book and their definitions.

Related Books

The following books provide information that you may also find useful:

Title	Author and Publisher	ISBN Number
Sun Performance and Tuning (2nd Edition)	Adrian Cockroft and Richard Pettit, Sun Microsystems Press/Prentice Hall: 1998	ISBN 0-13-095249-4

Title	Author and Publisher	ISBN Number
Configuration and Capacity Planning for Solaris Servers	Brian L. Wong, Sun Microsystems Press/Prentice Hall: 1997	ISBN 0-13-349952-9
Solaris Survival Guide for Windows NT Administrators	Tom Bialaski, Prentice Hall, Inc.: 1999	ISBN 0-13-025854-7
Guide to High Availability: Configuring boot/root/swap	Jeannie Johnstone, Prentice Hall, Inc.: 1999	ISBN 0-13-016306-6

What Typographic Changes Mean

The following table describes the typographic changes used in this book.

TABLE P-1 Typographic Conventions

Typeface or Symbol	Meaning	Example
AaBbCc123	The names of commands, files, and directories; on-screen computer output	Edit your .login file. Use ls -a to list all files. machine_name% You have mail.
AaBbCc123	What you type, contrasted with on-screen computer output	machine_name% **su** Password:
AaBbCc123	Command-line placeholder: replace with a real name or value	To delete a file, type rm *filename*.
AaBbCc123	Book titles, new words or terms, or words to be emphasized	Read Chapter 6 in *User's Guide*. These are called *class* options. You *must* be root to do this.

xxvi   Resource Management

Shell Prompts in Command Examples

The following table shows the default system prompt and superuser prompt for the C shell, Bourne shell, and Korn shell.

TABLE P-2   Shell Prompts

Shell	Prompt
C shell prompt	`machine_name%`
C shell superuser prompt	`machine_name#`
Bourne shell and Korn shell prompt	`$`
Bourne shell and Korn shell superuser prompt	`#`

PART I Architecture

This section describes the overall architecture of resource management solutions. It introduces policy definition and resource control and describes a selection of workloads and common methods of measurement.

CHAPTER 1

Introduction

This chapter introduces the business problems that resource management addresses and explains the scope of this book.

Business Problems

If you work in a large data center environment, the following questions might be familiar to you.

- The data center is full of systems. Many of those systems are lightly used, and more applications are always waiting to be brought online. There is no room to add more systems, and the available systems are getting more powerful. How can we add a new application to an existing system, without affecting the level of service provided to its users?
- There are so many small server systems that they are a nightmare to manage. Each server has its own custom setup, and unlike an environment containing desktop machines, it's hard to automate a cloned installation process. How can we combine lots of small servers into a few big ones?
- Very large systems are installed in the data center, and many applications share their resources. How can we measure and control these applications to meet a service level agreement (SLA) that we have with users?
- The Solaris operating environment is being installed as a replacement for mainframes running MVS. How can mainframe techniques be applied to a UNIX system? What is the same and what is new?
- Sun provides a base-level operating environment with many facilities and several unbundled products that extend its capability. How can we tell what combinations of products work together to solve our business problems?

These are the questions answered by this book.

Scope

The scope of this book can be summarized as:

- The best way to use combinations of Sun Microsystems products to manage resources.
- Generic resource management concepts and methods.
- Comparison of UNIX system practices with mainframe class practices.

Sun's range of products provide a lot of built-in flexibility that can be deployed in many ways to meet the requirements of several markets. The documentation for these product covers all the options but normally provides only basic information about how these product can be used with other products. This book, on the other hand, focuses on resource management, looks at products that are relevant, gives detailed and specific information about how to choose the right set of products and features to solve resource management problems.

To solve the problem, products must fit into an overall methodology that addresses the processes of workload consolidation and service level management. The principles are explained with reference to tools and products that can help implement each scenario. To manage the service level you provide, you must be able to measure and control the resources consumed by it.

Resource management is an established discipline in the mainframe operations arena. As Solaris systems are deployed in the data center, mainframe staff must figure out how to apply existing management practices to these unfamiliar systems. One of the common complaints voiced by mainframe staff confronted with UNIX systems is that they don't have the measurement data they need to do capacity planning and performance management properly. These techniques are critical parts of a consolidation and resource management process. Thus, this book provides detailed information on the tools and measurements available for Solaris systems. The Solaris operating environment is one of the best instrumented UNIX implementations, and it is supported by all the vendors of performance tools. However, not all commercial tools report Solaris-specific metrics.

Resource management for UNIX systems is in its infancy compared to common practices under MVS. We are all trying to solve the same set of problems. So over time, the Solaris operating environment will provide comparable resource and service level management features.

CHAPTER 2

Service Level Management

This chapter describes the overall methodology of service level management so that the resource management component can be put into a wider context. It also describes and compares several approaches to resource management.

Service Level Definitions and Interactions

This section starts with a high level view of service level management and defines a terminology that is based on existing practices.

Computer systems are used to provide a service to end users. System and application vendors provide a range of components that can be used to construct a service. System managers are responsible for the quality of this service. A service must be available when it is needed and must have acceptable performance characteristics.

Service level management is the process by which information technology (IT) infrastructure is planned, designed, and implemented to provide the levels of functionality, performance, and availability required to meet business or organizational demands.

Service level management involves interactions between end users, system managers, vendors and computer systems. A common way to capture some of these interactions is with a service level agreement (SLA) between the system managers and the end users. Often, many additional interactions and assumptions are not captured formally.

Service level management interactions are shown in FIGURE 2-1. Each interaction consists of a service definition combined with a workload definition. There are many kinds of service definitions and many views of the workload. The processes involved in Service Level Management include creating service and workload definitions and translating from one definition to another.

The workload definition includes a *schedule* of the work that is run at different times of the day (for example, daytime interactive use, overnight batch, backup, and maintenance periods). For each period, the workload mix is defined in terms of applications, transactions, numbers of users, and work rates.

The service level definition includes availability and performance for *service classes* that map to key applications and transactions. Availability is specified as uptime over a period of time and is often expressed as a percentage (for example 99.95 percent per month). Performance may be specified as response time for interactive transactions or throughput for batch transactions.

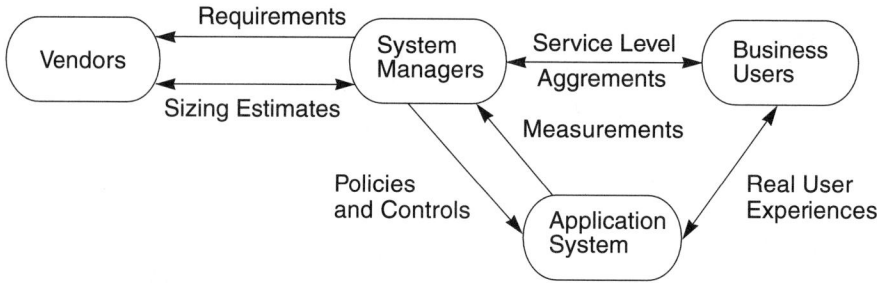

FIGURE 2-1 Service Level Management Interactions

System Level Requirements

System managers first establish a workload definition and the service level requirements. The requirements are communicated to vendors, who respond by proposing a system that meets these requirements.

Sizing Estimates

Vendors measure the system performance using generic benchmarks. They may also work with system managers to define a customer-specific benchmark test. Vendors provide a sizing estimate based on the service level requirements and workload definition. The basis of the sizing estimate can be a published benchmark performance. In some cases, the measured performance on a customer-defined benchmark is used as the basis of a sizing estimate. Vendors provide reliability data for system components. They can also provide availability and performance guarantees for production systems with a defined workload (at a price). Vendors cannot provide unqualified guarantees because typically, many application and environmental dependencies are outside their control.

Service Level Agreements

System managers and end users negotiate an SLA that establishes a user-oriented view of the workload mix and the service levels required. This may take the form: 95th percentile response time of under two seconds for the new-order transaction with up to 600 users online during the peak hour. It is important to specify the workload (in this case the number of users at the peak period), both to provide bounds for what the system is expected to do and to be precise about the measurement interval. Performance measures averaged over shorter intervals will have higher variance and higher peaks.

The agreed-upon service levels could be too demanding or too lax. The system may be quite usable and working well, but still failing an overly demanding service level agreement. It could also be too slow when performing an operation that is not specified in the SLA or whose agreed-to service level is too lax. The involved parties must agree to a continuous process of updating and refining the SLA.

Real User Experiences

The actual service levels experienced by users with a real workload are subjective measures that are very hard to capture. Often problems occur that affect parts of the system not covered explicitly by the service level agreement, or the workload varies from that defined in the service level agreement. One of the biggest challenges in performance management is to obtain measurements that have a good correlation with the real user experience.

Service Level Measurements

The real service levels cannot always be captured directly, but the measurements taken are believed to be representative of the real user experience. These measurements are then compared against the service level agreement to determine whether a problem exists. For example, suppose downtime during the interactive shift is measured and reported. A problem could occur in the network between the users and the application system that causes poor service levels from the end-user point of view but not from the system point of view. It is much easier to measure service levels inside a backend server system than at the user interface on the client system, but it is important to be aware of the limitations of such measurements. A transaction may take place over a wide variety of systems. An order for goods will affect systems inside and outside the company and across application boundaries. This problem must be carefully considered when the service level agreement is made and when the service level measurements are being defined.

Policies and Controls

System managers create policies that direct the resources of the computer system to maintain service levels according to the workload definition specified in those policies. A policy workload definition is closely related to the service level agreement workload definition, but may be modified to satisfy operational constraints. It is translated into terms that map oto system features. Example policies include:

- A maximum of 600 interactive users of the order entry application at any time.
- Order entry application has a 60 percent share of CPU, 30 percent share of network, and 40 percent share of memory.
- If new-order response time is worse than its target, steal resources from other workloads that are overachieving.

The policy is only as effective as the measurements available to it. If the wrong things are being measured, the policy will be ineffective. The policy can control resources directly or indirectly. For example, direct control on CPU time and network bandwidth usage might be used to implement indirect control on disk I/O rates by slowing or stopping a process.

Capacity Planning and Exception Reporting

The measured workload and service levels should be analyzed to extract trends. A capacity planning process can then be used to predict future scenarios and determine action plans to tune or upgrade systems, modify the service level agreement, and proactively avoid service problems.

In cases where the measured workload from the users exceeds the agreed-upon workload definition or where the measured service level falls short of the defined level, an exception report is produced.

Accounting and Chargeback

The accrued usage of resources by each user or workload may be accumulated into an accounting system so that projects can be charged in proportion to the resources they consume.

Resource Management Control Loop

To manage a resource, you must be able to measure and control it. A control loop is set up that measures the performance of an application subsystem, applies policies and goals to decide what to do, then uses controls to change the resources being provided to that subsystem. This loop can be implemented manually on a time scale measured in days or weeks (by reconfiguring and upgrading entire systems), or it can be automated in software and run as often as every few seconds. The control loop is shown in FIGURE 2-2.

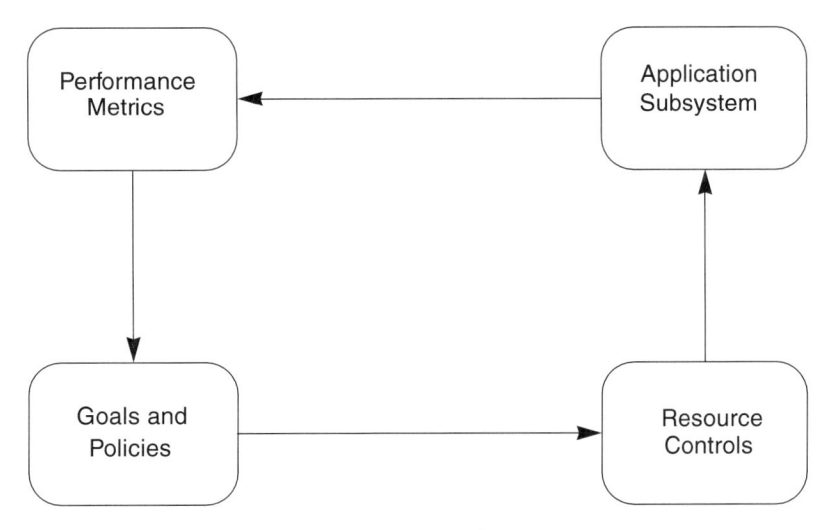

FIGURE 2-2 Resource Management Control Loop

A complete system implements many control loops. A brief digression into basic control theory is provided at this point to help explain the behavior of such systems.

A Simple Approach to Control Theory

We spend so much of our lives operating control loops that it is actually quite intuitive to most people. Designing a control loop is more complex and requires a more explicit understanding of the situation.

You start with an objective, such as to steer a car around a corner while staying in the lane. You apply a control input by turning the steering wheel to the point that will get you around the corner. After a delay. the car responds, You measure the response, compare it with what you wanted, and obtain the error difference. If the difference is zero you don't need to change the control input. If the turn is too tight, you need to reduce the input. If the turn is too wide, you need to increase the input. You have to decide how much extra correction is needed to compensate for being wrong the first time, and also decide whether the car has finished responding fully to the initial input. You may decide to over- or under-correct, and apply the correction gradually or quickly (for example, if you are heading straight for a lamp post!).

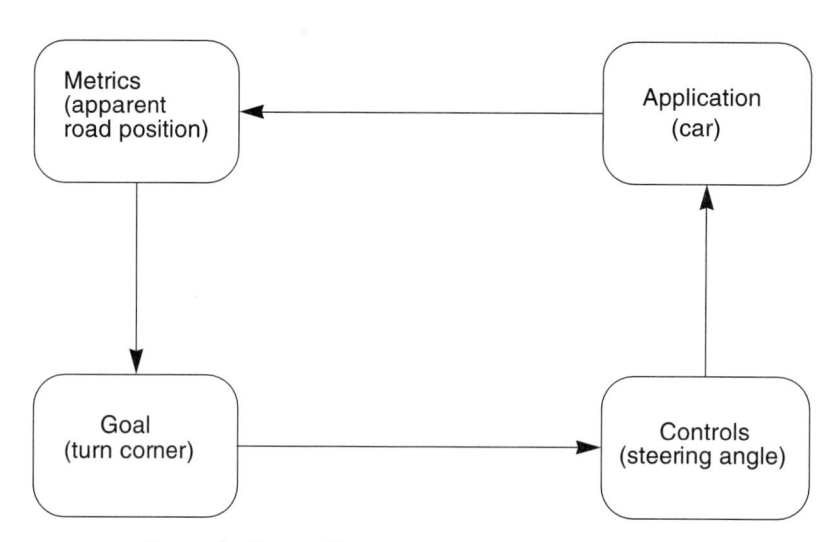

FIGURE 2-3 Example Control Loop

The first time you tried a car driving game on a computer, you probably swung wildly from side to side. This wild swinging is caused by over-correcting too late because you don't have the same motion sensing inputs you have in a real car. When the car is oscillating, your corrections may end up being delayed to the point that you are turning the wheel the wrong way at the wrong time, and you might spin off or crash. Eventually, you learn to react based on what you see on the screen and make smaller corrections more quickly to keep the car on track and stable.

In control terms, you are applying *negative feedback* to the system. You take the error difference between what you wanted and what you got, and apply the inverse of the error to the system to reduce the error in the future. The rate at which you measure and apply corrections is called the *control interval,* and the rate at which the system responds to changes is called the *time constant* for the loop. The amount of the error that you feed back changes the characteristic behavior of the control loop. If you feed back a large proportion of the error with a short control interval, the system is *lightly damped* and will be very responsive to sudden changes but will probably oscillate back and forth. If you feed back a small proportion of the error over a longer control interval, the system is *heavily damped* and will tend to be sluggish and unresponsive with a large time constant.

When you apply these principles to computer system resource management you can see that it is important to average measurements over an appropriate time scale and get the damping factor right. The resource manager needs to respond quickly enough to cope with sudden changes in the workload such as many simultaneous user logins at the start of a shift, while maintaining a steady flow of resources to all the workloads on the system so that response times are consistent and predictable.

Viewpoints of Resource Management

You can measure and control a computer system in many ways. This section examines various approaches to solving resource management problems. The methodology used depends upon the starting point of the developers, for example a network-centric methodology can be extended for use in other areas, so can a storage-centric or server-centric viewpoint.

Diverse Methods

This diversity of approach occurs both because of the products that are available and because of the expectations of the end users who are purchasing solutions. In a large organization, several groups (such as system administrators, network managers, database administrators, and security managers) are responsible for different parts of operations management.

In some organizations, each group is free to use its own methods and obtain its own tools. This can cause demarcation problems because there is so much overlap in the scope of each method. Or a single methodology and tool could be imposed by the dominant group. The problem with such an aproach is that the methodology may be optimal for managing one aspect of the system only and could do a poor job in other areas.

In an ideal world, one all-encompassing mega-tool would implement an integrated methodology and solve all resource management problems. The closer you get to this ideal, the more expensive and complex the tool becomes. And you may not want all of its features. So it is harder to justify purchasing it.

A more pragmatic approach is to integrate simpler, more specialized tools that share information with each other, have a similar look and feel, and can be used as a standalone product as needed.

Today's diverse set of methodologies and tools have very little integration between them and several different user interfaces. The products produced at Sun Microsystems, Inc. are converging on a common user interface style and on common technologies for sharing information to provide better integrated resource management components. This book's primary role is to explain to data center operations managers how to use combinations of the current set of products and technologies. It also indicates the direction of the development and integration work that will produce the next generation of products.

The System-Centric Viewpoint

The system-centric viewpoint focuses on what can be done on a single server using a mixture of hardware and operating system features. The operating system provides basic management capabilities for many components such as attached network and storage devices. But it specializes in managing CPU and memory resources for a single desktop or server system. Dynamic Reconfiguration (DR), processor sets, Solaris Resource Manager™, and Sun Enterprise™ 10000 (also known as Starfire™) Dynamic System Domains (DSDs) are all system-centric resource management technologies. The Sun hardware system-centric resource management tool is the Sun Enterprise SyMON™ 2.0 software. It is based on the Simple Network Management Protocol (SNMP), so it also has some network management capabilities. The Solaris Management Console™ software provides a more generic framework for gathering together operating system administration tools and interfacing to industry standard initiatives such as the web-based management initiative (WebM) and the Common Information Model (CIM). The Starfire system currently uses its own HostView interface running on a separate system service processor (SSP) to manage domains.

The system-centric viewpoint runs into problems when a lot of systems must be managed. Coordinating changes and allocating resources becomes complex quite rapidly. Tools like the Sun Enterprise SyMON 2.0 software can view many systems on one console, but cannot replicate and coordinate changes over multiple systems. One reason why the Sun Enterprise SyMON 2.0 software does not fully support management of the Starfire system is because each domain on the system runs a separate copy of the Solaris operating environment and sees a different subset of the hardware configuration. The next release of this software will be extended to view an SSP and all the domains in a Starfire system as a special kind of cluster so it can be used in place of the HostView interface.

The operating system and devices provide a large number of measurements of utilization, throughput, and component-level response times. There are several good ways to control CPU resources, but at present, there is no way to control the usage of real memory by a workload. The only way to constrain a workload that is using too much memory is to slow down or stop its CPU usage so that it stops referencing its memory, which will then be stolen by other, more active processes.

Manual resource management policies can be implemented using the Sun Enterprise SyMON Health Monitor, which generates alerts when a component of the system becomes overloaded. The system administrator can then tune or reconfigure the system to avoid the problem. Automatic resource management policies are implemented by Solaris Resource Manager, which dynamically adjusts the priorities of processes to ensure that their recent CPU usage tracks the share of the system that has been given as a goal for that user.

The Cluster-Centric Viewpoint

The cluster-centric viewpoint concentrates on coordinating resource management across the cluster. Systems are clustered together to provide higher availability and higher performance than that provided by a single system. A cluster is more complex to install and administer, so tools and methods attempt to automate cluster management to make it more like a single system. From a resource-management viewpoint, the primary issue is load balancing and the extra costs of accessing nonlocal information over the cluster interconnect. Sun has two kinds of clusters. The highly integrated SPARCcluster™ product range is focused on improved availability in commercial environments. Its management tools will eventually become an integrated extension to the SyMON software. For high performance computing, Sun HPC Servers use the platform computing load share facility (LSF) to perform load balancing on much larger and more loosely coupled clusters.

At a cluster level, multiple system level measurements are compared to measure load balance and look for spare resources. The cluster interconnect utilization and proportion of remote data access are important additional measures. The primary resource management control is the choice of where to run new work. It is not currently possible to migrate a running job from one node in a cluster to another, or to checkpoint a job to disk and restart it again later, either on the same node or on a different one.

When deciding on the resources that are available on a node, it is easy to decide if there is some spare CPU power, but very hard to decide if there is enough available real memory. The kernel maintains a free list of memory, but there is also some proportion of memory in use as a file system cache that could be reclaimed to run a new job if there was a way to measure it. This is a current issue for the LSF product.

The Network-Centric Viewpoint

From a network point of view, there are a large number of devices to manage. Many of them are network components with limited monitoring capabilities, such as bridges and routers. The primary resource that is managed is network capacity. At the intersection of servers and networks, there are products that perform protocol based bandwidth management on a per-server basis (such as Solaris™ Bandwidth Manager software) or act as secure firewalls. In the telecommunications industry, network management encompasses all the equipment required to run a global system where the end-points are mostly telephones or mobile cellphones, and the traffic is a mixture of speech and data. In this environment, SNMP is too simple, so the more scalable OSI-based CMIP management protocol is often used. The Solstice™ Enterprise Manager product is a Telco-oriented CMIP and SNMP management system that is used to manage cellular networks. In theory it could be used to manage computer systems and local area networks, but it was not developed to do this. Computer-oriented local and wide area networks are normally managed using SNMP protocols, with the Solstice SunNet Manager™ or HP OpenView products collecting and displaying the data. Both products provide some visibility into what is happening in the computer systems on the network, but they are much more focused on network topology. At this level, resource management is done on a per-network basis, often by controlling the priority of data flows through intelligent routers and switches. The Sun Enterprise SyMON 2.0 software can act as a network management platform as well as a system hardware management platform, which may help to integrate these two viewpoints.

Protocol information along with the information found in packet headers and network addresses form the basis for network measurements. There is no user or process identifier in a packet, so it is hard to directly map network activity to system level activity unless an identifiable server process is dedicated to each protocol. Some protocols measure round trip times for their acknowledgments. This can provide an estimate of network latency between two systems.

Network controls are based on delaying and prioritizing packets based on the protocol and destination data in the packet headers. This can occur at the servers that make up the end points or in the routers that connect them.

Storage-Centric Viewpoint

Storage has recently moved from being a simple attached computer system peripheral to a complex managed entity in its own right. Networked storage using fibre channel puts an interconnection layer in between multiple servers or clusters and multiple storage subsystems. This storage area network (SAN) can contain switches and routers just like local or wide area networks, but the protocol in common use is SCSI over fibre channel rather than IP over Ethernet. A SAN may also span multiple sites, for example, where remote mirroring is being used for disaster recovery. Storage is also now open for access in a heterogeneous multi-vendor environment, where multiple server and storage vendors can all be connected over the SAN. This is an emerging technology, and tools to manage a SAN are still being developed. Sun provides one approach with an industry-wide initiative called Jiro. It is based on a distributed pure Java™ technology platform that can run anywhere a JVM is available, scaling from embedded devices through open systems into mainframe and enterprise environments. Jiro enables management of any storage resource in a heterogeneous distributed environment, from storage hardware, like devices and switches, to storage software like backup solutions and volume managers. Jiro is being promoted as an open multi-vendor standard.

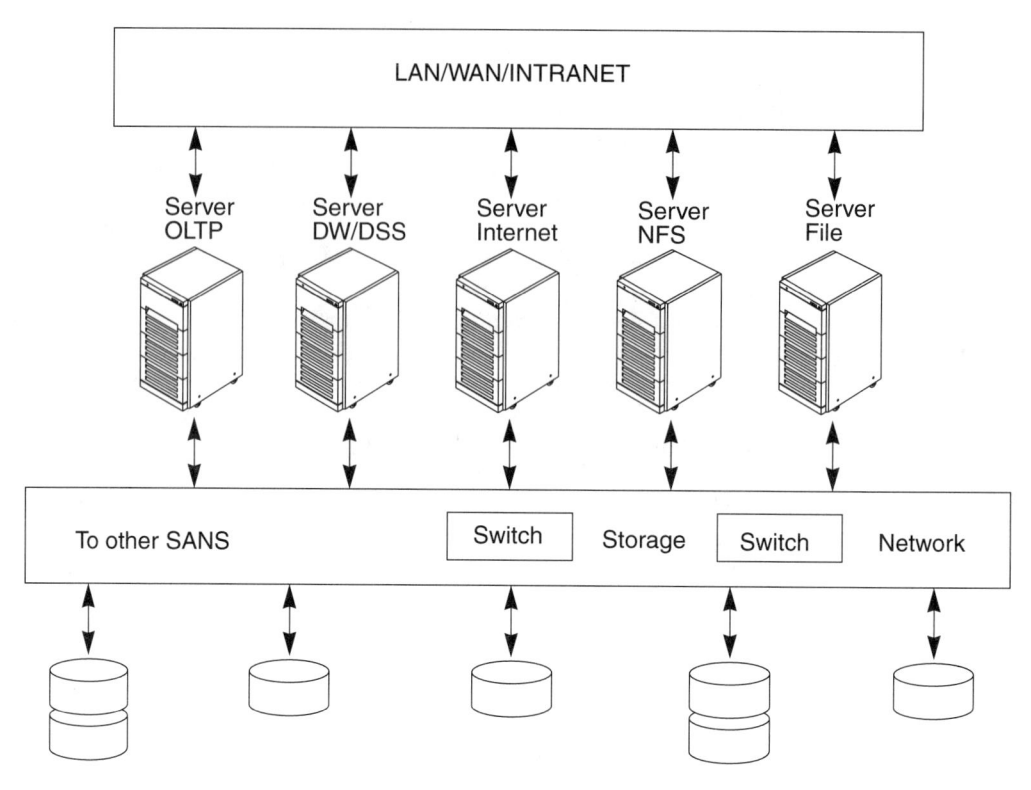

FIGURE 2-4 Storage Area Network

Storage management has two constraints that make it interesting: one is that it must be distributed over many server systems and storage devices to be useful. The other is that these servers and devices come from many vendors and run different operating software. So Jiro cannot include a core dependency on the Solaris operating environment or other Sun products. Jiro must solve some of the generic problems of clustered and networked resource management. In particular, it manages the state of distributed devices in a persistent manner. Jiro must be capable of stand-alone operation, with component management interfaces to other products.

Jiro enables resource management of capacity, performance, and availability of data storage. Backup and archival policies can be used to automate migration of data to a tape library. Measurements of capacity and performance characteristics can be combined with availability policies, so the operator will be alerted of any problems. Ultimately storage subsystems will be reconfigured automatically.

At present, Jiro does not include a general purpose rule script-based policy engine. It does provide the infrastructure necessary to create polices, allowing the view of storage to be elevated to the Storage Service level.

Integration between the system viewpoint and the storage viewpoint has some of the same problems as the integration of system and network viewpoints. The traffic on the SAN does not contain any indication of which user or process generated the request. Within the Solaris software, it is possible to trace storage accesses on a per-process, per device basis. But the overhead of collecting and analyzing this data is quite high. There may be a need for a Jiro Solaris Storage Bandwidth Manager to bridge the two management viewpoints in a way that accounts for, prioritizes, and controls SAN bandwidth on a per process or per user basis.

Database-Centric Viewpoint

A database management system has its own notion of users, manages its own memory and storage allocation, and can appear as a "black box" to the server system on which it runs. Some database vendors have implemented their own resource management capability on a per user or per transaction basis. This may take the form of priorities, shares, or limits on CPU usage per user or per transaction. The database also contains its own logic that implements policies and dynamically controls resources.

The database implementation can sometimes work well with server-based resource management. This is described in more detail in Chapter 4.

Integration is needed between the internal database resource management capabilities and the other resource management viewpoints.

Application-Centric Viewpoint

Large and complex applications such as SAP R/3, Baan, and Oracle Financials contain their own resource management concepts and controls. For example, Oracle Financials implements its own batch queue system to decouple the generation of large reports from the interactive response time of the users. A report is sent to a subsystem called the concurrent manager, which is configured to have a number of parallel streams of work of various types according to the local policy. Concurrent manager activity can be scheduled to occur outside normal working hours, or it can be used to soak up spare cycles during the day.

SAP R/3 measures the response time of important transactions and breaks these down into application server time and backend database server time. As many users connect to an application server and many database servers connect to a single backend database, there is no concept of which user is doing work on the backend system. The application itself must have the instrumentation to keep track of what is going on. The application directly implements the policies and controls.

Integrated Methods

In a large organization, all of the above viewpoints are useful, and some combination of methodologies is probably implemented already. FIGURE 2-5 indicates the relative breadth of coverage of each methodology. A darker box shows that better coverage is available, a white box indicates that little or no support is provided for a combination.

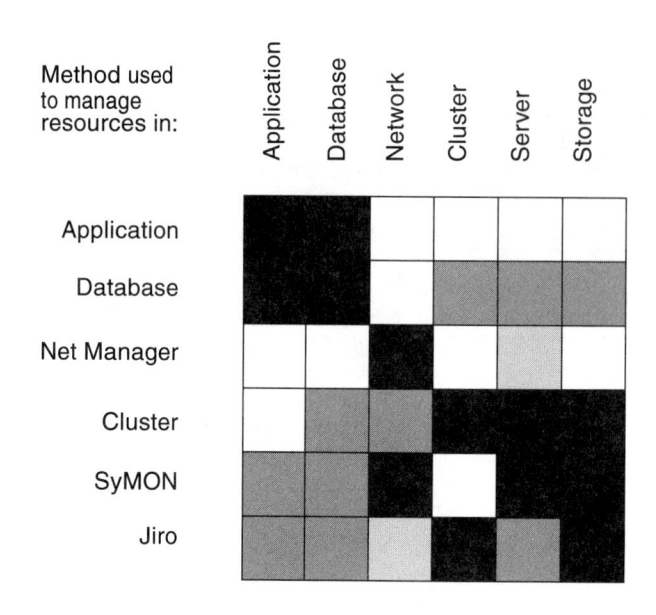

FIGURE 2-5   Integrated Methodology by Viewpoint

The mature methods have remained specialized, but the emerging technologies of Sun Enterprise SyMON 2.0 and Jiro address a much broader scope of problems. The product overview section of this book discusses their capabilities in much greater detail.

So far the discussion has been quite abstract. The next chapter introduces several example workloads, showing the appropriate methodologies to manage resources for them.

The Consolidation Process

The consolidation process starts when you identify candidate systems and applications. First measure the resource usage and service levels of those systems so you can see which application workloads will fit together best.

Next, migrate those systems to a common Solaris release and patch revision and do some testing so you can be sure that everything works correctly in the same environment. You also need to make sure that there are no conflicts in the name service configuration and network services files. For example, local password files may need to be merged, and any conflicting port numbers specified in the /etc/services file may need to be cleared. If you use a name service such as NIS for all your password and services information, then the systems should already be seeing the same name space and definitions. Using a common name service eases the consolidation process. If you prefer to make all the changes at one time, then you can upgrade as the application is consolidated, but allow for more testing time and a more incremental installation process on the consolidated system

For each group of consolidated applications, you must choose appropriate resource management controls. Once you have consolidated your applications to fewer systems, monitor and re-size the consolidated systems to allow for peak loads. You can either remove excess resources for use elsewhere or identify additional candidate applications to be consolidated onto these systems. Treat this as a rolling upgrade program rather than a one-time big change.

An obvious question that arises is how many systems should the new consolidation contain. Circumstances vary, but the basic principles remain the same. If you treat consolidation as a process, then the number of systems decreases over time and the size of systems increases.

Downtime impacts multiple applications on the consolidated systems. Therefore, when you increase the resources by adding an extra application, you want to do so without rebooting. Consolidated upgrades benefit from systems that can perform dynamic reconfiguration. The midrange Sun Ultra™ Enterprise™ E3000-E6500 servers can perform I/O board reconfiguration with the Solaris 2.6 release, but they require the Solaris 7 release for dynamic reconfiguration of CPU and memory, which causes some application availability issues. The number of system footprints may be too high with midrange servers, and it is hard to reduce the total number of servers effectively. With the high-end Starfire system, Dynamic System Domains (DSDs) solve these problems. DSDs are supported on the Solaris 2.5.1, 2.6, and 7 releases. The total number of DSDs can be reduced as applications are consolidated.

One approach is to use each DSD for a different Solaris revision. You may have a large DSD for the bulk of your Solaris 2.6 applications, a smaller one for applications that have not yet migrated from the Solaris 2.5.1 release, and a development and test

DSD for the Solaris 7 release. Over time, the Solaris 2.5.1 DSD will shrink away and its resources will migrate into the other DSDs. Applications will also migrate into the Solaris 7 DSD. The key benefit here is that this all happens under software control, using a single system footprint in the data center. DSDs are described in detail Chapter 8.

Use the Solaris Resource Manager or the Solaris Bandwidth Manager software or processor sets to control applications within a single copy of the Solaris operating environment.

A consolidated system runs a mixture of workloads. You have to choose relevant processes and aggregate to measure them. The remainder is overhead or unplanned activity. If it is significant, it should be investigated. Break down network workloads as well so that you know which applications are generating the network traffic.

There is a common set of measurements to collect per workload.

- Number of processes and number of users
- End user response times for a selection of operations
- User and System CPU usage
- Real and virtual memory usage and paging rates
- I/O rates to disk and network devices
- Microstate wait timers to see which resources are bottlenecks

To actually perform workload aggregation you have to match patterns in the data.

- match processes on user name
- match processes on command name and arguments
- match processes using processor set binding
- match system accounting data using user and command name
- match network packets on port number and protocol

You usually have to assign disks and file systems to workloads manually. Dealing with shared memory, libraries, and code makes RAM breakdown hard.

When you are accumulating measurements don't accumulate the `ps` command `CPU%`. It's a decayed average of recent CPU usage, not an accurate measure of actual CPU usage over an interval. You need to measure the actual process CPU time used in each interval by taking the difference of two measurements. There is more detail on the available measurements and what they mean in Chapter 5.

CHAPTER **3**

Policies and Controls

To manage the resources of a system, you must be able to measure and control resource usage. You must also establish policies that determine the controls that are invoked once the available measurements are interpreted. This chapter examines various types of policies and controls and ways to implement them. It also looks at each subsystem in turn to see the resources that can be managed.

Policy Types

There are many types of policies and many ways to implement them. Some of the main classifications are explained below. A recent draft standard defines the terminology of each kind of policy. That terminology has been adopted in this book, and the standard is summarized in this section.

Limits and Error Event Rules

One of the simplest policies is to define limits on a measurement and associate it with an action. This is often implemented as an "if measure passes threshold then action" rule. Products such as the Sun Enterprise SyMON 2.0 software (referred to hereafter as SyMON) predefine many simple limit rules and allow new rules to be set on any measurement. A limit can be defined as a simple rule with a single input measurement. It is also common to have several thresholds with a warning level action and a critical problem level action for the same measure.

An error event is different because it is treated as a discrete on/off event rather than a continuous variable to be compared against a limit.

In either case, an alert is generated and logged. The alert can be transitory and go away when the rule is re-evaluated, or it can be persistent and require a user to acknowledge that it has been seen.

Complex Rules and Hierarchies

More complex rules take several inputs and can maintain historical information such as previous state and running averages. They can also be built out of several simple limit rules. A complex rule is used to establish the state of a component or a subsystem. When rules are combined, they are ranked so that critical problems take precedence over warnings. A hierarchy of rules can be built for a network of systems so that the overall state of the network is indicated by the state of the system that has the worst problem. In turn, that state is based on the state of the subsystem that has the worst problem. A rule state propagation hierarchy is provided as part of the Sun Enterprise SyMON 2.0 product, and many other commercial tools implement this mechanism.

The policy is inherent in the set of rules that are implemented, the thresholds that the rules use, and the actions that occur when a rule becomes active.

Priority

A relative importance level can be given to the work done by a system as part of a policy that prioritizes some activities over others. The Solaris Resource Manager product and others like it assign shares to each user according to a policy decided by the administrator, then accumulate the CPU usage at a per-user level and implement a control based on the number of shares held by each user and the user's place in the hierarchy.

An alternative approach is to specify percentages directly. The Solaris Bandwidth Manager software uses this mechanism to provide a way to specify policies on a per-network packet basis. Each packet is classified by address or protocol and each class is given a priority and a percentage of the total bandwidth that it can use.

Goals

Goal-based policies are prescriptitive rather than reactive. They operate at a higher level. A goal can be translated into a mixture of limits, priorities, and relative importance levels. Goals can include actions for when the goal cannot be met.

A goal can also be thought of as a control loop, where the policy manipulates controls when a measurement deviates from its desired range. As described in Chapter 3, a control loop is a complex thing to manage because its stability characteristics, time constant, and damping factor must be set correctly. The interaction of multiple inter-linked control loops can be problematic.

Goals can be expressed in several ways:

- Response time goals try to monitor the end user response time of a system and control resources so that high priority work maintains its response time goal by taking resources from lower priority work.
- Throughput goals monitor the rate of consumption of a resource for long running jobs and control the relative priority to maintain the desired balance.
- Deadline goals have a way of telling how far a repetitive batch job has gone through its work, and control resources to ensure that the entire job completes by a deadline. For example, a payroll application must complete on time and generate the correct number of pay slips. A goal-based workload manager could monitor the running total.

At present, automated goal-based workload management is a feature found only on mainframes running OS/390 software.

Operational Policies

Some policies are implemented manually as part of operations management. For example, an availability policy can include a goal for uptime and an automatic way to measure and report the uptime over a period. There is no direct control in the system that affects uptime. It is handled by operations staff, who will reconfigure software to work around problems, swap out unreliable hardware, or reconfigure the system into a more resilient configuration if the availability goal is not being met.

In most cases, goal-based policies require manual intervention to complete the control loop. A measure of response time is monitored, and if its goal is not being met, the administrator manually varies the CPU shares, moves work from an overloaded system to another system, or performs a hardware upgrade.

Networked Security Policies

Access to a system varies according to the role of the user. A security policy can prevent access to certain resources or allow designated users to manage subsystems. For example, the SyMON software includes access control lists for operations that change the state of a system, and multiple network domain views to give different administrative roles their own view of the resources being managed. Security and network-based policies can be stored in an LDAP based name service. When users dial into an Internet service provider, they are looked up in a RADIUS authentication database, which can extract a profile from an LDAP server to configure the systems each user is allowed to access and the Solaris Bandwidth Manager configuration is updated to take into account that user's network address.

Controls

Controls are used to limit or redirect resources.

Limits

A limit prevents a resource from exceeding a preset value. Some limits are system wide (such as the total number of processes allowed on a system) and some operate on a per-user basis (such as a file system quota). Since many limits are implemented by the Solaris software, the action, when a limit is reached, is to return an error code inside the application and possibly send a signal to the process. Well-written applications handle the errors and catch the signals, but applications that do not expect to ever run into a limit might misbehave or abort. During testing, it is a good idea to run with very tight limits and test the behavior of applications as they hit those limits.

Direct and Indirect Controls

A direct control operates on the resource you want to control. For example, the Solaris Resource Manager software controls CPU usage per user by implementing a scheduling class that determines each user's share of the CPU. An indirect control works via dependent resources. For example, to limit the I/O throughput of a process, it is sufficient to be able to measure the I/O throughput and limit the CPU resources for that process. The process could be stopped temporarily to prevent it from issuing read and write system calls at too high a rate. It might be more efficient to add a direct measurement and control capability to the code that implements read and write calls, but that is a more invasive approach that requires changes to the Solaris software itself.

The Solaris Bandwidth Manager product implements a direct control on network packet rates. This can be used to implement an indirect control on the CPU resources taken up by the NFS server code in the kernel. The Solaris Resource Manager software cannot control NFS service directly as NFS is implemented using kernel threads that do not have an associated user-level process.

Standardized Policy Definitions

The Internet draft policy framework standard by Strassner and Ellesson defines its scope thus:

> This document defines a set of terms that the Internet community can use to exchange ideas on how policy creation, administration, management, and distribution could work among policy servers and multiple device types.

The terminology definitions are network oriented but apply equally well to system level policies. Some of the terms defined in this standard are listed here.

- Administrative Domain: A collection of network elements under the same administrative control and grouped together for administrative purposes.
- Network Element (also called a Node): A networking device, such as a router, a switch, or a hub, where resource allocation decisions have to be made and the decisions have to be enforced.
- Policy: The combination of rules and services where rules define the criteria for resource access and usage.
- Policy control: The application of rules to determine whether or not access to a particular resource should be granted.
- Policy Object: Contains policy-related info such as policy elements and is carried in a request or response related to resource allocation decision.
- Policy Element: Subdivision of policy objects; contains single units of information necessary for the evaluation of policy rules. A single policy element carries an user or application identification whereas another policy element may carry user credentials or credit card information. Examples of policy elements include identity of the requesting user or application, user/app credentials, and so on. The policy elements themselves are expected to be independent of which Quality of Service signaling protocol is used.
- Policy Decision Point (PDP): The point where policy decisions are made.
- Policy Enforcement Point (PEP): The point where the policy decisions are actually enforced.
- Policy Ignorant Node (PIN): A network element that does not explicitly support policy control using the mechanisms defined in this standard.
- Resource: Something of value in a network infrastructure to which rules or policy criteria are first applied before access is granted. Examples of resources include the buffers in a router and bandwidth on an interface.
- Service Provider: Controls the network infrastructure and may be responsible for the charging and accounting of services.

General Policy Architecture

The general architecture shown FIGURE 3-1 illustrates one common implementation of a policy that combines the use of a policy repository, a PDP, and a PEP. This diagram is not meant to imply that these entities must be located in physically separate devices, nor is it meant to imply that the only protocols used for communicating policy are those illustrated. Rather, it simply shows one implementation containing the three important entities fundamental to policy: a repository, a PDP, and a PEP.

```
┌─────────────────────┐
│  Management tool    │
├─────────────────────┤
│  Repository client  │
└─────────┬───────────┘
          │◄────── Repository access protocol
┌─────────┴───────────┐
│  Policy repository  │
│  (directory server, │
│   database, etc.)   │
└─────────┬───────────┘
          │◄────── Repository access protocol
┌─────────┴───────────┐
│  Repository client  │
│ Policy Decision Point│
│       (PDP)         │
└─────────┬───────────┘
          │◄────── Policy protocol
┌─────────┴───────────┐
│ Policy Enforcement  │
│    Point (PEP)      │
└─────────────────────┘
```

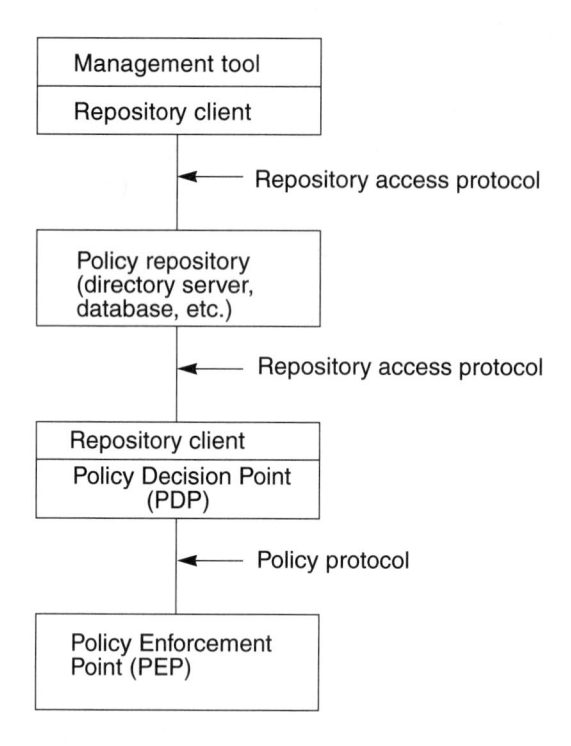

FIGURE 3-1   Example Policy Architecture

It is assumed that policy decisions will always be made in the PDP and implemented in the PEP. Specifically, the PEP cannot make decisions on its own. This simplifies the definition and modeling of policy while leaving open the possibility for a single device to have both a local PDP (LPDP) as well as a PEP.

In general, the repository access protocol and the policy protocol are different protocols. If the policy repository is a directory, then LDAP is one example of a repository access protocol. However, the policy protocol can be any combination of COPS, SNMP, and Telnet/CLI. Given this rich diversity, a common language is needed to represent policy rules. The rest of the standard document describes the terminology necessary to enable the definition of such a language and discusses how policy is defined, manipulated, and used in the PDP and PEP. For more information, see the complete document at http://www.ietf.org/internet-drafts/draft-strassner-policy-terms-01.txt.

Subsystem Policies and Controls

Each component and subsystem implements a set of measurements and controls that allows a policy to manage them.

User-Level Controls

User-level controls include limits on the number of logins and limits on the resources used by each user.

Login Limits

The Solaris software implements a blanket login ban for non-root users as described in the nologin(4) manual page. It also limits the total number of processes that can be started via the nproc kernel tunable. This feature scales with the memory configuration. A further limit is placed on the total number of processes per user using the maxuprc kernel tunable. This is a single global limit. The total number of logins per user can also be limited. The current limit can be viewed with sysdef or sar. The example in FIGURE 3-2 was run on a 64 Mbyte desktop system.

```
% sysdef -i | grep processes
    1002maximum number of processes (v.v_proc)
     997maximum processes per user id (v.v_maxup)
% sar -v 1

SunOS maddan 5.6 Generic sun4m    03/18/99

18:25:12   proc-sz     ov  inod-sz    ov  file-sz    ov  lock-sz
18:25:13   108/1002     0  4634/4634   0  495/495     0  0/0
```

FIGURE 3-2 Determining Solaris Process Limits

When the SRM software is in use, you can view the maximum number of processes that can be limited on a per-user basis using the `limadm` command. You can view the current number and limit using the `liminfo` command, as described in Chapter 7.

Application-Level Controls

The main class of application-level controls are those provided by relational databases and transaction processing monitors. These consist mainly of access controls, but the Oracle8*i* database also implements controls on resource consumption and policies for relative importance. This is described in more detail in the Chapter 7.

CPU Power-Level Controls

There are many ways to control CPU power. The most basic one is to physically change the CPU configuration itself. A faster CPU shortens the CPU-intensive component of response times. Additional CPUs allow more concurrent work to take place with a similar response time.

Physically changing the CPU configuration requires a power down and reboot on many computer systems. But the Sun Enterprise Server systems allow CPU boards to be added and removed from a running system without powering it down or rebooting it. On the Starfire system, the CPUs can be partitioned into dynamic system domains, and a separate copy of the Solaris operating environment booted in each domain. CPU boards can then be moved from one dynamic system domain to another. This is described in detail in Chapter 8.

With a single copy of the Solaris software, the CPUs can be partitioned into processor sets as described in Chapter 7. Each process is bound to a processor set and constrained to run only on the CPUs that are members of that set. Sets are created and removed dynamically. If one set is overloaded, its processes cannot make use of the CPU power in a different set without manual intervention. Processor sets are most useful when there are a large number of CPUs to partition. This technique is obviously not useful on a uniprocessor system.

The SRM software also works within a single copy of the Solaris operating environment. Unlike sets, it has fine granularity and can be used on a uniprocessor system. When a system gets busy, all CPU power is used automatically. SRM works by biasing CPU usage on a per-user basis, using shares to determine the relative importance of each user.

The `kill` command sends a stop signal to a process and suspends it in the same way that typing Control-Z does in an interactive shell session. Sending a start signal lets the process continue. Stopping and starting processes in this way can control the concurrency of CPU-bound jobs on a system.

The Load Share Facility (LSF) software is described in detail in Chapter 10. LSF software implements a distributed batch queuing system where jobs are submitted and, when resources are available, sent to be run on a system. LSF software implements its own set of policies and controls.

Disk I/O Policies

Access controls via file permissions and access control lists (ACLs) control who can read and write to a file system.

Currently, no direct measures or controls of the rate at which a process is writing to a file system exist. The only information provided for each process is the total read plus write data rate. Block input and output counters are not incremented correctly in current releases of the Solaris operating environment. The block counter problem is filed as bugid 1141605 and is fixed in the next release of Solaris software. This data is not made available by the standard commands; it is part of the "usage" structure that includes microstate accounting as described in Chapter 5.

Because the Solaris software does not have any direct measurements or controls, additional application-specific information is required (such as configuring the location of data files manually) to implement policies.

Disk Space

See Chapter 6 for a description of the disk quota system. Disk quotas are currently implemented separately on each file system type. They are available on the UFS file system and remote mounts of UFS via NFS only. Other file system types either have no quota system or have a separately administered implementation.

Virtual Memory

An application consumes virtual memory when it requests memory from the operating system, and the memory is allocated from a central pool of resources. Virtual memory usage, however, is not directly related to physical memory usage because not all virtual memory has physical memory associated with it. If an application requests 16 Mbytes from the operating system, the operating system will create 16 Mbytes of memory within that application's address space, but will not allocate physical memory to it until that memory is read from or written to.

When you restrict or control the amount of virtual memory that an application can have, you are not controlling the amount of RAM that application can have. Rather you are implementing a policy limit on the maximum amount of virtual address space that process can have. This is an important difference because the limit is enforced when the application first requests memory not while it is using it. When the application hits the limit, it will probably fail because its requests to extend its virtual address space will fail. This may be what you want if the application is likely to impact higher priority work. But careful testing and debugging is required to make applications recover gracefully from memory allocation failures.

Virtual memory can be limited at the system level and at the process level. At a system level, the total amount of virtual memory available is equal to the total amount of swap space available. Each time virtual memory is used, the amount of swap space available drops by the same amount. If one application requests a large amount of virtual memory (for example, `malloc` (1 Gbyte), there is potential for that application to exhaust the system-wide swap space, which will then cause other applications to fail when they request memory.

You can use resource management of virtual memory to prevent a single process from growing too large and consuming all virtual memory resources by limiting the maximum amount of memory that a process or group of processes can use. This can be useful in two cases: to prevent any one user from using all of the available swap space (a denial of service attack) and to prevent a runaway process or leaking process from consuming all of the available swap space.

Base Solaris software can do simple resource management of a process's virtual memory usage. The limits information described in Chapter 6 can be used to limit the maximum amount of virtual memory used by a process. Limits are enforced per process, thus preventing any one process from using an unreasonably large amount of virtual memory. But a user can run many processes, so this does not prevent denial of service attacks.

The SRM software has a mechanism that can limit the maximum amount of virtual memory per user. This implements a similar limits policy as the per-process limit built into the Solaris operating environment, but it can be used to limit a user, regardless of how many processes are running. FIGURE 3-3 shows the three levels of virtual memory that can be controlled.

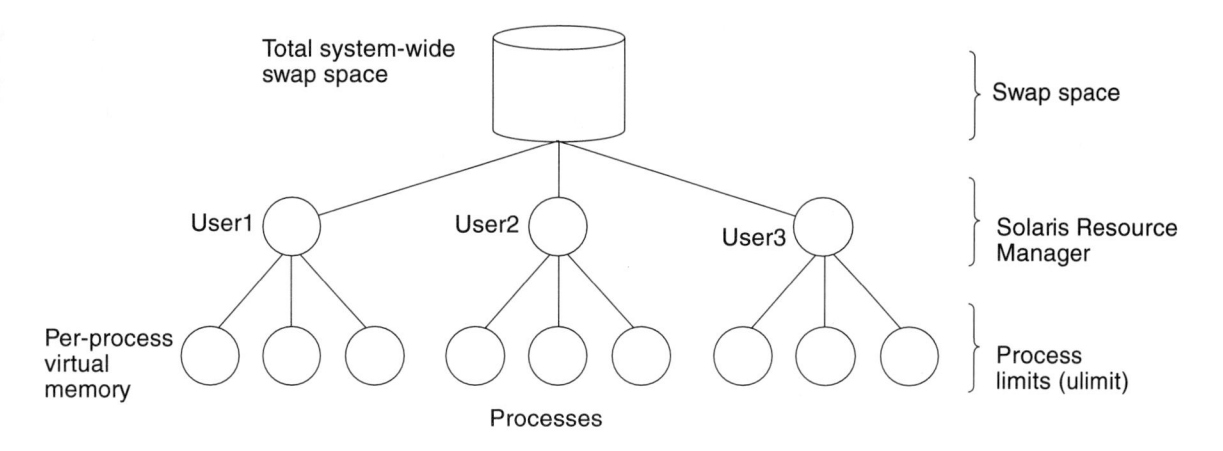

FIGURE 3-3 Three Levels of Virtual Memory Limits

Relationship Between Virtual Memory and Swap Space

Note that the amount of swap space used by a user does not correlate directly to the sum of all that user's processes. A user may have three processes, where each shares a single shared memory segment among them. Each process has the shared memory segment mapped to its address space, but swap space is only accounted for once within these processes. For example, three users each have a one Gbyte shared global area mapped to their address space, but each incremental user is not consuming an additional one Gbyte of swap from the system-wide pool. They use three Gbytes of virtual memory space, but only one Gbyte of swap space.

It is important to factor this in when using products like SRM software to control a user's virtual memory usage. The virtual memory accounted for by the SRM software is different from the amount of swap space used by the user. Since we are trying to control virtual memory in an attempt to prevent a single user from consuming all of the swap space, we must take care to apply the correct virtual memory limit policy. This sometimes makes it extremely difficult to control swap space usage with SRM software, but the right parameters provide adequate control in most environments.

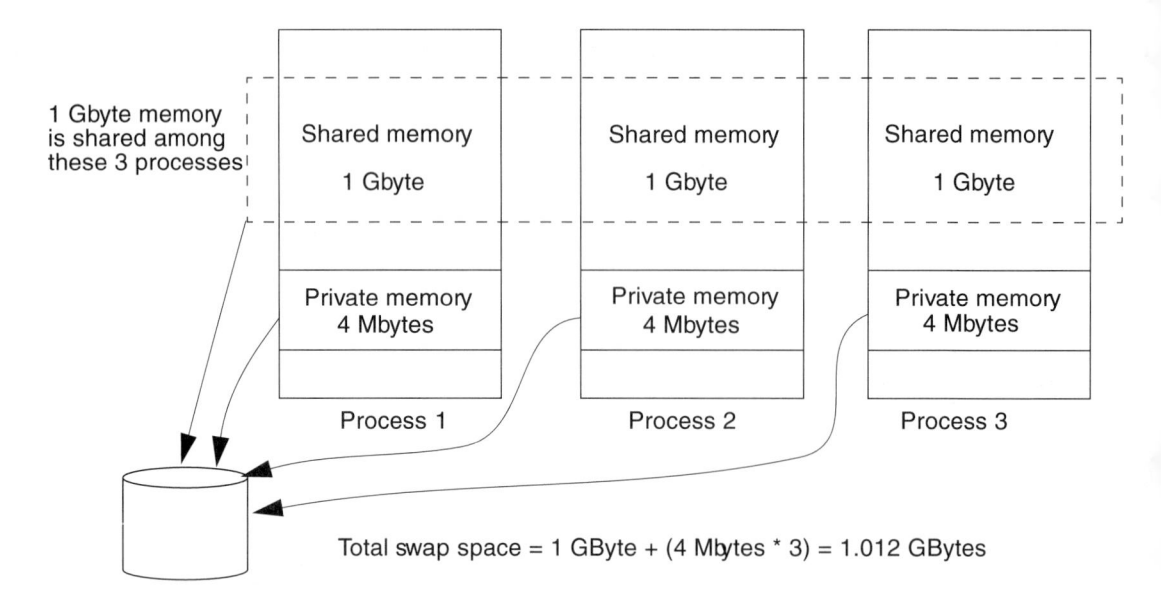

FIGURE 3-4 Swap Usage Only Accounts for Shared Segments Once

In the example illustrated in FIGURE 3-3 and FIGURE 3-4, the SRM software is configured to limit the total virtual memory to 1.012 GBytes, which allows all three processes to execute normally. If one of the three processes has a memory leak, the limit would be hit for that user, affecting only the processes owned by that user. The disadvantage is that if the user starts another process, the same limit is reached. The per-user limits must take into account the number of processes each user is expected to run.

Physical Memory

Resource Management of physical memory means defining policies and controlling the amount of RAM that is allocated to different workloads. In contrast to the virtual memory limit policies, physical memory is controlled by applying importance policies to different types of memory. In the future, it may be possible to apply limit or allocation style policies to physical memory, but that capability is not available in the Solaris operating environment today.

The physical memory management system in the Solaris operating environment can implement different policies for different memory types. By default, the memory management system applies an equal importance policy to different memory subsystems, which sometimes results in unwanted behavior. Before we look at the policies, let's take a quick look at the different consumers of memory.

The most important consumers of memory in the Solaris operating environment are:

- Kernel memory, used to run the operating system
- Process memory, allocated to processes and applications
- System V shared memory, allocated by the shared memory subsystem by applications such as databases
- Memory used for file system caching

The Default Memory Allocation Policy

Memory in the Solaris operating environment is, by default, allocated on a demand basis with equal importance to each subsystem. When a subsystem requests memory, it is allocated from a central pool of free memory. If sufficient memory is available in the free pool, then an application's request is granted. If free memory is insufficient, then memory is taken from other subsystems to satisfy the request. The equal-importance policy means that the application with the most aggressive memory requests gets the majority of the memory assigned to it. For example, suppose a user starts a `netscape` process that uses 20 Mbytes of memory. That memory is taken from the free pool of memory and allocated to the `netscape` process. When the user starts a `gimp` image editor tool, if there is no free memory in the free memory pool, then memory will be taken from the `netscape` browser and allocated to the `gimp` image editor tool. The Solaris memory allocation policy takes into account recent usage in an attempt to choose the correct application from which to steal memory, but the usage history is very short (less than one minute) in most circumstances.

FIGURE 3-5 shows an example where the memory allocated to the `netscape` process is reduced when the `gimp` process is started.

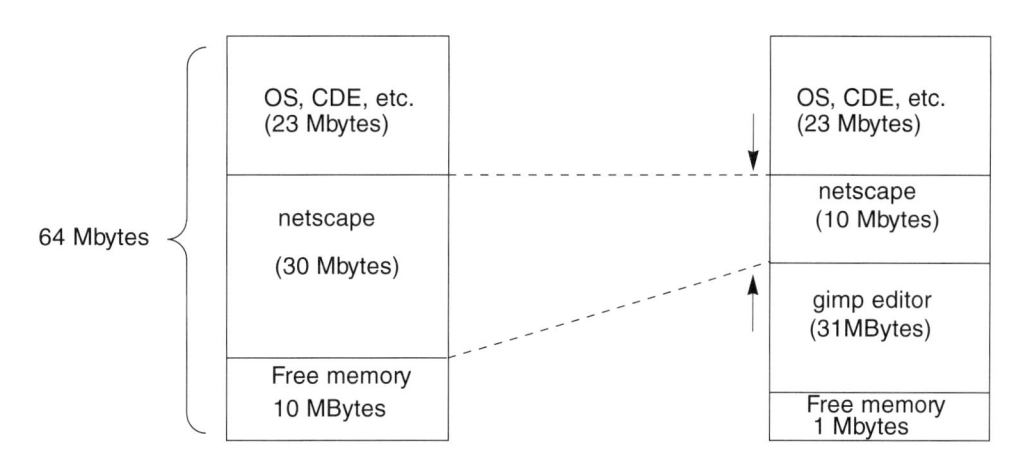

FIGURE 3-5 Memory Allocation with `netscape` and `gimp`

This situation can be avoided by configuring physical memory in the system so that there is always enough memory for each application's requirements. In example shown in FIGURE 3-5, if we configured the system with 128 Mbytes of memory, then both `netscape` and `gimp` could execute at the same time without affecting each other.

However, there is another consumer of memory in the operating system that often causes application memory starvation. That consumer is the file system. The file system uses memory from the free memory pool just like any other application in the system. Because the memory system implements equal importance by default, the file system can squeeze applications in the same way `gimp` did in FIGURE 3-5. Reading a file through the file system causes the file system to use physical memory to cache the file. This memory is consumed in 8-kilobyte chunks as the file is read. The free memory pool is thus depleted and the memory system starts looking for memory that it can use to replenish the free pool. The memory system will take memory from other applications that haven't used portions of their memory recently. For example, if you start a file-based mail tool such as `dtmail`, the memory used to cache the file when `dtmail` reads a 23-Mbyte mail file will be taken from other portions of the system.

Let's revisit the example shown FIGURE 3-5 and look at what happens when we factor in the file system memory usage. FIGURE 3-6 shows the same 64-Mbytes system where we start `dtmail` while `netscape` is running. Again, if we increase the memory to 128 Mbytes, we will provide enough memory for `netscape`, the `dtmail` application, and the `/var/mail` file. What happens if the file we are accessing is many times larger than the memory in the system (for example, several gigabytes)?

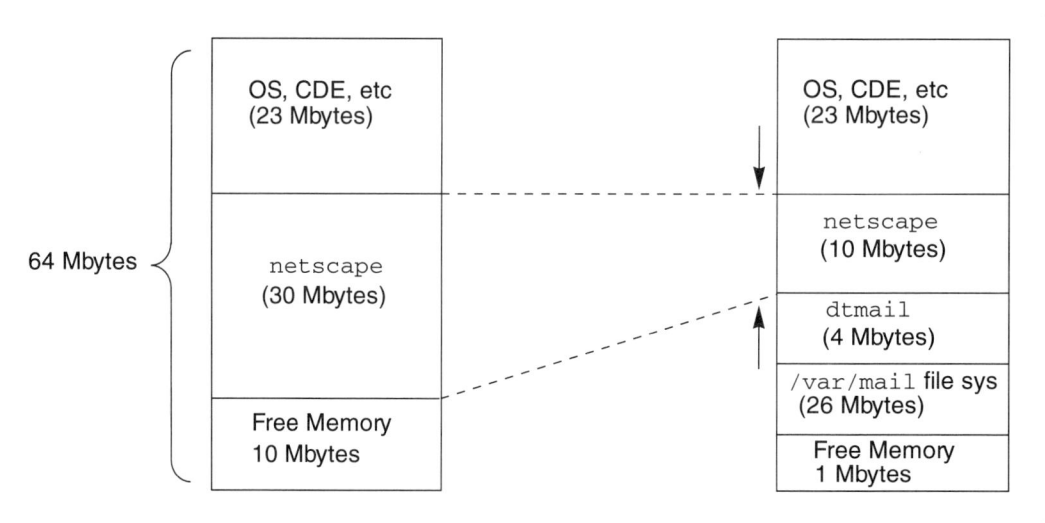

FIGURE 3-6 Memory Allocation with `netscape` and `dtmail`

Priority Paging—Memory Policy by Importance

The Solaris feature priority paging prevents the file system from consuming too much memory. Priority paging implements a memory policy with different importance factors for different memory types. Application memory is allocated at a higher priority than file system memory thus preventing the file system from stealing memory from other applications. Priority paging is implemented in the Solaris 7 operating environment, but it must be enabled with an /etc/system parameter as follows:

```
*
* /etc/system file
*
set priority_paging=1
```

To use priority paging with the Solaris 2.6 release, use kernel patch 105181-13; with the Solaris 2.5.1 release, use kernel patch 103640-26 or higher.

With priority paging enabled, the memory system behaves differently. In our example, rather than shrinking Netscape from 30 Mbytes to 10 Mbytes, the system limits the amount of memory that is allocated to the file system. FIGURE 3-7 shows how both netscape and dtmail can exist on the same system, while the size of the file system cache is held to a reasonable limit.

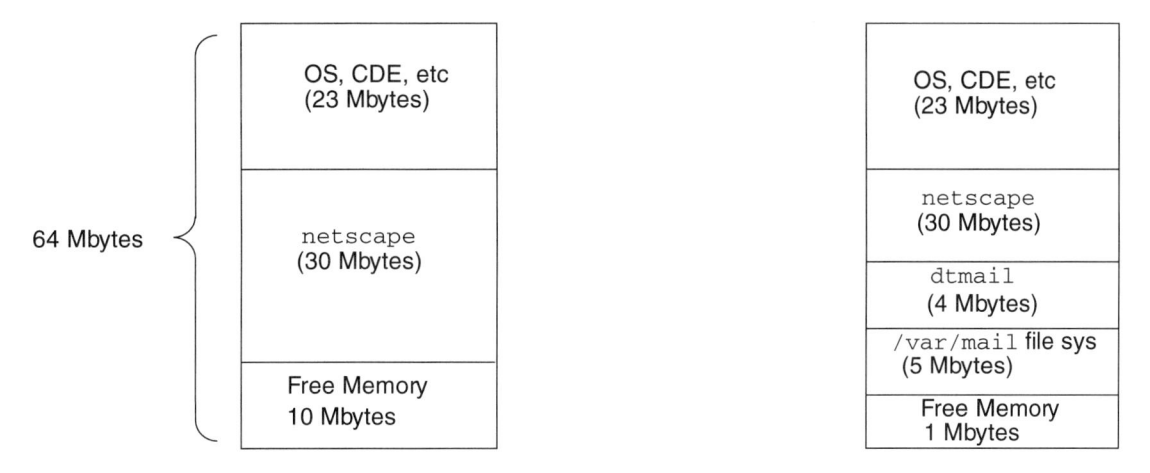

64 Mbytes

| OS, CDE, etc (23 Mbytes) |
| netscape (30 Mbytes) |
| Free Memory 10 Mbytes |

| OS, CDE, etc (23 Mbytes) |
| netscape (30 Mbytes) |
| dtmail (4 Mbytes) |
| /var/mail file sys (5 Mbytes) |
| Free Memory 1 Mbytes |

FIGURE 3-7 Memory Allocation with Priority Paging Enabled

The new memory allocation policy can be extremely important for larger systems, where memory paging problems cannot be resolved by adding additional memory. A large database system with a 50 Gbyte+ database on the file system will continuously put memory pressure on the database application with the default memory allocation policy. But priority paging will ensure that the file system only uses free memory for file system caching. As the application grows and shrinks, the size of the file system cache will grow and shrink in keeping with the amount of free memory on the system.

Network Interfaces and Network Services

TCP/IP-based network services are configured using the `/etc/services` and `/etc/inetd.conf` files so that the server responds on a particular port number. Access controls are implemented by removing and enabling particular port specifications from these files. In addition, more sophisticated access control can be implemented using TCP wrappers. These wrappers look at the incoming request packets and can deny access from unauthorized networks. To relay high volumes of traffic in and out of a secured network, a firewall is used. Access policies can be based on the destination address, protocol, or port number.

The Solaris Bandwidth Manager product provides controls on network traffic on each interface of a server. Chapter 9 explains how this product can be used as part of a resource control framework.

Network level resource managers can distribute incoming traffic over multiple systems according to the current load on each system and the network delays between the end user and the available servers. Cisco Local Director and Resonate Central Dispatch, among other products, can be used to direct traffic within a single web site, while Cisco's Distributed Director and Resonate's Global Dispatch products distribute traffic over wide areas, optimizing the wide area network delays. Cisco's products are implemented as hardware routers, while Resonate's products run as a software package on the existing server systems.

CHAPTER **4**

Workload Management

Application workloads can be understood in terms of the resources they consume on each of the systems that they are distributed across.

Resource measurements are available at the system level and at the per-process level. Analysis of per-process measurements separates the raw data into application workloads. When several applications are consolidated onto a single system, resource contention can occur. Analysis determines which resource is suffering from contention and which application workloads are involved. This chapter describes several tools that help perform process-based analysis.

This chapter also describes several diverse, real-life situations and the appropriate tools to use with them.

- The first scenario covers resource management issues that occur in Internet service provider (ISP) environments.
- The second scenario portrays at consolidated commercial workloads, which include databases and file services for UNIX systems using NFS and batch workloads.
- The third scenario looks at batch workloads, which are required by most commercial installations.

Workload Analysis Tools

In a distributed environment with discrete applications on separate systems, workloads are analyzed by monitoring the total resource usage of each whole system. The busiest systems can be identified and tuned or upgraded. This approach does not work when multiple workloads are combined on a single system. While all performance monitoring tools can tell you how busy the CPU is in total, few of them can aggregate all the processes that make up a workload and tell you the amount of resource per-user that workload is using.

Sun Enterprise SyMON 2.0 Software

The Sun Enterprise SyMON 2.0 software is described in detail in Chapter 12. This section briefly introduces the product and concentrates on the specific process of performing a workload analysis breakdown using SyMON as the example tool.

Sun Enterprise SyMON 2.0 software is a three-tier application. A customizable agent process runs on each system to be monitored. All agents report back to a centralized server process. Multiple graphical consoles can be started to view or customize the data. The console is written in Java and can be installed to run on the Solaris operating environment or the Windows NT environment.

The main console window shows all the systems in an administrative domain that are being monitored. A separate window shows a particular system in detail. A sample main window is shown in FIGURE 4-1.

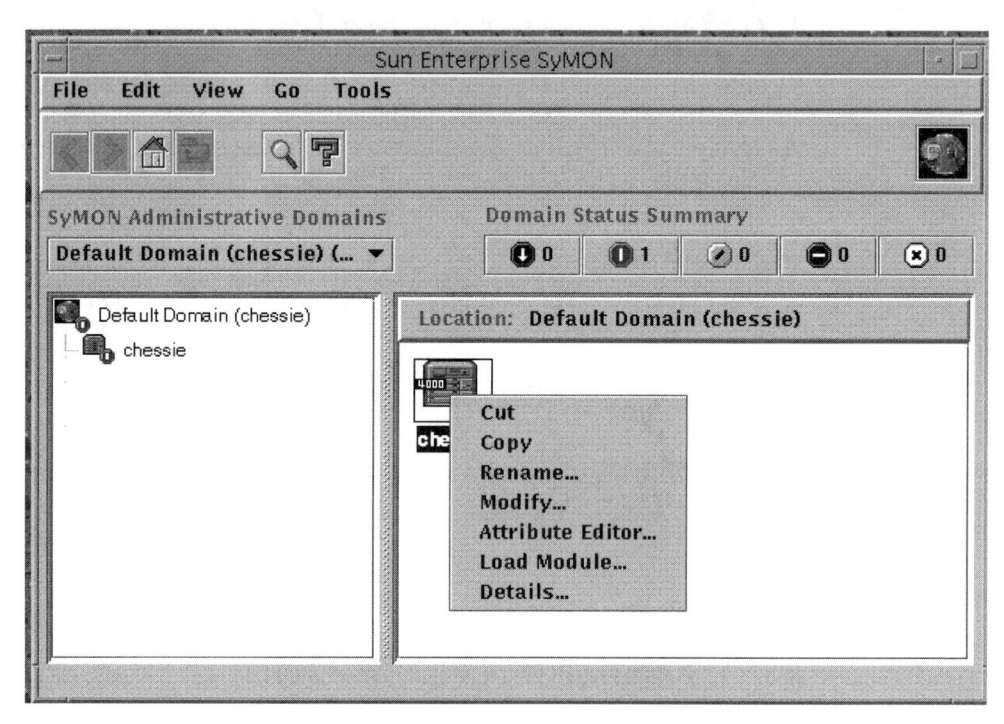

FIGURE 4-1   Sun Enterprise SyMON 2.0 Main Console Window

The agent on each system can be dynamically customized by loading additional modules at any time and by configuring the modules to monitor specific metrics and generate alarms if problems occur. Metrics can also be logged to a file.

Monitoring Processes

One optional module is a process monitor. It can be used to view all the processes on a system. It can also be configured to pattern match and accumulate all the processes that make up a workload. To load the process monitor, select the system and choose the Load Module option from the menu. A Load Module window is displayed, as shown in FIGURE 4-2.

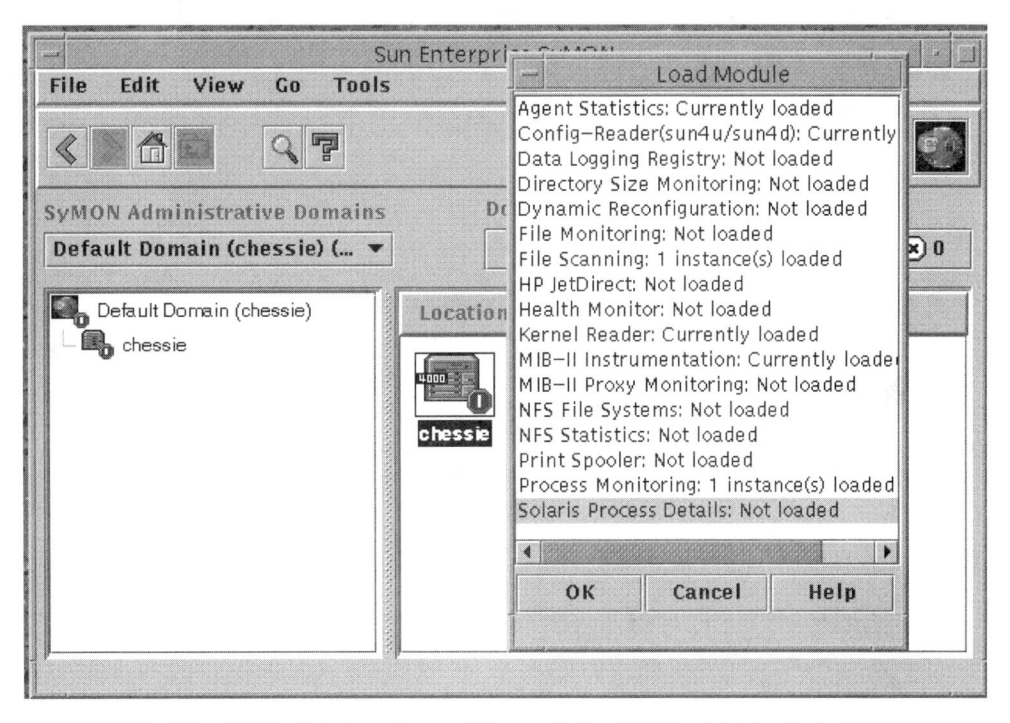

FIGURE 4-2 Sun Enterprise SyMON 2.0 Load Solaris Process Details Module

Select the Solaris Process Details module as shown in FIGURE 4-2. This module must be configured to give an initial sorting order metric for the display and the number of processes to list. The attributes configuration screen is shown in FIGURE 4-3.

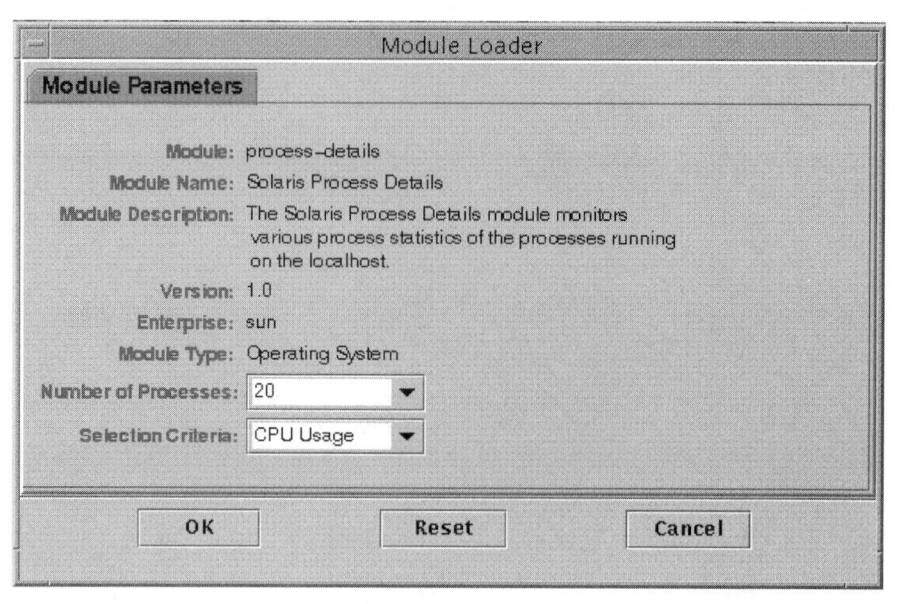

FIGURE 4-3 Process Details Module Parameters

The detailed window for each system has several tabs for looking at different kinds of data. Select the system and choose the Details option from the menu. When the new window opens choose the Processes tab. The Processes tab display is shown in FIGURE 4-4.

Note – If the Process Monitoring module has not been loaded for the selected system, an error message is displayed.

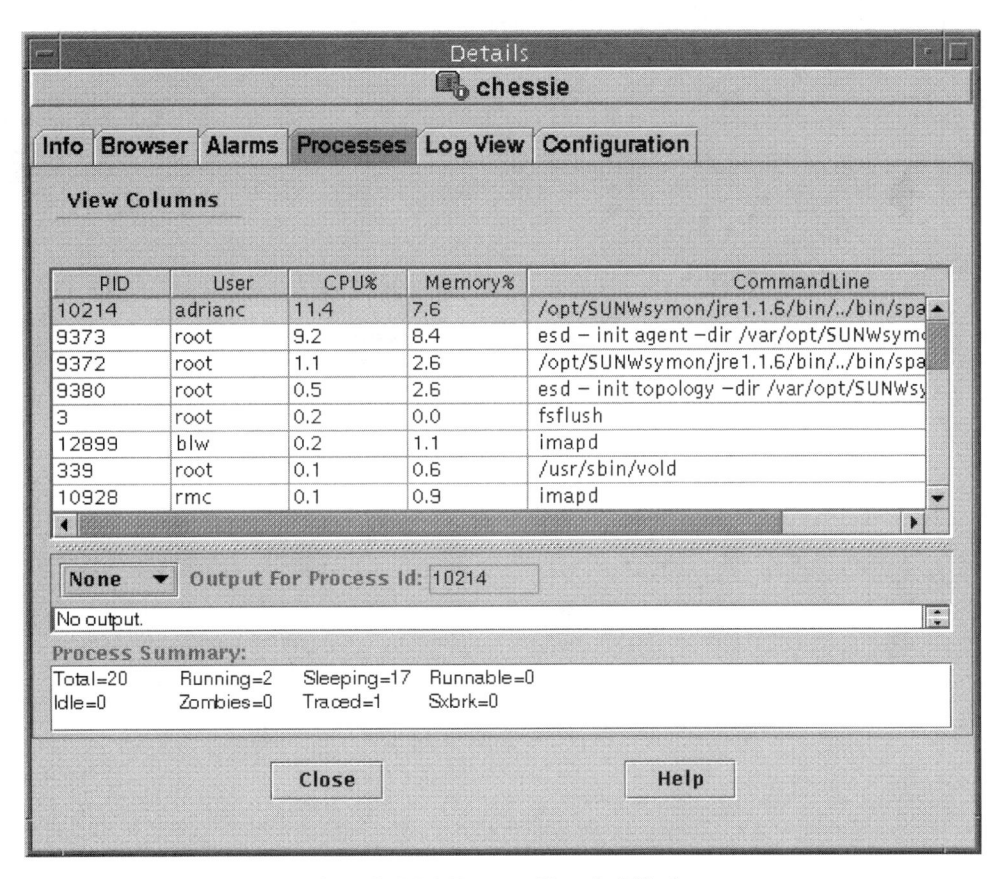

FIGURE 4-4 Sun Enterprise SyMON 2.0 Process Details Window

When you can see all the processes and users on the system, group them together. For example, all the system daemons that run as root can be gathered into a "system overhead" workload, or all the processes that make up a web server can be accumulated. A good approach is to sort the global process list by the recent CPU usage field and pick off the active processes into workloads until all the significant activity has been accounted for.

Monitoring Workloads

To configure the SyMON workload monitor, select a system and choose the Load Module option. Then choose the Process Monitoring option from the menu as shown in FIGURE 4-5.

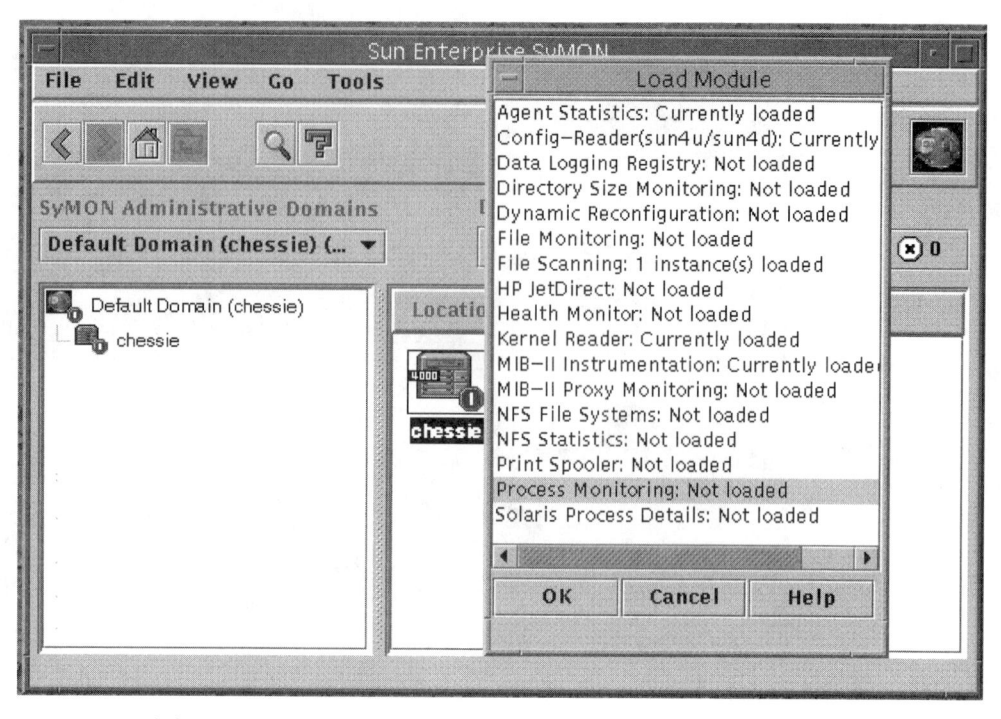

FIGURE 4-5 Selecting the Process Monitoring Option

You must first give a name to the definition you are creating by setting the module parameters as shown in FIGURE 4-6.

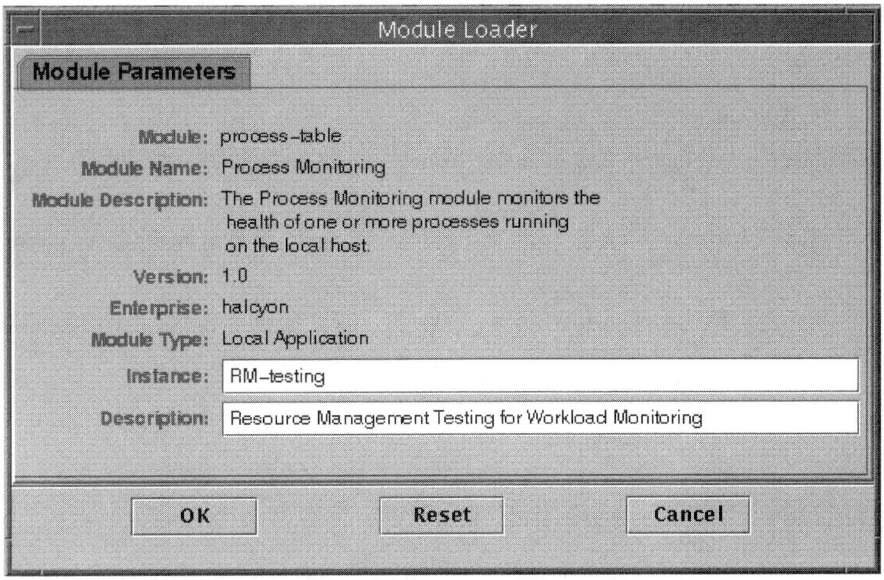

FIGURE 4-6 Process Monitor Parameters Setup

Once the Process Monitoring module has been set up, view the details window for the system again. This time select the Browser tab rather than the Processes tab, and find the Process Monitoring data under Local Applications as shown in FIGURE 4-7.

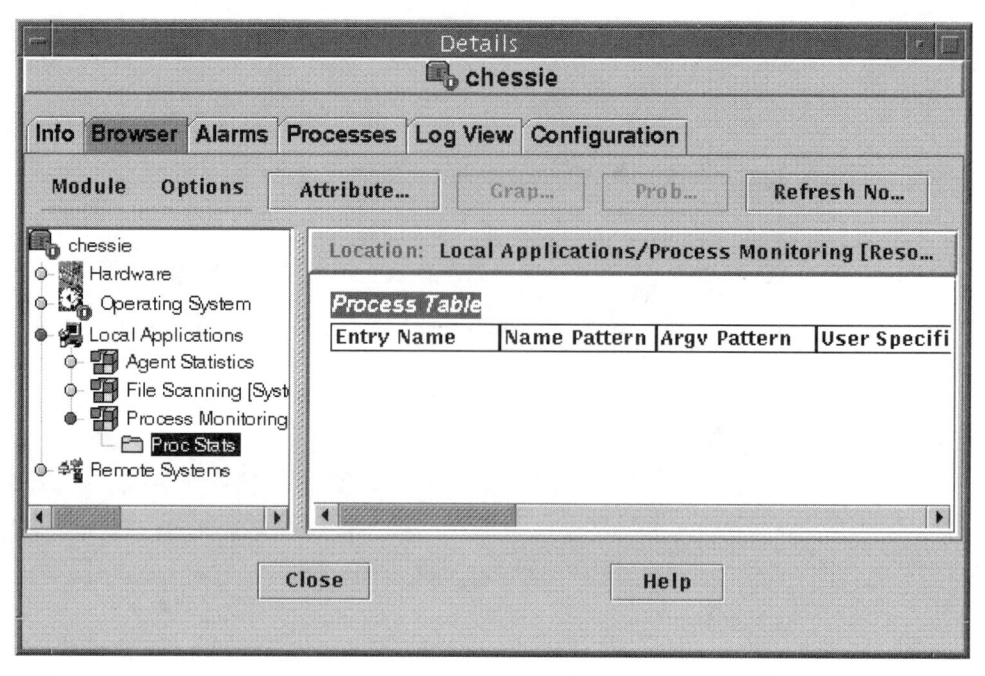

FIGURE 4-7 Unconfigured Process Monitoring Display

Now, configure the process monitor. Pop up a menu over the Process table as shown in FIGURE 4-8 and choose Add Row. A Row Adder window is displayed.

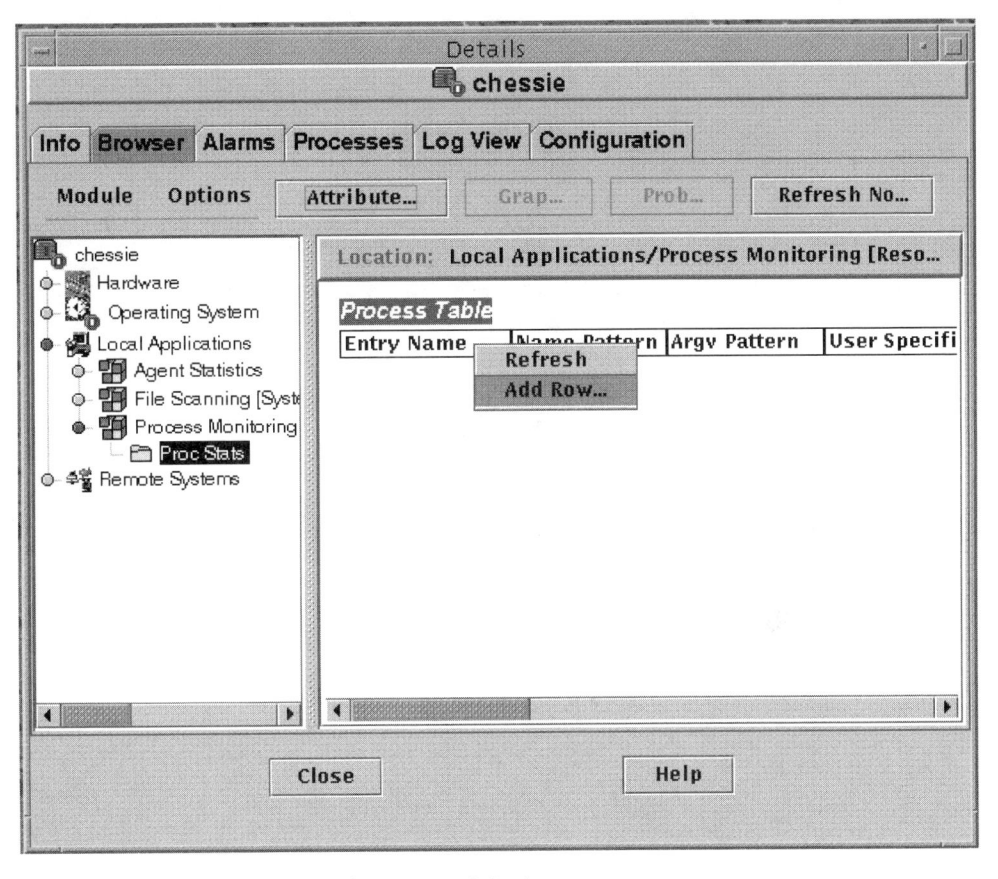

FIGURE 4-8 Adding a Row to the Process Monitor

Type in the name of a user, command, or arguments to be pattern matched against the processes on the system. The easiest way to do this is to keep the Row Adder window visible and switch back to the Processes tab so you can see the processes that are running. This is shown in FIGURE 4-9, where the Java Runtime Environment (jre) process that makes up part of the SyMON application has been selected.

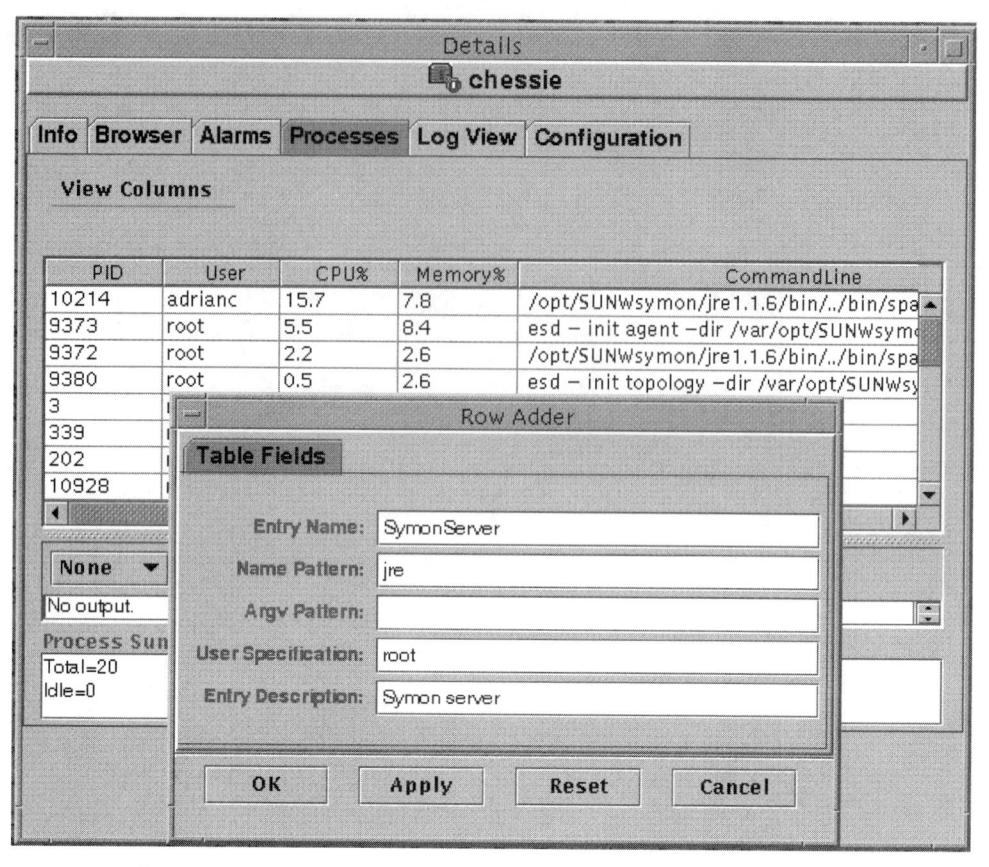

FIGURE 4-9 Setting Up Process Details for a Row

More complex pattern matching capabilities are available, including the ability to or together multiple argument names. In the example in FIGURE 4-10, a selection of argument values are used to select the SyMON server helper processes.

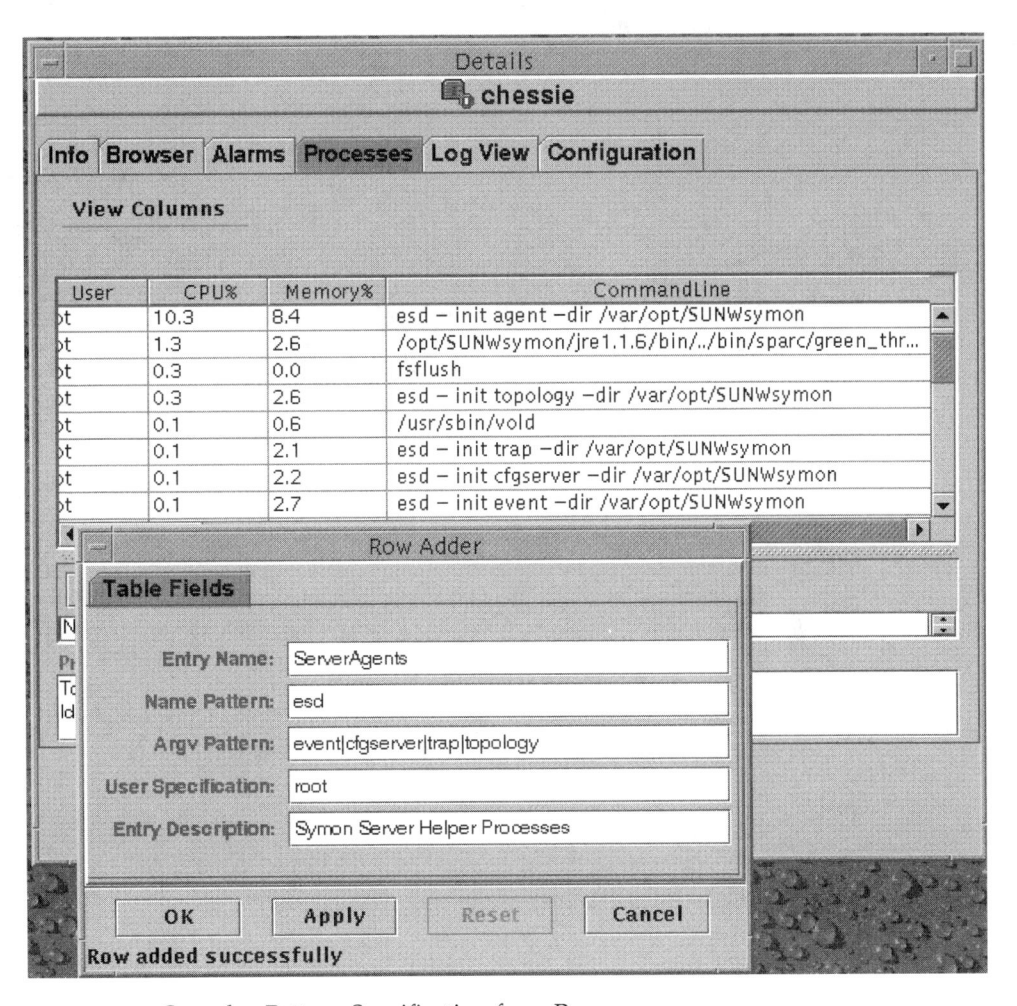

FIGURE 4-10 Complex Pattern Specification for a Row

Once you have created a workload definition, use the Browser tab to view the number of processes it matches and the accumulated resource usage for the workload. An example is shown in FIGURE 4-11.

Chapter 4   Workload Management   45

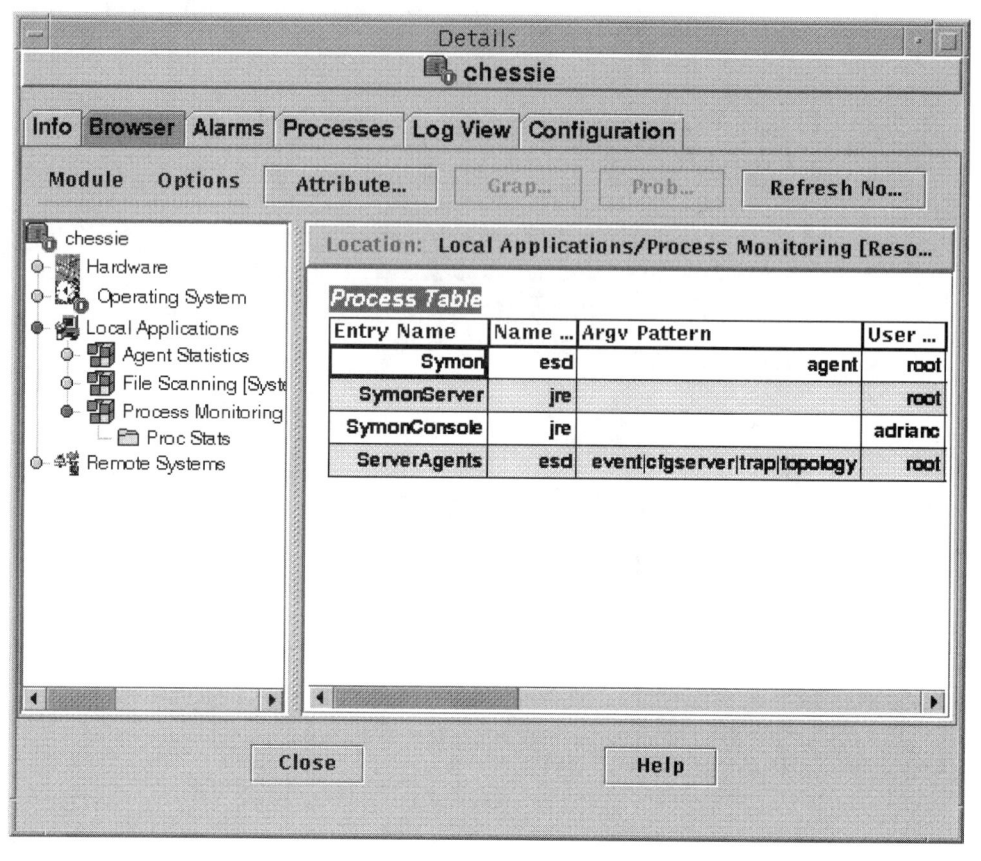

FIGURE 4-11 Initial Process Monitoring Display

FIGURE 4-11 shows the configuration information, but all the data is scrolled to the right. You can adjust the position and order of any table by selecting the headers with the cursor and sliding them until you get the desired view. A better optimized display layout is shown in FIGURE 4-12.

46   Resource Management

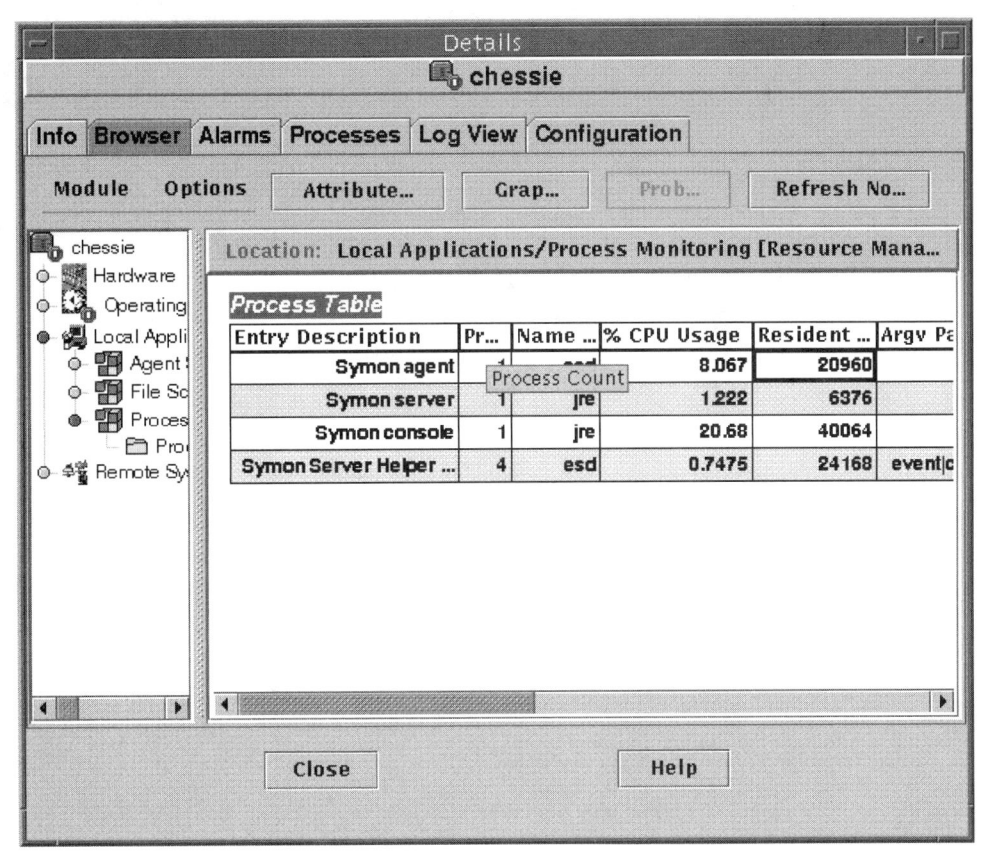

FIGURE 4-12 Optimized Layout Process Monitoring Display

You can select a metric and graph it or place a threshold and an alarm on it. To do this, pop up a menu over a specific row item so that the Attribute Editor for that item appears. FIGURE 4-13 shows how a CPU usage threshold can be placed on a row that could match a group of processes. The number in the row of the table has changed color to indicate that the threshold has been reached and a caution alarm has been raised. (This figure contains two overlapping windows.) It is also possible to configure long term logging of a particular value using the History tab shown in this display.

Chapter 4   Workload Management   47

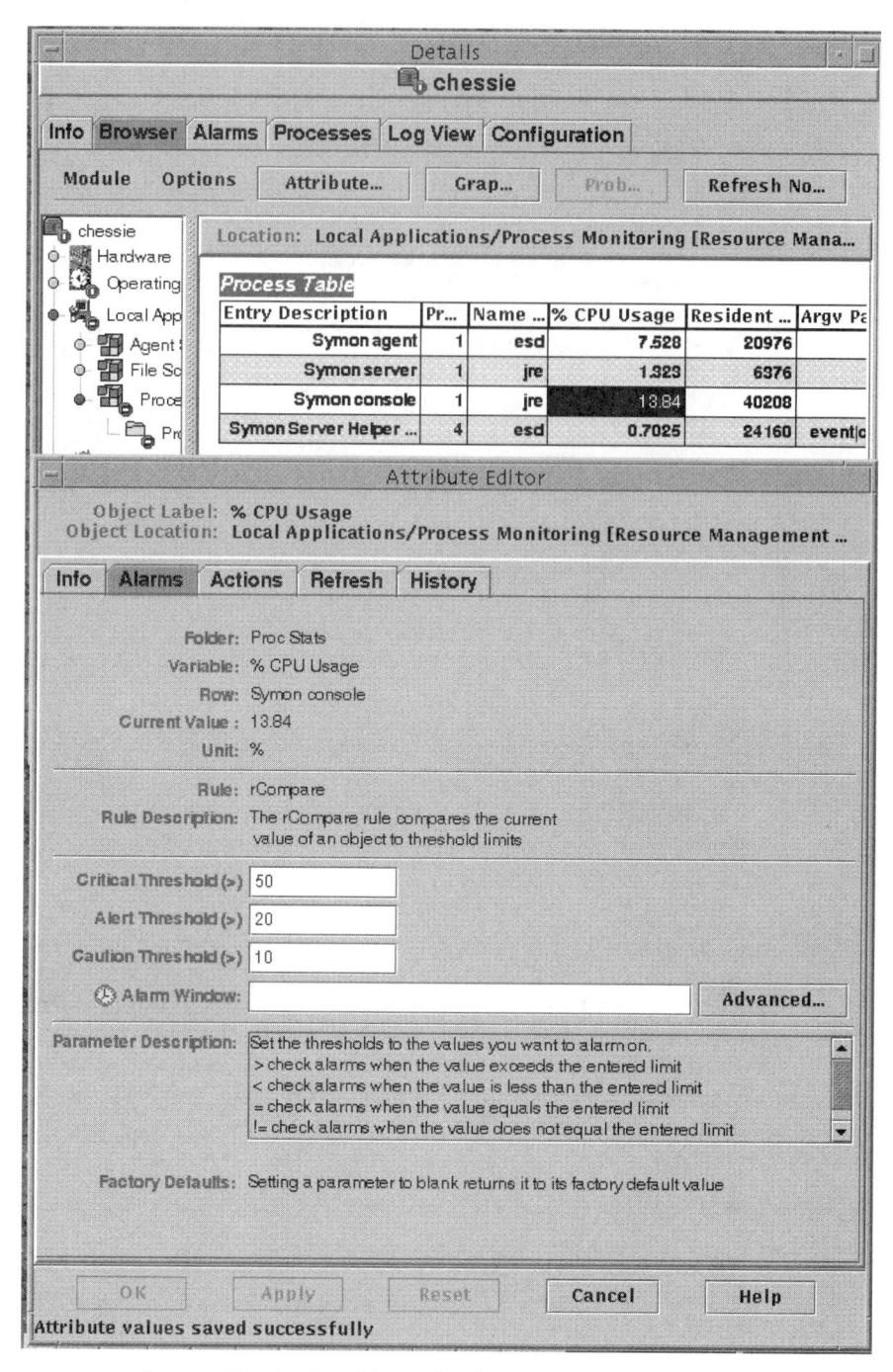

FIGURE 4-13 Process Monitoring Alarm Configuration

48   Resource Management

Finally, it is easy to create a graph that monitors any of the values in the table and to add other values to the graph. The example in FIGURE 4-14 combines data from a process monitor with system level information on CPU usage.

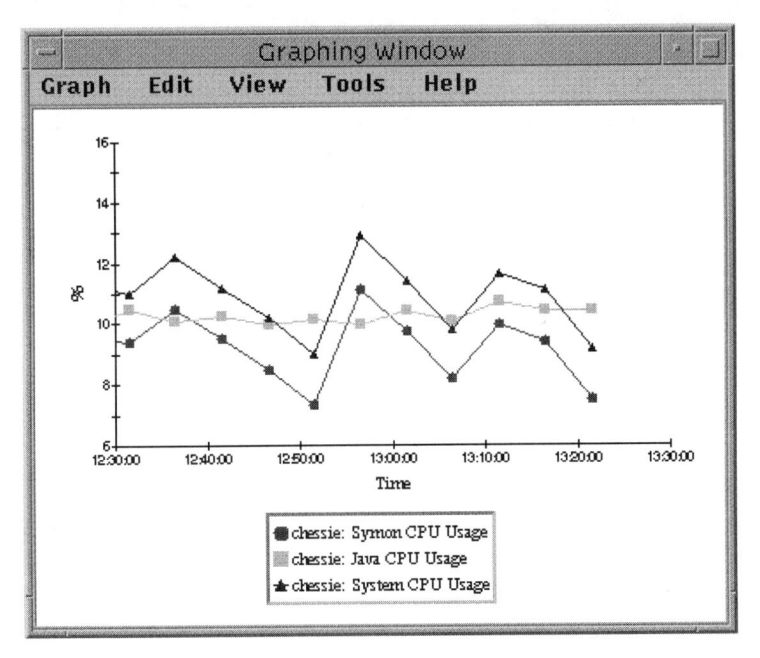

FIGURE 4-14 Workload Graph Example

Chapter 12 provides more information on how to configure and use SyMON.

Workload Analysis Products

Other commercial products incorporate process analysis capabilities similar to those of SyMON software then also store long term historical data and build capacity planning models that can be used to do trend analysis and predict future scenarios. Three products with this capability are:

- BMC Best/1—see http://www.bmc.com
- Teamquest—see http://www.teamquest.com
- Metron Athene (This product is also the basis of Landmark Predictor)— see http://www.metron.co.uk and http://www.landmark.com

Customized Process Monitors

The Solaris software provides a great deal of per-process information that is not collected and displayed by the `ps` command or the SyMON software. The data can be viewed and processed by a custom-written process monitor. You could write one from scratch or use the experimental scripts provided as part of the SE (SymbEl Engine) Toolkit. The SE Toolkit is freely available for Solaris systems and is widely used. However, it is not a Sun-supported product. It can be downloaded from the URL `http://www.sun.com/sun-on-net/performance/se3`. The SE Toolkit is based on an interpreter for a dialect of the C language and provides all the per process information in a convenient form that can then be processed further or displayed. The available data and the way the SE Toolkit summarizes it is explained in detail in Chapter 5. For now, we are only interested in how this tool can be used.

The SE Process Class

The basic requirement for the process class is that it should collect both the `psinfo` and `usage` data for every process on the system. The `psinfo` data is what the `ps` command reads and summarizes. The `usage` data is extra information that includes the microstate accounting timers. Sun's developer-oriented Workshop Analyzer uses this data to help tune code during application development, but it is not normally collected by system performance monitors. For consistency, all the data for all processes should be collected at one time and as quickly as possible, then offered for display, one process at a time. This avoids the problem in the `ps` command where the data for the last process is measured after all the other processes have been measured and displayed, so the data is not associated with a consistent timestamp.

The `psinfo` data contains a measure of recent average CPU usage, but what you really want is all data measured over the time interval since the last reading. This is complex because new processes arrive and old ones die. Matching all the data is not as trivial as measuring the performance changes for the CPUs or disks in the system. Potentially, tens of thousands of processes must be tracked.

The code that implements this is quite complex, but all the complexity is hidden in the class code in `/opt/RICHPse/include/process_class.se`. The result is that the most interesting data is available in a very easy-to-use form and a simple script can be written in SE to display selected process information in a text based format similar to the `ps` command. To change the displayed data, it is easy to edit the `printf` format statement in the script directly.

Using the `pea.se` Script

The `pea.se` script is an extended process monitor that acts as a test program for `process_class.se` and displays useful information that is not extracted by standard tools. It is based on the microstate accounting information described in Chapter 5.

```
Usage: se [-DWIDE] pea.se [interval]
```

The script runs continuously and reports on the average data for each active process in the measured interval. This reporting is very different from tools such as ps, that print the current data only. There are two display modes: an 80-column format (which is the default and is shown in FIGURE 4-15) and the wide mode, which displays much more information and is shown in FIGURE 4-16. The initial data display includes all processes and shows their average data since the process was created. Any new processes that appear are also treated this way. When a process is measured a second time and is found to have consumed some CPU time, its averages for the measured interval are displayed. Idle processes are ignored. The output is generated every ten seconds by default. The script can report only on processes that it has permission to access. So it must be run as root to see everything in the Solaris 2.5.1 operating environment. However, it sees everything in the Solaris 2.6 operating environment without root permissions.

```
% se pea.se
09:34:06 name    lwp    pid   ppid    uid    usr%   sys%  wait%  chld%   size    rss   pf
olwm              1     322    299   9506    0.01   0.01   0.03   0.00   2328   1032  0.0
maker5X.exe       1   21508      1   9506    0.55   0.33   0.04   0.00  29696  19000  0.0
perfmeter         1     348      1   9506    0.04   0.02   0.00   0.00   3776   1040  0.0
cmdtool           1     351      1   9506    0.01   0.00   0.03   0.00   3616    960  0.0
cmdtool           1   22815    322   9506    0.08   0.03   2.28   0.00   3616   1552  2.2
xterm             1   22011   9180   9506    0.04   0.03   0.30   0.00   2840   1000  0.0
se.sparc.5.5.1    1   23089  22818   9506    1.92   0.07   0.00   0.00   1744   1608  0.0
fa.htmllite       1   21559      1   9506    0.00   0.00   0.00   0.00   1832     88  0.0
fa.tooltalk       1   21574      1   9506    0.00   0.00   0.00   0.00   2904   1208  0.0
nproc 31    newproc 0    deadproc 0
```

FIGURE 4-15 Output from the `pea.se` Command

Note – The font size in FIGURE 4-16 has been severely reduced.

```
% se -DWIDE pea.se
09:34:51 name    lwp    pid   ppid   uid    usr%   sys%  wait%  chld%  size   rss   pf   inblk  outblk  chario  sysc   vctx
ictx     msps
maker5X.exe      1 21508   1   9506   0.86   0.36   0.10  0.00  29696  19088  0.0  0.00  0.00   5811    380    60.03  0.30  0.20
perfmeter        1   348   1   9506   0.03   0.02   0.00  0.00   3776   1040  0.0  0.00  0.00    263     12     1.39  0.20  0.29
cmdtool          1 22815 322   9506   0.04   0.00   0.04  0.00   3624   1928  0.0  0.00  0.00    229      2     0.20  0.30  0.96
se.sparc.5.5.1   1  3792 341   9506   0.12   0.01   0.00  0.00   9832   3376  0.0  0.00  0.00      2      9     0.20  0.10  4.55
se.sparc.5.5.1   1 23097 22818 9506   0.75   0.06   0.00  0.00   1752   1616  0.0  0.00  0.00    119     19     0.10
0.30   20.45
fa.htmllite      1 21559   1   9506   0.00   0.00   0.00  0.00   1832     88  0.0  0.00  0.00      0      0     0.10  0.00  0.06
nproc 31  newproc 0  deadproc 0
```

FIGURE 4-16 Output from the `-DWIDE pea.se` Command

The `pea.se` script is 90 lines of code containing a few simple `printfs` in a loop. The real work is done in `process_class.se` (over 500 lines of code). It can be used by any other script. The default data shown by `pea.se` consists of:

- Current time and process name
- Number of lwps for the process, so you can see which are multithreaded
- Process ID, parent process ID, and user ID
- User and system CPU percentage measured accurately by microstate accounting
- Process time percentage spent waiting in the run queue or for page faults to complete
- CPU percentage accumulated from child processes that have exited
- Virtual address space size and resident set size, in Kbytes
- Page fault per second rate for the process over this interval

When the command is run in wide mode, the following data is added:

- Metadata input and output blocks per second
- Characters transferred by read and write calls
- System call per second rate over this interval
- Voluntary context switches, where the process slept for a reason
- Involuntary context switches where the process was interrupted by higher priority work or exceeded its time slice
- Milliseconds per slice or the calculated average amount of CPU time consumed between each context switch

Several additional metrics are available and can be substituted or added to the display by editing a copy of the script.

Workload Based Summarization

When you have numerous processes, group them together to make them more manageable. If you group them by user name and command, then you can form workloads, which is a powerful way to view the system. The SE Toolkit also includes a workload class, which sits on top of the process class. It pattern matches on user name, command and arguments, and processor set membership. It can work on a first-fit basis, where each process is included only in the first workload that matches. It can also work on a summary basis, where each process is included in every workload that matches. By default, the code allows up to 10 workloads to be specified.

The `pw.se` Test Program for Workload Class

Specifying workloads is the challenge. For simplicity, `pw.se` uses environment variables. The first variable is PW_COUNT, the number of workloads. This is followed by PW_CMD_n, PW_ARGS_n, PW_USER_n, and PW_PRSET_n where n goes from 0 to PW_COUNT -1. If no pattern is provided, `pw.se` automatically matches anything. If you run `pw.se` with nothing specified all processes are accumulated into a single catch-all workload. The `size` value is accumulated because it is related to the total swap space usage for the workload although it is inflated due to shared memory. The `rss` value is not, as too much memory is shared for the result to have any useful meaning. The final line also shows the total accumulated over all workloads.

```
16:00:09 nproc 61    newproc 0   deadproc 0
wk  command    args    user procs   usr%   sys% wait% chld%    size    pf
 0                                59    26.3    2.0   5.6   0.0  180900    2
 1                                 0     0.0    0.0   0.0   0.0       0    0
 2                                 0     0.0    0.0   0.0   0.0       0    0
 3                                 0     0.0    0.0   0.0   0.0       0    0
 4                                 0     0.0    0.0   0.0   0.0       0    0
 5                                 0     0.0    0.0   0.0   0.0       0    0
 6                                 0     0.0    0.0   0.0   0.0       0    0
 7                                 0     0.0    0.0   0.0   0.0       0    0
 8                                 0     0.0    0.0   0.0   0.0       0    0
 9                                 0     0.0    0.0   0.0   0.0       0    0
10  Total        *         *      59    26.3    2.0   5.6   0.0  180900    2
```

FIGURE 4-17 Example Output from pw.se

It is easier to use the `pw.sh` script that sets up a workload suitable for monitoring a desktop workstation that is also running a Netscape web server.

```
% more pw.sh
#!/bin/csh

setenv PW_CMD_0 ns-httpd
setenv PW_CMD_1 'se.sparc'
setenv PW_CMD_2 'dtmail'
setenv PW_CMD_3 'dt'
setenv PW_CMD_4 'roam'
setenv PW_CMD_5 'netscape'
setenv PW_CMD_6 'X'
setenv PW_USER_7 $USER
setenv PW_USER_8 'root'
setenv PW_COUNT 10
exec /opt/RICHPse/bin/se -DWIDE pw.se 60
```

FIGURE 4-18 Sample `pw.se` Configuration Script

The script runs with a one minute update rate and uses the wide mode by default. It is useful to note that a workload that has a high `wait%` is either being starved of memory (waiting for page faults) or of CPU power. A high number of page faults for a workload indicates that it is either starting a lot of new processes, doing a lot of file system I/O, or that it is short of memory.

```
16:00:09 nproc 61  newproc 59   deadproc 0
wk  command    args      user count    usr%   sys%  wait%  chld%    size    pf pwait% ulkwt% chario   sysc   vctx   ictx   msps
 0  ns-httpd                        0    0.0    0.0    0.0    0.0       0     0    0.0    0.0      0      0      0      0   0.00
 1  se.sparc                        1   26.0   13.8    0.8   24.4    2792     6    0.8    0.0  20531      0      9     15  16.55
 2  dtmail                          0    0.0    0.0    0.0    0.0       0     0    0.0    0.0      0      0      0      0   0.00
 3        dt                        3    0.0    0.0    0.0    0.0   11132     0    0.0    0.0     64      0      0      0   0.00
 4     roam                         2    1.3    0.2    0.0    0.0   31840     0    0.0    0.0   8978      0      2      2   3.74
 5  netscape                        2    0.1    0.0    0.0    0.0   34668     0    0.0    0.0   1081      0      0      0   0.00
 6         X                        2    3.2    0.8    0.0    0.0   27188     0    0.0    0.0   4571      0     10      3   3.09
 7              adrianc            16    0.0    0.0    0.1    0.8   32048     1    0.1    0.0    102      0      9      3   0.03
 8                 root            33    0.0    0.0    0.0    6.4   41224     1    0.0    0.0     47      0      0      3   0.09
 9                                  0    0.0    0.0    0.0    0.0       0     0    0.0    0.0      0      0      0      0   0.00
10     Total       *      *        59   30.6   14.9    0.9   31.5  180892     7    0.9    0.0  35375      0     21     23  10.32
```

FIGURE 4-19 Example Output from Configured pw.se

Process Rule

Once you have collected the data, you can write a rule that examines each process or workload and determines, using thresholds, whether that workload is CPU-bound, memory-bound, I/O bound, or suffering from some other problem. This information can then be used as input to determine the resources that must be increased for workloads that are under-performing. A prototype of this rule is implemented in the SE Toolkit, and it can produce the kind of information shown in FIGURE 4-20. The example was taken while saving changes to a large file, hence the process was detected to be I/O bound. In this example the threshold is set to zero. In practice, you would set higher thresholds.

```
% se pry.se 791
...
monpid 791  nproc 94  newproc 0  deadproc 0
15:34:45 name lwmx    pid  ppid   uid    usr%   sys% wait% chld%   size     rss    pf   inblk outblk chario
 sysc   vctx    ictx    msps
maker5X.exe     1     791     1   9506    4.77   1.41  0.45  0.00   25600   22352  1.7    0.00   0.00 139538
 858  27.13    5.84    1.87
  amber: IObound

amber:  0.2%    [ 0.0% ] process is delayed by page faults in data file access
```

FIGURE 4-20 Sample Process Monitoring Rule

Now we will look at some sample workloads and see how the tools for workload analysis can be used in practice.

Internet Service Provider Workloads

The Internet provides a challenge for managing computer systems. Instead of a small population of known users who can connect to a server system, millions of users can connect to any server that is on the Internet. External synchronizing events can cause a tidal wave of users to arrive at the server at the same time, as shown in the following examples.

- Sports-related web sites in the USA get a peak load during key games in the "March madness" college basketball season. In general, any television or news media event may advertise a URL to which users can connect, and cause a spike in activity.

- In countries where local phone calls are charged by the minute, the onset of cheap rate calls at 6:00 p.m. each day causes a big spike in the number of dial-in connections at an ISP, creating a major load on the local servers at that time.

- Proxy caching web servers sit between a large number of users and the Internet and funnel all activity through the cache. They are used in corporate intranets and at ISPs. When all the users are active at once, regardless of where they are connecting to, these proxy cache servers get very busy.

On the other hand, many web sites get little or no activity most of the time. It is too expensive to dedicate a single computer system to each web site, so a single system may be configured to respond to hundreds or thousands of internet addresses. This is sometimes known as virtual web hosting. From a user perspective it is not possible to tell that accesses to the different web sites are going to the same physical system. If one of the virtual web sites becomes very busy, the performance of accesses to all the other virtual sites can be affected, and resource management tools are needed to help maintain a fair quality of service for all the sites.

This section looks at three case studies: a proxy web cache workload, virtual web hosting, and a content provider site.

Proxy Web Cache Workload

A caching web server acts as an invisible intermediary between a client browser and the servers that provide content. It cuts down on overall network traffic and provides administrative control over web traffic routing. Performance requirements are quite different from those for a regular web server. After discussing the issues, we'll look at several metrics that must be collected and analyzed to determine the workload mix and the management of resources.

We start by remembering the caching principle of temporal and spacial locality. In the case of a web cache, cacheable objects are always separate and are always read in their entirety with no prefetching. The proxy web cache mostly works by using temporal locality. If cached items are read more than once by different users in a reasonably short time interval, the cache will work well. If every user reads completely different pages, the cache will just get in the way. If one user rereads the same pages, that browser will tend to cache the pages on the client. So the proxy server cache won't be used effectively.

Not all web content is cacheable. Some of the busiest traffic is dynamic by nature, and caching it would prevent the browser from seeing an update.

Cache Effectiveness

Caches commonly have a hit rate of about 20 to 30 percent, with only 60 percent of the data being cacheable. That figure does not take into account the size of each access—just the total number of accesses. Each cache transaction takes some time to complete and adds significant latency to the connection time. In other words, the cache slows down end users significantly, and only a small proportion of the data read is supplied from the cache. All the users go through the cache regardless of their final destination. This funnel effect can increase network load at a local level because accesses to local web servers will normally go via the cache, causing two trips over the local network rather than one.

Direct web service, as shown in FIGURE 4-21, allows the browser to contact web servers directly whenever possible. This contact may involve a firewall proxy that does not provide caching to get out to the public Internet.

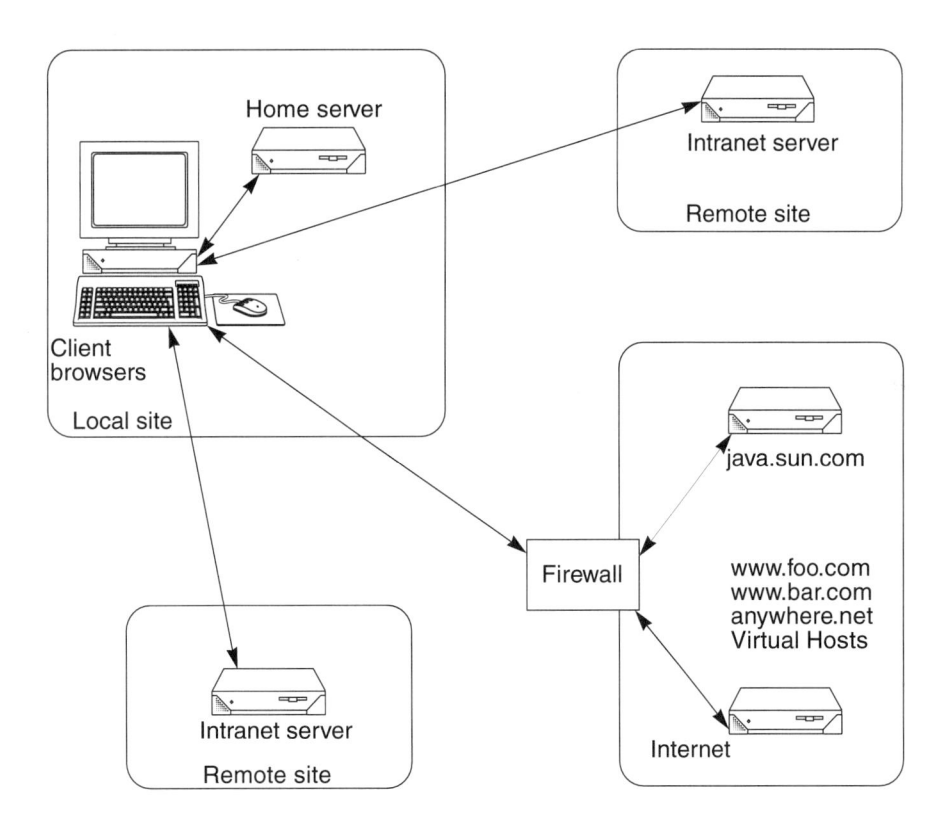

FIGURE 4-21 Direct Web Service without Proxy Cache

In contrast, when a proxy is introduced, as shown in FIGURE 4-22, all the browsers connect to the proxy by default. An exception can be made for named systems and domains that can be accessed more efficiently by a direct connection.

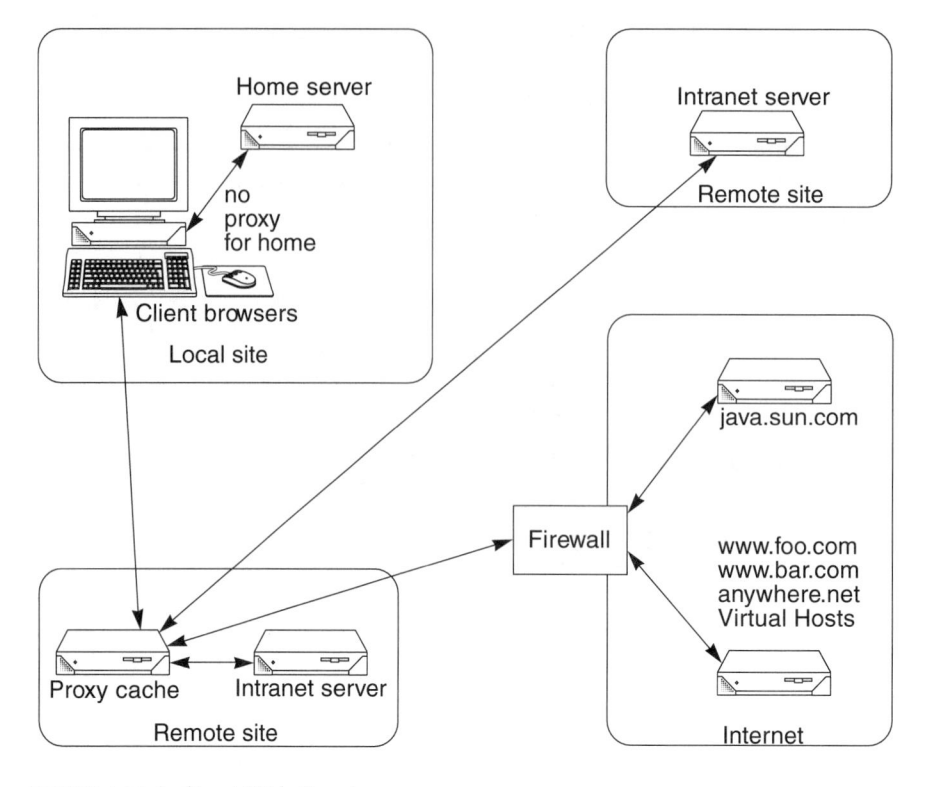

FIGURE 4-22 Indirect Web Service

Caching for Administrative Control

The reduction in wide-area network traffic from a 20 to 30 percent hit rate is worth having, especially since wide-area links are expensive and may be saturated at peak times.

The real reason to set up a proxy cache intranet infrastructure is the administrative control. Security is a big problem. One approach is to set up the firewall gateways to the Internet so that they route web traffic only to and from the proxy caches. The proxy caches can make intelligent routing decisions. For example, Sun has connections to the Internet in Europe and the USA. If a user in Europe accesses an Internet web site in Europe, that access is routed via the local connection. When an access is made to a site in the USA, a choice can be made. The route could go to the USA over Sun's private network to the USA-based gateway, or it could go directly to the Internet in Europe and find its own way to the USA. The second option reduces the load on expensive private transatlantic links, but the first option can be used as a fallback if the European connection goes down.

Restricted routing also forces every end user who wants to get out to the Internet to do so via a proxy cache. The cache makes routing and filtering decisions and logs every access with the URL and the client IP address (which is usually sufficient to identify the end user). If the corporate policy is "Internet access is provided for business use only during business hours," then employees who clog up the networks with non-business traffic can be identified. It is probably sufficient to make it known to the employees that their activity is being logged and that they can be traced. Posting an analysis of the most visited sites during working hours for everyone to look at would probably have a sobering effect. Filtering can be added to deny access to popular but unwelcome sites.

The point is that you have a limited amount of expensive wide-area network capacity. There is a strong tendency for end users to consume all the capacity that you provide. Using gentle peer pressure to keep the usage productive seems reasonable and can radically improve the performance of your network for real business use.

Solaris Bandwidth Manager software can be used effectively in this environment to implement policies based on the URL, domain or protocol mix that is desired. For example, if traffic to an Internet stock quote server is crowding out more important traffic in the wide area links of a company intranet, Solaris Bandwidth Manager software can throttle access to that site to a specified percentage of the total. The combination of proxy cache controls and bandwidth management is a powerful and flexible way to optimize use of wide area network and Internet gateway bandwidth.

Clustered Proxy Cache Architectures

The Apache and Netscape™ proxy caches are extensions of a conventional web server. They are used singly, and although they can be used in a hierarchy of caches, there is no optimization between the caches. An alternative is a clustered cache. The Harvest Cache was the original development and is now a commercial product. The Squid cache is a freely available spin-off and is the basis for some commercial products. Squid is used at the biggest cache installations, caching traffic at the country level for very large Internet service providers.

Clustered caches use an intercache protocol (ICP) to talk among themselves and form an explicit hierarchy of siblings and parents. If the load would overwhelm a single machine or if high availability is important, multiple systems are configured as siblings. Each sibling stores data in its cache but also uses the ICP to search the caches of other siblings. The net result: the effective cache size is that of all the siblings combined, the hit rate is improved, and it doesn't matter which sibling a client visits. The parent-child relationships also form a more efficient hierarchy because the ICP-based connections are much more efficient than individual HTTP transfers. ICP connections are kept open, and transfers have lower latency. When using bandwidth management in a clustered cache architecture, give the inter-cache protocol high priority so that the response time for cache queries does not get affected when the caches are generating a lot of network traffic.

Virtual Web Hosting

A huge number of people and businesses have registered their own personal domain names and want the domain to be active on the internet with a home page. In many cases, there is little activity on these names, but they are assigned a fixed IP address, and somewhere a web server must respond to that address. In the Solaris operating environment, it is possible to configure more than one IP address on a single network interface. The default limit is 256 virtual addresses per interface, but it has tested up to 8000 addresses per interface and could go higher. Use the `ifconfig` command to assign IP addresses to an interface and specify virtual interfaces with a trailing colon and number on the interface name. Use the `ndd` command to query or set the maximum number of addresses per interface. In the example below, two addresses are configured on hme0, and the default of up to 256 addresses is set.

```
% ifconfig -a
lo0: flags=849<UP,LOOPBACK,RUNNING,MULTICAST> mtu 8232
        inet 127.0.0.1 netmask ff000000
hme0: flags=863<UP,BROADCAST,NOTRAILERS,RUNNING,MULTICAST> mtu 1500
        inet 129.136.134.27 netmask ffffff00 broadcast 129.136.134.255
hme0:1: flags=863<UP,BROADCAST,NOTRAILERS,RUNNING,MULTICAST> mtu 1500
        inet 129.136.134.26 netmask ffffff00 broadcast 129.136.134.255
hme1: flags=863<UP,BROADCAST,NOTRAILERS,RUNNING,MULTICAST> mtu 1500
        inet 129.136.23.11 netmask ffffff00 broadcast 129.136.23.255

# /usr/sbin/ndd -get /dev/ip ip_addrs_per_if
256
```

The real limit to the number of virtual addresses is the time it takes to run `ifconfig` command on all of them. When thousands of virtual addresses are configured, the reboot time is affected, which can be a significant problem in a high availability failover scenario. The Solaris 2.6 operating environment was tuned to speed up this process.

Web servers can be configured in several ways to manage many virtual addresses. The most efficient way is to use a feature of the web server so that a single instance of the server listens to many addresses and responds with the appropriate home page. With a multithreaded web server, one process can support many addresses. With web servers like Apache that use a separate process for each connection, more processes are spawned for the addresses that are most active at any point.

Administrative problems may rule out this approach. It may be necessary to run a completely separate web instance of the web server for each address. This way the web server runs using a distinct userid. The administrator of the web site can log in as that user to configure their own site. The web server and any search engine or `cgi-bin` scripts that it starts all run as that user so that accounting, performance monitoring and resource management tools can manage each virtual web site's activity separately. It is common for `cgi-bin` scripts to have errors and be resource intensive. They can get stuck in infinite loops and consume an entire CPU. With thousands of customer web sites setup on a single system, the central administrator cannot control the quality of the custom `cgi-bin` code that is set up on each site.

In the end, this workload is similar in many ways to an old-fashioned central timeshare system. Resource management using the SRM software to control the CPU usage and the number of processes and logins on a per-user basis is extremely effective. The Solaris Bandwidth Manager software can also be used effectively, as there is an explicit administrative mapping from each network address to the userid that is running that web server. Users can be allocated shares of the CPU and network resources according to their need, or can pay more for a larger share and be confident that they will get a better quality of service if the server saturates.

Managing Web Servers with SRM Software

The SRM software manages resources on web servers by controlling the amount of CPU and virtual memory. Three basic topologies are used on systems hosting web servers.

Resource Managing a Consolidated Web Server

A web server can be managed by controlling the resources it can use. In an environment where a web server is being consolidated with other workloads, this basic form of resource management prevents other workloads from affecting the performance of the web server, and vice versa.

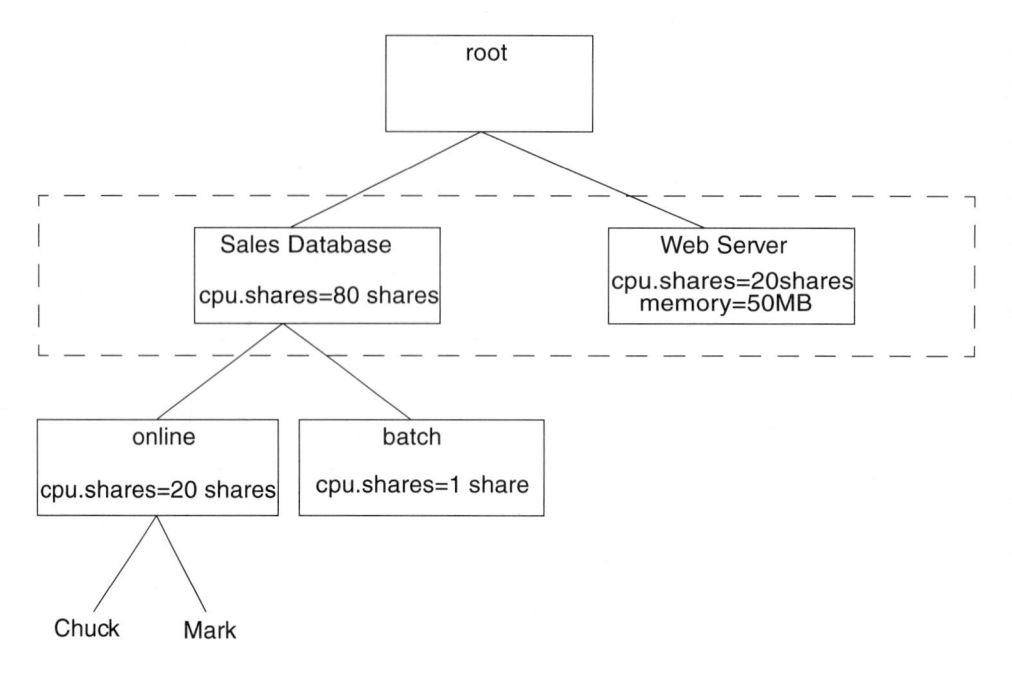

```
                         ┌─────────┐
                         │  root   │
                         └─────────┘
                         ╱         ╲
        ┌───────────────╱───────────╲──────────────────┐
        │   ┌──────────────────┐   ┌──────────────────┐│
        │   │  Sales Database  │   │   Web Server     ││
        │   │cpu.shares=80 shares│ │cpu.shares=20shares││
        │   │                  │   │   memory=50MB    ││
        │   └──────────────────┘   └──────────────────┘│
        └──────────╱──────╲─────────────────────────────┘
              ╱            ╲
   ┌──────────────────┐  ┌──────────────────┐
   │     online       │  │      batch       │
   │cpu.shares=20 shares│ │cpu.shares=1 share│
   └──────────────────┘  └──────────────────┘
        ╱    ╲
     Chuck  Mark
```

FIGURE 4-23 Resource Management of a Consolidated Web Server

In FIGURE 4-23, the web server is allocated 20 shares, which means that it is guaranteed at least 20 percent of the processor resources should the database place excessive demands on the processor. In addition, if a `cgi-bin` process in the web server runs out of control with a memory leak, the entire system will not run out of swap space; only the web server will be affected.

Managing Resources within a Single Web Server

It is often necessary to use resource management to control the behavior within a single web server. For example, a single web server may be shared among many users, each with their own CGI-BIN programs. An error in one CGI-BIN program could cause the entire web server to run slowly or, in the case of a memory leak, could even bring down the web server. To prevent this from happening, use the per-process limits.

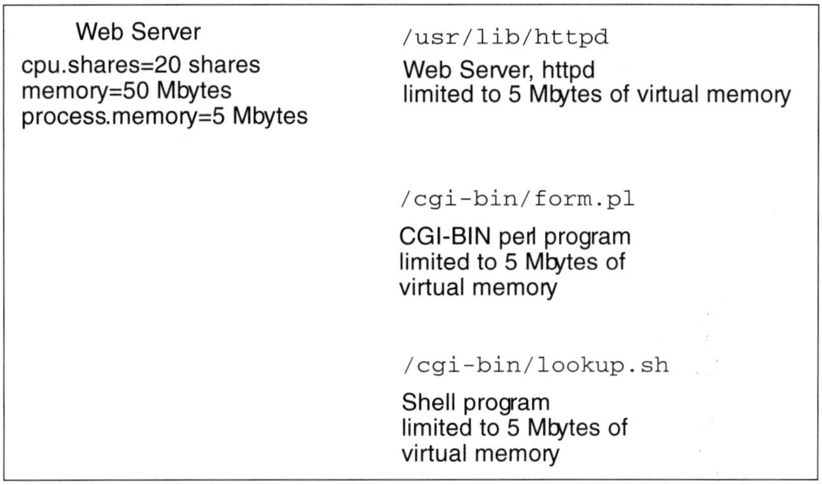

```
        Web Server                  /usr/lib/httpd
   cpu.shares=20 shares             Web Server, httpd
   memory=50 Mbytes                 limited to 5 Mbytes of virtual memory
   process.memory=5 Mbytes


                                    /cgi-bin/form.pl

                                    CGI-BIN perl program
                                    limited to 5 Mbytes of
                                    virtual memory


                                    /cgi-bin/lookup.sh

                                    Shell program
                                    limited to 5 Mbytes of
                                    virtual memory
```

FIGURE 4-24 Resource Management of a Single Web Server

Resource Management of Multiple Virtual Web Servers

Single machines often host multiple virtual web servers. In such cases, there are multiple instances of the `httpd` web server process, and far greater opportunity exists to exploit resource control using the SRM software.

You can run each web server as a different UNIX userid by setting a parameter in the web server configuration file. This effectively attaches each web server to a different lnode in the SRM hierarchy. For example, the Solaris Web Server has the following parameter, as shown in FIGURE 4-25, in the configuration file, `/etc/http/httpd.conf`

```
# Server parameters
server  {
  server_root                      "/var/http/"
  server_user                      "webserver1"
  mime_file                        "/etc/http/mime.types"
  mime_default_type                text/plain
  acl_enable                       "yes"
  acl_file                         "/etc/http/access.acl"
  acl_delegate_depth               3
  cache_enable                     "yes"
  cache_small_file_cache_size      8              # megabytes
  cache_large_file_cache_size      256            # megabytes
  cache_max_file_size              1              # megabytes
  cache_verification_time          10             # seconds
  comment                          "Sun WebServer Default Configuration"

  # The following are the server wide aliases

  map    /cgi-bin/            /var/http/cgi-bin/                    cgi
  map    /sws-icons/          /var/http/demo/sws-icons/
  map    /admin/              /usr/http/admin/

# To enable viewing of server stats via command line,
# uncomment the following line
  map    /sws-stats           dummy                                 stats
}
```

FIGURE 4-25 Solaris Web Server Parameter File

By configuring each web server to run as a different UNIX userid, you can set different limits on each web server. This is particularly useful for control and for accounting for resource usage on a machine hosting many web servers. You can make use of most or all of the SRM resource controls and limits:

Shares [cpu.shares] The CPU shares can proportionally allocate resources to the different web servers.

Mem limit [memory.limit] The memory limit can limit the amount of virtual memory that the web server can use. This prevents any one web server from causing another to fail from memory allocation.

Proc mem limit [`memory.plimit`] The per-process memory limit can limit the amount of virtual memory a single `cgi-bin` process can use. This stops any `cgi-bin` process from bringing down its respective web server.

Process limit [`process.limit`] The maximum number of processes allowed to attach to a web server. It effectively limits the number of concurrent `cgi-bin` processes.

Commercial Workloads

If you want to consolidate or control the relative importance of applications in commercial workloads, you must manage system resources. For example, if you want to mix decision support and OLTP applications on the same system, you need resource management so that the decision support does not affect the response times for the users of the OLTP system. Even without consolidation, workload resource management is an important tool that can provide resource allocation for users according to importance. (For example, in the case where telesales order users have a higher importance than general accounting users.)

This section examines some aspects of the resource management that apply to these types of problems. It focuses on workload consolidation and resource management of databases and analyzes the following workloads:

- NFS Servers
- Databases
- Batch workloads
- Mail servers

Workload Consolidation

Workload consolidation is the most requested form of commercial workload resource management. It allows multiple applications to co-exist in the same Solaris operating environment with managed resource allocation so that one workload does not adversely affect another. The success of workload consolidation is bound closely to the ability to partition resources between the applications, and it is important to understand the types of resources being managed and how they interact.

The resources used by commercial applications fall into the following categories:

- CPU cycles

- Physical memory
- Virtual memory and swap space
- Disk bandwidth
- Disk space
- Network bandwidth

Each application uses these resources differently, and the ability to consolidate one application with another is governed by how effectively you can manage each resource. Sometimes resources cannot be managed by the Solaris operating environment. These types of applications cannot be mix with others. However, in most cases, combinations of resource management products can solve this problem.

The NFS Server Workload

The unique characteristics of an NFS workload place multiple resource demands on the system. No single product can provide complete resource management of an NFS workload. The resources used by NFS and the different products or techniques that can be used to manage them are shown in TABLE 4-1.

TABLE 4-1 NFS Workload Resources

Resource Type	Management Product/ Method	Comments and Issues
CPU	Processor Sets / nfsd/ Solaris Bandwidth Manager	Limit by constraining the system processor set. Control the number of nfsd threads nfsd(1M). Indirectly limit the number of NFS operations by using Solaris Bandwidth Manager.
Physical Memory	Priority Paging	Install and enable priority paging so that file systems will not consume all physical memory.
Swap Space	N/R	NFS uses very little swap space.
Disk Bandwidth	Separate Disks/ Solaris Bandwidth Manager	Either put the NFS file systems on a different storage device or indirectly use Solaris Bandwidth Manager to control the NFS request rate.
Disk Space	File System Quotas	Use file system quotas to limit disk space allocation. See "Base Solaris Operating Environment" on page 136.
Network Bandwidth	Solaris Bandwidth Manager	Use Solaris Bandwidth Manager to control the rate of NFS operations.

Controlling NFS CPU Usage

NFS servers are implemented in the Solaris kernel as kernel threads and run in the system class. You can control the amount of resource allocated to the NFS server in three ways:

- Limit the number of NFS threads with `nfsd`
- Limit the amount of CPU allocated to the system class with `psrset`
- Indirectly control the number of NFS ops with Solaris Bandwidth Manager.

You can control the number of NFS threads by changing the parameters to the NFS daemon when the NFS server is started. Edit the start-up line in `/etc/rc3.d/S15nfs.server`:

> **/usr/lib/nfs/nfsd -a 16** (change 16 to number of threads)

The actual number of threads required will vary according to the number of requests coming in and the time each thread spends waiting for disk I/O to service the request. There is no hard tie between the maximum number of threads and the number of NFS threads that will be on the CPU concurrently. The best approach is to approximate the number of threads required (somewhere between 16 to 64 per CPU), and then find out if the NFS server is doing its job or using too much CPU time.

NFS is a fairly lightweight operation, so it is unlikely that the NFS server CPU usage is an issue. The CPU time consumed by the NFS server threads accumulates as system time. If the system time is high, and the NFS server statistics show a high rate of NFS server activity, then curtail CPU usage by reducing the number of threads.

A far more effective way to control NFS servers is to use the Solaris Bandwidth Manager product to limit the traffic on the NFS port, 2049, and indirectly cap the amount of CPU used by the NFS server. The disadvantage is that spare CPU capacity can be wasted because managing by bandwidth usage does not reveal how much spare CPU is available.

To understand if you have over constrained NFS's allocation of resources you can use the new NFS `iostat` metrics and look at the `%busy` column.

NFS Metrics

Local disk and NFS usage are functionally interchangeable, so the Solaris 2.6 operating environment was changed to instrument NFS client mount points the same way it does disks. NFS mounts are *always* shown by `iostat` and `sar`. With automounted directories coming and going more often than disks coming online, that change may cause problems for performance tools that don't expect the number of `iostat` or `sar` records to change often.

The full instrumentation includes the wait queue for commands in the client (`biod wait`) that have not yet been sent to the server. The active queue measures commands currently in the server. Utilization (`%busy`) indicates the server mount-point activity level. Note that unlike the case with simple disks, *100% busy does not indicate that the server itself is saturated*; it just indicates that the client always has outstanding requests to that server. An NFS server is much more complex than a disk drive and can handle many more simultaneous requests than a single disk drive can. This is explained in more detail later in this chapter.

The following is an example of the new `-xnP` option, although NFS mounts appear in all formats. Note that the `P` option suppresses disks and shows only disk partitions. The `xn` option breaks down the response time, `svc_t`, into wait and active times and puts the device name at the end of the line. The `vold` entry automounts floppy and CD-ROM devices.

```
% iostat -xnP
                            extended device statistics
    r/s    w/s    kr/s    kw/s  wait  actv  wsvc_t  asvc_t   %w   %b device
    0.0    0.0     0.0     0.0   0.0   0.0     0.0     0.0    0    0 vold(pid363)
    0.0    0.0     0.0     0.0   0.0   0.0     0.0     0.0    0    0 servdist:/usr/dist
    0.0    0.5     0.0     7.9   0.0   0.0     0.0    20.7    0    1 servhome:/export/home2
    0.0    0.0     0.0     0.0   0.0   0.0     0.0     0.0    0    0 servmail:/var/mail
    0.0    1.3     0.0    10.4   0.0   0.2     0.0   128.0    0    2 c0t2d0s0
    0.0    0.0     0.0     0.0   0.0   0.0     0.0     0.0    0    0 c0t2d0s2
```

NFS Physical Memory Usage

NFS uses physical memory in two ways: In the kernel each NFS thread consumes some space for a stack and local data, and outside the kernel the data being served by NFS consumes memory as it is cached in the file system. The amount of kernel memory used by NFS is easily manageable because its size doesn't change much and the amount of memory required is small.

The amount of memory used by the file systems for NFS servers is, however, very large and much harder to manage. By default, any non-sequential I/O and non-8KB I/O uses memory at the rate of data passed though the file system. The amount of memory used grows continuously. When there is no more free memory, memory is taken from other applications on the system.

By using priority paging (see "Priority Paging—Memory Policy by Importance" on page 33) you can apply a different resource policy to the memory system to prevent this from happening. With priority paging, the file system can still grow to use free memory, but cannot take memory from other applications on the system. Priority paging should be mandatory for any system that has NFS as one of the consolidation applications.

NFS and Swap Space

NFS uses a very small amount of swap space, and there should be no inter-workload swap space issues from NFS.

NFS Disk Storage Management

You can manage NFS disk storage using UFS disk quotas. See "Disk Quotas" on page 130 for more information.

Controlling NFS with Solaris Bandwidth Manager Software

You can control amount of resources consumed by NFS indirectly by curtailing the amount of network bandwidth on port 2049. The Solaris Bandwidth Manager product provides the means to do this.

First assess the network interfaces that need to be controlled. If clients come in over several network interfaces, all of these interfaces must be brought under control by the Solaris Bandwidth Manager software.

When defining interfaces in the Solaris Bandwidth Manager software, you must specify whether incoming or outgoing traffic needs to be managed. In the case of NFS, network traffic could go in both directions (reads and writes). In the Solaris Bandwidth Manager configuration, this would look as follows:

```
interface hme0_in
    rate       100000000        /* (bits/sec) */
    activate   yes

interface hme_out
    rate       100000000
    activate   yes
```

Next define the service you want to manage. The Solaris Bandwidth Manager software already has two pre-defined classes for NFS:

```
service nfs_udp
    protocol udp
    ports 2049, *
    ports *, 2049

service nfs_tcp
    protocol tcp
    ports 2049, *
    ports *, 2049
```

Put in place a filter that can categorize network traffic in NFS and non-NFS traffic:

```
filter nfs_out
    src
        type     host
        address  servername
    dst
        type     subnet
        mask     255.255.255.0
        address  129.146.121.0
    service
        nfs_udp, nfs_tcp
```

The filter in the above example is for managing outgoing NFS traffic to the 129.146.121.0 network. You could decide to leave out the destination and manage NFS traffic to all clients, from wherever they come.

Create another `nfs_in` filter for NFS traffic in the opposite direction. Only the `src` and `dst` parts need to be reversed.

Lastly, create a class that will allocate a specific bandwidth to this filter:

```
class managed_nfs
    interface      hme_out
    bandwidth      10
    max_bandwidth  10
    priority       2
    filter         nfs_out
```

This class sets a guaranteed bandwidth of 10 percent of the available bandwidth (10 Mbytes in case of fast Ethernet). Control the maximum bandwidth by setting an upper bound to the CPU resources that NFS consumes on the host. The key variable is `max_bandwidth`; it specifies an upper bound to the consumed bandwidth that never will be exceeded. You could even set the `bandwidth` variable to 0, but this could lead to NFS starvation if other types of traffic will be managed as well.

The `priority` variable is less important. It will be a factor if other types of traffic are being managed. Generally, higher priorities will have lower average latencies, because the scheduler gives them higher priority if it has the choice (within the bandwidth limitations that were configured).

It is not easy to find a clear correlation between NFS network bandwidth and NFS server CPU utilization. That correlation depends very much on the type of NFS workload for your server. A data-intense NFS environment that moves large files and tends to saturate networks is very different from an attribute-intense environment, which tends to saturate CPUs with lots of small requests for file attributes, such as a software development compile and build server. Experimentation will determine what's good for you. Your administrator could even develop a program that monitors NFS CPU utilization, and if it gets too high, use the Solaris Bandwidth Manager APIs to dynamically limit the bandwidth more, all automatically and in real time.

Database Workloads

Resource management of databases can be somewhat simplified by viewing the database as a "black box" and managing resources around it. This strategy is particularly useful when doing server consolidation because the main objective with consolidation is to partition one workload from an other.

In most commercial database systems several packages interact with the database to provide the overall application environment to the user. The typical data center strategy is to consolidate more workloads onto each system. Resource management of the whole environment requires careful planning and a solid understanding of the interaction between these packages and the database.

A look at a typical example where a single database instance provides database services for two different applications that require access to the same data, uncovers some of the complexities of database resource management. FIGURE 4-26 shows a typical backend database server with a web application used for customer order entry and an ad-hoc decision support user that generates large queries against a database.

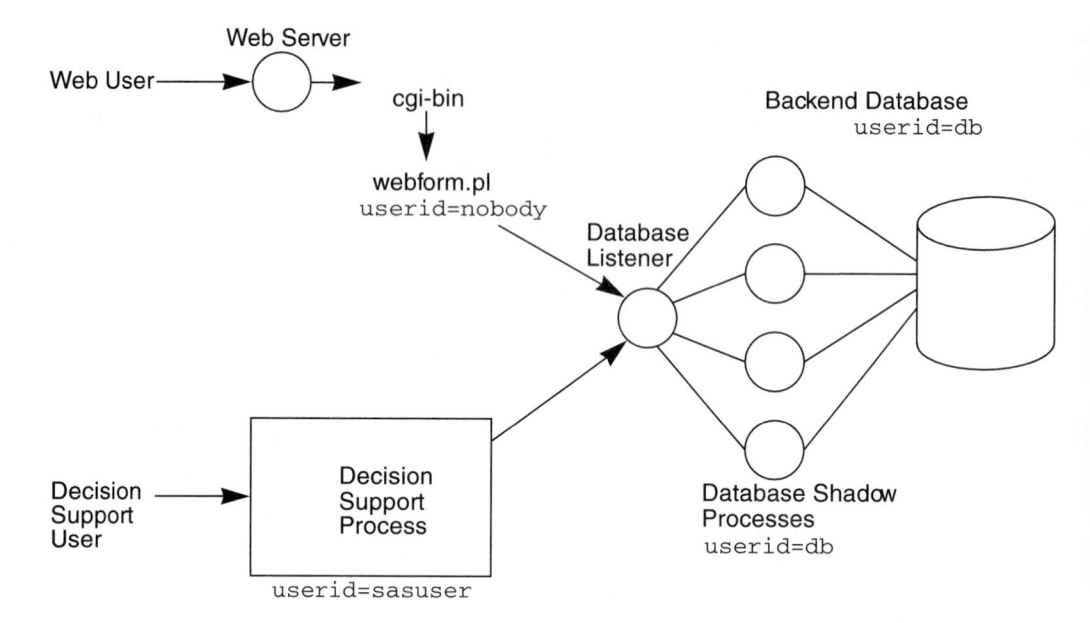

FIGURE 4-26 Practical Example with a Database Server and a Decision Support Process

The life cycle of each transaction crosses several management boundaries. No single control or policy can assign resources to ensure that adequate CPU is provided to meet response times. For example, if the decision support user is retrieving a large number of transactions from the database, the web user may not be able to get adequate response from the database during that time. Ideally, you want to control the allocation of resources as the transaction proceeds though the system. A time line of the transaction though the system is shown in FIGURE 4-27.

SBM URL Filter	SRM userid=nobody	SRM Inode per script	DB Resource Manager prset per instance		SRM userid=nobody	SBM URL Filter
1. Network Latency	2. Web server	3. cgi-bin Perl exec time and script execution	4. DB Listener connect	5. DB SQL txn latency	6. Web server response	7. Network Latency

FIGURE 4-27 Transaction Flow and Resource Management Product Assignment

1. Network Latency—The user issues an `http` request from the desktop, which must travel across the intranet/Internet to the web server. This component can be managed by controlling the bandwidth and network priorities into the web server

with the Solaris Bandwidth Manager software. Often the network infrastructure between the client browser and the web server is outside the control of management (for example, the internet). Managing the bandwidth on the network port on the machine that hosts the web server is a useful strategy to ensure that key `http` requests get the required bandwidth, while other lower priority data transfers (such as an `ftp` transfer) are constrained. The Solaris Bandwidth Manager software can control the bandwidth allocation into the web server, and `cgi-bin` can be controlled using bandwidth manager URL prioritization. (See Chapter 4.)

2. The Web Server—The web server usually runs as a single user, and often as the user `nobody`. Ensure that the web server as a whole gets a sufficient share of CPU. Use SRM software to ensure that adequate CPU is allocated by assigning CPU shares to the `nobody` user.

3. The Web Server `cgi-bin` script—The `cgi-bin` script is forked by the web server, and by default also runs as the userid `nobody`. Use the SRM software to limit the amount of CPU the `cgi-bin` script uses by creating a node in the SRM hierarchy for that `cgi-bin` script and using the `srm` user command as a wrapper to the `cgi-bin` script to assign resource control limits to that point in the hierarchy. See "Managing Resources within a Single Web Server" on page 62 for more information on how to control `cgi-bin` scripts.

4. The Database Listener—The database listener process accepts the incoming connection from database client applications. (in this case the `cgi-bin` Perl script). The database listener forks a database process and connects the client application to the database.

5. The Database Server Session—The Database session can either be a new per-client process or some portion of the existing server processes. You can control the amount of CPU allocated to the database processes by using database vendor-specific resource control tools.

6. Web Server Response—Control passes back to the web server to output the data to the client browser. The same control as in the web server component (2) is implemented here.

7. Network Latency—The response from the web server is transmitted over the network. The Solaris Bandwidth Manager software again controls the bandwidth out of the port on the host to the internet/intranet.

Each stage of the transaction uses different resources. You can apply different techniques to each stage. The more difficult part of using today's technologies is managing the priority of the transaction once it enters the database. You can use fine-grained resource management to control the amount of CPU allocated to the users in the database, but you must ensure that external control of the database by resource management products is fully supported for the database in question.

Virtual Memory and Databases

The SRM software and resource limits can limit the amount of virtual memory used by processes, users, and workloads. This capability does not manage physical memory, but it effectively restricts the amount of global swap space consumed by each user.

When a user or workload reaches the virtual memory limit, the system returns a memory allocation error to the application, that is calls to `malloc()` fail. The same error code is reported to the application as if the application had run out of swap space.

In practice, many applications do not respond well to memory allocation errors because it is very hard to recover from a lack-of-memory error without making some additional demand for memory. Because of this, it is a high risk to ever let a database server reach its virtual memory limit. If the limit is reached, the database engine may hang or crash, and the database may have to be restarted.

It is best to set a high virtual memory limit so that the limit can never be reached under normal circumstances. However, the virtual memory limit can be used to place a ceiling on the entire database server to stop a user with a memory leak from affecting other databases or workloads on the system.

Database Consolidation

You can consolidate databases using a number of resource management techniques. Choose the technique based on the supportability and functionality of the solution. Not all databases are supported under each of the resource management facilities. Because most consolidated database servers are mission-critical production servers, this should be the primary concern.

The objective for successful consolidation is to provide strong insulation between each database instance. This requires careful resource management of CPU, memory, I/O, and network traffic.

Insulating CPU Usage

Processor usage is a relatively easy resource to isolate. There are several mechanisms by which this can be achieved. There is a trade-off between the strength of insulation and the flexibility of resource allocation. At one end of the scale is Starfire dynamic system domains, which provides the same level of insulation as separate machines but requires manual intervention to shift resources between database instances. There is also a large granularity of resource allocation, which is four processors at a time. At the other end of the spectrum is the SRM software, which provides fine-grained resource management with the ability to dynamically assign resources whenever they are needed. But it also provides much lower insulation between the applications.

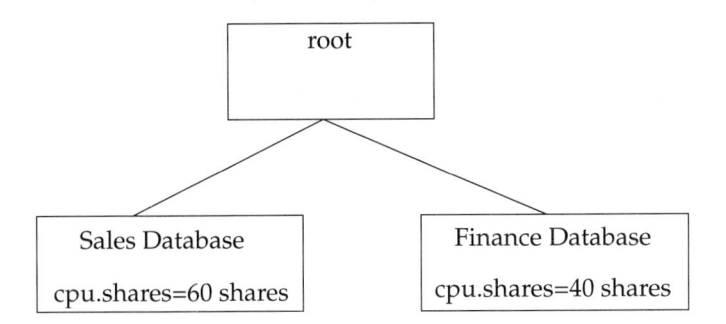

```
                    root
                   /    \
         Sales Database   Finance Database
         cpu.shares=60 shares   cpu.shares=40 shares
```

FIGURE 4-28 Consolidation of Two Databases with Solaris Resource Manager

The advantage with the SRM software is that resources are completely dynamic. If one database is not using the resources, they are available to the other database. System resources are not wasted because spare CPU cycles can be used by any other workload requiring them. The more workloads consolidated, the flatter the total resource usage becomes. By doing this, you can often size a system for the average resource requirements instead of the peaks.

Processor sets provide a middle ground. The granularity is one CPU, and the resources are easier to reallocate than with domains, but still relatively static in nature. Processor sets and domains, however, provide the static processor assignment and granularity required by some databases. In some cases, this is the only supported way of dividing resources between databases. Unfortunately, resources are statically assigned. Although some movement of resources is possible, it means that you must size each database instance for most of its peak requirements.

Insulating Memory Usage

Databases have three types of memory usage, which have very different characteristics:

- shared memory area
- private memory area
- file system paging memory

The shared memory area is often the largest component of the database's memory requirements. It is the easiest to insulate between instances because the memory is allocated as shared memory. All mainstream databases allocate this as intimate shared memory (ISM), which wires down the memory so that it can't be paged. Because this memory is wired down, the memory allocated to each instance stays allocated. One instance cannot steal memory from another. However, this poses a challenge for dynamic memory resource allocation, such as dynamic reconfiguration because the wired-down memory must be unallocated before it can be removed from the system, requiring quiescing of the database.

The private memory is the additional memory that a database uses, over and above the large shared memory segment that is typical of most databases. The private memory is the regular process memory used by each process that the database engine comprises, and it is regular pageable memory. For example, the Oracle shadow processes have a small private memory size of about 500k per process. The Oracle parallel query processes may use several megabytes per process. The private memory area requirements for each database vary, but they are generally many times smaller than the global shared memory requirements. The amount of memory used is sometimes configurable. Simple capacity planning ensures that sufficient system-wide memory exists to cater to all of the database private memory requirements. Take care when including Decision Support System (DSS) database instances because they often have huge private memory requirements.

Often overlooked are the memory requirements of the file system. By using raw devices for all tablespaces or by using the direct I/O feature of the UFS file system, the file system bypasses the Solaris page cache. In this case, we do not need to take into consideration the memory use of the file system.

The Solaris page cache causes a huge memory demand, which places undue pressure on the database private memory and breaks down any insulation between established databases. Priority paging puts a hard fence between the file systems and applications, and the file system will only use free memory in the system for its cache. If you plan to run a database on file systems, consider this a mandatory requirement. See Chapter 3 for more information.

In summary, to provide proper memory insulation between databases, ensure the following:

- Use ISM for the shared global areas to wire down memory.
- Use proper capacity planning and parameters to ensure there is sufficient RAM for private memory requirements.
- Use either raw disk devices or ensure that priority paging is installed to prevent file system memory pressure.

Insulating I/O

Ensure that I/O activity from one application does not affect another application in an undesirable way. The best way to insulate I/O within a single database instance is to make sure that application tables are placed on separate I/O devices. This still leaves shared log devices, which can be a source of I/O contention. Ensure that adequate I/O bandwidth, spindles, and, where possible, hardware caching are provided for adequate performance for the log devices.

Databases can be consolidated by simply ensuring that each database is assigned its own I/O devices. This completely insulates one database from another. However, you must also make sure that all data paths from the server to the storage device are carefully isolated. For example, two databases can be placed on their own set of disks within a Sun StorEdge™ A3500 storage system. However, because both sets of disks use the same SCSI channel to the host the databases, I/O is not properly insulated.

If you must use a single storage controller, use capacity planning so that sufficient bandwidth is available to combine both. For OLTP applications this is rarely an issue because the bandwidth requirements are so low. For example, an OLTP system generating 2000 8-kilobyte IOPS only requires 16 Mbytes of I/O bandwidth. A decision support application is completely different. A single decision support workload can generate several hundred megabytes a second of I/O. In addition to this, decision support often generates enough I/O to overwrite the cache continuously (cache wiping), which hurts the OLTP random I/O that makes extensive use of the storage cache. Do not consider a single storage controller for consolidation of decision support workloads with OLTP workloads.

Databases in a Resource Managed Environment

Relationships with databases and resource management products are many and vary with each database type. For example, if you add CPU resources to an instance of Oracle 7, the Oracle engine automatically picks up those resources, whereas some other databases must be restarted to use the newly available resources. (Note, however, that internal table sizes and latch sizing will not be automatically adjusted, and performance may improve after a restart of the database.) To understand how different databases work within a resource management environment, look at the different database topologies and explore what happens to each database when you add or remove CPU, memory, or I/O resources.

Database Resource Management Compatibility

TABLE 4-2 Database Resource Management Vendor Support

Vendor	Version	Resource Type	Support Statement
Oracle	7.3	CPU	Dynamic addition of CPU resources with processor sets, DR, and SRM software works and is supported by Oracle. New resources are automatically used within the target instance.
		Memory	Dynamic addition of physical memory through DR requires an `init.ora` change and a database restart before it can be used by Oracle. Dynamic detach of physical memory requires the Oracle instance to be shut down first.
Oracle	8.0	CPU	Dynamic addition of CPU resources with processor sets, DR, and SRM software works and is supported by Oracle. New resources are automatically used within the target instance.
		Memory	Dynamic addition of physical memory though DR requires an `init.ora` change and a database restart before it can be used by Oracle. Dynamic detach of physical memory requires the Oracle instance to be shut down first.
Oracle	8i	CPU	If the Oracle 8i Resource Manager software is not running, dynamic addition of CPU resources with processor sets, DR, and SRM software works and is supported by Oracle. New resources are automatically used within the target instance.
		Memory	Dynamic addition of physical memory though DR requires an `init.ora` change and a database restart before it can be used by Oracle. Dynamic detach of physical memory requires the Oracle instance to be shut down first.

TABLE 4-2 Database Resource Management Vendor Support *(Continued)*

Vendor	Version	Resource Type	Support Statement
Oracle	8*i* Resource Manager	CPU	Oracle 8*i* resource manager requires the CPU resources to be static and does not co-exist with any Solaris dynamic resource addition or removal. If processor sets, SRM software or DR of CPUs is to be used, Oracle 8*i* resource manager software is not supported.
		Memory	Dynamic addition of physical memory though DR requires an `init.ora` change and a database restart before it can be used by Oracle. Dynamic detach of physical memory requires the Oracle instance to be shut down first.
Oracle	OPS	-	Not Covered in this BluePrint
Informix	7.x 8.x 9.x	CPU	Informix engines (processes) must be configured as the number of CPUs + 1. Adding processors via processor sets requires a command line Informix adjustment to increase or decrease the number of engines. Informix and SRM software pose a more complex problem and care must be taken to ensure the number of engines interacts correctly with the shares allocated.
		Memory	Addition of shared memory via DR requires an Informix command before the shared memory can be used.
Sybase	11.x 12.x	CPU	See Chapter 8 for information on Dynamic System Domains for Sybase.
DB2	5.2	CPU	The number of processors per DB2 logical partition is established via a fixed DB configuration parameter. Changing the number of CPUs per logical partition requires restarting the database.
		Memory	DB2 memory parameters are established via static configuration files. Resizing DB2 memory parameters requires restarting the database.

Resource Manager of the Oracle Database

Managing resources in an Oracle database provides the means to meet service levels and response times in commercial systems. However, you must consider architectural and support issues when planning to implement resource management. There are two ways to manage resources of a database: the black box approach, where you manage a whole instance as a single managed entity or using resource management products to manipulate resources within an Oracle instance.

Oracle versions 7.3, 8.0, and 8*i* must be managed as a black box, which allows you to implement server consolidation by using Solaris resource management products. If you require fine-grained resource management within Oracle, use Oracle's resource manager software, which ships with Oracle versions starting at 8*i*.

Oracle8*i* Resource Manager Software

The Oracle8*i* Resource Manager software ensures system resources are applied to the most important tasks of the enterprise at the levels required to meet enterprise goals.

In Oracle8*i*, a new Database Resource Manager software allocates and manages CPU resources among database users and applications. In addition, the Oracle8*i* Database Resource Manager software enables you to limit the degree of parallelism of any operation. You can balance one user's resource consumption against other users and partition system resources among tasks of varying importance to achieve overall enterprise goals.

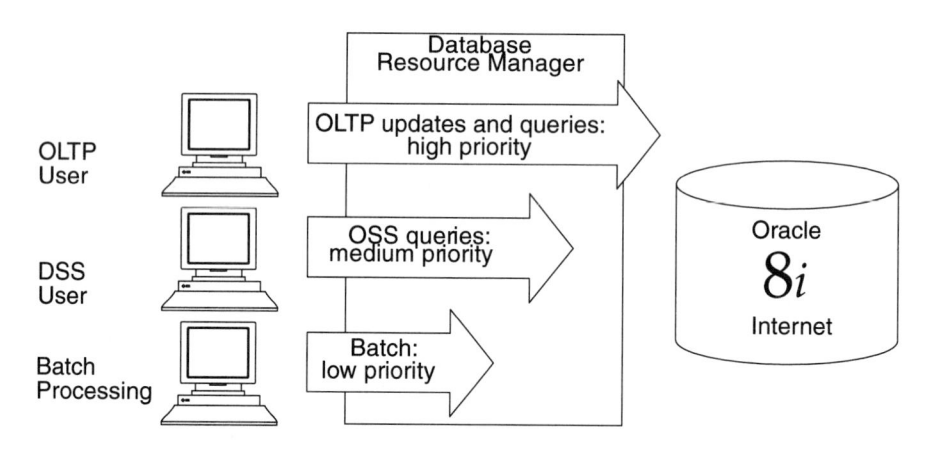

FIGURE 4-29 Oracle8*i* Resource Manager

Establishing Resource Plans and Policies

Resources are allocated to users based on a plan specified by the database administrator. User sessions and groups of user sessions are assigned to resource consumer groups. Resource consumer groups are separate from user roles. This separation allows one user to have different sessions assigned to different resource consumer groups. An overall resource plan is defined specifying how resources are distributed among the different resource consumer groups. Subplans allow the further subdivision of CPU resources within a resource consumer group. Up to eight levels of resource allocation can be defined. Levels allow the further subdivision of CPU resources between resource consumer groups. Levels specify both resource consumer group allocation limits and distribution of unused resources. Subplans and levels can be used together. These capabilities allow simple, yet powerful allocation policies to be implemented for database resources.

Oracle8i Database Resource Manager Functionality

Let us look at the example of Company XYZ that sells widgets directly to customers over the Internet. To assure optimum performance for customers placing orders, 80 percent of the CPU is allocated to service customer orders. The remainder of the CPU resource is divided between the processing required to ship the widgets and bill for them. To implement this resource policy, the following plan is created.

TABLE 4-3   Company XYZ Resource Plan

Resource Consumer Groups	CPU Resource Allocations
Web Based Order Entry	80%
Shipping	15%
Billing	5%

The Company XYZ resource plan can be refined by specifying how resources are allocated between different classes of customers or how resources are allocated within a resource consumer group. Company XYZ categorizes its customers into two groups based on their purchase volume: premium and standard. To ensure a higher level of service for premium customers, the company creates an order entry subplan. The order entry subplan dictates how resources allocated to the order entry resource consumer group are subdivided. In this case, premium customers are allocated 60 percent of the order entry resources and the standard customers are allocated the remaining 40 percent.

TABLE 4-4 Order Entry Subplan

Resource Consumer Groups	CPU Resource Allocations
Premium Customers	60%
Standard Customers	40%

Using a subplan is different from creating two different order entry resource consumer groups in the primary plan. If that were done, any resources allocated but not used by the standard customers would be distributed across all the other resource consumer groups. With the order entry subplan, resources unused by the standard customers are made available to the premium customers before making them available to other resource consumer groups. It is also possible to create additional subplans to benefit premium customers with priority shipping and billing resources.

This resource plan can be refined by specifying how unused resources are allocated between resource consumer groups. Company XYZ wants to ensure that at least five percent of the resources are always available to service the billing functions. It also wants any unused resources from order entry and shipping made available to billing. This is done by placing the order entry and shipping resource consumer groups in one level and the billing resource consumer group in a second level, as shown in TABLE 4-5.

TABLE 4-5 Company XYZ Resource Plan

Resource Consumer Groups	Level 1 CPU Resource Allocation	Level 2 CPU Resource Allocations
Web-based Order Entry	80%	0%
Shipping	15%	0%
Billing	0%	100%

While this revised plan may appear to provide the same allocation of resources as the first plan, it is different. Unused resources allocated to the order entry or shipping resource consumer group are made available to the billing resource consumer group. The levels also establish a maximum level of CPU consumption for the order entry and shipping resource consumer groups. In the first plan, unused resources from any one consumer group are proportionally divided among the other resource consumer groups.

Flexible and Adaptable Resource Management

The only constant is change. Resource plans and policies that achieve the desired results in the morning, may not do so in the evening. All aspects of the Oracle8*i* Database Resource Manager settings can be changed while the database is running without shutting down and restarting the database. Plans, subplans, levels, membership in resource consumer groups, and resource allocations can be dynamically altered on a production database without quiescing the system.

The database administrator can create many different plans and resource consumer groups. These definitions are stored in the data dictionary. A default plan, specified by the administrator, is activated when the database is started. This allows alternate plans for day time, night time, weekends, quarter end, or other times that require a different set of priorities.

Unlike conventional priority schemes, all resource consumer groups will receive, if required, their allotment of resources and cannot be starved by a high demand for resources from other resource consumer groups. Using percentages to allocate CPU resources ensures this. In addition, it allows resource allocation policies to remain static across hardware changes to the computer system.

Database Integration

The Oracle8*i* Database Resource Manager is fully integrated into the database security system. A PL/SQL package lets you to create, update, and delete resource plans and resource consumer groups. You define a user's default consumer group and privileges. Users can switch resource consumer groups to increase execution priority if they have the necessary privileges. In addition, CPU resource usage can change dynamically because an administrator on a production system can move users from group to group.

Oracle database versions prior to Oracle8*i* support the ability to set hard resource limits for each user. Oracle8*i* continues this support. These fixed ceilings, specified in each user's profile, provide a separate and different capability from Oracle8*i* Database Resource Manager's flexible allocation of unused resources to consumer groups. To maximize system throughput, this allocation can be well above specified resource plan percentages when other user groups use less than their allocation.

Finally, the Oracle8*i* Database Resource Manager software and the Oracle8*i* automatic degree of parallelism (ADOP) feature have been integrated. ADOP attempts to optimize system utilization by automatically adjusting the degree of parallelism for parallel query operations. ADOP takes into account resource consumer group allocations before choosing a degree of parallelism to ensure CPU targets are met.

Support for Oracle8i Resource Manager with SRM Software

At the time of this writing, Oracle 8*i* Resource Manager should not be used when other resource management tools are managing the database instance. Do not use Oracle Resource Manager and SRM software at the same time.

Using Processor Sets and Domains to Allow Use of Oracle8i Database Resource Manager

To overcome the Oracle8*i* Database Resource Manager compatibility restrictions, it is possible to isolate the database so that it is responsible for managing its resources. Two approaches can be used to do this: processor sets and dynamic system domains.

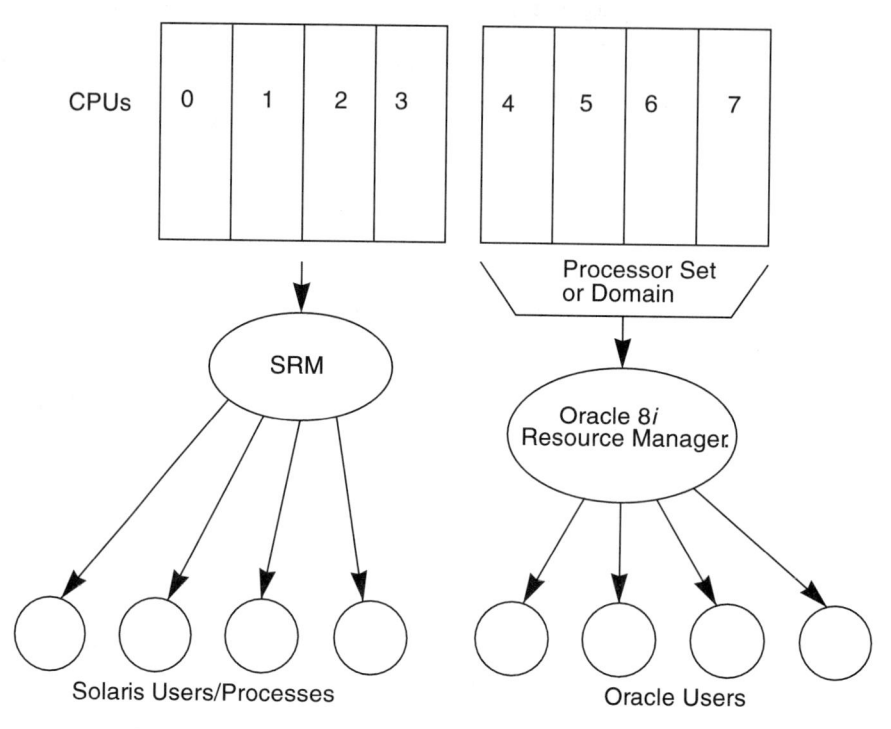

FIGURE 4-30 Using Processor Sets or Domains to Allow Oracle8*i* Resource Manager

Using this approach, you partition the database from other resource demands on the system and provide a consistent resource allocation to the database (a requirement of Oracle Resource Manager software). Oracle Resource Manager software can then be used to allocate resources to each authenticated Oracle user. In the case of the Perl script, the user's identity may not be known, so a special user can be created within Oracle's user database specifically for that Perl script, and resources can be assigned against it.

Note that the size of the processor set or dynamic system domain cannot change once Oracle is started. A change in the number of processors must be followed by a restart of the database instance.

Resource Manager of the Informix Database

Informix uses a fixed number of server engines (processes), which are configured at start-up as number of CPUs plus one. Take care to ensure that the right number of engines are running for the allocated resources. This is straight forward when using processor sets and dynamic domains because the resource allocation is done on a processor boundary and at specific times. Each time the processor allocation is changed, the Informix command line interface can alter the number of engines to correctly reflect the new CPU allocation.

The SRM software provides a more dynamic environment with no fixed boundaries around resource allocation. This means that the amount of CPU available to the Informix instance varies and cannot be easily predicted. The maximum amount of CPUs that an informix instance will use is governed by two factors: the configured number of Informix engines, and the resource limits imposed by the resource manager (processor sets, SRM software).

Batch Workloads

Most commercial installations require batch processing. Batch processing is typically done at night, after the daily online load has diminished. This is usually for two reasons: to consolidate the day's transactions into reports and to prevent batch workloads from affecting the on-line workload.

A batch workload runs unconstrained and attempts to complete in the shortest time possible. This means that batch is your worst resource consumer, because it attempts to consume all other resources it needs until it is constrained by some system bottleneck. (The bottleneck for batch is the smallest dataflow point in the system.)

Batch presents two problems to system managers: it can affect other batch jobs that are running concurrently and it can never be run together with the online portion of the workload during business hours.

Good planning schedules batch jobs to run outside work hours (for example, 12:00 midnight to 6:00 a.m.). But a simple hiccup or day of high sales could make the batch workload spill over into business hours. This is not as bad as downtime, but if your batch workload is still running at 10:30 a.m. the next day, it could make online customers wait several minutes for each sales transaction. This could ultimately leading to lost sales.

Both these problems require resource management to allow proper control over the workloads. In an MVS environment, IBM Workload Manager can specify target completion times and job velocity for batch workloads (see Chapter 13 for more details). With the Solaris operating environment, you can to control the allocation of resources to the batch workloads to constrain them. This requires more administration of resource management, but achieves a similar result.

Resources Used by Batch Workloads

Batch workloads are a hybrid between OLTP and DSS workloads, and their effect on the system lies somewhere between the two. A batch workload can consist of many repetitive transactions to a database, with some heavy computational work for each. A simple example may be the calculation of total sales for the day. In such a case, the batch process must retrieve every sales transaction for the day from two databases, extract the sales amount, and maintain a running sum.

Batch typically places high demands on both processor and I/O resources because a large amount of CPU is required for the batch process and the database, and a large amount of I/Os are generated from the backend database for each transaction retrieved.

To control a batch workload, you must effectively limit the rate of consumption of both CPU and I/O. At the time of writing, the Solaris operating environment allows fine-grained resource control of CPU. However, I/O resources must be managed by allocating different I/O devices to each workload.

Two methods are typically used to isolate batch resource impact: one is to copy the database onto a separate system and run the batch and reporting workloads on that separate system; the other is to use CPU resource control. Copying the database onto a separate system presents a problem because, in most situations, the batch process updates portions of the online database and cannot be separated.

Since the amount of I/O generated from a batch workload is proportional to the amount of CPU consumed, you can indirectly control the I/O rate of the batch workload. However, you must ensure that excessive I/O is not generated on workloads with very light CPU requirements.

CHAPTER **5**

Workload Measurements

If you want to manage a resource, you must measure its usage.

The generic types of measurements that you can obtain directly or indirectly via related measurements are throughput, utilization, queue length and response time. These measurements are made at several levels, including business operations, application, user, system, network, process, and device level.

This chapter discusses measurement sources and the meaning of the available measurements that are important for resource management.

One problem in documenting the details of Solaris measurements is that far more measurements are available than can be displayed by the standard tools such as `vmstat`, `sar`, and `ps`. Most commercial performance tools read the kernel directly and have access to the full range of measurements, although they do not use all of them. The SyMON product collects a large proportion of the available measurements. The most convenient way to explore this data is to use the SE Toolkit. This freely available but unsupported tool provides full access to all the raw data sources in the Solaris operating environment and generates higher level processed data. It is used to prototype ideas that can then be promoted for incorporation in products, in particular for the Sun Enterprise SyMON 2.0 software.

The SE Toolkit

The SE Toolkit is based on a C language interpreter that is extended to make all the Solaris measurement interfaces available in an easy form. The code that takes metrics and processes them is provided as C source code and runs on the interpreter so that it is easy to trace where data comes from and how it is processed. You can then write your own programs in any language to obtain the same data. The SE Toolkit has been jointly developed by Richard Pettit and Adrian Cockcroft as a "spare time" activity since 1993. Richard worked at Sun but is currently at Foglight Software, and

Adrian is one of the authors of this book. The SE Toolkit can be downloaded from `http://www.sun.com/sun-on-net/performance/se3`. Detailed information and examples of how to write code that reads the kernel and the SE Toolkit itself can be found in *Sun Performance and Tuning, Java and the Internet*, by Adrian Cockcroft and Richard Pettit, Sun Press 1998.

Measurement Levels

Measurements can be classified into several levels. Data from lower levels is aggregated and merged with new data as more valuable higher level measurements are produced.

- Business operations

    Business workloads are broad-based and are not only computer oriented. Use a form that makes sense to managers and non-technical staff to represent the part of the business that is automated by the computer system.

- Applications

    The business operation can be broken down into several applications such as sales and distribution, e-commerce web service, email, file, and print. Examples of application-specific measurements are order entry rate, emails relayed, and web server response time.

- Users

    Each class of user interacts with several applications. The number of users and the work pattern of each class of users should be understood.

- Networks

    Networks connect the users to the applications and link together multiple systems to provide applications that are replicated or distributed. Measure traffic patterns and protocol mixes for each network segment.

- Systems

    System-level measurements show the basic activity and utilization of the memory system and CPUs. Some network measurements, such as TCP/IP throughput, are also available on a per system basis. Per process activity can be aggregated at a per system level then combined with network measurements to measure distributed applications.

- Processes

    Process measurements show the activity of each user and each application. Current process activity can be monitored, and accounting logs provide a record of who ran what when.

- Devices

    Devices, such as disks and network interfaces, are measured independently and aggregated at the system level. There are few ways to link the usage of a device to a process or a user automatically, so detailed information about the configuration of devices and the usage of file systems by applications is needed.

The Application Resource Measurement Standard

The Application Resource Measurement (ARM) standard aims to instrument application response times. The intent is to measure end-to-end response time by tagging each ARM call with a transaction identifier and tracking these transactions as they move from system to system. If a user transaction slows down, the system in the end-to-end chain of measurements that shows the biggest increase in response time can be pinpointed.

This technique sounds very useful, and there is both good and bad news about ARM. The good news is that all vendors support the one standard, and several implementations exist, from Hewlett-Packard and Tivoli (who jointly invented the standard) to the more recently developed BMC Best/1 and Landmark. The bad news is that application code must be instrumented to measure user response time, and sophisticated tools are needed to handle the problems of distributed transaction tracking. Application vendors have shown interest, so more measurements will become available. The latest versions of Baan products include ARM-based instrumentation.

SAP R/3 Measurements

The SAP R/3 enterprise resource planning package has three tiers of systems: user desktops, application servers, and a backend database. The application instruments itself and measures the performance of key user transactions and the response time of the backend database for each application. This information is provided by a facility called CCMS, and it is used by several tools such as BMC Best/1 to provide more detailed application-level management than can be done with just system and device-level information.

Internet Server Measurements

An Internet server complex often provides a range of services and uses applications such as firewalls, web servers, and content generation databases. Each of these applications supports a range of operations that you can log or monitor to discover the rate of use and the mixture of operations. In some cases, the time taken for each operation is also logged, so you can obtain a response time measurement.

One of the most common applications is the proxy web cache service. Because this application often acts as a funnel for all the web traffic going out of a corporate intranet to the Internet itself, a good measure of overall Internet response time can be obtained. An example scenario follows.

Configuring and Monitoring a Proxy Cache

Data is collected on a Netscape 2.5 proxy cache that is serving most of the thousand or so employees in Sun's United Kingdom facility. The server is situated at the largest site, so some users have LAN-based access speeds. However, several other sites in the UK, run over wide area links to the central site. Additionally, a number of users are connected over ISDN and modem dial-up connections.

The access log contains the same data that a normal web server log contains, but several additional values are logged. Netscape supports two extended formats and also allows a custom format to be specified. The interesting data to extract is the mixture of possible cache outcomes that determines whether it is a cache hit or not, as well as the routing information and transfer time. The SE Toolkit `percollator.se` script can parse Netscape and Squid proxy cache log formats and summarize the data.

The route data is analyzed to count all the entries that go to PROXY or SOCKS and report the percentage that are indirect. This is the percentage that gets routed to the Internet, rather than being DIRECT references to other servers in the corporate intranet or incomplete transfers marked with a "-".

The cache finish status was analyzed, and operations are divided into four categories. The NO-CHECK and UP-TO-DATE states are cache hits. The WRITTEN, REFRESHED, and CL-MISMATCH states are misses that cause cache writes. The DO-NOT-CACHE and NON-CACHEABLE states are uncacheable, and anything else is an error or incomplete transfer. The percentages for the first three are recorded.

The total transfer time is recorded. The average transfer time can be calculated, but since the transfer size varies from zero to several megabytes, the average transfer time for each of the size ranges for the mix must also be worked out. The mix in the `percollator.se` code is based on the SPECweb96 size boundaries of up to

1 Kbyte, 1 Kbyte up to 10 Kbytes, 10 Kbytes up to 100 Kbytes, 100 Kbytes up to 1 Mbyte, and over 1 Mbyte. We end up with the percentage of `ops` and the average transfer time in each size range.

Observed Results in Practice

On a fairly quiet weekday, 280,000 accesses went via this cache, and 56 percent of the accesses went out to the Internet. The cache breakdown was as follows: 34 percent of the accesses hit in the cache, 16 percent missed and caused a cache write, 49 percent of the accesses were not cacheable, and 1 percent ended in some kind of error. A week's worth of data showed that the indirect and cache hit rates vary by 5 to 10 percent of the total from day to day.

The transfer time averaged about 2.3 seconds. The problem with this number is that it included a small number of very large or very slow transfers. The average for transfers up to 1 Kbyte was 1.8 seconds; for 1 to 10 Kbytes, it was 2.5 seconds; for 10 to 100 Kbytes, it was 6 seconds; for 100 Kbytes to 1 Mbyte, it was 40 seconds; and for over 1 Mbyte, it was 188 seconds. Within each of these size bands, connections to the client browser took place over everything from 100-Mbit Ethernet to 28.8-Kbit modems.

Transfer Time Versus Size Distribution

To calculate the transfer time versus size distribution, 10,000 access log entries were taken. After removing all zero content length and zero time transfers, size was plotted against transfer time using log-to-log axes. The result showed that transfer time is not very dependent on size until the size gets into the 10 to 100 Kbyte region, as shown in FIGURE 5-1.

FIGURE 5-1   Log-to-Log Plot of Response Time Versus Size

The plot in FIGURE 5-1 shows bands of transfer times that depend upon the user's location. Many users are locally connected, but others are operating over slower networks. The transfer time includes the time spent waiting for the remote server to respond. Although it does not represent the extra time imposed by the cache, it actually gives a reasonable summary of the response time that users are experiencing with their browsers. This information is useful because you can collect it at a central point rather than attempting to measure the response time at an individual user site.

A probability density histogram of the same data is shown in FIGURE 5-2.

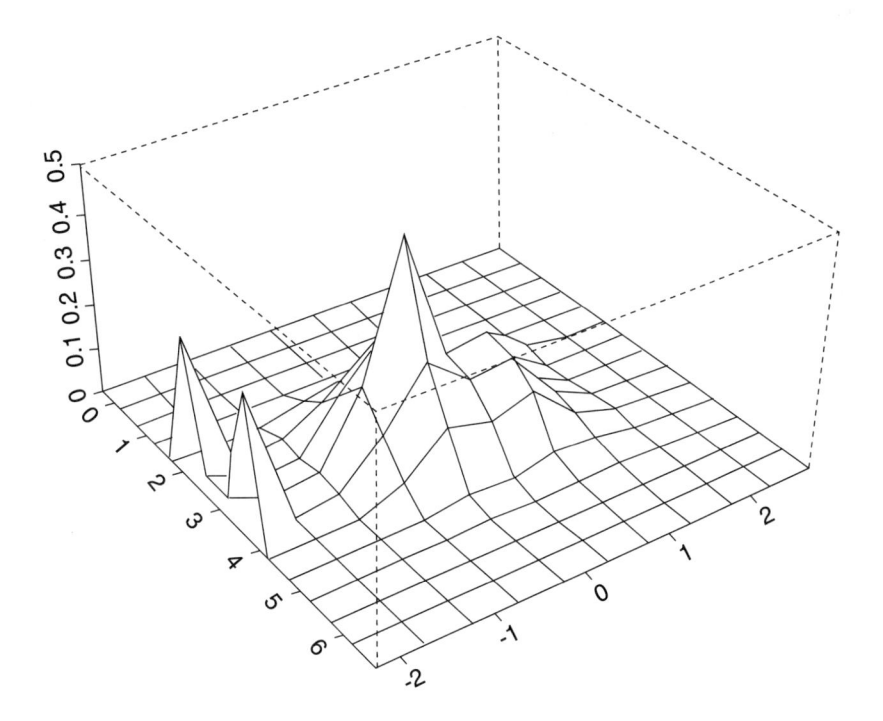

FIGURE 5-2 Perspective Log-Log Plot of Response Time Versus Size Distribution

The plot in FIGURE 5-2 shows that the most probable response is at about 0.5 seconds and 1 Kbyte. Remember that the average response time is 2.3 seconds on this data. It is clear that the average does not tell the whole story.

Internet Servers Summary

Log files are a rich source of performance information. Watching the rate at which they grow and breaking down the mix of logged operations is a powerful technique for getting good application-level performance measurements. You can apply this technique to many other applications, such as `ftp` and mail servers, as well as to any other application that can write a line to a file when it does some work.

Process Information

Many users are familiar with the `ps` process status command. But the `ps` command does not provide access to all the information available from the Solaris operating environment. It does provide a common set of data that is generally available on all UNIX systems, so we start by looking at that data, then move to the Solaris-specific data to gain a better insight into what is happening to a process.

The underlying data structures provided by the Solaris operating environment are described in full in the `proc(4)` manual page. The interface to `/proc` involves sending `ioctl` commands or opening special pseudo-files and reading them (a new feature of the Solaris 2.6 release). The data that `ps` uses is called `PIOCPSINFO`, and this is what you get back from `ioctl`. The data is slightly different if you read it from the pseudo-file.

```
proc(4)                     File Formats                    proc(4)

  PIOCPSINFO
     This returns miscellaneous process information such as that
     reported by ps(1). p is a pointer to a prpsinfo structure
     containing at least the following fields:

     typedef struct prpsinfo {
        char         pr_state;    /* numeric process state (see pr_sname) */
        char         pr_sname;    /* printable character representing pr_state */
        char         pr_zomb;     /* !=0: process terminated but not waited for */
        char         pr_nice;     /* nice for cpu usage */
        u_long       pr_flag;     /* process flags */
        int          pr_wstat;    /* if zombie, the wait() status */
        uid_t        pr_uid;      /* real user id */
        uid_t        pr_euid;     /* effective user id */
        gid_t        pr_gid;      /* real group id */
        gid_t        pr_egid;     /* effective group id */
        pid_t        pr_pid;      /* process id */
        pid_t        pr_ppid;     /* process id of parent */
        pid_t        pr_pgrp;     /* pid of process group leader */
        pid_t        pr_sid;      /* session id */
        caddr_t      pr_addr;     /* physical address of process */
        long         pr_size;     /* size of process image in pages */
```

FIGURE 5-3 Process Information Used as Input by the `ps` Command

```
        long            pr_rssize;      /* resident set size in pages */
        u_long          pr_bysize;      /* size of process image in bytes */
        u_long          pr_byrssize;    /* resident set size in bytes */
        caddr_t         pr_wchan;       /* wait addr for sleeping process */
        short           pr_syscall;     /* system call number (if in syscall) */
        id_t            pr_aslwpid;     /* lwp id of the aslwp; zero if no aslwp */
        timestruc_t pr_start            /* process start time,sec+nsec since epoch
*/
        timestruc_t pr_time;            /* usr+sys cpu time for this process */
        timestruc_t pr_ctime;           /* usr+sys cpu time for reaped children */
        long            pr_pri;         /* priority, high value is high priority */
        char            pr_oldpri;      /* pre-SVR4, low value is high priority */
        char            pr_cpu;         /* pre-SVR4, cpu usage for scheduling */
        u_short         pr_pctcpu;      /* % of recent cpu time, one or all lwps */
        u_short         pr_pctmem;      /* % of system memory used by the process */
        dev_t           pr_ttydev;      /* controlling tty device (PRNODEV if none) */
        char            pr_clname[PRCLSZ]; /* scheduling class name */
        char            pr_fname[PRFNSZ]; /* last component of exec()ed pathname */
        char            pr_psargs[PRARGSZ];/* initial characters of arg list */
        int             pr_argc;        /* initial argument count */
        char            **pr_argv;      /* initial argument vector */
        char            **pr_envp;      /* initial environment vector */
    } prpsinfo_t;
```

FIGURE 5-3 Process Information Used as Input by the `ps` Command *(Continued)*

For a multithreaded process, you can get the data for each lightweight process separately. There's a lot more useful-looking information there, but no sign of the high-resolution microstate accounting that /usr/proc/bin/ptime and several SE Toolkit scripts display. They use a separate `ioctl`, PIOCUSAGE.

```
proc(4)                         File Formats                        proc(4)

    PIOCUSAGE
       When applied to the process file descriptor, PIOCUSAGE
       returns the process usage information; when applied to an
       lwp file descriptor, it returns usage information for the
       specific lwp.  p points to a prusage structure which is
       filled by the operation. The prusage structure contains at
       least the following fields:

       typedef struct prusage {
            id_t             pr_lwpid;    /* lwp id.  0: process or defunct */
            u_long           pr_count;    /* number of contributing lwps */
```

FIGURE 5-4 Additional Microstate-Based Process Information

```
        timestruc_t   pr_tstamp;    /* current time stamp */
        timestruc_t   pr_create;    /* process/lwp creation time stamp */
        timestruc_t   pr_term;      /* process/lwp termination timestamp */
        timestruc_t   pr_rtime;     /* total lwp real (elapsed) time */
        timestruc_t   pr_utime;     /* user level CPU time */
        timestruc_t   pr_stime;     /* system call CPU time */
        timestruc_t   pr_ttime;     /* other system trap CPU time */
        timestruc_t   pr_tftime;    /* text page fault sleep time */
        timestruc_t   pr_dftime;    /* data page fault sleep time */
        timestruc_t   pr_kftime;    /* kernel page fault sleep time */
        timestruc_t   pr_ltime;     /* user lock wait sleep time *
        timestruc_t   pr_slptime;   /* all other sleep time */
        timestruc_t   pr_wtime;     /* wait-cpu (latency) time */
        timestruc_t   pr_stoptime;  /* stopped time */
        u_long        pr_minf;      /* minor page faults */
        u_long        pr_majf;      /* major page faults */
        u_long        pr_nswap;     /* swaps */
        u_long        pr_inblk;     /* input blocks */
        u_long        pr_oublk;     /* output blocks */
        u_long        pr_msnd;      /* messages sent */
        u_long        pr_mrcv;      /* messages received */
        u_long        pr_sigs;      /* signals received */
        u_long        pr_vctx;      /* voluntary context switches */
        u_long        pr_ictx;      /* involuntary context switches */
        u_long        pr_sysc;      /* system calls */
        u_long        pr_ioch;      /* chars read and written */
    } prusage_t;
```

PIOCUSAGE can be applied to a zombie process (see PIOCPSINFO).

Applying PIOCUSAGE to a process that does not have microstate accounting enabled will enable microstate accounting and return an estimate of times spent in the various states up to this point. Further invocations of PIOCUSAGE will yield accurate microstate time accounting from this point. To disable microstate accounting, use PIOCRESET with the PR_MSACCT flag.

FIGURE 5-4 Additional Microstate-Based Process Information *(Continued)*

There is a lot of useful data here. The time spent waiting for various events is a key measure. It is summarized by `msacct.se` in the following figure:

```
Elapsed time              3:20:50.049   Current time Fri Jul 26 12:49:28 1996
User CPU time                2:11.723   System call time              1:54.890
System trap time                0.006   Text pfault sleep               0.000
Data pfault sleep               0.023   Kernel pfault sleep             0.000
User lock sleep                 0.000   Other sleep time            3:16:43.022
Wait for CPU time               0.382   Stopped time                    0.000
```

FIGURE 5-5   Summary of Microstate Process Data Reported by `msacct.se`

Data Access Permissions

To access process data you must have access permissions for entries in /proc or run as a setuid root command. In the Solaris 2.5.1 release, using the ioctl access method for /proc, you can only access processes that you own, unless you log in as root, and the ps command is setuid root. In the Solaris 2.6 release, although you cannot access the /proc/pid entry for every process, you *can* read /proc/pid/psinfo and /proc/pid/usage for every process. This means that any user can use the full functionality of ps and the process. The code for process_class.se conditionally uses the new Solaris 2.6 access method and the slightly changed definition of the psinfo data structure.

Microstate Accounting

Microstate accounting is not turned on by default. It slows the system down slightly. It was on by default until the Solaris 2.3 release. From the Solaris 2.4 release on, it is enabled the first time you issue an ioctl to read the data. For the Solaris 2.6 access method, the process flags that enable microstate data collection and an inherit on fork option must be set directly via the /proc/pid/ctl interface.

The CPU time is normally measured by sampling 100 times a second, the state of all the CPUs from the clock interrupt. Microstate accounting works as follows: A high-resolution timestamp is taken on every state change, every system call, every page fault, and every scheduler change. Microstate accounting doesn't miss anything, and the results are much more accurate than those from sampled measurements. The normal measures of CPU user and system time made by sampling can be wrong by 20 percent or more because the sample is biased, not random. Process scheduling uses the same clock interrupt used to measure CPU usage. This approach leads to systematic errors in the sampled data. The microstate-measured CPU usage data does not suffer from those errors.

For example, consider a performance monitor that wakes up every ten seconds, reads some data from the kernel, then prints the results and sleeps. On a fast system, the total CPU time consumed per wake-up might be a few milliseconds. On exit from the clock interrupt, the scheduler wakes up processes and kernel threads that have been sleeping until that time. Processes that sleep then consume less than their allotted CPU time quanta always run at the highest timeshare priority. On a lightly loaded system there is no queue for access to the CPU, so immediately after the clock interrupt, it is likely that the performance monitor will be scheduled. If it runs for less than 10 milliseconds, it will have completed and be sleeping again before the next clock interrupt. If you remember that the only way CPU time is allocated is based on what was running when the clock interrupt occurs, you can see that the performance monitor could be sneaking a bite of CPU time whenever the clock interrupt isn't looking. When there is a significant amount of queuing for CPU time, the performance monitor is delayed by a random amount of time, so sometimes the clock interrupt sees it, and the error level decreases.

The error is an artifact of the dual functions of the clock interrupt. If two independent, unsynchronized interrupts are used (one for scheduling and one for performance measurement), then the errors will be averaged away over time. Another approach to the problem is to sample more frequently by running the clock interrupt more often. This does not remove the bias, but it makes it harder to hide small bites of the CPU. The overhead of splitting up the interrupts is not worth implementing. You can increase the CPU clock rate to get more accurate measurements, but the overhead is higher than using direct microstate measurement, which is much more useful and accurate because it measures more interesting state transitions than just CPU activity.

The case where this problem matters most is when a sizing exercise occurs by measuring a lightly loaded system, then scaling the results up for a higher load estimate. Performance models that are calibrated at a light load also suffer from this problem. The best solution is to use a microstate accounting-based tool, or to disable some of the CPUs so that the measurements are made on a fairly busy system.

Some performance tool vendors are currently working to incorporate microstate-based data in their products. An example implementation of a microstate-based monitor was built using the SE Toolkit. The data provided by the SE process monitoring class is shown in FIGURE 5-6.

```
    /* output data for specified process */
    double interval;         /* measured time interval for averages */
    double timestamp;        /* last time process was measured */
    double creation;         /* process start time */
    double termination;      /* process termination time stamp */
```

FIGURE 5-6 Combined Process Information from SE Toolkit Process Class

```
    double elapsed;         /* elapsed time for all lwps in process */
    double total_user;      /* current totals in seconds */
    double total_system;
    double total_child;     /* child processes that have exited */
    double user_time;       /* user time in this interval */
    double system_time;     /* system call time in this interval */
    double trap_time;       /* system trap time in interval */
    double child_time;      /* child CPU in this interval */
    double text_pf_time;    /* text page fault wait in interval */
    double data_pf_time;    /* data page fault wait in interval */
    double kernel_pf_time;  /* kernel page fault wait in interval */
    double user_lock_time;  /* user lock wait in interval */
    double sleep_time;      /* all other sleep time */
    double cpu_wait_time;   /* time on runqueue waiting for CPU */
    double stoptime;        /* time stopped from ^Z */
    ulong syscalls;         /* syscall/interval for this process */
    ulong inblocks;         /* input blocks/interval - metadata only - not interesting */
    ulong outblocks;        /* output blocks/interval - metadata only - not interesting */
    ulong vmem_size;        /* size in KB */
    ulong rmem_size;        /* RSS in KB */
    ulong maj_faults;       /* majf/interval */
    ulong min_faults;       /* minf/interval - always zero - bug? */
    ulong total_swaps;      /* swapout count */
    long  priority;         /* current sched priority */
    long  niceness;         /* current nice value */
    char  sched_class[PRCLSZ];/* name of class */
    ulong messages;         /* msgin+msgout/interval */
    ulong signals;          /* signals/interval */
    ulong vcontexts;        /* voluntary context switches/interval */
    ulong icontexts;        /* involuntary context switches/interval */
    ulong charios;          /* characters in and out/interval */
    ulong lwp_count;        /* number of lwps for the process */
    int   uid;              /* current uid */
    long  ppid;             /* parent pid */
    char  fname[PRFNSZ];    /* last component of exec'd pathname */
    char  args[PRARGSZ];    /* initial part of command name and arg list */
```

FIGURE 5-6 Combined Process Information from SE Toolkit Process Class *(Continued)*

Most of the data in FIGURE 5-6 is self explanatory. All times are in seconds in double precision with microsecond accuracy. The minor fault counter seems to be broken because it always reports zero. The `inblock` and `outblock` counters are not interesting because they only refer to file system metadata for the old-style buffer cache. The `charios` counter includes all read and write data for all file descriptors, so you can see the file I/O rate. The `lwp_count` is not the current number of lwps. It is a count of how many `lwps` the process has ever had. If the count is more than one, then the process is multithreaded. It is possible to access each `lwp` in turn and read its `psinfo` and `usage` data. The process data is the sum of these.

Child data is accumulated when a child process exits. The CPU used by the child is added into the data for the parent. This can be used to find processes that are forking many short-lived commands.

Accounting

Who ran what, when, and how much resource was used?

Many processes have very short life spans. You cannot see such processes with `ps`, but they may be so frequent that they dominate the load on your system. The only way to catch them is to have the system keep a record of every process that has run, who ran it, what it was, when it started and ended, and how much resource it used. The answers come from the system accounting subsystem. While you may have some concerns about accounting because of the "big brother is watching you" connotation or the cost of additional overhead, the information is important and valuable. The overhead of collecting accounting data is *always present but is insignificant*. When you turn on accounting, you are just enabling the storage of a few bytes of useful data when a process exits.

Accounting data is most useful when it is measured over a long period of time. This temporal information is useful on a network of workstations as well as on a single, time-shared server. From this information, you can identify how often programs run, how much CPU time, I/O, and memory each program uses, and what work patterns throughout the week look like. To enable accounting to start immediately, enter the three commands shown below.

```
# ln /etc/init.d/acct /etc/rc0.d/K22acct
# ln /etc/init.d/acct /etc/rc2.d/S22acct
# /etc/init.d/acct start
Starting process accounting
```

Refer to the accounting section in the *Solaris System Administration Answerbook* and see the `acctcom` command. Add some `crontab` entries to summarize and checkpoint the accounting logs. Collecting and checkpointing the accounting data itself puts a negligible additional load onto the system, but the summary scripts that run once a day or once a week can have a noticeable effect, so schedule them to run outside business hours.

Your `crontab` file for the `adm` user should contain the following:

```
# crontab -1 adm
#ident    "@(#)adm       1.5    92/07/14 SMI"    /* SVr4.0 1.2    */
#min      hour    day    month    weekday
0         *       *      *        *         /usr/lib/acct/ckpacct
30        2       *      *        *         /usr/lib/acct/runacct 2> /var/adm/
acct/nite/fd2log
30        9       *      *        5         /usr/lib/acct/monacct
```

You get a daily accounting summary, but it is best to keep track of the monthly summary stored in `/var/adm/acct/fiscal`. Following is an excerpt from `fiscrpt07`, which is the report for July on this desktop system.

```
Jul 26 09:30 1996                         TOTAL COMMAND SUMMARY FOR FISCAL 07 Page 1

                 TOTAL COMMAND SUMMARY
COMMAND  NUMBER        TOTAL    TOTAL      TOTAL    MEAN     MEAN    HOG       CHARS  BLOCKS
   NAME    CMDS     KCOREMIN  CPU-MIN   REAL-MIN  SIZE-K  CPU-MIN FACTOR      TRNSFD    READ

 TOTALS   26488  16062007.75  3960.11  494612.41  4055.95    0.15   0.01  17427899648   39944

mae          36   7142887.25  1501.73    2128.50  4756.45   41.71   0.71   2059814144    1653
sundgado     16   3668645.19   964.83    1074.34  3802.36   60.30   0.90    139549181      76
Xsun         29   1342108.55   251.32    9991.62  5340.18    8.67   0.03   2784769024    1295
xlock        32   1027099.38   726.87    4253.34  1413.04   22.71   0.17   4009349888      15
fountain      2    803036.25   165.11     333.65  4863.71   82.55   0.49       378388       1
netscape     22    489512.97    72.39    3647.61  6762.19    3.29   0.02    887353080    2649
maker4X.     10    426182.31    43.77    5004.30  9736.27    4.38   0.01    803267592    3434
wabiprog     53    355574.99    44.32     972.44  8022.87    0.84   0.05    355871360     570
imagetoo     21    257617.08    15.65     688.46 16456.60    0.75   0.02     64291840     387
java        235    203963.64    37.96     346.35  5373.76    0.16   0.11    155950720     240
aviator       2    101012.82    22.93      29.26  4406.20   11.46   0.78      2335744      40
se.sparc     18     46793.09    19.30    6535.43  2424.47    1.07   0.00    631756294      20
xv            3     40930.98     5.58      46.37  7337.93    1.86   0.12    109690880      28
```

The commands reported are sorted by KCOREMIN, which is the product of the amount of CPU time used and the amount of RAM used while the command was active. CPU-MIN is the number of minutes of CPU time. REAL_MIN is the elapsed time for the commands. SIZE-K is an average value for the RSS over the active lifetime of the process. It does not include times when the process was not actually running. (In Solaris 2.4 and earlier releases, a bug causes this measure to be invalid.) HOG FACTOR is the ratio of CPU-MIN to REAL-MIN; a high factor means that this command hogs the CPU whenever it is running. CHARS TRNSFD counts the number of characters read and written. BLOCKS READ counts data read from block devices (basically, local disk file system reads and writes). The underlying data that is collected can be seen in the acct(4) manual page. The data structure is very compact—about 40 bytes, as shown FIGURE 5-7:

```
DESCRIPTION
     Files produced as a result of calling acct(2) have records
     in the form defined by <sys/acct.h>, whose contents are:

  typedef ushort  comp_t;       /* pseudo "floating point" representation */
                                /* 3-bit base-8 exponent in the high */
                                /* order bits, and a 13-bit fraction */
                                /* in the low order bits. */

     struct   acct
     {
              char     ac_flag;        /* Accounting flag */
              char     ac_stat;        /* Exit status */
              uid_t    ac_uid;         /* Accounting user ID */
              gid_t    ac_gid;         /* Accounting group ID */
              dev_t    ac_tty;         /* control tty */
              time_t   ac_btime;       /* Beginning time */
              comp_t   ac_utime;       /* accounting user time in clock */
                                       /* ticks */
              comp_t   ac_stime;       /* accounting system time in clock */
                                       /* ticks */
          comp_t   ac_etime;      /* accounting total elapsed time in clock */
                                       /* ticks */
              comp_t   ac_mem;         /* memory usage in clicks (pages) */
              comp_t   ac_io;          /* chars transferred by read/write */
              comp_t   ac_rw;          /* number of block reads/writes */
              char     ac_comm[8];     /* command name */
     };
```

FIGURE 5-7 Accounting Data Format

Solaris Resource Manager Accounting

The SRM software provides the ability to generate accounting data based on resource usage. This is made available by the accumulation of resource information in the lnode tree. Although the SRM software does not provide resource accounting, it does provide the data and data-extraction tools used to develop a system to generate accounting (or billing) information. See Chapter 7 for more information on SRM Accounting.

Network Accounting Using NetFlow

The Solaris Bandwidth Manager software has built-in support for Cisco NetFlow™ software. This feature allows for detailed network measurements that can be sent to other software packages that can process and analyze this data.

Besides the Solaris Bandwidth Manager software, NetFlow data collection is supported on a variety of Cisco devices, such as the Cisco 7000 and 7500 series routers.

When NetFlow is enabled on the Solaris Bandwidth Manager software or any Cisco equipment supporting NetFlow, network packets are processed and classified into flows. A flow is a unidirectional series of packets that have several parameters in common:

- Source and destination IP address
- Source and destination application port number
- IP protocol type
- IP ToS (Type of Service)

A flow ends when either a FIN or RST packet is received for that flow, or when it times out.

NetFlow-enabled devices send out NetFlow datagrams, which contain records for one or more flows. Combining multiple flow records in one datagram reduces network overhead caused by NetFlow. These datagrams are UDP based, so they can get lost in transit in case of a busy network. NetFlow version 5 and higher add a sequence number to the datagram header, so the receiver of these datagrams can at least know that a datagram was lost.

Each NetFlow datagram record contains detailed flow information, such as the number of bytes in the flow, the number of packets, the duration, source and destination IP address, and so on.

Cisco offers applications that read and process NetFlow datagrams. NetFlow FlowCollector™ is a NetFlow datagram consumer for one or more NetFlow devices. These devices simply point to the host and port number on which the FlowCollector software is running. The FlowCollector aggregates this data, does preprocessing and filtering, and provides several options to save this data to disk (such as flat files). Other applications, such as network analyzing, planning, and billing, can use these files as input.

The NetFlow FlowAnalyzer™ application uses the output from NetFlow FlowCollector. It provides elaborate processing, graphing, and reporting options for network analysis, planning, troubleshooting, and more.

You can run the Solaris Bandwidth Manager software in statistics mode, where it will process packets but not provide the priority scheduling. By using the NetFlow output of the Solaris Bandwidth Manager software, you can obtain detailed network measurements that are not easily measured otherwise. For example, you can find out the bandwidth used by a specific application or user by using NetFlow data analysis. The flow data can also provide latency information of specific applications. Trend data can show the long term impact of the deployment of certain applications.

For more information about Cisco NetFlow, see
http://www.cisco.com/warp/public/732/netflow/index.html.

Storage Measurements

Individual disks are well instrumented, but storage subsystems are now much more complex than a few individual disks. This section explains the basic Solaris software measures and discusses more complex disk subsystems.

Disk Workloads

There are six basic disk access patterns. Read, write, and update operations can either be sequentially or randomly distributed. Sequential read and write occur when files are copied and created or when large amounts of data are processed. Random read and write can occur in indexed database reads or can be due to page-in or page-out to a file. Update consists of a read-modify-write sequence and can be caused by a database system committing a sequence of transactions in either a sequential or random pattern. When you are working to understand or improve the performance of your disk subsystem, spend some time identifying which of the access-pattern categories are most important to you.

You cannot automatically tell which processes are causing disk activity. The kernel does not collect this information. You may be able to work out where the workload comes from by looking at how an application was installed, but often you must resort to using truss on a process or the TNF tracing system. The Solaris software does not offer a way of getting I/O activity on a per-file descriptor basis, so application-specific instrumentation is all we have. Databases such as Oracle can collect and report data on a per-tablespace basis, so if you can map the tablespaces to physical disks, you can tell what is going on programmatically. Such collection and analysis is performed by the BMC Best/1 performance modeling tool so that changes in disk workload can be modeled.

Output Formats and Options for `iostat`

The `iostat` command produces output in many forms. When a large number of disks are being reported, the `iostat -x` variant provides extended statistics and is easier to read because each disk is summarized on a separate line (see FIGURE 5-8). The following values are reported: the number of transfers and kilobytes per second with read and write shown separately, the average number of commands waiting in the queue, the average number of commands actively being processed by the drive, the I/O service time, and the percentages of the time that commands were waiting in the queue, and commands that were active on the drive.

```
% iostat -txc 5
                         extended disk statistics         tty          cpu
disk   r/s   w/s   Kr/s   Kw/s wait actv  svc_t  %w  %b  tin tout us sy wt id
fd0    0.0   0.0   0.0    0.0  0.0  0.0   0.0    0   0    0   77 42  9  9 39
sd0    0.0   3.5   0.0   21.2  0.0  0.1  41.6    0  14
sd1    0.0   0.0   0.0    0.0  0.0  0.0   0.0    0   0
sd3    0.0   0.0   0.0    0.0  0.0  0.0   0.0    0   0
                         extended disk statistics         tty          cpu
disk   r/s   w/s   Kr/s   Kw/s wait actv  svc_t  %w  %b  tin tout us sy wt id
fd0    0.0   0.0   0.0    0.0  0.0  0.0   0.0    0   0    0   84 37 17 45  1
sd0    0.0  16.8   0.0  102.4  0.0  0.7  43.1    2  61
sd1    0.0   0.0   0.0    0.0  0.0  0.0   0.0    0   0
sd3    0.0   1.0   0.0    8.0  0.0  0.1 114.3    2   4
```

FIGURE 5-8 `iostat -x` Output

Disk configurations have become extremely large and complex on big server systems. The Starfire system supports a maximum configuration of several thousand disk drives, but dealing with even a few hundred is a problem. When large numbers of disks are configured, the overall failure rate also increases. It is hard to keep an inventory of all the disks, and tools like the SyMON software have to depend upon parsing messages from `syslog` to see if any faults are reported. The size of each disk is also growing. When more than one type of data is stored on a disk, it's hard to determine which disk partition is active. A series of new features has been introduced in the Solaris 2.6 release to help solve these problems.

- Per-partition data identical to existing per-disk data

  It is now possible to separate root, swap, and home directory activity even if these file systems are on the same disk.

- New "error and identity" data per disk

  You no longer need to scan `syslog` for errors. Full data is saved from the first SCSI probe to a disk. This data includes vendor, product, revision, serial number, RPM, heads, and size. Soft, hard, and transport error counter categories sum up any problems. The detail option adds the Media Error, Device not ready, No device, Recoverable, Illegal request, and Predictive failure analysis information. Dead or missing disks can still be identified because there is no need to send them another SCSI probe.

- New `iostat` options to present these metrics

    One option (`iostat -M`) shows throughput in Mbytes/s rather than Kbytes/s for high-performance systems. Another option (`-n`) translates disk names into a more useful form, so you don't have to deal with the sd43b format—instead, you get c1t2d5s1. This feature makes it easier to keep track of per-controller load levels in large configurations.

Fast tapes now match the performance impact of disks. We recently ran a tape backup benchmark to see if there were any scalability or throughput limits in the Solaris software, and we were pleased to find that the only real limit is the speed of the tape drives. The final result was a backup rate of an Oracle database at 1 terabyte/hour or about 350 Mbytes/s, which was as fast as the disk subsystem we had configured could perform. To sustain this rate, we used every accessible tape drive, including 24 StorageTEK Redwood tape transports, which run at around 15 Mbytes/s each. We ran this test using the Solaris 2.5.1 operating environment, but there are no measurements of tape drive throughput in the Solaris 2.5.1 release. Tape metrics were added to the Solaris 2.6 release, and you can see the tape drive that is active, the throughput, average transfer size, and service time for each tape drive.

Tapes are instrumented in the same way as disks; they appear in `sar` and `iostat` automatically. Tape read/write operations are instrumented with all the same measures that are used for disks. Rewind and scan/seek are omitted from the service time.

The output format and options of `sar(1)` are fixed by the generic UNIX standard SVID3, but the format and options for `iostat` can be changed. In the Solaris 2.6 release, existing `iostat` options are unchanged. Apart from extra entries that appear for tape drives and NFS mount points, anyone storing `iostat` data from a mixture of Solaris 2.x systems will get a consistent format. New options that extend `iostat` are as follows:

- `-E` full error statistics
- `-e` error summary statistics
- `-n` disk name and NFS mount point translation, extended service time
- `-M` Mbytes/s instead of Kbytes/s
- `-P` partitions only
- `-p` disks and partitions

Here are examples of some of the new `iostat` formats:

```
% iostat -xp
                              extended device statistics
device    r/s   w/s   kr/s   kw/s  wait  actv  svc_t   %w   %b
sd106     0.0   0.0   0.0    0.0   0.0   0.0   0.0     0    0
sd106,a   0.0   0.0   0.0    0.0   0.0   0.0   0.0     0    0
sd106,b   0.0   0.0   0.0    0.0   0.0   0.0   0.0     0    0
sd106,c   0.0   0.0   0.0    0.0   0.0   0.0   0.0     0    0
st47      0.0   0.0   0.0    0.0   0.0   0.0   0.0     0    0
```

```
% iostat -xe
                              extended device statistics ---- errors ----
device    r/s   w/s   kr/s   kw/s  wait  actv  svc_t   %w   %b  s/w  h/w  trn  tot
sd106     0.0   0.0   0.0    0.0   0.0   0.0   0.0     0    0   0    0    0    0
st47      0.0   0.0   0.0    0.0   0.0   0.0   0.0     0    0   0    0    0    0
```

```
% iostat -E

sd106   Soft Errors: 0 Hard Errors: 0 Transport Errors: 0
Vendor: SEAGATE   Product: ST15230W SUN4.2G Revision: 0626 Serial No:
00193749
RPM: 7200 Heads: 16 Size: 4.29GB <4292075520 bytes>
Media Error: 0 Device Not Ready: 0 No Device: 0 Recoverable: 0
Illegal Request: 0 Predictive Failure Analysis: 0

st47    Soft Errors: 0 Hard Errors: 0 Transport Errors: 0
Vendor: EXABYTE   Product: EXB-8505SMBANSH2 Revision: 0793 Serial No:
```

The Solaris 2.5 Trace Capability

UNIX systems have had a kernel trace capability for many years. It was designed for development and debugging, not for end users. The production kernel is normally built without the trace capability for performance reasons. One of the first production kernels to include tracing was IBM's AIX kernel on the RS/6000 servers. They left it on during early releases to assist in debugging, then decided that tracing was useful enough to pay its way, and the overhead was low. So it is now a permanent feature. Sun also recognized the value of trace information but decided to extend the trace capability to make it more generally useful and to implement it alongside the existing kernel trace system. It was introduced in the Solaris 2.5 operating environment and consists of the following features.

- A self-describing trace output format, called Trace Normal Form (TNF), allows data structures to be embedded in the trace file without the need for an external definition of their types and contents.
- A set of libraries allows user-level programs to generate trace data. In particular, this trace data helps analyze and debug multithreaded applications.

- A well-defined set of kernel probe points covering most important events was implemented.
- A program `prex`(1) controls probe execution for both user and kernel traces.
- A program `tnfxtract`(1) reads out the kernel trace buffer, and `tnfdump`(1) displays TNF data in human-readable ASCII.
- Manual pages exist for all the commands and library calls. The set of implemented kernel probes is documented in `tnf_probes`(4).

A few things about kernel probes are inconvenient. While user-level probes can write to trace files, the kernel probes write to a ring buffer. This buffer is not a single global ring; it is a buffer per kernel thread. This buffer scheme avoids any need to lock the data structures, so there is no performance loss or contention on multiprocessor systems. You cannot easily tell how big the buffer needs to be. One highly active probe point might loop right round its buffer while others have hardly started. If you are trying to capture every single probe, make the buffer as big as you can. In general, it is best to work with low event rate probes or rely on sampling and put up with missing probes. The `tnfxtract` routine just takes a snapshot of the buffer, so a second snapshot will include anything left over from the first one. The `tnfdump` program does quite a lot of work to sort the probe events into time order.

I/O Trace: Commands and Features

The command sequence to initiate an I/O trace is quite simple. You run the commands as root, and you need a directory to hold the output. It's easiest to have two windows open: one to run `prex`, and the other to go through a cycle of extracting, dumping, and viewing the data as required. The command sequence for `prex` is to first allocate a buffer (the default is 384 Kbytes; you can make it bigger), enable the `io` group of probes, make them trace accesses, then turn on the global flag that enables all kernel tracing.

```
# prex -k
Type "help" for help ...
prex> buffer alloc
Buffer of size 393216 bytes allocated
prex> enable io
prex> trace io
prex> ktrace on
```

Now, wait a while or run the program you want to trace. In this case, we ran `iostat -x 10` in another window, didn't try to cause any activity, and waited for some slow service time to appear. After approximately one minute, we stopped collecting.

```
prex> ktrace off
```

In the other window we extracted and dumped the data to take a look at it.

```
# mkdir /tmp/tnf
# cd /tmp/tnf
# tnfxtract io.tnf
# tnfdump io.tnf | more
```

Understanding I/O Measurements

To really understand the data presented by `iostat`, `sar`, and other tools, you must look at the raw data being collected by the kernel, remember some history, and do some simple mathematics.

In the old days, disk controllers controlled the disks directly. All the intelligence was in the controller. The disk heads were directly connected to the controller, and the device driver knew exactly which track the disk was reading. As each bit was read from disk, it was buffered in the controller until a whole disk block was ready to be passed to the device driver.

The device driver maintained a queue of waiting requests, which were serviced one at a time by the disk as shown in FIGURE 5-9. From this, the system could report the service time directly as milliseconds-per-seek. The throughput in transfers per second was also reported, as was the percentage of the time that the disk was busy (the utilization). The terms *utilization, service time, wait time, throughput,* and *wait queue length* have well-defined meanings in this scenario because the setup is so simple that a very basic queueing model fits it well. A set of simple equations from queuing theory can be used to derive these values from underlying measurements.

I/Os waiting in device driver queue

I/Os being serviced one at a time by the disk

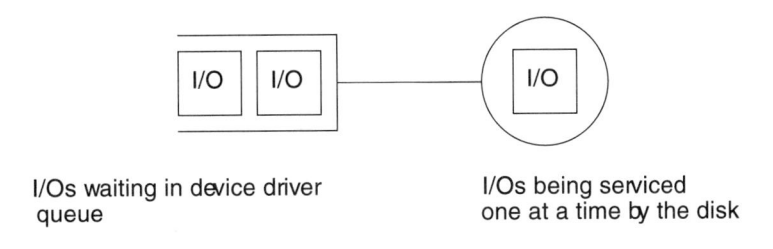

FIGURE 5-9 Simple Old Disk Model

Nowadays, a standard disk is SCSI based and has an embedded controller. The disk drive contains a small microprocessor and about 1 Mbyte of RAM. It can typically handle up to 64 outstanding requests via SCSI tagged-command queuing. The system uses a SCSI Host Bus adapter (HBA) to talk to the disk. In large systems, there is another level of intelligence and buffering in a hardware RAID controller. The simple model of a disk used by `iostat` and its terminology have become confused. In addition, the same reporting mechanism is used for client side NFS mount points and complex disk volumes setup using Solstice™ DiskSuite™ software.

In the old days, if the device driver sent a request to the disk, the disk would do nothing else until it completed the request. The time it took was the service time, and the average service time was a property of the disk itself. Disks that spin faster and seek faster have lower (better) service times. With today's systems, if the device driver issues a request, that request is queued internally by the RAID controller and the disk drive, and several more requests can be sent before the first one comes back. The service time, as measured by the device driver, varies according to the load level and queue length and is not directly comparable to the old-style service time of a simple disk drive.

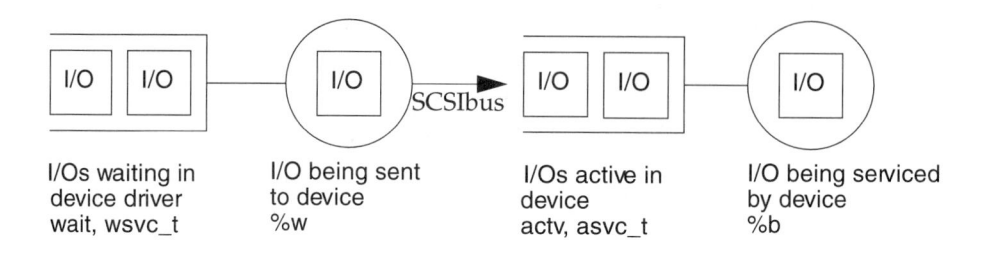

```
┌───┬───┐      ╱‾‾‾╲          ┌───┬───┐      ╱‾‾‾╲
│I/O│I/O│─────│ I/O │────▶   │I/O│I/O│─────│ I/O │
└───┴───┘      ╲___╱SCSIbus  └───┴───┘      ╲___╱
```

I/Os waiting in   I/O being sent   I/Os active in   I/O being serviced
device driver   to device   device   by device
wait, wsvc_t   %w   actv, asvc_t   %b

FIGURE 5-10 Two-Stage Disk Model Used by Solaris 2

The instrumentation provided in the Solaris operating environment takes this change into account by explicitly measuring a two-stage queue: one queue, called the wait queue, in the device driver; and another queue, called the active queue, in the device itself. A read or write command is issued to the device driver and sits in the wait queue until the SCSI bus and disk are both ready. When the command is sent to the disk device, it moves to the active queue until the disk sends its response. The problem with `iostat` is that it tries to report the new measurements in some of the original terminology. The "wait service time" is actually the time spent in the "wait" queue. This is not the right definition of service time in any case, and the word "wait" is used to mean two different things. To sort out what we really have, we must do some mathematics.

Let's start with the actual measurements made by the kernel. For each disk drive (and each disk partition, tape drive, and NFS mount in the Solaris 2.6 release), a small set of counters is updated. An annotated copy of the `kstat(3K)`-based data structure that the SE Toolkit uses is shown in FIGURE 5-11.

```
struct ks_disks {
    long        number$;     /* linear disk number */
    string      name$;       /* name of the device */

    ulonglong   nread;       /* number of bytes read */
    ulonglong   nwritten;    /* number of bytes written */
    ulong       reads;       /* number of reads */
    ulong       writes;      /* number of writes */
    longlong    wtime;       /* wait queue - time spent waiting */
    longlong    wlentime;    /* wait queue - sum of queue length multiplied
by time at that length */
    longlong    wlastupdate; /* wait queue - time of last update */
    longlong    rtime;       /* active/run queue - time spent active/running */
    longlong    rlentime;    /* active/run queue - sum of queue length * time
at that length */
    longlong    rlastupdate; /* active/run queue - time of last update */
    ulong       wcnt;        /* wait queue - current queue length */
    ulong       rcnt;        /* active/run queue - current queue length */
};
```

FIGURE 5-11 Kernel Disk Information Statistics Data Structure

None of these values are printed out directly by iostat, so the basic arithmetic starts here. The first thing to note is that the underlying metrics are cumulative counters or instantaneous values. The values printed by iostat are averages over a time interval. We need to take two copies of the above data structure together with a high resolution *timestamp* for each and do some subtraction. We then get the average values between the *start* and *end* times. We'll write it out as plainly as possible, with pseudocode that assumes an array of two values for each measure, indexed by *start* and *end*. T_{hires} is in units of nanoseconds, so we divide to get seconds as T.

T_{hires} = hires elapsed time = $EndTime - StartTime$ = $timestamp[end] - timestamp[start]$

$T = \dfrac{T_{hires}}{100000000}$

B_{wait} = hires busy time for wait queue = $wtime[end] - wtime[start]$

B_{run} = hires busy time for run queue = $rtime[end] - rtime[start]$

QB_{wait} = wait queue length * time = $wlentime[end] - wlentime[start]$

QB_{run} = run queue length * time = $rlentime[end] - rlentime[start]$

We assume that all disk commands complete fairly quickly, so the arrival and completion rates are the same in a steady state average, and the throughput of both queues is the same. We'll use completions below because they seem more intuitive in this case.

C_{read} = completed reads = $reads[end] - reads[start]$

X_{read} = read throughput = iostat rps = $\dfrac{C_{read}}{T}$

C_{write} = completed writes = $writes[end] - writes[start]$

X_{write} = write throughput = iostat wps = $\dfrac{C_{write}}{T}$

C = total commands completed = $C_{read} + C_{write}$

X = throughput in commands per second = iostat tps = $\dfrac{C}{T}$ = $X_{read} + X_{write}$

A similar calculation gets us the data rate in kilobytes per second.

K_{read} = Kbytes read in the interval = $\dfrac{nread[end] - nread[start]}{1024}$

X_{kread} = read Kbytes throughput = iostat Kr/s = $\dfrac{K_{read}}{T}$

K_{write} = Kbytes written in the interval = $\dfrac{nwritten[end] - nwritten[start]}{1024}$

X_{kwrite} = write Kbytes throughput = iostat Kw/s = $\dfrac{K_{write}}{T}$

X_k = total data rate in Kbytes per second = iostat Kps = $X_{kread} + X_{kwrite}$

Next, we obtain the utilization or the busy time as a percentage of the total time:

U_{wait} = wait queue utilization = iostat %w = $\dfrac{100 \times B_{wait}}{T_{hires}}$

U_{run} = run queue utilization = iostat %b = $\dfrac{100 \times B_{run}}{T_{hires}}$

Now, we get to service time, but it is *not* what `iostat` prints out and calls service time. This is the real thing!

$$S_{wait} = \text{average wait queue service time in milliseconds} = \frac{B_{wait}}{C \times 100000}$$

$$S_{run} = \text{average run queue service time in milliseconds} = \frac{B_{run}}{C \times 100000}$$

The meaning of S_{run} is as close as you can get to the old-style disk service time. Remember that the disk can run more than one command at a time and can return those commands in a different order than they were issued.

The data structure contains an instantaneous measure of queue length, but we want the average over the time interval. We get this from that strange "length time" product by dividing it by the busy time:

$$Q_{wait} = \text{average wait queue length} = \text{iostat wait} = \frac{QB_{wait}}{B_{wait}}$$

$$Q_{run} = \text{average run queue length} = \text{iostat actv} = \frac{QB_{run}}{B_{run}}$$

Finally, we get the number that `iostat` calls service time. It is defined as the queue length divided by the throughput, but it is actually the residence or response time and includes all queuing effects:

$$R_{wait} = \text{average wait queue response time} = \text{iostat wsvc\_t} = \frac{Q_{wait}}{X}$$

$$R_{run} = \text{average run queue response time} = \text{iostat asvc\_t} = \frac{Q_{run}}{X}$$

Another way to express response time is in terms of service time and utilization:

$$R_{wait} = \text{average wait queue response time prediction} = \text{iostat wsvc\_t} = \frac{S_{wait}}{1 - B_{wait}}$$

$$R_{run} = \text{average run queue response time prediction} = \text{iostat asvc\_t} = \frac{S_{run}}{1 - B_{run}}$$

This uses a theoretical model of response time that assumes that as you approach 100 percent utilization with a constant service time the response time increases to infinity.

The real definition of service time is the time taken for the first command in line to be processed. Its value is not printed out by `iostat`. Using the SE Toolkit, this deficiency is easily fixed. A corrected version of `iostat` written in SE prints out the data, using the format shown in FIGURE 5-12.

```
% se siostat.se 10
03:42:50   ------throughput------ -----wait queue----- ----active queue----
disk       r/s   w/s   Kr/s    Kw/s qlen res_t svc_t %ut qlen res_t svc_t %ut
c0t2d0s0   0.0   0.2   0.0     1.2 0.00 0.02  0.02   0 0.00 22.87 22.87   0
03:43:00   ------throughput------ -----wait queue----- ----active queue----
disk       r/s   w/s   Kr/s    Kw/s qlen res_t svc_t %ut qlen res_t svc_t %ut
c0t2d0s0   0.0   3.2   0.0    23.1 0.00 0.01  0.01   0 0.72 225.45 16.20   5
```

FIGURE 5-12 SE-Based Rewrite of `iostat` to Show Service Time Correctly

The Solaris 2.6 disk instrumentation is complete and accurate. Now that it has been extended to tapes, partitions, and client NFS mount points, there much more can be done with it.

Understanding Resource Utilization Characteristics

One important characteristic of complex I/O subsystems is that the utilization measure can be confusing. When a simple system reaches 100 percent busy, it has also reached its maximum throughput. This is because only one thing is being processed at a time in the I/O device. When the device being monitored is an NFS server, hardware RAID disk subsystem, or a striped volume, it is clearly a much more complex situation. All of these can process many requests in parallel.

I/Os waiting in device driver
$Q_{wait}, R_{wait}, U_{wait}$

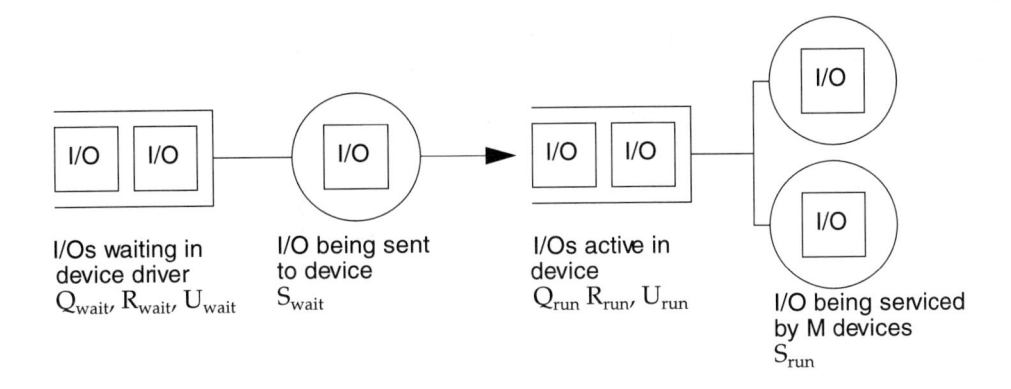

I/O being sent to device
S_{wait}

I/Os active in device
$Q_{run}, R_{run}, U_{run}$

I/O being serviced by M devices
S_{run}

FIGURE 5-13 Complex I/O Device Queue Model

As long as a single I/O is being serviced at all times, the utilization is reported as 100 percent. This makes sense because it means that the pool of devices is always busy doing something. However, there is enough capacity for additional I/Os to be serviced in parallel. Compared to a simple device, the service time for each I/O is the same, but the queue is being drained more quickly so the average queue length and response time is less, and the peak throughput is more. In effect, the load on each disk is divided by the number of disks, so the underlying utilization is U/M. The approximated model for response time in this case changes so that response time stays lower for longer, but it still heads for infinity at a true 100 percent utilization.

$$R_{wait} = \text{average wait queue response time prediction} = \text{iostat wsvc\_t} = \frac{S_{wait}}{1 - (B_{wait}/M)^M}$$

$$R_{run} = \text{average run queue response time prediction} = \text{iostat asvc\_t} = \frac{S_{run}}{1 - (B_{run}/M)^M}$$

In practice, some other effects come into play. The drives optimize head movement, so that as the queue gets longer, the average service time decreases, since it is more likely that there is a block nearby to make a shorter seek to. This in itself increases throughput more than traditional simple queueing models would predict.

Network Measurements

The way network measurements can and should be made depends on the objective of the measurement. Do you want to manage the overall health of a network link? Are you interested in the TCP/IP statistics of your server? Do you want to know how much bandwidth is used by a specific application? Each of these questions can be answered if the right tools and techniques are used to do the measuring.

Network Throughput

Using SNMP counters is a good way to get an overall view of network throughput. The Solaris software provides an SNMP daemon which provides the data you need. If your host is managed by the SyMON software, you can browse the SNMP counters through the SyMON GUI, and it is very easy to graph network throughput data by combining some of these counters in a simple formula. For example, to get a graph depicting how much percent of the (half duplex) network segment that is busy, use the following formula:

```
((ifInOctets + ifOutOctets) / time_interval)/ ifSpeed) * 100
```

Most networking devices support SNMP, and the SyMON software can incorporate any third-party MIBs so all links from a switch can be monitored at the same time.

Besides the SyMON software, many other commercial and free applications and utilities manage SNMP devices. One example of an excellent free utility is MRTG and can be downloaded from
http://ee-staff.ethz.ch/~oetiker/webtools/mrtg/mrtg.html.

Ethernet Statistics

Traditionally, administrators have used collisions as an indicator of network health for Ethernet networks. Collisions are reported using `netstat` with the `-i` flag.

```
doghouse% netstat -i

Name  Mtu   Net/Dest   Address    Ipkts      Ierrs  Opkts      Oerrs  Collis  Queue
lo0   8232  loopback   localhost  40986      0      40986      0      0       0
hme0  1500  doghouse   doghouse   128128305  0      125004514  0      77754   0
```

The collision rate is (Collis / Opkts) * 100%. In our case, that is less than a tenth of a percent. Collisions are absolutely normal and should cause no concern unless collision rates become very high (in the order of 10 to 20 percent or higher). If you have high collision rates, check the total bandwidth utilization on your network link.

Today, more and more switched and full duplex Ethernet networks are being deployed. In these environments, there are no collisions since each port on the switch has its own dedicated bandwidth, and hosts can send network packets whenever they want. If a switch gets overloaded, it just drops packets that it can't process fast enough. Dropped packets have to be retransmitted by the sender.

Netstat has an undocumented option that is invoked with the -k flag. It will dump a lot of statistics that are kept in kernel structures (the kstats). You can look at for example the statistics from the hme card as follows:

```
doghouse% netstat -k hme0
hme0:
ipackets 133465658 ierrors 0 opackets 130244542 oerrors 0
collisions 83672 defer 115 framing 0 crc 0 sqe 0 code_violations
0 len_errors 0 ifspeed 10 buff 0 oflo 0 uflo 0 missed 0
tx_late_collisions 0 retry_error 0 first_collisions 0 nocarrier 0
inits 6 nocanput 0 allocbfail 0 runt 0 jabber 0 babble 0 tmd_error
0 tx_late_error 0 rx_late_error 0 slv_parity_error 0
tx_parity_error 0 rx_parity_error 0 slv_error_ack 0 tx_error_ack
0 rx_error_ack 0 tx_tag_error 0 rx_tag_error 0 eop_error 0 no_tmds
0 no_tbufs 0 no_rbufs 0 rx_late_collisions 0 rbytes 1523404831
obytes 813184078 multircv 33440 multixmt 3 brdcstrcv 3312500
brdcstxmt 14694 norcvbuf 0 noxmtbuf 0 phy_failures 0
```

Most of these statistics are related to the Ethernet MAC and the network interface card hardware itself. In general, these counters help troubleshoot hardware problems. Every network interface card typically has different counters, which can change with the operating system releases. Sun does not officially support the netstat option.

Protocol Statistics

To view TCP, UDP, IP, ICMP, and IGMP statistics, you can use `netstat -s`. The command prints lots of protocol-specific information. Adrian Cockcroft and Rich Pettit describe this in their book *Sun Performance and Tuning, Java and the Internet*. The more interesting counters are incorporated into the SE Toolkit script `nx.se`. The output of `nx.se` looks as follows:

```
% /opt/RICHPse/bin/se nx.se
Current tcp RtoMin is 200, interval 5, start Thu Aug 27 00:23:09 1998
00:23:14 Iseg/s Oseg/s InKB/s  OuKB/s Rst/s  Atf/s  Ret%  Icn/s  Ocn/s
tcp        0.0    0.2    0.00    0.01  0.00   0.00   0.0   0.00   0.00
Name     Ipkt/s Opkt/s InKB/s  OuKB/s IErr/s OErr/s Coll% NoCP/s Defr/s
hme0       1.2    1.2    0.09    0.20  0.000  0.000  0.0   0.00   0.00
hme1       0.0    0.0    0.00    0.00  0.000  0.000  0.0   0.00   0.00
hme2       0.0    0.0    0.00    0.00  0.000  0.000  0.0   0.00   0.00
```

The script lists TCP as if it were an interface, with input and output segment and data rates, resets per second, outgoing connection attempt fails per second, percentage of bytes retransmitted, and incoming and outgoing connections per second. It then lists all the interfaces. For interfaces that provide this information (at present, only `le` and `hme`) `nx.se` reports kilobytes in and out. NoCP is nocanput. This counts the number of times a received packet was discarded due to slow processing in the TCP/IP stack and lack of buffering on input. `Defr` shows the number of defers that took place. A defer happens when an Ethernet tries to send out a packet, but it finds the medium to be busy, and it has to hold off (defer) the sending until the line is clear.

PART II Products

This section describes the products available for resource management and explains how they work alone and together.

CHAPTER **6**

Solaris Operating Environment

This chapter discusses the Solaris operating environment, focusing on several standard capabilities that are useful for resource management. The Solaris operating environment provides a foundation for all the other products that manage resources.

When to Use Basic Solaris Features

The basic facilities of the Solaris operating environment are sufficient for simple resource management that can be partly implemented manually, where low system cost is more of an issue than automating and controlling the management process.

On a large multiprocessor system, you can use processor partitioning at the per-CPU level. This obviously doesn't work on uniprocessors and is too coarse in granularity with small numbers of CPUs.

Some of the software controls such as limits can be set globally, so if the same limit is appropriate for all the users, the basic limits set by Solaris software might be useful.

With a simple workload that is performance sensitive, the additional overhead of measuring and controlling resources can be an issue. The basic Solaris features are always present and have low overhead when enabled.

Relationship to Other Resource Control Features

Although the Solaris operating environment provides the foundation, some hardware and optional software features extend that capability. In some cases, the Solaris operating environment itself is a limiting factor. Each of the following products is described in detail in its own chapter.

Solaris Resource Manager Software

Solaris Resource Manager (SRM) extends some of the resource management concepts of the Solaris operating environment by managing resources on a per-user basis rather than having a single global default for limits. It also completely replaces the regular Solaris timeshare scheduler with its own hierarchical share based scheduler. SRM software also maintains accrued usage accounting information for each user, which is much more detailed and accurate than the regular Solaris accounting information.

Dynamic System Domains and Dynamic Reconfiguration

The Sun Enterprise 10000 server implements dynamic system domains, where each domain runs its own copy of the Solaris operating environment. Domains can grow and shrink at runtime without requiring a reboot. The Sun Enterprise 3500 to 6500 servers implement a single domain but still allow CPUs, memory, and I/O boards to be dynamically added or removed from a running system. This requires considerable support in the Solaris software, and in particular all device drivers must implement extra functionality that allows them to be dynamically reconfigured. Old and third-party devices still work but require a full reboot if they need to be reconfigured in or out of a system.

Solaris Bandwidth Manager Software

Solaris Bandwidth Manager software uses the Solaris streams networking infrastructure. It pushes extra streams modules onto the protocol stack that instruments and controls packets coming and going on each network interface.

Processor Partitioning

When several workloads compete for CPU time on a large system, you can divide the CPUs into sets and bind each workload to a different set to constrain it. This section describes how this works and where it can be used effectively.

In the past, it was common to use several systems, one to run each workload. Modern computer systems are so powerful and scalable, that it becomes more efficient to consolidate workloads onto fewer, larger, systems. A new feature in the Solaris 2.6 operating environment allows a multiprocessor machine to be partitioned into *processor sets*, where each workload is constrained to use only the processors in one set. The Solaris 7 version adds some interrupt management capabilities.

Processor Sets

Let's start by taking a look at the manual page for the Solaris 7 version of the `psrset` command.

```
Maintenance Commands                                      psrset(1M)

NAME
     psrset - creation and management of processor sets

SYNOPSIS
     psrset -c [ processor_id ... ]
     psrset -d processor_set_id
     psrset -a processor_set_id processor_id ...
     psrset -r processor_id ...
     psrset -p [ processor_id ... ]
     psrset -b processor_set_id pid ...
     psrset -u pid ...
     psrset -e processor_set_id command [argument(s)]
     psrset -f processor_set_id
     psrset -n processor_set_id
     psrset -q [ pid ... ]
     psrset [ -i ] [ processor_set_id ... ]

DESCRIPTION
     The psrset utility controls the management of processor
     sets.  Processor sets allow  the  binding of processes to
     groups of processors, rather than just a  single  processor.
     There  are two types of processor sets, those created by the
     user using the psrset command or the  pset_create(2)  system
     call,  and  those automatically created by the system.  Pro-
     cessors assigned to user-created  processor  sets  will  run
     only  LWPs  that  have been bound to that processor set, but
     system processor sets may run other LWPs as well.

     System-created processor sets will not  always  exist  on  a
     given  machine.  When  they  exist,  they will generally
     represent particular characteristics  of  the  underlying
     machine,  such  as groups of processors that can communicate
     more quickly with each other  than  with  other  processors  in
     the  system.  These  processor  sets  cannot be modified or
     removed, but processes may be bound to them.

OPTIONS
     The following options are supported:

     -a   Assigns the specified processors to the specified  pro-
          cessor set.
```

-b   Binds all the LWPs of the specified processes to the specified processor set.

-c   Creates a new processor set.

-d   Removes the specified processor set, releasing all processors and processes associated with it.

-e   Executes the given command in the specified processor set.

-f   Disables interrupts for all processors within the specified processor set.

-i   Displays the type and processor assignments of the specified processor sets, or of all processor sets.

-n   Enables interrupts for all processors within the specified processor set.

-p   Displays the processor set assignments of the specified processors, or of all processors.

-q   Displays the processor set bindings of the specified processes, or of all processes.

-r   Removes the specified processors from the processor sets to which they are assigned.

-u   Removes the processor set bindings of all LWPs of the specified processes.

USAGE

The -a option assigns a list of processors to a processor set. Processor sets automatically created by the system cannot have processors assigned to them. However, processors belonging to system processor sets may be assigned to user-created processor sets. This option is restricted to use by the super-user.

The -b option binds all of the LWPs of the specified processes to the specified processor set. LWPs bound to a processor set will be restricted to run only on the processors in that set unless they require resources available only on another processor. Processes may only be bound to non-empty processor sets, that is, processor sets that have had processors assigned to them.

Bindings are inherited, so new LWPs and processes created by a bound LWP will have the same binding. Binding an interactive shell to a processor, for example, binds all commands executed by the shell.

The -c option creates a processor set and displays the new processor set ID. If a list of processors is given, it also attempts to assign those processors to the processor set. If this succeeds, the processors will be idle until LWPs are bound to the processor set. This option is restricted to use by the super-user.

The -d option removes a previously created processor set. Processor sets automatically created by the system cannot be removed. This option is restricted to use by the super-user.

The -e option executes a command (with optional arguments) in the specified processor set. The command process and any child processes are executed only by processors in the processor set.

The super-user may execute a command in any active processor set. Other users may only execute commands in system processor sets.

The -f option disables interrupts for all possible processors in the specified processor set. See psradm(1M). If some processors in the set cannot have their interrupts disabled, the other processors will still have their interrupts disabled, and the command will report an error and return non-zero exit status. This option is restricted to use by the super-user.

The -i option displays a list of processors assigned to each named processor set. If no argument is given, a list of all processor sets and the processors assigned to them is displayed. This is also the default operation if the psrset command is not given an option.

The -n option enables interrupts for all processors in the specified processor set. See psradm(1M). This option is restricted to use by the super-user.

The -p option displays the processor set assignments for the specified list of processors. If no argument is given, the processor set assignments for all processors in the system is given.

The -q option displays the processor set bindings of the

specified processes. If a process is composed of multiple
LWPs, which have different bindings, the bindings of only
one of the bound LWPs will be shown. If no argument is
given, the processor set bindings of all processes in the
system is displayed.

The -r option removes a list of processors from their
current processor sets. Processors that are removed will
return to either the system processor set to which they previously belonged, or to the general pool of processors if
they did not belong to a system processor set. This option
is restricted to use by the super-user.

Processors with LWPs bound to them using pbind(1M) cannot be
assigned to or removed from processor sets.

The -u option removes the processor set bindings from all
the LWPs of the specified processes, allowing them to be
executed on any on-line processor if they are not bound to
individual processors through pbind.

The super-user may bind or unbind any process to any active
processor set. Other users may only bind or unbind
processes to system processor sets. Furthermore, they may
only bind or unbind processes for which they have permission
to signal, that is, any process that has the same effective
user ID as the user.

The initial state is that all CPUs belong to a default system processor set. You can create additional sets by taking CPUs away from the system set. The kernel only uses the system set for normal operations, although interrupts are handled by processors regardless of which set they belong to. At least one CPU will always remain in the system processor set. For example, NFS services will run only on the system processor set.

If you have a mix that includes some NFS service that needs to be constrained, this is one way to accomplish that. In general, the system set should be as large as possible, perhaps shared with one of your regular workloads so that you don't starve the kernel of CPU time.

Published Dual TPC-C and TPC-D Results

Sun has published a fully audited benchmark in which an online transaction processing TPC-C workload was run on the same machine at the same time as a data warehouse TPC-D workload. This was managed using processor sets. A 16-CPU Sun Enterprise 6000 was divided into an 8-CPU system processor set and an additional 8-CPU user-created set. A single copy of the IBM DB2 Universal Server database code was used to create two database instances on separate parts of the disk subsystem. When the benchmark was run, the continuous small TPC-C transactions ran at a constant rate, providing good response times to the online users The large and varied TPC-D transactions were constrained and did not affect the online user response times. The overall throughput was less than it might have been if the idle time in each set had been used by the other workload, but consistency of steady state response times and throughput is a requirement for an audited TPC-C result, and it could not be achieved without using processor sets in this way.

The TPC-C summary is at:

http://www.tpc.org/results/individual_results/Sun/sun.ue6000.ibm.es.pdf

The TPC-D summary is at:

http://www.tpc.org/results/individual_results/Sun/sun.ue6000.ibm.d.es.pdf

How Process Partitioning Works

The Solaris operating environment maintains a queue of jobs that are ready to run on a per-CPU basis. There is no single global run queue. Older versions of the Solaris operating environment implement processor binding using the `pbind` command and underlying system calls. A process is bound to a CPU with `pbind`, but it isn't exclusive. Other work can also run on that CPU. With `psrset`, the binding is to a group of CPUs, but it is also an exclusive binding, and nothing else will be scheduled to run on that set. You can use `pbind` within any set, to give a further level of control over resource usage.

The way `psrset` works is to create a kind of virtual machine for scheduling purposes. Once a process is bound to that set, all child processes are also bound to that set, so it is sufficient to bind a shell or startup script for an application. You must have root permissions to make bindings.

The system normally keeps a linked list of the online processors. Each processor has its own run queue. When a kernel thread is to be placed on a run queue, it goes through some various machinations and decides where the thread should be placed. Normally, this is the same processor on which it last ran, but sometimes it changes processors (migrates) for various reasons (load balancing, for example).

With processor sets, you can split up the list of processors into disjoint subsets. When you create a processor set, you create a new list with the processors that are in the set. The processors are taken out of the normal list of processors that run everything not in the set. Processes assigned to the set run on the processors in the set's list and can migrate between them. Other processes and normal (non-interrupt) kernel threads cannot run on those processors; they no longer have access to them. It's as if the processors have been taken off-line. The exception is kernel threads that can be bound to a specific processor for one reason or another, but this is unusual.

Interrupts are taken on whichever CPU normally takes that interrupt, but any subsequent activity will take place in the system processor set. Use the `mpstat` command to view the distribution of interrupts and load over all the CPUs.

```
% mpstat 5
CPU minf mjf xcal  intr ithr  csw icsw migr smtx srw syscl usr sys wt idl
  0   58   8 1459   822  610 1306  171  242   96  30   609   6  67 27   0
  1   36   8 1750  1094  657 1100  151  238  104  28   717   6  76 18   0
  4   53   7 1518   951  759 1111  155  226   95  29   642   6  69 24   0
  5   25   7 1715  1067  765 1104  178  232  111  23   552   7  65 28   0
```

Limits

The `sysdef -i` command shows the default limits, listing the values in hexadecimal, as shown in FIGURE 6-1. The shell commands `limit` or `ulimit` also show the default limits, as shown in FIGURE 6-2.

```
% sysdef -i
...
        Soft:Hard           Resource
Infinity:Infinity           cpu time
Infinity:Infinity           file size
1fefe000:1fefe000           heap size
  800000: ff00000           stack size
Infinity:Infinity           core file size
      40:     400           file descriptors
Infinity:Infinity           mapped memory
```

FIGURE 6-1 Example Systemwide Resource Limits Shown by `sysdef`

```
% limit
cputime         unlimited
filesize        unlimited
datasize        2097148 kbytes
stacksize       8192 kbytes
coredumpsize    0 kbytes
descriptors     64
memorysize      unlimited
% limit -h
```

FIGURE 6-2 Per Shell Current and Hard Limits

```
cputime      unlimited
filesize     unlimited
datasize     unlimited
stacksize    2097148 kbytes
coredumpsize unlimited
descriptors  1024
memorysize   unlimited
```

FIGURE 6-2 Per Shell Current and Hard Limits *(Continued)*

Let us examine the capabilities of each limit in turn. They exist in this form for historical reasons and have several limitations.

CPU Time

The maximum CPU time specified in total CPU seconds can be specified. Any process reaching this limit is sent a SIGXCPU signal, and will terminate with a core dump unless it catches the signal.

File Size

The maximum size in bytes of any single file can be specified. Any process reaching this limit is sent a SIGXFSZ signal, and will terminate with a core dump unless it catches the signal.

Data Size and Stack Size

The maximum size in bytes of the data segment of a process can be specified. If this limit is reached, a call to `malloc` will fail and the process may terminate. A stack space overrun causes a segmentation violation and a core dump. The hard limits for data size and stack size vary according to the hardware architecture of the system.

Core Dump Size

This sets the maximum size of a core dump. It can be set to zero if core dumps are unwanted and there is a danger that they may accumulate and fill up the disk. It also takes some time to write the core dump to disk, so it is quicker to recover from a failed application such as a web browser that dies and needs to be restarted.

File Descriptors

To increase the default number of file descriptors per process, you can set the kernel tunables `rlim_fd_cur` and `rlim_fd_max` in `/etc/system`.

The definition of `FILE` for the `stdio` library can handle only 256 open files at most, but raw read/write will work above that limit. The `select` system call uses a fixed-size bitfield that can only cope with 1024 file descriptors; the alternative is to use `poll`, which has no limit.

It is dangerous to set `rlim_fd_cur` to more than 256. Programs that need more file descriptors should either call `setrlimit` directly or have their own limit set in a wrapper script. If you need to use many file descriptors to open a large number of sockets or other raw files, it is best to force all of them to file descriptors numbered above 256. This lets system functions such as name services, which depend upon `stdio` file operations, continue to operate using the low-numbered file descriptors.

Programs compiled in the 64-bit execution using the Solaris 7 operating environment do not have the above limitations. The definition of FILE is opaque and has no practical limit on open files. The definition of the select bitfield is increased to 65536 bits.

Memory Size

This limit operates on the total size of the process address space. It can be used to prevent leaky processes from growing to consume all of the swap space, but it has no effect on real resident set memory usage. This is due to a fundamental limitation of the Solaris operating environment. We understand that it would be very useful to be able to control real physical memory usage per process, but it requires a substantial rewrite of the way Solaris software handles virtual memory.

Disk Quotas

The Solaris disk quota system is based directly on the Berkeley UNIX quota system developed many years ago. It provides limits on the total size of the files owned by a user on a UFS file system, and the total number of files. There is a soft limit that causes warnings to be printed out, and a hard limit that cannot be exceeded. After a grace period the soft limit is also enforced, and the user must free enough space to go below the soft limit again to reset this timer.

When a UFS file system is exported over NFS, the quotas of the underlying file system are inherited by the NFS mount, and quotas work in basically the same way as they would on a local UFS disk. This is not true for other file systems such as Veritas VxFS, which provides its own local quota system, which is not integrated into the NFS export mechanism in the current release.

Quotas are setup using the `edquota(1M)` command. A user can view quotas using the `quota(1M)` command. By default quotas are displayed when the user logs into the system.

In practice, quotas are not used very often. The mere threat of imposing quotas on a disk that is being overused is an effective way to motivate users to clear up their directory spaces.

When large numbers of uncontrolled users share a large system, it is a good idea to set up disk quotas from the beginning. Two environments where this is important are the home directories of university student populations and internet service providers that provide space for home pages, and charge more for extra space.

SRM is based on the ShareII product from Softway. ShareII contains its own disk quota functionality, but this was not carried over into SRM. The thinking was that a more general quota mechanism is needed, one that works across all file system types. Rather than introduce a new mechanism in SRM and change it again in a future release, it was decided to just make a single change.

Configurable Kernel Limits

There are a few kernel variables that limit the resources a user can request. If they are set too high, the system can be susceptible to denial of service attacks.

System V Shared Memory

The normal semantics for System V Shared Memory allow any user to request a memory segment to be shared. Ultimately if too many large processes try to run they will be paged out. The shared memory requests are limited by the amount of swap space that can be reserved to backup the memory.

A special option for System V Shared Memory called Intimate Shared Memory (ISM) is implemented in the Solaris operating environment to increase performance for database applications. When ISM is requested by setting a special SHM_SHARE_MMU flag in the call to `shmat(2)` memory is allocated that is locked in RAM and shares its memory management mappings with every process. ISM has evolved over the years.

- Solaris 2.5.1 ISM reserves an equal amount of swap space but never uses it.
- Solaris 2.6 ISM does not reserve any swap space and uses 4-Mbyte pages to map large ISM segments, which greatly reduces memory management overheads.

The resource management implications are that end users could consume all the memory in a system with calls to allocate ISM, and this memory is not pagable. In the Solaris 2.5.1 ISM this memory also consumes swap space.

The kernel variable that limits all System V memory allocation can be set in `/etc/system`. Its default value is one megabyte, which prevents any problems:

```
set shmsys:shminfo_shmmax=1048576
```

FIGURE 6-3 Setting for System V shared Memory Size Limit

When running databases, this value is normally increased to allow several gigabytes of ISM to be allocated.

Maximum User Process Count Limit

There is a systemwide limit on the total number of processes that each user is allowed to have. By default this limit is set to five less than to total process count limit, which effectively means that there is no limit. It can be useful to set this limit to a low value on student timesharing systems.

```
set maxuprc=20
```

FIGURE 6-4 Setting for Maximum User Process Count Limit

The current count and total process limit is shown by `sar -v` in the `proc-sz` column. Use `sysdef -i` to view the value of `maxuprc`. For example, on the small desktop system shown in FIGURE 6-5 there are 83 processes in existence out of a maximum of 1002, and the maximum number for a single user is set at 997. The process count limits scale up as the amount of memory in the system is increased to one gigabyte, and there is also a hard limit of 32000 processes set by the Solaris 7 software at present. In the future this limit will be raised.

```
% sar -v 1

SunOS hostname 5.6 Generic sun4m    02/02/99

10:13:36  proc-sz     ov  inod-sz      ov  file-sz    ov  lock-sz
10:13:37  83/1002      0  4831/4831     0  462/462     0  0/0

% sysdef -i | grep processes
    1002maximum number of processes (v.v_proc)
     997maximum processes per user id (v.v_maxup)
```

FIGURE 6-5 Monitoring Process Count Settings

CHAPTER **7**

Solaris Resource Manager Software

This chapter discusses the Solaris Resource Manager (SRM) software, which controls major system resources. SRM software also implements administrative policies that govern which resources users can access, and more specifically, what level of those resources each user is permitted to consume.

The SRM product is based on ShareII technology from Softway Pty. Limited, Australia.

When to Use SRM Software

The SRM software is the Sun resource management extension for the Solaris operating environment and should be used when more advanced resource management and control is required.

For example, two workloads can be consolidated onto a single system using processor sets to manage the CPU resource by allocating 10 processors to workload A and 8 processors to workload B. Although this would provide processor limits for each workload, resources could be potentially wasted if one of the workloads is not using all of its share of the processors because the spare CPU cannot be used by any other workload.

The SRM software provides the following advantages over base Solaris resource control:

- Better utilization of system resources
- Dynamic control of system resources
- More flexible resource allocation policies
- Fine-grained control over resources
- Decayed usage of resources
- Accounting data for resource usage

Relationship to Other Solaris Resource Control Features

Base Solaris Operating Environment

The Solaris operating environment includes several features that provide control over certain types of resources. Some features, such as `nice(1)` and processor sets, are part of the basic Solaris software and allow a limited form of resource management.

The `nice(1)` command permits users to manipulate program execution priority. Unless superuser privilege is invoked, this command only permits the user to lower the priority. This can be a useful feature (for example, when a user starts a low-priority batch job from an interactive login session), but it relies on the cooperation of the user. The SRM software enforces administrative policies, even without the cooperation of the user.

Processor sets were introduced in the Solaris 2.6 release. This feature allows you to divide multiprocessor systems into logical groups and permits users to launch processes into those groups. The advantage is that workloads running in one processor set are protected from CPU activity taking place in any other processor set. In some ways, this is similar to what the SRM software does, but the two features operate on a completely different basis. Processor sets control only CPU activity. The control is at a relatively coarse-grained hardware level, because processors can belong to exactly one processor set at a time. Especially in the case of relatively small systems, the granularity may be quite high: on a 4-processor system, the minimum resource that can be assigned is 25 percent of the system.

The SRM software has much finer-grained control. Each user is allocated a share of the system. The shares can be distributed arbitrarily on a fine granularity, and the scheduler will allocate resources accordingly. For example, if 50 shares are granted, and one user has 40 of them, that user will get 40 / 50 = 80 percent of the resource. Similarly, if 67 total shares are granted, a user with 57 shares will get 85 percent of the resource. In addition, the SRM software can control resources other than CPU.

Dynamic System Domains

The Sun Enterprise 10000 server has a feature called dynamic system domains, which allows you to logically divide a single system rack into one or more independent systems, each running its own copy of the Solaris operating environment. For example, a system with 32 CPUs on 8 system boards might be operated as 1 system with 16 CPUs, and 2 other systems with 8 CPUs each. In this configuration, three copies of the Solaris software would be running. The dynamic system domains feature also permits controlled movement of resources into and out of each of the Solaris images, thus creating a relatively coarse-grained facility for managing physical resources. (The minimum unit of inter-domain allocation is an entire system board.) The SRM software is similar to dynamic system domains in that it provides the mechanisms to allocate resources, but it does so in very different ways. The SRM software runs within a single instance of the Solaris operating environment, and provides fine-grained administrative control to the resources in the system. Dynamic system domains divide a single piece of hardware into multiple instances of the Solaris operating environment. Dynamic system domains provides tools to manage the transfer of resources between instances of the Solaris operating environment running on the same Sun Enterprise 10000 frame. The SRM software can be run in each instance of the Solaris operating environment within a Sun Enterprise 10000 system and used in conjunction with dynamic system domains.

Dynamic Reconfiguration

The dynamic reconfiguration feature of Sun Enterprise servers enables users to dynamically add and delete system boards, which contain hardware resources such as processors, memory, and I/O devices. The effect of a dynamic reconfiguration operation on memory has no impact on SRM memory-limit checking.

Solaris Bandwidth Manager Software

The Solaris Bandwidth Manager software is a product that works with the Solaris kernel to enforce limits on the consumption of network bandwidth. The Solaris Bandwidth Manager software is a form of resource management software that applies to a different class of resources. The SRM software and the Solaris Bandwidth Manager software have different and separate management domains: the SRM software operates on a per-user or per-application basis, while the Solaris Bandwidth Manager software manages on network identities, including combinations of per-port, per-service, and per-protocol bases.

Solaris Resource Manager Functions

This section describes the SRM software capabilities as outlined in TABLE 7-1.

TABLE 7-1 Solaris Resource Manager Functions

	Policy	Control	Measurement	Accounting
CPU Usage	Per userid	X	Per userid	X
Virtual Memory	per-user per-process	per-user per-process	per-user per-process	X
Number of processes	X	X	X	X
Maximum Logins	X	X	X	X
Connect Time	X	X	X	X

Solaris Resource Manager Policies

The SRM software is built around a fundamental addition to the Solaris kernel called an lnode (limit node). Lnodes correspond to UNIX userids, and may represent individual users, groups of users, applications, and special requirements. The lnodes are indexed by userid and are used to record resource allocations policies and accrued resource usage data by processes at the user, group of users, and/or application level.

Hierarchical Structure

The SRM management model organizes lnodes into a hierarchical structure called the scheduling tree. The scheduling tree is organized by userid: each lnode references the userid of the lnode's parent in the tree. Each sub-tree of the scheduling tree is called a scheduling group, and the user at the root of a scheduling group is the group's header. The root user is the group header of the entire scheduling tree.

A group header can be delegated the ability to manage resource policies within the group. The lnodes are initially created by parsing the /etc/passwd file. An lnode administration command (limadm(1MSRM)) will create additional lnodes after the SRM software is installed and assign lnodes to parents.

The scheduling tree data is stored in a flat file database that can be modified as required.

Though userids used by lnodes do not have to correspond to a system account, with an entry in the system password map, it is strongly recommended that a system account is created for the userid of every lnode. A non-leaf lnode (those with subordinate lnodes) account can be purely administrative because no one ever logs in to it. However, it is equally possible that it can be the lnode of a real user who does log in and run processes attached to this non-leaf lnode.

Note that SRM scheduling groups and group headers have nothing to do with the system groups defined in the /etc/group database. Each node of the scheduling tree, including group headers, corresponds to a real system user with a unique userid.

Hierarchical Limits

If a hierarchical limit is assigned to a group header in an lnode tree (scheduling group), then it applies to the usage of that user plus the total usage of all members of the scheduling group. This allows limits to be placed on entire groups, as well as on individual members. Resources are allocated to the group header, who may allocate them to users or groups of users that belong to the same group.

Delegated Administration of Policies

The system administrator can set administrative privileges for any lnode, including assigning administrative privileges selectively to users. A user with hierarchical administrative privilege is called a sub-administrator. A sub-administrator may create, remove, and modify the lnodes of users within the sub-tree of which they are the group header.

Sub-administrators cannot normally alter their own limits or flags, and cannot circumvent their own flags or limits by altering flags or usages within their group.

The central administrator (or super-user) can alter the limits, usages, and flags of any user, including itself. Ordinary users can be granted this privilege by setting a flag.

Policies by Executable Name

Resource policies that are not restricted to userids can be created by attaching workloads to lnodes. For example, a policy based on application executable name can be created by creating lnodes for each application executable and then attaching the executable to the correct lnode.

A wrapper script can be required to implement this policy using the `srmuser` command.

Controls Available with SRM Software

The SRM software provides control of the following system resources: CPU (rate of processor) usage, virtual memory, number of processes, number of logins, and terminal connect-time.

The SRM software keeps track of each user's usage of each resource. For all resources except CPU usage, users may be assigned hard limits on their resource usages. A hard limit causes resource consumption attempts to fail if the user allows the usage to reach the limit. Hard limits are directly enforced by either the kernel or whatever software is responsible for managing the respective resource. A limit value of zero indicates no limit. All limit attributes of the root lnode should be left set to zero.

The SRM software progressively decays past usage so that only the most recent usage is significant. The system administrator sets a half-life parameter that controls the rate of decay. A long half-life favors even usage, typical of longer batch jobs, while a short half-life favors interactive users.

The CPU resource is controlled using the SHR scheduler. Users are allocated CPU time dynamically in proportion to the number of shares they possess (analogous to shares in a company), and in inverse proportion to their recent usage. The important feature of the SHR scheduler is that while it manages the scheduling of individual threads (technically, in the Solaris software, the scheduled entity is a lightweight process (LWP)), it also portions CPU resources between users.

Each user also has a set of flags that are boolean-like variables used to enable or disable selective system privileges, for example, login. Flags can be set individually per user or inherited from a parent lnode.

The usages, limits, and flags of a user can be read by any user, but can be altered only by users who have administrative powers.

Decay of Renewable Resources

The SRM software employs a usage, limit, and decay model to control a user's rate of consumption of a renewable resource. Usage is defined as the total resource used, with a limit set on the ratio of usages in comparison to other users. Decay refers to the period by which historical usage is discounted. The next resource quantum, for example, clock tick, will be allocated to the active lnode with the lowest decayed total usage value in relation to its allocated share. The decayed usage value is a measure of the total usage over time less some portion of historical usage determined by a half-life decay model.

CPU Resource Management

The primary advantage of the SRM scheduler over the standard Solaris scheduler is that it schedules users or applications rather than individual processes. Every process associated with an lnode is subject to a set of limits. For the simple case of one user running a single active process, this is the same as subjecting each process to the limits listed in the corresponding lnode. When more than one process is attached to an lnode, as when members of a group each run multiple processes, all of the processes are collectively subject to the listed limits. This means that users or applications cannot consume CPU at a greater rate than their entitlements allow, regardless of how many concurrent processes they run. The method for assigning entitlements as a number of shares is simple and understandable, and the effect of changing a user's shares is predictable.

The allocation of the renewable CPU service is controlled using a fair share scheduler. Each lnode is assigned a number of CPU shares, analogous to shares in a company. The processes associated with each lnode are allocated CPU resources in proportion to the total number of outstanding active shares, where active means that the lnode has running processes attached. Only active lnodes are considered for an allocation of the resource, as only they have active processes running and need CPU time. As a process consumes CPU ticks, the CPU usage attribute of its lnode increases.

The scheduler regularly adjusts the priorities of all processes to force the relative ratios of CPU usages to converge on the relative ratios of CPU shares for all active lnodes at their respective levels. In this way, users can expect to receive at least their entitlements of CPU service in the long run, regardless of the behavior of other users. The scheduler is hierarchical, because it also ensures that groups receive their group entitlement independently of the behavior of the members.

The SRM software has a long-term scheduler; it ensures that all users and applications receive a fair share over the course of the scheduler term. This means that when a light user starts to request the CPU, that user will receive commensurately more resource than heavy users until their comparative usages are in line with their relative fair share allocation. The more you use over your entitlement now, the less you will receive in the future. Additionally, you can set the decay period so that the scheduler forgets about past usage.

The decay model is one of half-life decay, where 50 percent of the resource has been decayed away within one-half life. This ensures that steady, even users are not penalized by short-term, process-intensive users. The half-life decay period sets the responsiveness or term of the scheduler; the default value is 120 seconds. Shorter values tend to provide more even response across the system, at the expense of slightly less accuracy in computing and maintaining system-wide resource allocation. Regardless of administrative settings, the scheduler tries to prevent marooning (resource starvation) and ensure reasonable behavior, even in extreme situations.

The SRM scheduler will never waste CPU availability. No matter how low a user's allocation, that user will always be given all the available CPU if there are no competing users. One of the consequences of this is that users may notice performance that is less smooth than they are used to. If a user with a very low effective share is running an interactive process without any competition, it will appear to run quickly. However, as soon as another user with a greater effective share demands some CPU time, it will be given to that user in preference to the first user, so the first user will notice a marked job slow-down. Nevertheless, SRM scheduler goes to some lengths to ensure that legitimate users are not marooned and unable to do any work. All processes being scheduled by the SRM software (except those with a maximum `nice` value) will be allocated CPU regularly by the scheduler. There is also logic to prevent a new user who has just logged on from being given an arithmetically fair, but excessively large, proportion of the CPU to the detriment of existing users.

Virtual Memory (Per-User and Per-Process Limits)

Virtual memory is managed using a fixed resource model. The virtual memory limit applies to the sum of the memory sizes of all processes attached to the lnode. In addition, there is a per-process virtual memory limit that restricts the total size of the process's virtual address space size, including all code, data, stack, file mappings, and shared libraries. Both limits are hierarchical. Limiting virtual memory is useful for avoiding virtual memory starvation. For example, the SRM software will stop an application that is leaking memory from consuming unwarranted amounts of virtual memory to the detriment of all users. Instead, such a process only starves itself or, at worse, others in its resource group.

Number of Processes

The number of processes that users may run simultaneously is controlled using a fixed resource model with hierarchical limits.

Terminals and Login Connect-Time

The system administrator and group header can set terminal login privileges, number of logins, and connect-time limits, which are enforced hierarchically by the SRM software. As a user approaches a connect-time limit, warning messages are sent to the user's terminal. When the limit is reached, the user is notified, then forcibly logged out after a short grace period.

Processes

Every process is attached to an lnode. The `init` process is always attached to the root lnode. When processes are created by the fork(2) system call, they are attached to the same lnode as their parent. Processes can be re-attached to any lnode using a SRM system call, given sufficient privilege. Privileges are set by root or by users with the correct administrative permissions enabled.

Measurement

Resource usage information is exposed to the administrators of the system, and provides two views of resource usage information: a per-user view and a workload view of resource usage.

Per-User Resource Usage

Use the `liminfo` command to obtain a report of a individual user's current usages, limits, privileges, and so on. You can also use the `liminfo` command to inquire on the attributes of other users.

You can request a number of different report formats, including options that make the output of `liminfo` suitable for processing by a pipeline of filters. Refer to the manual page for `liminfo(1SRM)` for details of the options and their meanings, and for a description of the fields that can be displayed.

Workload View of Resource Usage

The workload view of resource usage is based on the lnode resource hierarchy tree. The SRM software does this by recording accrual of resource usage in the lnode tree.

The lnode's `cpu.accrue` attribute contains the accrued CPU usage for all lnodes within the group as well as that of the current lnode. When any of an lnode's accrue attributes are updated, the change is also applied to the lnode's parent (as with changes to the usage attribute) and so on up to the root lnode so that the accrued usage at each level in the scheduling tree is the sum of the accrued usage for the lnode and its children, if any.

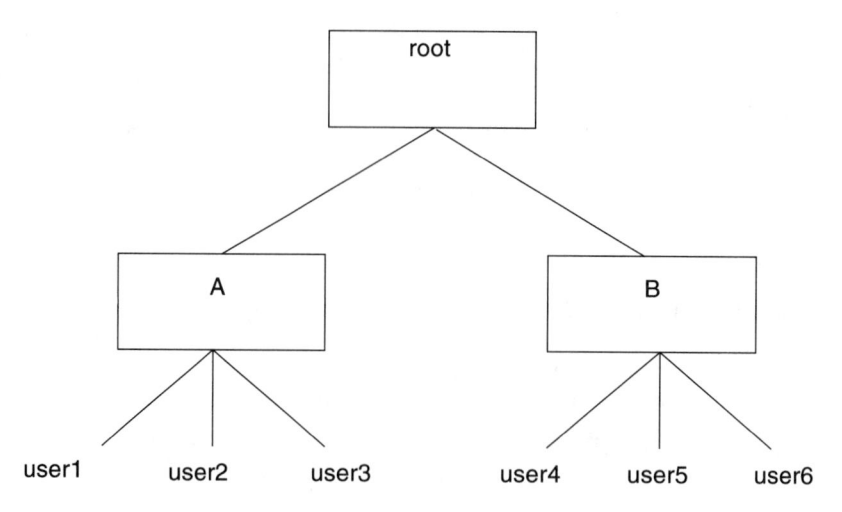

FIGURE 7-1 Accounting Based on the Workload Hierarchy

For example, a system with two workloads A and B can have an lnode hierarchy with lnodes A and B reporting to the root node, and then individual users reporting into node A and B. The CPU usage of each user can be observed via the usage fields in the lnode of each user, but the sum total of CPU used for workload A is available by looking at the accrued CPU usage in the lnode for workload A.

System Resource Accounting Information

The SRM system maintains information (primarily current and accrued resource usage) that you can use to conduct comprehensive system resource accounting. No accounting programs are supplied as part of the SRM software, but its utility programs provide a base for the development of a customized resource accounting system.

Workload Configuration

The key to effective resource management using the SRM software is a well designed resource hierarchy.

Mapping the Workload to the lnode Hierarchy

The SRM software uses the lnode tree to implement the resource hierarchy. Each node in the lnode tree maps to userid in the password database. This means workloads must be mapped to align with entries in the password database. In some cases, you might have to create additional users to cater to the leaf nodes in the hierarchy. These special users will not actually run processes or jobs, but will act as an administration point for the leaf node.

A Simple Flat Hierarchy

A simple hierarchy would, for example, control the processing resources of two users, Chuck and Mark. Both of these users are notorious for using large amounts of CPU at different times, and hence have an impact on each other at different times of the day. To resolve this, construct a single level hierarchy and allocate equal shares of CPU to each user.

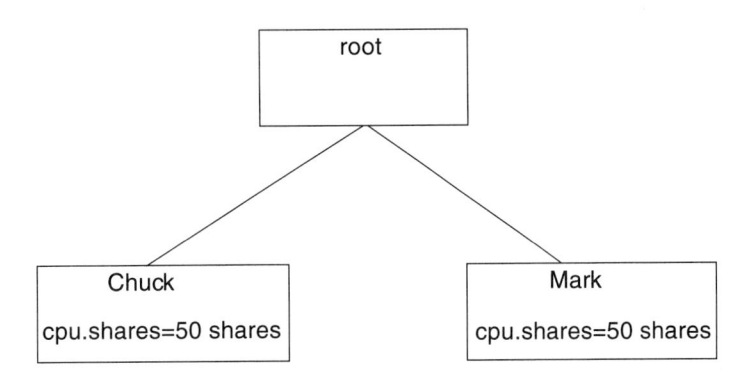

```
                    ┌─────────┐
                    │  root   │
                    └────┬────┘
                   ┌─────┴─────┐
         ┌─────────┴──┐   ┌────┴────────┐
         │   Chuck    │   │    Mark     │
         │cpu.shares= │   │cpu.shares=  │
         │ 50 shares  │   │ 50 shares   │
         └────────────┘   └─────────────┘
```

FIGURE 7-2   A Simple Flat Solaris Resource Manager Hierarchy

This simple hierarchy is established using the limadm command to make Chuck and Mark children of root:

```
# limadm set sgroup=root chuck
# limadm set sgroup=root mark
```

Now that both Chuck and Mark are children of the root share group, you can allocate resource shares against them. For example, to allocate 50 percent of the resources to each, give the same number of CPU shares to each. (There is no reason you could not allocate one share to each user to achieve the same). Use the limadm command to allocate the shares:

```
# limadm set cpu.shares=50 chuck
# limadm set cpu.shares=50 mark
```

You can observe the changes to the lnode associated with Chuck with the liminfo command:

```
# liminfo -c chuck
Login name:              chuck            Uid (Real,Eff):      2001 (-,-)
Sgroup (uid):            root (0)         Gid (Real,Eff):       200 (-,-)

Shares:                       50          Myshares:                1
Share:                      41 %          E-share:                 0 %
Usage:                         0          Accrued usage:           0

Mem usage:                   0 B          Term usage:             0s
Mem limit:                   0 B          Term accrue:            0s
Proc mem limit:              0 B          Term limit:             0s
Mem accrue:                0 B.s

Processes:                     0          Current logins:          0
Process limit:                 0

Last used: Tue Oct 4 15:04:20 1998
Directory: /users/chuck
Name:      Hungry user
Shell:     /bin/csh

Flags:
```

The fields from the `liminfo` command are explained below. Refer to manual page on `liminfo` for more information. The first two lines of output from the `liminfo` command relate to aspects of the lnode userid and its position in the lnode tree.

Login name	The login name and initial GID from the password map that corresponds to the userid of the attached lnode. Every lnode is associated with a system userid. Create a system account for the userid of every lnode. In this instance a placeholder userid is used for the Database1 of db1.
	Note that the default PAM configuration under the SRM software creates an lnode for any user who logs in without one. By default, lnodes created by root or by a user with the `uselimadm` flag set are created with the lnode for the user other as their parent, or if that does not exist, with the root lnode as their parent. Lnodes created by a user with the administration flag set are created with that user as their parent. The parent of an lnode can be changed with the general command for changing lnode attributes, `limadm`.
Uid	The userid of the lnode attached to the current process. Normally, this will be the same as that of the real userid of the process (the logged in user), but in some circumstances (described later) it may differ.
R,Euid and R,Egid	The real and effective userid and GID of the current process. This is the same information that is provided by the standard system `id(1M)` command. It is not strictly related to the SRM software, but it is displayed for convenience. These fields are not displayed if `liminfo(1SRM)` is displaying information on a user other than the default (that is, it was provided with a login name or userid as an argument).
Sgroup (uid) [sgroup]	The name and userid of the parent lnode in the lnode tree hierarchy. This will be blank for the root lnode. Many SRM features depend on the position of an lnode within the tree hierarchy, so it is useful for a user to trace successive parent lnodes back to the root of the tree.

Chapter 7   Solaris Resource Manager Software   **147**

After the blank line, the next two lines of the liminfo(1SRM) display show fields relating to CPU scheduling.

Shares [cpu.shares]
: The number of shares of CPU entitlement allocated to this user. It is only directly comparable to other users with the same parent lnode, and to the Myshares value of the parent lnode itself. You might normally set the shares of all users within a particular scheduling group to the same value (giving those users equal entitlements). This value will normally be something greater than 1, so that you have some leeway to decrease the shares of specific users when appropriate.

Myshares [cpu.myshares]
: This value is used only if this user has child lnodes (that is, if there are other lnodes that have an sgroup value of this user) that are active (that is, have processes attached). Where this is the case, this value gives the relative share of CPU for processes attached to this lnode, compared with those attached to its child lnodes.

Share
: The calculated percentage of the system CPU resources to which the current user is entitled. As other users log on and log off (or lnodes become active or inactive), this value will change, because only active users are included in the calculation. Recent usage by the current user is not included in this calculation.

E-Share
: This is the effective share of this user (that is, the actual percentage of the system CPU resources which this user would be given in the short term if the user required it and all other active users were also demanding their share). It can be thought of as the current willingness of the SRM software to allocate CPU resources to that lnode. This value will change over time as the user uses (or refrains from using) CPU resources. Lnodes that are active but idle (that is, with attached processes sleeping), and so have a low usage, will have a high effective share value. Correspondingly, the effective share can be very small for users with attached processes that are actively using the CPU.

Usage [cpu.usage]   The accumulated usage of system resources that are used to determine scheduling priority. Typically, this indicates recent CPU usage, though other parameters may also be taken into account. The parameter mix used can be viewed with the `srmadm(1MSRM)` command. Each increment to this value decays exponentially over time so that eventually the SRM software will forget about the resource usage. The rate of this decay is most easily represented by its half-life, which you can see with the `srmadm` command.

Accrued usage [cpu.accrue]   This is the same resource accumulation measurement as Usage, but it is never decayed. It is not used directly by the SRM software but may be used by administration for accounting purposes. Unlike usage, this value represents the sum of the accrued usages for all lnodes within the group, as well as that of the current lnode.

After the second blank line, the next four lines of the `liminfo` display show four fields relating to virtual memory:

Mem usage [memory.usage][memory.myusage]

The combined memory usage of all processes attached to this lnode.

If two values are displayed, separated by a frontslash (/) character, then this lnode is a group header and the first value is the usage for the whole scheduling group, while the second value is that of just the current user.

Mem limit [memory.limit]   The maximum memory usage allowed for all processes attached to this lnode and its members (if any). That is, the sum of the memory usage for all processes within the group plus those attached to the group header will not be allowed to exceed this value. Note that in this instance, a 0 value indicates that there is no limit.

Proc mem limit [memory.plimit]   The per-process memory limit is the maximum memory usage allowed for any single process attached to this lnode and its members.

Mem accrue [memory.accrue]   The memory accrue value is measured in byte-seconds and is an indication of overall memory resources used over a period of time.

After the third blank line, the next four lines of the `liminfo` display show fields relating to the user and processes.

Processes [process.usage][process.myusage]

> The number of processes attached to this lnode. Note that this is processes, not counting threads within a process.
>
> If two values are displayed, separated by a frontslash (/) character, then this lnode is a group header and the first value is the usage for the whole scheduling group, while the second value is that of just the current user.

Process limit [process.limit]

> The maximum total number of processes allowed to attach to this lnode and its members.

Current logins [logins]

> Current number of simultaneous SRM login sessions for this user. When a user logs in through any of the standard system login mechanisms (including `login(1)`, `rlogin(1)`, and so on.) basically anything that uses PAM for authentication and creates a `utmp(4)` entry) then this counter is incremented. When the session ends, the count is decremented.

If a user's `flag.onelogin` flag evaluates to set, the user is only permitted to have a single SRM login session.

Last used [lastused]

> This field shows the last time the lnode was active. This will normally be the last time the user logged out.

Directory

> The user's home directory (items from the password map rather than from SRM software are shown for convenience).

Name

> This is the `finger` information, which is usually the user's name (items from the password map rather than from the SRM software are shown for convenience).

Shell

> The user's initial login shell (items from the password map rather than from the SRM software are shown for convenience).

Flags

> Flags that evaluate to set or group in the lnode is displayed here. Each flag displayed is followed by suffix characters indicating the value and the

150 Resource Management

way in which the flag was set (for example, whether it was explicitly from this lnode (+) or inherited (^)).

A Simple Form of Batch Management

You can create a simple hierarchy to control the environment in which batch jobs are run. To do this, add an extra layer in the hierarchy to divide the computational requirements of online and batch using the `limadm` command:

```
# limadm set sgroup=root online
# limadm set sgroup=root batch
# limadm set cpu.shares=20 online
# limadm set cpu.shares=1 batch
# limadm set sgroup=online chuck
# limadm set sgroup=online mark
```

In the example above, the `limadm` command was used to create a new leaf in the hierarchy for online and batch, and put Chuck and Mark into the online group.

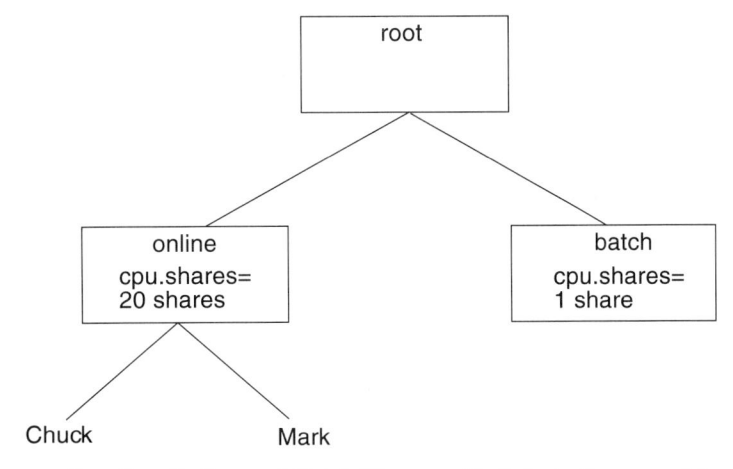

FIGURE 7-3 Creating Online and Batch Shares with Solaris Resource Manager Software

By using the described hierarchy, you can ensure that the online users get their share of the processor resource. Without any further changes, both Chuck and Mark will have access to 20 times the processing resource than does batch because their userid's map to lnodes that are under the online lnode. You must, however, ensure that the batch processes run against the batch lnode. To do this simply start the batch jobs under the batch userid.

```
# srmuser batch /export/database/bin/batchjob
```

For further information on batch management and batch management tools, see Chapter 4.

Consolidation

Since SRM software is a key component of batch management, we will discuss how SRM can be used to implement portions of workload consolidation.

The SRM software allows system resources to be allocated at a system-wide level, sometimes in proportion with business arrangements of machine allocation between departments. An additional layer in the SRM hierarchy is used to achieve this.

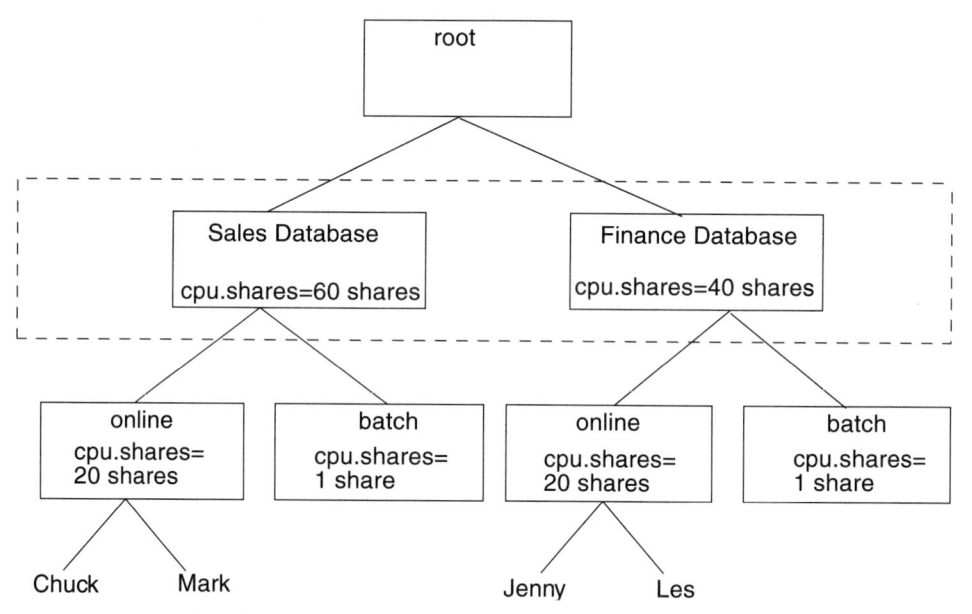

FIGURE 7-4 Consolidation of Two Databases with Solaris Resource Manager Software

152   Resource Management

A Multi User Workload Example

A simple example is to split a single machine into two separate share groups, for example, BATCH and ONLINE. Using the simple batch/online example, we can allocate different shares to each of these two different workloads. In this example, 5 shares were given to batch, and 95 shares were given to online. The actual total number of shares is arbitrary, but in this example they total 100 to look like percentages. Given that batch and online have different shares on the machine, the scheduler can now allocate work depending on two things: the share apportioned to that workload and the amount of free CPU available.

Note that the workload depends on both items, rather than just its share. On a machine that is 100 percent busy, our example will allocate 5 percent of the resource to the batch workload. However, on a machine that is not 100 percent busy more CPU can be allocated to batch without affecting any other workload. This gives the effect of soft-partitioning, where a workload can be constrained to a maximum (for example 5 percent), but can use more if more is available. FIGURE 7-5 shows our example using OLTP application in timeshare (TS) mode.

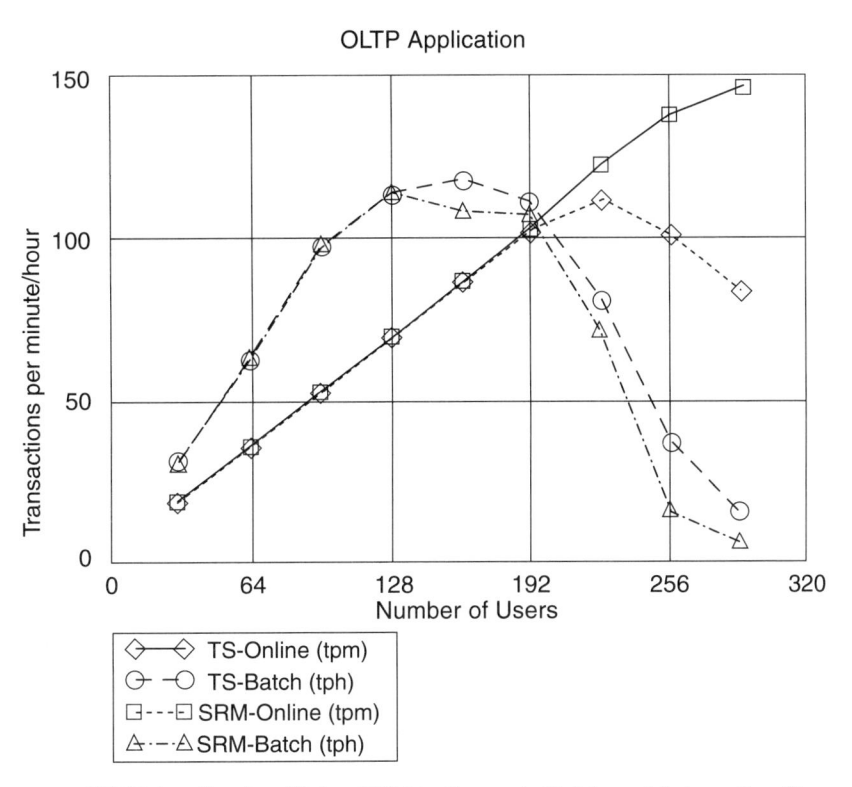

FIGURE 7-5 OLTP Application Using SRM to Separate Batch and Interactive Users

Chapter 7   Solaris Resource Manager Software   153

The OLTP application has a batch and interactive portion, each of which typically has some sort of impact on their respective throughputs. FIGURE 7-5 shows the batch and interactive curves for both timeshare and using the SRM software. Looking at the batch timeshare workload, note that while the CPU is not 100 percent busy, batch is free to consume CPU as it requires. When the CPU becomes 100 percent utilized (at about 192 users), we see the effect of the soft partitioning. As demand for CPU increases, the online users see totally different effects with and without share. Online throughput and performance drops off dramatically on the machine without the SRM software, but with the SRM software, batch is limited to 5 percent, and will not affect the throughput of the interactive workload.

Databases

Databases are typically configured as '"black boxes" when used with SRM, and SRM is used to manage the amount of CPU given to each instance of the database. Some of the database vendors offer resource management features, which are discussed in more detail in "Database Workloads" on page 71.

Note that the SRM scheduler does impose a small system scheduling overhead, which may need to be taken into account. Most database measurements done to date reflect an overhead of less than 5 percent. However different workloads behave in different ways and may show different results.

SRM and Preemption Control

Oracle8*i* implements preemption control to allow high-end scalability. Preemption control is an interface between the Oracle kernel and the Solaris scheduler that allows Oracle to provide hints to the scheduler to prevent the Solaris software from stopping process execution at critical times. For example, with no hints the Solaris scheduler could deschedule a thread just after it has acquired a row latch in the database, holding up all other processes until that process is rescheduled. To avoid this problem, Oracle can tell the Solaris scheduler that it's holding a critical resource and should not stop running, and if possible, the process will be allowed to run until it gives up its context.

The Solaris Resource Manager 1.0 software needs a patch to support preemption control. Note that there are some performance implications of running Oracle8*i* on the SRM 1.0 software without the preemtion control patch. Refer to Sun RFE 4223677 for further information.

Managing NFS

The Network File System (NFS) runs as kernel threads, and uses the kernel scheduling class SYS. This means that scheduling allocation for NFS is not managed by the SRM SHR class, and hence no CPU resource control of NFS is possible.

However, NFS can be controlled by using network port resource management. For example, the Sun Bandwidth Allocator product can control the number of NFS packets on the server. In some cases, NFS can also be managed by limiting the number of CPUs available in the system class with processor sets.

Managing Web Servers

The SRM software can manage resources on web servers by controlling the amount of CPU and virtual memory. Three basic topologies are used on systems hosting web servers.

Resource Management of a Consolidated Web Server

A single web server can be managed by controlling the amount of resources that the entire web server can use. This is useful in an environment where a web server is being consolidated with other workloads. This most basic form of resource management prevents other workloads from affecting the performance of the web server and vice versa.

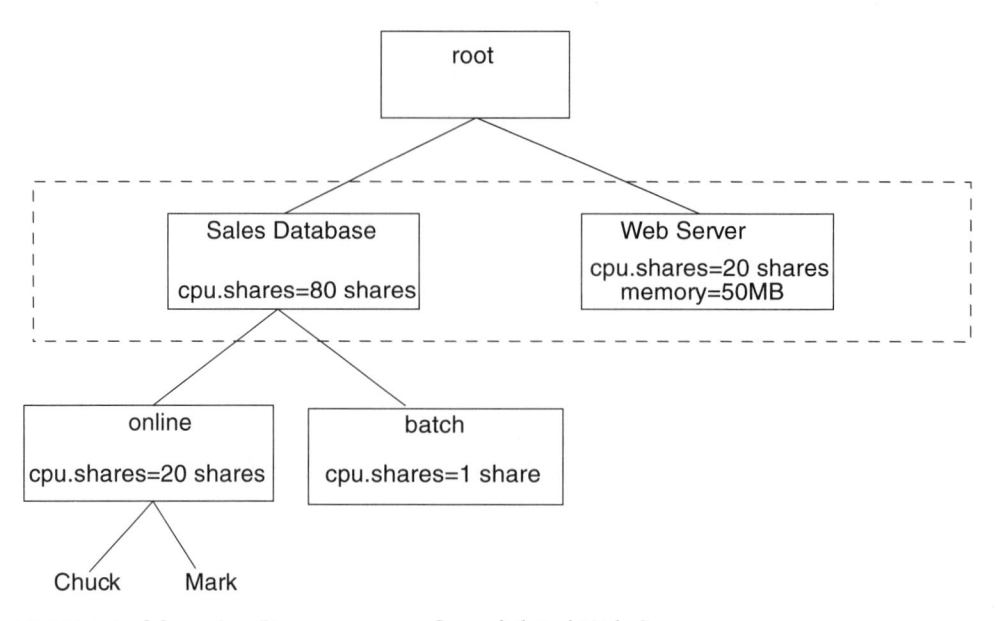

```
                          root
                           |
        ┌──────────────────┴──────────────────┐
        |                                     |
   Sales Database                        Web Server
                                    cpu.shares=20 shares
   cpu.shares=80 shares                  memory=50MB
        |
   ┌────┴────┐
   |         |
 online    batch
cpu.shares=20 shares   cpu.shares=1 share
   |
 ┌─┴─┐
Chuck Mark
```

FIGURE 7-6 Managing Resources on a Consolidated Web Server

In FIGURE 7-6, the web server is allocated 20 shares. This means that it is guaranteed at least 20 percent of the processor resources if the database places excessive demands on the processor.

In addition, if a CGI-BIN process in the web server runs out of control with a memory leak, the entire system will not run out of swap space. Only the web server will be affected.

Fine Grained Resource Management of a Single Web Server

Often resource management is needed to control the behavior within a single web server. For example, a single web server can be shared among many users, with each running their own CGI-BIN programs.

An error in a CGI-BIN program could cause the entire web server to run slowly. In case of a memory leak, could even bring down the web server. To prevent this from happening, use the per-process limits.

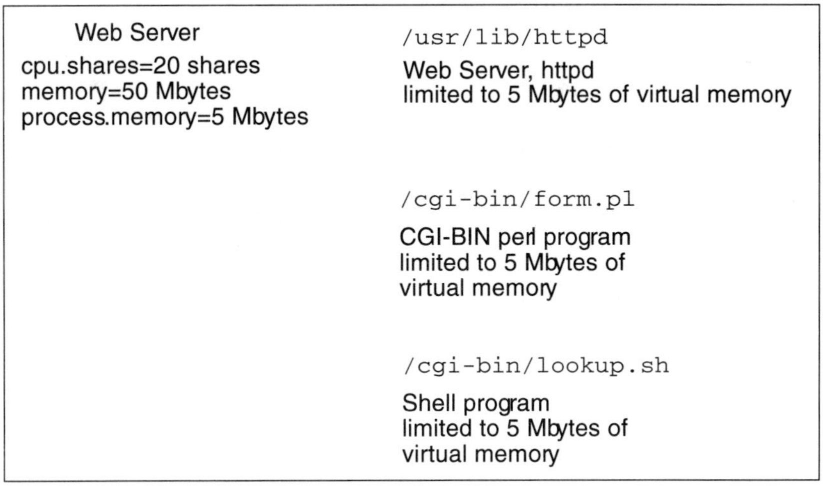

```
     Web Server              /usr/lib/httpd
   cpu.shares=20 shares      Web Server, httpd
   memory=50 Mbytes          limited to 5 Mbytes of virtual memory
   process.memory=5 Mbytes


                             /cgi-bin/form.pl
                             CGI-BIN perl program
                             limited to 5 Mbytes of
                             virtual memory


                             /cgi-bin/lookup.sh
                             Shell program
                             limited to 5 Mbytes of
                             virtual memory
```

FIGURE 7-7 Fine Grained Resource Management of a Single Web Server

Resource Management of Multiple Virtual Web Servers

Single machines are often used to host multiple virtual web servers In such cases, there are multiple instances of the `httpd` web server. There is also greater opportunity to exploit resource control using the SRM software.

Each web server can run as a different UNIX userid by setting a parameter in the web server configuration file. This effectively attaches each web server to a different lnode in the SRM hierarchy.

For example, the Solaris web server has the following parameters in the configuration file, /etc/http/httpd.conf:

```
# Server parameters
server  {
  server_root                   "/var/http/"
  server_user                   "webserver1"
  mime_file                     "/etc/http/mime.types"
  mime_default_type             text/plain
  acl_enable                    "yes"
  acl_file                      "/etc/http/access.acl"
  acl_delegate_depth            3
  cache_enable                  "yes"
  cache_small_file_cache_size   8              # megabytes
  cache_large_file_cache_size   256            # megabytes
  cache_max_file_size           1              # megabytes
  cache_verification_time       10             # seconds
  comment                       "Sun WebServer Default Configuration"

  # The following are the server wide aliases

  map     /cgi-bin/             /var/http/cgi-bin/              cgi
  map     /sws-icons/           /var/http/demo/sws-icons/
  map     /admin/               /usr/http/admin/

# To enable viewing of server stats via command line,
# uncomment the following line
  map     /sws-stats            dummy                           stats
}
```

FIGURE 7-8 Solaris Web Server Parameter File

By configuring each web server to run as a different UNIX userid you can set different limits on each web server. This is especially useful for controlling and accounting for resource usage on a machine hosting many web servers.

You can use most or all of the SRM resource controls and limits as follows:

Shares [cpu.shares]   Proportionally allocate resources to the different web servers

Mem limit [memory.limit]   Limit the amount of virtual memory that the web server can use. This will prevent any single web server from causing another one to fail.

Proc mem limit [memory.plimit]	Limit the amount of virtual memory a single `cgi-bin` process can use. This will stop any `cgi-bin` process from bringing down its respective web server.
Process limit [process.limit]	Set the maximum number of processes allowed to attach to a web server. This will effectively limit the number of concurrent `cgi-bin` processes.

Creating a Policy on Executable Name

In some cases, it may be useful to construct a hierarchy which allocates resources based on the application which each user is executing. Use the `srmuser` command and wrappers around the executables.

Create a different point in the hierarchy for each application type. Then authorize users to switch lnodes as they execute each application.

```
                        root
                       /    \
                   Users    Applications
                   /  \        /      \
                Mark  Chuck  /usr/bin/app1    /usr/bin/app2
                             cpu.shares=20 shares   cpu.shares=1 share
```

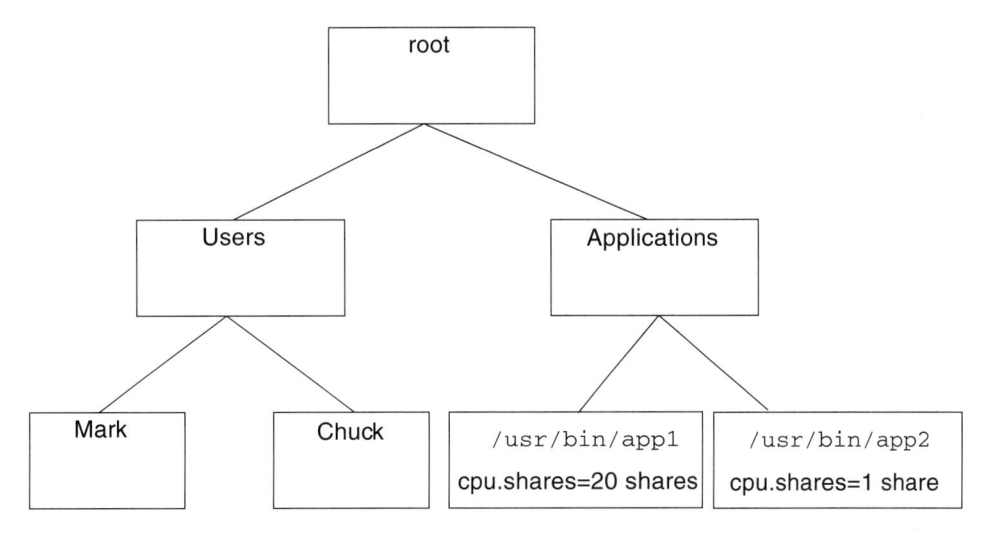

FIGURE 7-9 A Hierarchy Allowing Policies by Executable Name

The simple hierarchy shown in FIGURE 7-9 is established using the limadm command and makes Chuck and Mark children of the users group, and makes app1 and app2 children of the applications group:

```
# limadm set sgroup=root users
# limadm set sgroup=users chuck
# limadm set sgroup=users mark

# limadm set sgroup=root apps
# limadm set sgroup=apps app1
# limadm set sgroup=apps app2
```

Give both Chuck and Mark permission to switch lnodes on their child processes. This allows you to attach /usr/bin/app1 to the app1 lnode and /usr/bin/app2 to the app2 lnode.

```
# limadm set flag.admin=s chuck
# limadm set flag.admin=s mark
```

Allocate shares to both applications in the desired proportions:

```
# limadm set cpu.shares=20 app1
# limadm set cpu.shares=1 app2
```

Now use the srmuser command to create a simple wrapper script to set the appropriate lnodes upon execution of the applications:

```
#!/bin/sh
#
# Execute /usr/bin/app1 and attach it to the app1 lnode
#

/usr/srm/bin/srmuser app1 /usr/bin/app1
```

The Role and Effect of Processor Sets

Even with the SRM software in effect, processor sets may still play an important role. Sometimes a system must have hard limits applied to the resource policies. Suppose a company purchases a single 24-processor system, and then hosts two different business units from the same machine. Each of the business units pays for a proportion of the machine, 40 percent and 60 percent in our example. In this case, the IT department may want to enforce that the business that payed for 40 percent of the machine never gets more than 40 percent. This might seem selfish, but in reality if the second business unit only uses 10 percent of the machine for the first two months, the first business unit will become accustomed to 90 percent of the machine. When they are eventually reduced to their allocated 40 percent, response times will increase and users will complain.

With processor sets, it is possible to divide the workloads into 40 percent and 60 percent by allocating 10 and 14 processors to each of the business units. At no point in the future will either of the business units allocation of processor resource reduce, avoiding the drop in response times.

See "Processor Sets" on page 123 for detailed information on the use of processor sets for resource management.

Processor sets were introduced in the Solaris 2.6 release, and can co-exist with the SRM software. Some attention should be made to the interaction between these two technologies, as in some circumstances the net effect can be different from what was originally expected.

SRM Software and Processor Sets: A Simple Example

FIGURE 7-10 shows a simple scenario where processor sets and SRM CPU shares are mixed. User 1 has 25 SRM shares, and is restricted to processor set A (1 CPU). User 2 has 75 SRM shares, and is restricted to processor set B (1 CPU).

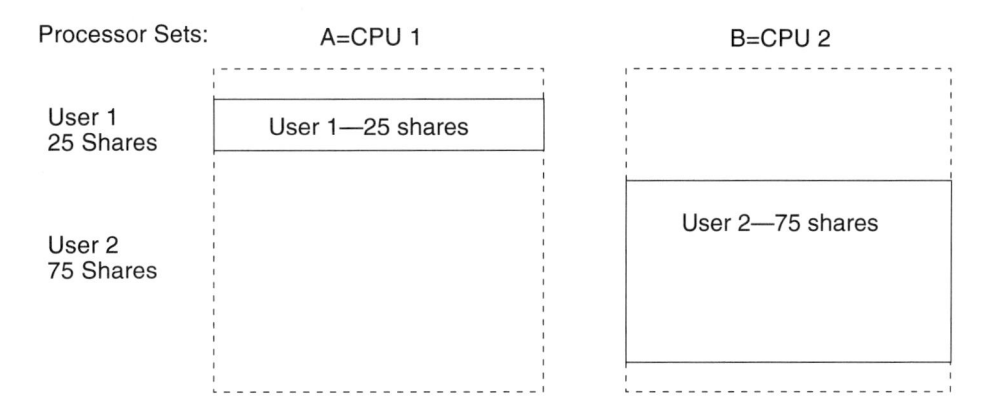

FIGURE 7-10 Simple Combination of Solaris Resource Manager and Processor Sets

In this example, user 2 will consume its entire processor set (50 percent of the system). Because user 2 is only using 50 percent (rather than its allocated 75 percent), user 1 is able to use the remaining 50 percent. In summary, each user will be granted 50 percent of the system.

SRM Software and Processor Sets: A More Complex Example

FIGURE 7-11 shows a more complex scenario where processor sets and SRM CPU shares are mixed. User 1 and 3 have 10 SRM shares each, and are restricted to processor set A (1 CPU). User 2 has 80 SRM shares and is restricted to processor set B (1 CPU).

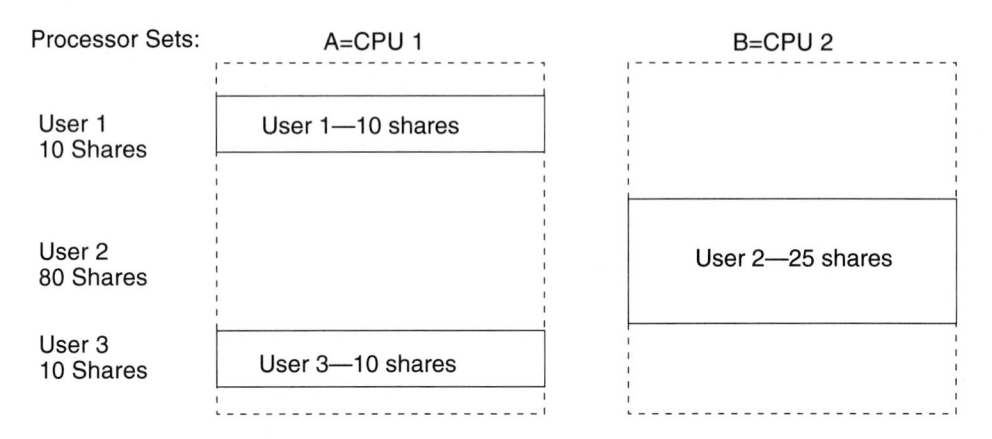

FIGURE 7-11 Complex Combination of Solaris Resource Manager and Processor Sets

In this example, user 2 will consume its entire processor set (50 percent of the system). Because user 2 is only using 50 percent (rather than its allocated 80 percent), user 1 and 3 are able to use the remaining 50 percent. This means that user 1 and 3 get 25 percent of the system, even though they are allocated only 10 shares each.

162 Resource Management

SRM and Processor Sets: Something to Avoid

FIGURE 7-12 shows a scenario to avoid. In this scenario, one user has processes in both processor sets. User 1 has 20 SRM shares, and has processes in each processor set. User 2 has 80 SRM shares, and is restricted to processor set B (1 CPU).

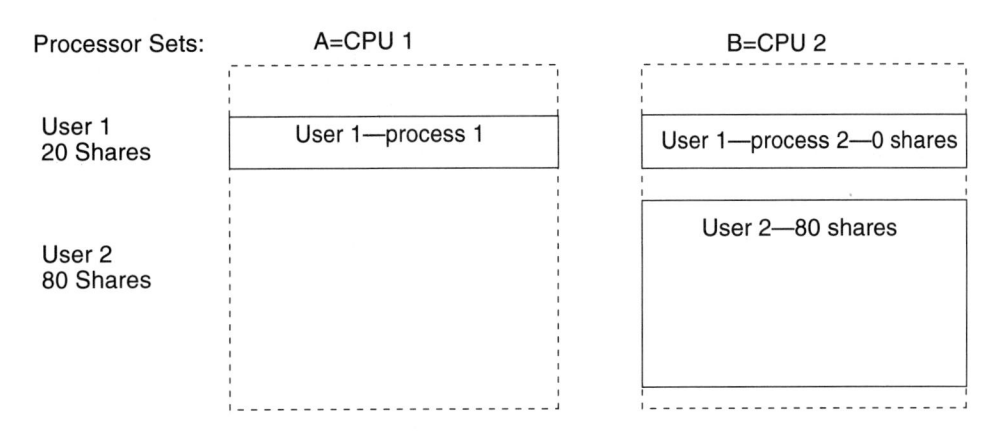

Processor Sets:	A=CPU 1	B=CPU 2
User 1 20 Shares	User 1—process 1	User 1—process 2—0 shares
User 2 80 Shares		User 2—80 shares

FIGURE 7-12 Something to Avoid: Users Spanning Multiple Processor Sets

In this example, user 1's process 1 will consume its entire processor set (50 percent of the system). Since User 2 is allowed 80 shares, user 2 will consume its entire processor set (50 percent). User 1's process 2 will get no share of the CPU.

Decay Factors and Parameters

The SRM software is designed to run with minimal or no tuning. However, a number of configurable parameters govern the way the scheduler apportions shares. These parameters can be used to influence the way the scheduler reacts to dynamic workloads, and different parameters can sometimes benefit particular workloads.

The SRM scheduler is a complete replacement for the Solaris timeshare scheduler (TS), and hence does not use any of the existing parameters provided with the TS scheduler module. On systems where SRM is installed, use the `dispadmin` command to display the configured scheduling classes:

```
# dispadmin -l
CONFIGURED CLASSES
==================

SYS     (System Class)
SHR     ((SHR) SRM Scheduler)
TS      (Time Sharing)
IA      (Interactive)
```

At boot time, the Solaris kernel starts all non-kernel processes in the SHR class instead of the traditional TS class. You can see this with the ps command.

```
# ps -cafe
    UID    PID  PPID  CLS  PRI     STIME TTY          TIME CMD
   root      0     0  SYS   96    Mar 12 ?            0:00 sched
   root      0     0  SYS   96    Mar 12 ?            0:00 sched
   root      1     0  SHR   59    Mar 12 ?            1:03 /etc/init -
   root      2     0  SYS   98    Mar 12 ?            0:00 pageout
   root      3     0  SYS   60    Mar 12 ?            7:19 fsflush
   root      4     0  SYS   60    Mar 12 ?            1:05 srmgr
   root    563     1  SHR   60    Mar 12 console     0:00 /usr/lib/saf/ttym
   root    313     1  SHR   59    Mar 12 ?            0:04 /usr/lib/utmpd
   root    201     1  SHR   59    Mar 12 ?            0:00 /usr/sbin/keyserv
   root     14     1  SHR   59    Mar 12 ?            0:00 vxconfigd -m boot
   root    159     1  SHR   59    Mar 12 ?            0:23 limdaemon
   root    199     1  SHR   59    Mar 12 ?            0:00 /usr/sbin/rpcbind
   root    252     1  SHR   59    Mar 12 ?            1:24 automountd
ctd...
```

The TS scheduler is configured by altering the dispatcher table that controls how process priorities are decayed. The TS scheduler uses a variable time quantum and adjusts process priorities as their time quantum expires. You can see the existing dispatcher table with the `dispadmin` command.

```
# Time Sharing Dispatcher Configuration
RES=1000

# ts_quantum  ts_tqexp  ts_slpret  ts_maxwait  ts_lwait  PRIOR LEVEL
       200       0        50          0          50       #    0
       200       0        50          0          50       #    1
       200       0        50          0          50       #    2
       200       0        50          0          50       #    3
       200       0        50          0          50       #    4
(snip)
        40      44        58          0          59       #   54
        40      45        58          0          59       #   55
        40      46        58          0          59       #   56
        40      47        58          0          59       #   57
        40      48        58          0          59       #   58
        20      49        59       32000         59       #   59
```

Process priorities are shown by the priority levels, which range from 0 through 59. The highest priority process (represented as 59) gets the most amount of CPU. A process starts with a normal priority inherited from its parent somewhere in the middle of the table. If the process uses its time quantum (each priority level has a different quantum represented by `ts_quantum`), it will be decayed to the priority in the `ts_tqexp` column. A process that has had no CPU will have its priority raised to `ts_lwait`. A process that has awakened after sleeping for an I/O will have its priority set to `ts_slpret`.

Decay Algorithms

If you were to use a fixed priority scheduler with no decaying of process priorities, a higher priority process would always get as much CPU as it wanted and could block all other lower priority processes from receiving any CPU. (The Solaris RT scheduler works this way.) The decay algorithm prevents any one process from hogging all of the CPU by decrementing its priority once it receives its allocation of CPU. This provides a fair allocation of CPU resources to each process, based on its priority. The amount of CPU allocated to each process can be influenced by setting the `nice` value between -19 and +19. The `nice` value is added to the process priority as it is scheduled. It allows one process to receive more CPU than another, but because of the decay model, it will not completely block other processes.

The table-based decay algorithms used in the Solaris software provide a flexible framework where the scheduler can be tuned for different workloads. The scheduler also replaces the BSD style scheduler's notion of a simple decay that does not use a table to calculate process priorities.

Comparison to BSD Style Priority Decay

The BSD UNIX scheduler decays the priority of each process by multiplying its priority by a fixed decay factor at a regular interval:

$$process\_pri = 0.66 * process\_pri + nice\_factor$$

We can compare what would happen if we varied the decay factor. At one end of the range, we could set the decay factor to 0.9 (slow decay), which would mean we almost have fixed process priorities. This would cause a process with a high priority to stay at a high priority for a long time and could allow a process to monopolize the CPU and starve other processes. At the other end of the range, we could decay process priorities very fast by using a decay factor of 0.1. This would prevent CPU monopolization but would cause all processes to receive similar amounts of CPU regardless of their nice factor. It would also allow a user who runs a large number of processes to get a large and unfair amount of CPU.

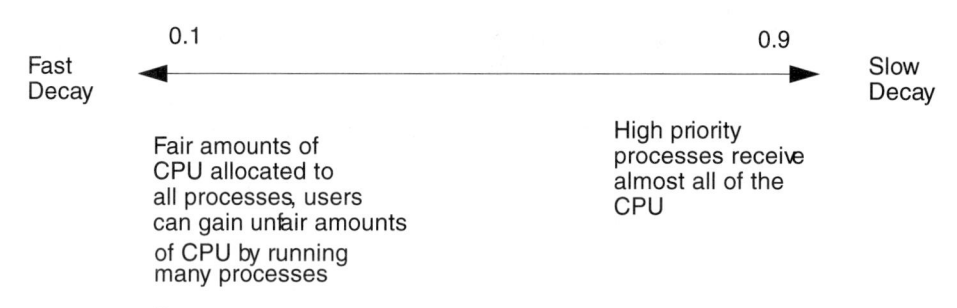

FIGURE 7-13 Effect of Decay Time on Allocation Fairness

Usage Decay and Process Priority Decay

The SRM scheduler has two different notions of decay that affect processes: one is the usage decay and the other is the process priority decay. This happens because the SRM software is implemented with two schedulers, the user scheduler and the process scheduler, each with its own set of parameters. The user scheduler calculates and attempts to bias *users* so that they each receive their share of allocated CPU according to the amount of shares allocated to them. The process scheduler sits underneath the user scheduler and manages fine-grained allocation of CPU to each process by using a BSD style decay model.

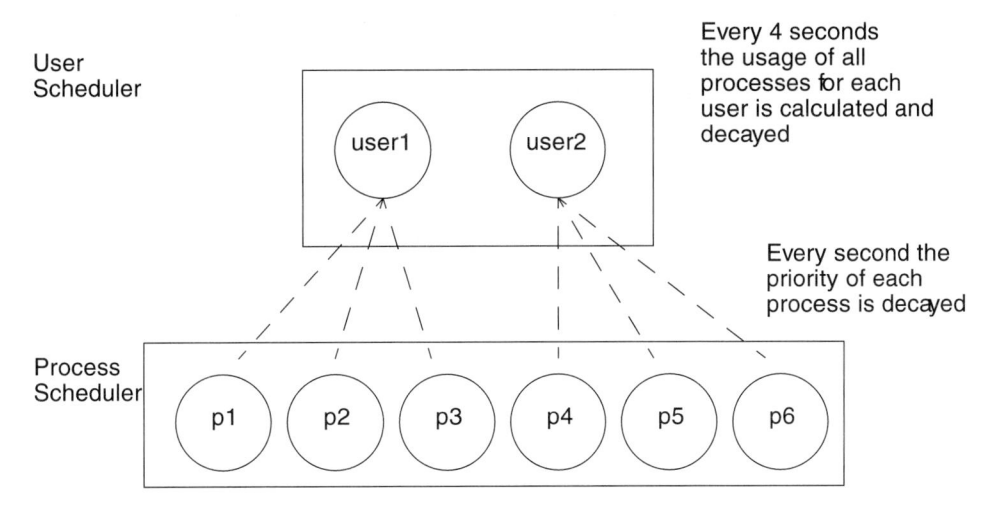

FIGURE 7-14 Two Levels of Scheduling in SRM

Process Priority Decay

If we ignore the user scheduler for the moment, we can look at the process scheduler as just another UNIX process scheduler that uses decay factors. The SHR scheduler does not use table driven decay. It uses a model closer to the BSD decay where each processes priority is decayed according to a fixed decay factor at regular intervals (each second). Internal process priorities in the SRM process scheduler are known as `userpri` and range from 0 to 10^{32}, where 0 is the highest priority

FIGURE 7-15 Effect of Decay on Process Priority

To prevent CPU monopolization, a low priority process (a high `userpri` value) has its `userpri` decayed each second by the fixed decay parameter so that it will eventually get some allocation of CPU. This prevents a process from CPU starvation in a way that is similar to the BSD scheduler. Use the `srmadm` command to view the process priority decay parameter:

```
# srmadm show -V3
Scheduling flags = -share, -limits, -adjgroups, -limshare, -fileopen
Idle lnode = root
Lost lnode = NONEXISTENT

Usage decay rate half-life = 120.0 seconds,
        (0.977159980000 - 4 second units, 0.999942239403 - 0 Hz units),

max. users                       = 12
active users                     = 0
active groups                    = 0
scheduler run rate               = 4 seconds
number of configured lnodes = 0

Process priority decay rate biased by "nice":-
   high priority (nice -20) 0.4044 (half-life   0.8 seconds)
   average priority (nice  0) 0.7039 (half-life   2.0 seconds)
   low priority (nice  19) 0.9885 (half-life  60.0 seconds)

Minimum group share factor         = 0.750
Maximum user share factor          = 2.000
Async-nice share factor            = 1.000e+07

Max. value for normal usage        = 1.000e+12
Max. value for normal p_sharepri   = 1.000e+28
Max. value for idle p_sharepri     = 1.000e+34

Cache hits on valid lnodes         = 0
Cache hits on invalid lnodes       = 0
Cache misses                       = 0
Number of lnodes replaced          = 0

Default system flags =  -admin, -uselimadm, -onelogin, -nologin,
                        -asynckill, -asyncnice, -noattach
```

The decay parameter for normal processes is 0.7039 by default. This means that every two seconds the `userpri` value for the process will halve (referred to as the half-life). The `nice` command can be used to alter process priorities. The decay values for processes depend on the `nice` factor assigned to each process. To give a process a higher priority, use the `nice` command to influence the decay value. For example running a command with `nice -19` causes the processes `sharepri` to drop faster. This occurs because you now multiply by a factor of 0.404, which allows the process to wait a shorter time before it gets access to the CPU again

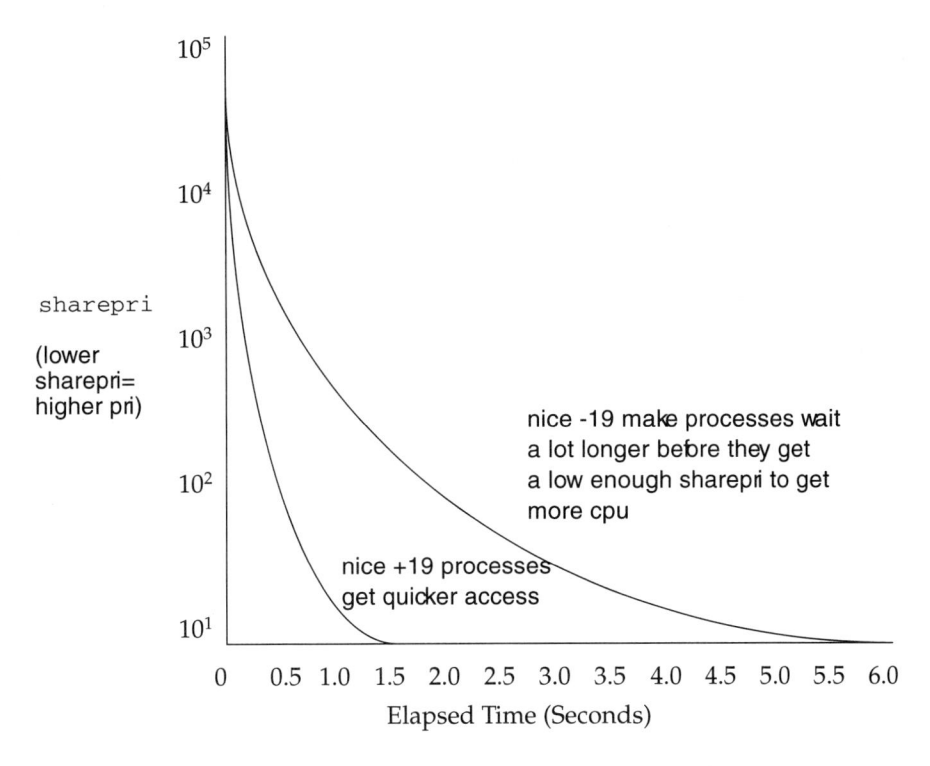

[Graph showing sharepri (lower sharepri = higher pri) on y-axis from 10¹ to 10⁵, versus Elapsed Time (Seconds) on x-axis from 0 to 6.0. Two decay curves are shown with annotations: "nice -19 make processes wait a lot longer before they get a low enough sharepri to get more cpu" and "nice +19 processes get quicker access".]

FIGURE 7-16 Process Priority Decay with Two Different nice Values

You can see how a process's sharepri is decayed every second using the priority decay factor. Now let's look at how process sharepri is increased. The sharepri for each process is increased at the same time according to the amount of CPU that it has used, just as we saw with the BSD scheduler equation. But the SHR scheduler includes a user usage factor that is derived from the user scheduler shown in FIGURE 7-14. This is how the SHR scheduler implements the notion of user based scheduling rather than just process-based scheduling. At each second, the scheduler manipulates the sharepri of each process by the following:

*sharepri = sharepri * decay_factor + users_usage_factor*

Consider a process that is using small amounts of CPU over the same period shown in FIGURE 7-16. You can see that the sharepri for each process increments as the process uses CPU and then decays while it does not.

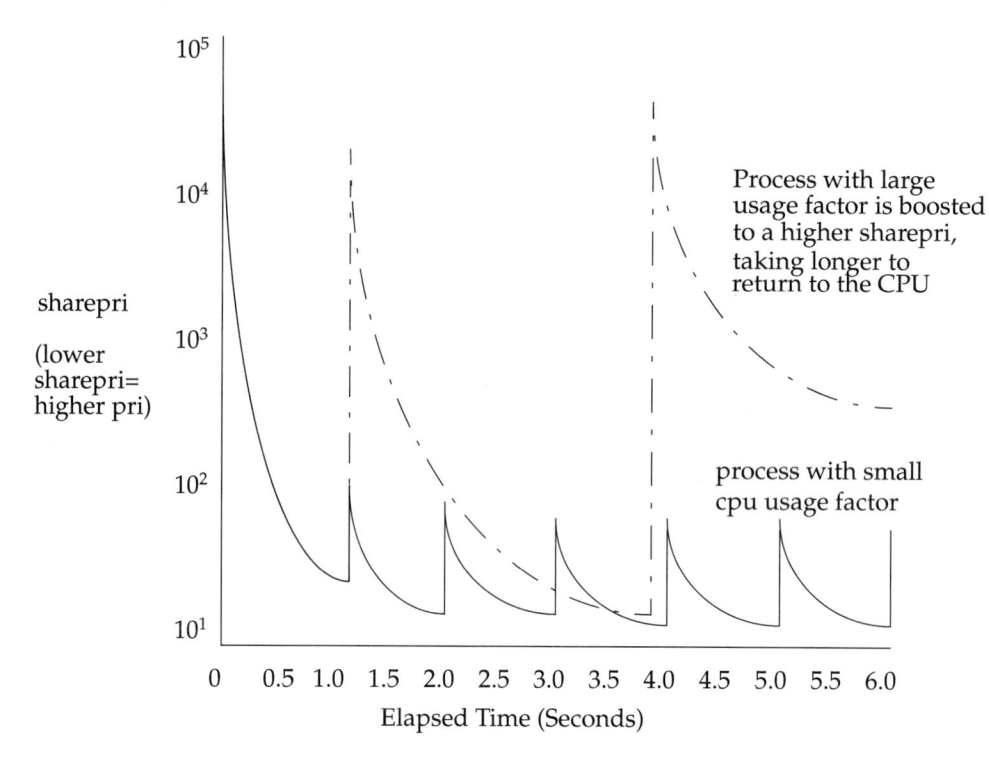

FIGURE 7-17 Process Priority Increase and Decay

A Note about /bin/ksh

The korn shell automatically sets the nice value of processes when they are sent to the background. This results in a slightly different process decay rate for foreground and background processes.

```
PID   USERNAME  THR  PRI  NICE  SIZE   RES   STATE  TIME   CPU     COMMAND
1599  user1     1    59   0     896K   560K  cpu/0  0:31   80.44%  t1spin
 425  user2     1    15   4     896K   560K  run    0:28    1.50%  spin
```

Usage Decay

So far we have focused on the process scheduler (bottom layer of FIGURE 7-14) and for the purpose of simplification we viewed the process scheduler as just another UNIX scheduler. The fair share features of the SRM software are implemented by factoring in the user usage, which is calculated in the top user scheduler layer. The user scheduler is the most important and visible portion of the SRM software and implements usage decays that control long term CPU allocation responsiveness. Short term (less then 4 second) responsiveness and individual process importance is controlled by the process priority decay parameters discussed in the previous section.

The user scheduler summarizes process usage across users and compares it to the shares allocated with the SRM policy hierarchy. This information is summarized as normalized usage and is passed to the process scheduler as a usage factor to control all of the processes within each user. User processes can be prioritized individually using the `nice` command to influence their priority decay.

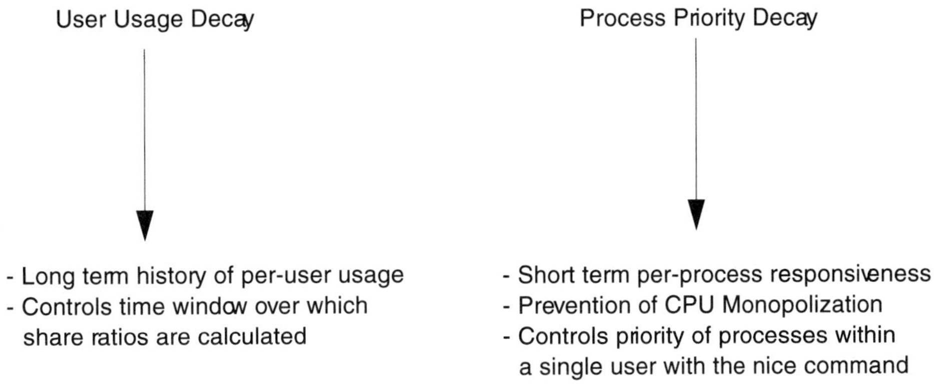

User Usage Decay

- Long term history of per-user usage
- Controls time window over which share ratios are calculated

Process Priority Decay

- Short term per-process responsiveness
- Prevention of CPU Monopolization
- Controls priority of processes within a single user with the nice command

FIGURE 7-18 Comparison of Usage Decay and Priority Decay

The user scheduler runs every four seconds and calculates the total CPU usage for all of the processes for each user. The usage is added to the usage and accrued fields in the lnode for that user. You can see the usage increment as a process executes by looking at the usage and accrued fields in the lnode with the `liminfo` command.

```
# liminfo -c chuck
Login name:            chuck          Uid (Real,Eff):     2001 (-,-)
Sgroup (uid):          root (0)       Gid (Real,Eff):      200 (-,-)

Shares:                    50         Myshares:                1
Share:                   41 %         E-share:                0 %
Usage:                 142302         Accrued usage:     4.23e+10
```

An example is a process that has been using CPU continuously for two seconds. This would incur a usage increment of 2 seconds x 1000 (SRM charge per tick) x 100 (ticks per second) = 2000.

If we were to allocate CPU resources based on instantaneous usage, we would only be able to allocate the proper shares to each user if both users were using CPU at the same time. In reality, this rarely happens unless both controlled users are running continuous batch-type jobs. More often, users use small portions of CPU at different intervals, and we want to allocate shares of CPU based on usage over a broader period of time. For example, if user 1 is using 1 second of CPU every ten seconds and user 2 is using CPU continuously, we would get incorrect results if we controlled the instantaneous CPU allocated to each user.

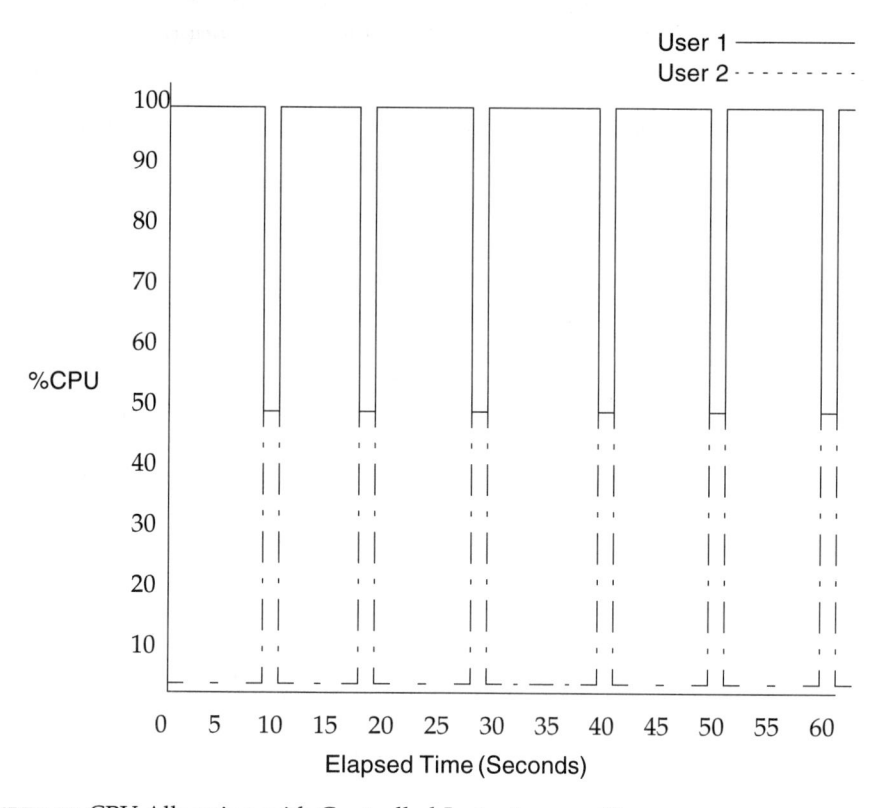

FIGURE 7-19 CPU Allocation with Controlled Instantaneous Use

FIGURE 7-19 shows that if we allocated 50 shares to user 1 and 50 shares to user 2, as described previously, and controlled their CPU instantaneously user 1 would get 100 percent of the CPU while user 1 is executing on its own, and then each user would get 50 percent while they are both busy. This means that even if user 2 is only using 10 percent of the CPU, user 2 is still being constrained by the resource manager. And user 2's one second request every ten seconds ends up taking two seconds.

By adding a decay factor we can average the CPU use over a larger time window. This gives us a true view of each users average use. If we revisit our example we could set a decay factor so that usage history is collected over the larger time window of 30 seconds. This would mean that user 1 would be recorded as using 90 percent of the CPU and user 2 would be recorded as using 10 percent. User 2 could use almost 100 percent of the CPU when it requests, and the one second request would complete in one second.

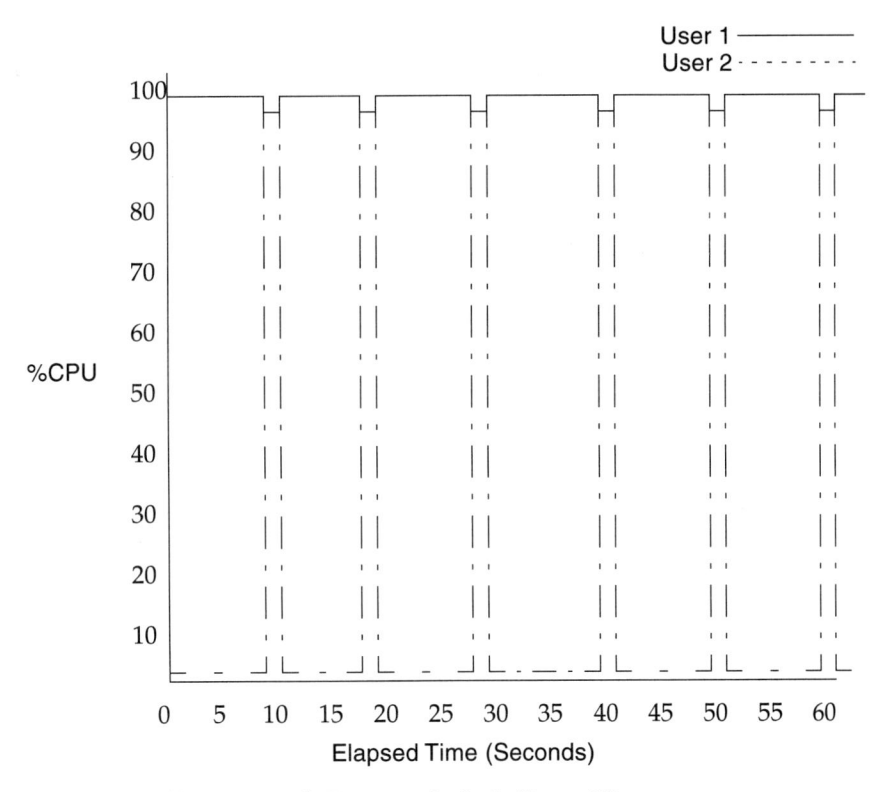

FIGURE 7-20 CPU Allocation with Decay to Include Usage History

User 1 can use close to 100 percent rather than 90 percent because of the process priority decay and the responsiveness of the process scheduler. Making the priority decay longer allows short term bursty users to get access to the CPU when they need it. This is particularly useful for interactive users or web servers.

If we were to keep too much usage history, then a user could be completely blocked from CPU resources for a long period if they over-consumed their share. This would happen if we set a very long decay time (almost no decay) and a user used more than its share while no other users were using their share. For example, if user 1 used 100 percent of the CPU over a weekend when no other users were on the system, user 1 could stop for up to two whole days when other users came back to work on Monday morning. Because of this, we need to choose a decay time that allows the scheduler to get the most useful average usage. The usage decay is set on a global basis. You can see it with the `srmadm` command.

```
# srmadm show -V3
Scheduling flags = -share, -limits, -adjgroups, -limshare, -fileopen
Idle lnode = root
Lost lnode = NONEXISTENT

Usage decay rate half-life = 120.0 seconds,
      (0.977159980000 - 4 second units, 0.999942239403 - 0 Hz units),

max. users                   = 12
active users                 = 0
active groups                = 0
scheduler run rate           = 4 seconds
number of configured lnodes  = 0

Process priority decay rate biased by "nice":-
   high priority (nice -20) 0.4044 (half-life   0.8 seconds)
average priority (nice    0) 0.7039 (half-life   2.0 seconds)
    low priority (nice   19) 0.9885 (half-life  60.0 seconds)

Minimum group share factor        = 0.750
Maximum user share factor         = 2.000
Async-nice share factor           = 1.000e+07

Max. value for normal usage       = 1.000e+12
Max. value for normal p_sharepri  = 1.000e+28
Max. value for idle p_sharepri    = 1.000e+34

Cache hits on valid lnodes        = 0
Cache hits on invalid lnodes      = 0
Cache misses                      = 0
Number of lnodes replaced         = 0

Default system flags = -admin, -uselimadm, -onelogin, -nologin,
                      -asynckill, -asyncnice, -noattach
```

You can see a demonstration of usage history in FIGURE 7-21. It shows two users with equal shares. User 1 has been consuming CPU for a very long time. A second user, user 2 has not. User 2 starts using CPU 5 seconds into the measured period. The large CPU usage history causes user's 1 usage factor to be high (calculated by the user scheduler). When this is passed to the process scheduler, it causes the process to have a high `sharepri`. Before user 2 starts, user 1 is the only user on the system, and even though user 1 has a high `sharepri` (low priority) user 1 can consume all of the CPU. User 2 starts with a usage history and usage factor of zero. When this is passed to the process scheduler, it results in a low `sharepri` (high priority). This means that user 2 can consume most of the CPU for a very short period. As the decay factor decays user 1's large usage history, user 1 is able to get more of the CPU. The default usage decay is 120 seconds, which, as shown in FIGURE 7-21 causes both users to end up at their equal allocation of shares after a commensurate amount of time.

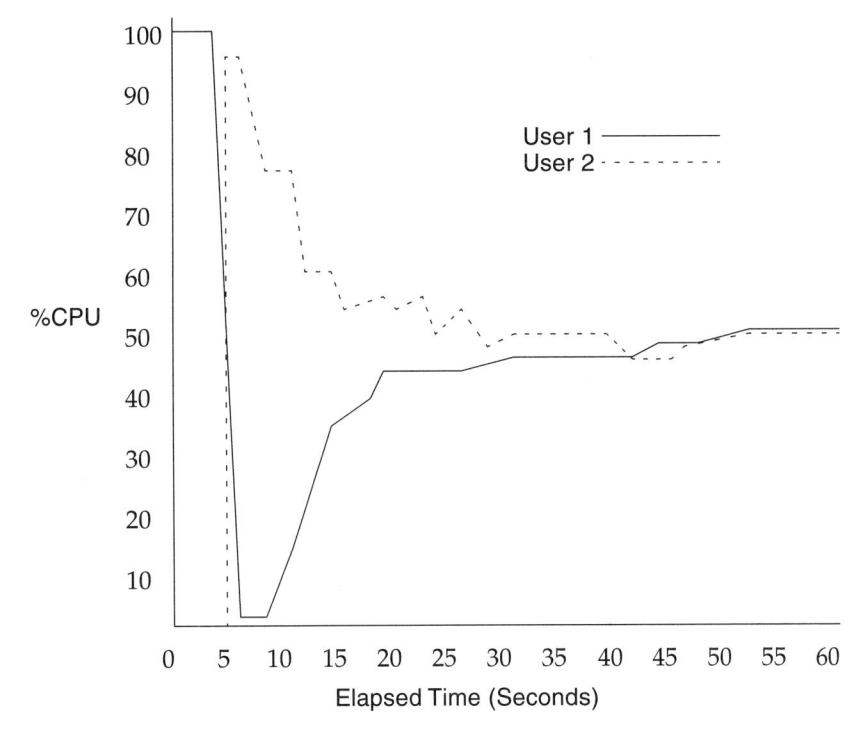

FIGURE 7-21 Throughput of a User Starting Affected by Decay

Note that two effects interplay here. The usage decay allows user 2 to almost monopolize the processor when user 1 over-consumes. But the process priority decay factor decays priorities fast enough so that user 1 still gets some of the CPU. Then user 1's `sharepri` is boosted high because user 1 has a large usage history. FIGURE 7-17 shows the interaction of the two processes described in this example. If we wanted to make user 2 consume 100 percent of the CPU and stop user 1 completely, we could set a long process priority decay time.

Setting Decay and Scheduler Parameters

The default values for usage decay and process priority decay are suitable in most situations because they include usage history over a relatively large window (about 1 minute) yet stop any one process from completely monopolizing the CPU for short periods. The default parameters particularly suit interactive workload environments, where different shares can be given to users without affecting keyboard response. Different behaviors can be achieved using different decay factors for other workloads, such as HPC or batch environments.

Decay and scheduler parameters are global, and may be set with the `srmadm` command, which must be run as root. The parameter changes take effect immediately and do not require a reboot or restarting of any srm processes.

```
# srmadm set usagedecay=240
```

The full list of parameters that can be set with the `srmadm` command are shown in TABLE 7-2.

TABLE 7-2 SRM Scheduler Parameters

Decay Parameter	Description
delta[=seconds]	The run interval for the SRM CPU scheduler. This is the time interval that elapses between recalculations of the normalized usages of all active users. The normalized usage affects the priorities of a user's processes, so larger values of delta effectively reduce the short-term responsiveness of the scheduler.
maxusage[=float]	The upper bound for CPU usages used in the priority calculation. Users with usages larger than this will use this value for their priority calculation. This prevents users with high CPU usages from skewing the priorities of other users.
usagedecay[={seconds | hours{h}}]	The decay rate for users' usages, expressed as a half-life in seconds. The optional suffix character h may be used to specify the value in hours.

TABLE 7-2 SRM Scheduler Parameters

Decay Parameter	Description
pridecay[={seconds | hours{h}}]	The decay rate for the priorities of processes with normal and maximum nice values respectively, expressed as half-lives. The rates for other nice values are interpolated between these two and extrapolated down to minimum nice. The second value must be greater than the first.
limshare[=y,n]	When this parameter is enabled, the SRM CPU scheduler applies its priority ceiling feature to limit all users' effective shares to prevent extremely low-usage users from briefly acquiring almost 100 percent of CPU. Use the enabled state.
	The rate of CPU service for a user is roughly inversely proportional to the user's usage. If users have not been active for a very long time, then their usage decays to near-zero. When such a user logs in (or the lnode becomes active in any way), then, for the duration of the next run interval, the user's processes could have such high priority that they monopolize the CPU.
	Enabling the limshare scheduling flag causes the scheduler to estimate the effective share that an lnode will receive before the next run interval. If the result exceeds the user's assigned entitlement by a given factor (see maxushare), then the user's normalized usage is readjusted to prevent this.
maxushare[=float]	f the limshare scheduling mode is enabled, the maximum effective share an individual user can have is limited to float times that user's allocated share. The maxushare default is 2.0, and it must not be set less than 1.0.

Changing the Default Process Priority Decay

The default configuration of decay parameters is a trade-off between process priority decay and usage decay to create an environment suitable for the short-term response required for interactive users. Sometimes the default parameters can provide incorrect results.

In "Comparison to BSD Style Priority Decay" on page 166 we discussed how process priority decay times have trade-offs at each extreme. A long process priority decay causes strict CPU allocation between processes. But it can cause a process to be marooned or starved of CPU if one user has priority over another. A short decay implements a fairer scheme where processes are biased but not starved. The latter is represented by the SRM defaults, which means that when a user starts a large number of processes the default setting can influence the amount of CPU that user is apportioned.

Consider an example where user 1 is given 99 shares, and user 2 is given 1 share. User 1 runs one CPU-bound process and user 2 runs 10 CPU bound processes. One would expect the SRM software to allocate 99 shares to user 1 and one share to user 2. But in reality, the rapid process priority decay tries to prevent marooning and gives each process a small amount of CPU. Thus user 1 gets closer to 80 percent and user 2 gets 20 percent

```
PID  USERNAME  THR  PRI  NICE  SIZE   RES   STATE  TIME   CPU     COMMAND
1599 user1      1   59    0    896K   560K  cpu/0  0:31   80.44%  t1spin
 425 user2      1   15    4    896K   560K  run    0:28    1.50%  spin
 460 user2      1   31    4    896K   560K  run    0:24    1.37%  spin
 465 user2      1   26    4    896K   560K  run    0:24    1.33%  spin
 462 user2      1   26    4    896K   560K  run    0:24    1.32%  spin
 464 user2      1   34    4    896K   560K  run    0:23    1.32%  spin
 451 user2      1   34    4    896K   560K  run    1:03    1.32%  spin
 459 user2      1   34    4    896K   560K  run    0:25    1.32%  spin
 466 user2      1   34    4    896K   560K  run    0:23    1.32%  spin
 444 user2      1   34    4    896K   560K  run    0:26    1.31%  spin
 446 user2      1   34    4    896K   560K  run    0:26    1.31%  spin
```

The default process priority decay parameters decay processes over a short period (two seconds). This means each process will decay fast enough to get some CPU. By changing the scheduler to use a longer decay parameter you can cause the scheduler to enforce strict share allocation, which will maroon other processes.

```
# srmadm set pridecay=60,120

# srmadm show -V 3
Scheduling flags = -share, -limits, -adjgroups, -limshare, -
fileopen
Idle lnode = root
Lost lnode = NONEXISTENT

Usage decay rate half-life = 120.0 seconds,
(0.977159980000 - 4 second units, 0.999942239403 - 0 Hz units),

max. users                          = 12
active users                        = 0
active groups                       = 0
scheduler run rate                  = 4 seconds
number of configured lnodes         = 0

Process priority decay rate biased by "nice":-
   high priority (nice -20) 0.9825 (half-life  39.2 seconds)
average priority (nice   0) 0.9885 (half-life  60.0 seconds)
    low priority (nice  19) 0.9942 (half-life 120.0 seconds)
```

By making the priority decay time very long you cause the scheduler to allocate CPU according to the shares. User 1 gets 99 shares and user 2 gets one.

```
PID USERNAME THR PRI NICE  SIZE  RES STATE  TIME   CPU COMMAND
1599 user1     1   59    0  896K 560K cpu/0  0:31 99.10% t1spin
 460 user2     1   31    4  896K 560K run    0:24  0.07% spin
 465 user2     1   26    4  896K 560K run    0:24  0.03% spin
 462 user2     1   26    4  896K 560K run    0:24  0.02% spin
 464 user2     1   34    4  896K 560K run    0:23  0.02% spin
 451 user2     1   34    4  896K 560K run    1:03  0.02% spin
 459 user2     1   34    4  896K 560K run    0:25  0.02% spin
 466 user2     1   34    4  896K 560K run    0:23  0.02% spin
 444 user2     1   34    4  896K 560K run    0:26  0.01% spin
 446 user2     1   34    4  896K 560K run    0:26  0.01% spin
 425 user2     1   15    4  896K 560K run    0:28  0.00% spin
```

Changing the Default User Usage Decay

The default usage decay parameters are appropriate for consolidating typical commercial workloads such as OLTP, batch, web servers and so on. However they may be inappropriate for timeshare environments such as universities and HPC environments. Where the usage history is decayed over a period of minutes, it means that over the period of an hour or a day users may overconsume their share of the machine.

A larger usage decay time will resolve such a problem and must be set on a global basis. The decay time can be set in hours or seconds.

```
# srmadm set usagedecay=4h

# srmadm show -V 3

Usage decay rate half-life = 4.0 hours,
(0.999807477651 - 4 second units, 0.999999518648 - 100 Hz units)
```

Note that there are side effects of setting a large usage decay. Users can over consume their share without knowing it. For example, a user can use 100 percent of the CPU for a sustained period when there are no other users on the system. Suppose that a user was granted 5 percent of the system but used 100 percent for two hours when no other users were logged in. Then, when other users log in the first user will almost stop until his usage is decayed.

Changing the Maximum User Share

Another interesting factor is the maximum user share clamp. This limits the maximum amount of share a user can get in a CPU constrained environment. The `maxushare` parameter, by default, limits users from exceeding 2.0 times their share. This parameter does not affect users in a case where each of two users is given 50 percent of the system, allowing either to swing to 100 percent. If you repeated the example with different shares, the results would be quite different. FIGURE 7-22 shows an example where user 1 is given 90 shares and user 2 is given 10 shares. Notice that even though user 2 has had no usage history and should be able to use 100 percent for a short duration, only 20 percent is realized.

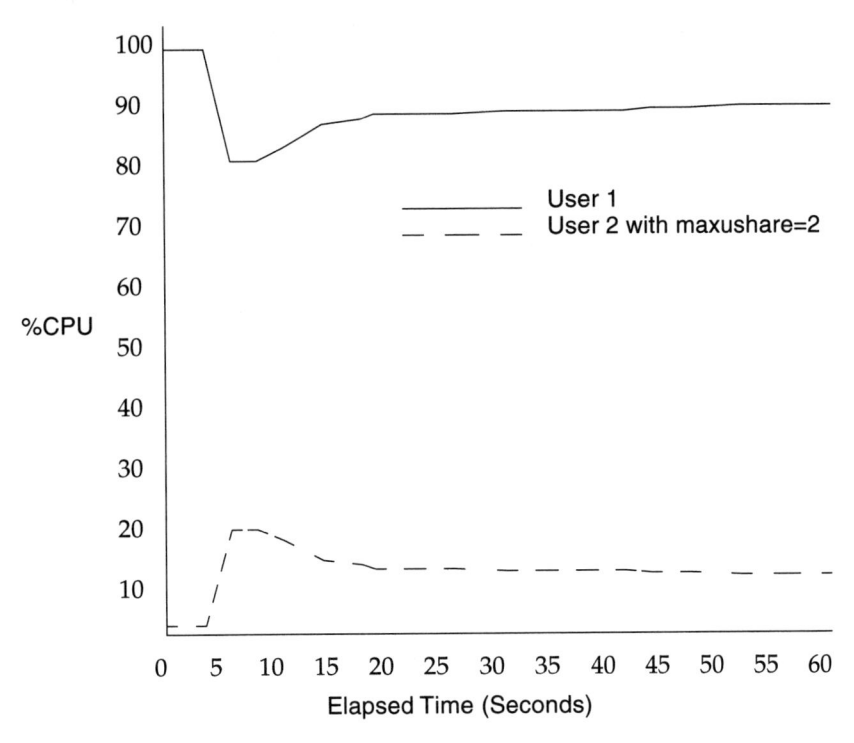

FIGURE 7-22 Effect of Maximum User Share Clamping (default maxushare=2)

You can set the maximum share clamp in two ways. You can adjust the maxushare parameter.

```
# srmadm set maxushare=10
```

Or completely remove the clamp.

```
# srmadm show limshare
yes
# srmadm set limshare=n

# srmadm show limshare
no
```

Both these parameters are global.

If you change the `maxushare` parameter to 10, you now let user 2 use up to 10 times its share allocation or 100 percent. FIGURE 7-23 shows the effect of setting maxushare higher. Notice that the behavior is similar to the example shown in FIGURE 7-21 where the users were not affected by the usage clamp.

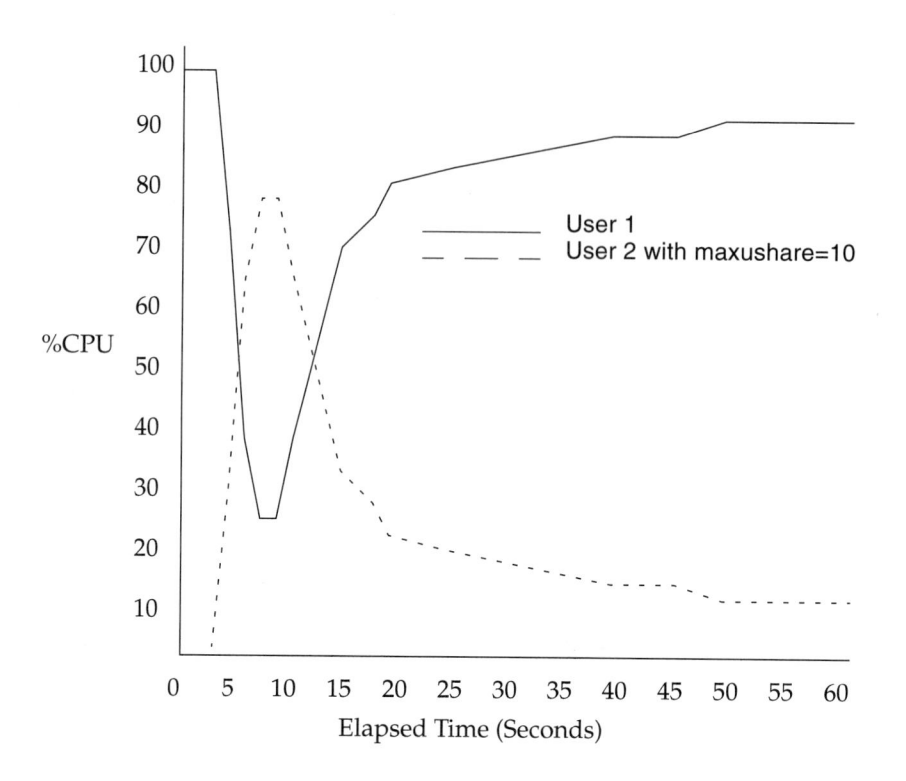

FIGURE 7-23 Effect of Setting `maxushare` to 10

Another important factor is that the `maxushare` clamp works for groups when the group scheduler is enabled. This can sometimes provide unexpected results. For example, a hierarchy similar to the one shown in FIGURE 7-24 has shares allocated at two levels: the group level (batch and interactive) and the user level (user1, user2, batch1, batch2).

If you allocate one share each to batch and interactive at the group level, and then 99 shares to batch1 and one share to batch2, you would expect that with nothing else running on the system, batch1 could use 100 percent of the CPU. This is true. However, you would expect that even if batch2 launched several jobs, batch 1 would still get 99 percent of the CPU since it has 99 shares at that level. This is not true because of the interaction of the group scheduler and the `maxushare` clamp. At the group level, at least three top level groups (batch, interactive, and other SRM default groups such as `srmother`). This means that the batch group has, at most, one in three shares, or 33 percent. And rather than 99 out of 100 shares at its level, batch1 really has 99/100 * 1/3 = 32 percent. The `maxushare` clamp by default allows a user to use 2.0 times its share, or 64 percent. The batch2 user gets 1/100 * 1/3 * 2.0 = 0.6 percent, but because not all the CPU is allocated (64% + 0.6%), batch1 ends up getting about 80 percent and batch2 about 20 percent.

In situations like this, you can get the correct behavior by increasing `maxushare` or disabling the `limshare` option.

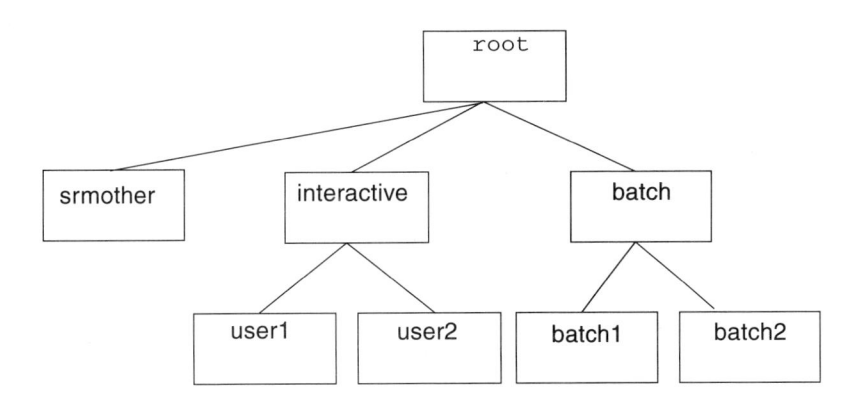

FIGURE 7-24 The Effect of the `maxushare` with Group Scheduler Enabled

Changing the User Scheduler Run Rate

The scheduler run rate is the frequency at which the user scheduler is run to summize process usage per user. It is four seconds by default. The CPU overhead of doing this is minimal, and there is little reduction in overhead by slowing down the scheduler run rate. Do not change the default of four seconds.

Changing the Scheduler Quantum

The scheduler is configured by default for a time quantum of 11 ticks, which with the default system clock rate of 100Hz, is 110ms. The scheduler quantum can be changed, and ideally should not be a divisor of the system clock (100) to prevent possible beat effects with the per-second process scheduler and the per-4-second user scheduler. The scheduler quantum can be changed with a parameter in /etc/system or with the dispadmin command, as shown in the following examples:

```
# dispadmin -g -c SHR

(SHR) SRM Scheduler Configuration

Resolution=1000                 # Resolution
Quantum=110                     # Global time quantum for all processes

# cat >/tmp/shr
Resolution=1000
Quantum=60
# dispadmin -c SHR -s /tmp/shr
# dispadmin -g -c SHR

(SHR) SRM Scheduler Configuration


Resolution=1000                 # Resolution
Quantum=60                      # Global time quantum for all processes
```

Setting the default share quantum via /etc/system:

```
* /etc/system
* Set SRM Scheduler Quantum
*
set shr_quantum = 59
```

Performance and Scalability Factors

Two factors affect the performance and scalability of SRM software: hierarchy tree depth and kernel memory.

Hierarchy Tree Depth

The amount of overhead caused by the SRM scheduler is minimal in most situations, and is proportional to the number of processes and the depth of the hierarchy tree. Hierarchies with trees deeper than about 7 layers impose a significant overhead and should be avoided. It is best to keep the hierarchy tree as flat as possible.

Kernel Memory

The amount of kernel memory used by the SRM software can be significant in some cases where a large number of lnodes are created. This is most likely on systems with large number of users in the password database. An SRM lnode is about 3 kilobytes.

Monitoring SRM Software

Implementing the SRM software can introduce some interesting new challenges for performance monitoring and management.

The question is often asked "How do I determine that the SRM software is constraining a workload?". The answer is simple. If the run queue is greater than the number of CPUs and the CPU is almost 100 percent busy (usr+sys>95 percent) then SRM is constraining a workload somewhere. This is no different from the standard Solaris scheduler since the SRM software allows a user to consume more than that user's share when there are spare CPU cycles available. The difference with the SRM software is which workloads are constrained, and that depends on how the shares are apportioned.

The lnode provides some information about which workloads are being constrained and by how much. The `srmstat` command can monitor the allocation of CPU against each SRM group The STU and LTU columns show the short term and long term CPU usage. See `srmstat(1SRM)` manual page for further information.

```
# srmstat -ac

User/group    No.  Proc  %Cpu   STU   LTU
System        7    59    0.8    0.0   0.0
daemon        1    1     0.0    0.0   0.5
srmidle       1          0.0    0.0   0.0
rmc           1    66    10.7   0.0   0.0
interactive   1          0.0    0.0   0.5
user1         1    3     84.8   1.0   0.0
user2         1    3     3.8    0.0   0.0
```

System Resource Accounting Information

The SRM software provides the ability to generate accounting data based on resource usage. This is made available by the accumulation of resource information in the lnode tree. Although the SRM software does not provide resource accounting, it does provide the data and data extraction tools that can be used to develop a system to generate accounting (or billing) information.

Billing Issues

You must decide which lnodes are to be billed for resource usage. For example, you may only be concerned with billing entire departments, so they may only want to bill the group headers of the topmost groups, whose accrued usage will include all the accrued usage of the lnodes at lower levels within their departments.

To implement a billing system, you must determine a costing function for each resource to be billed. This can be a simple linear relationship (where unit cost is the same, regardless of the amount used), or it can be a non-linear relationship, such as a step function, or a curve where unit cost varies as the amount of usage varies.

In deciding upon a costing function for each resource, the administrator should keep in mind that the costing function will not only control the assignment of cost to accrued resource usage, but can also have an impact on the way in which a user uses the resource. For example, if the costing function for virtual memory usage causes the unit cost to increase as the amount of usage increases, there is a strong incentive for the users to keep virtual memory usage low. Therefore, you can control user behavior through an appropriate costing strategy.

There is only one accrue attribute per resource. It contains the accrued usage for the resource based on the usage attribute for the resource. This means that there is no accrued usage corresponding to the `myusage` attribute. For group headers, there is no accrued usage for the user as an individual, since the accrue attribute holds the group's accrued usage. For lnodes with no children, leaf lnodes, this does not matter because the `myusage` attribute and the usage attribute are identical. If a bill is required for the individual accrued usage for a group header, it must be calculated from the group total less the sum of the individual totals of each child in the group.

Extracting Accounting Data

The `limreport` command allows you to query any attributes, including the accrue attributes, of any user. The command provides a executable method for the selection of information to be displayed from the chosen lnodes.

The `limadm` command provides a mechanism to reset the usage data of each user at an appropriate point, the timing of which will depend on the billing strategy.

1. Zero Usage Counters   # limadm set cpu.accrue=0 sales

2. Usage is accrued up the tree

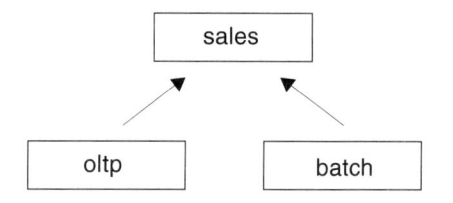

    sales
    ├── oltp
    └── batch

3. Usage may be reported with   # liminfo sales
   liminfo or limreport   # limreport 'uid==5000' '%f' cpu.accrue

FIGURE 7-25 Life Cycle of Usage Data

For example, if bills are to be produced at a group level, and then individual bills are to be produced for the group members, the accrue attributes of the group members would not be cleared until after both bills have been produced. However, if individual bills are not to be produced, the group members' accrue attributes may be cleared at the same time as the group header's, even though they may not have been individually used.

If we take a look at one of the previous examples that use a multi level hierarchy we can look at the points of the hierarchy from which we would want to take usage information.

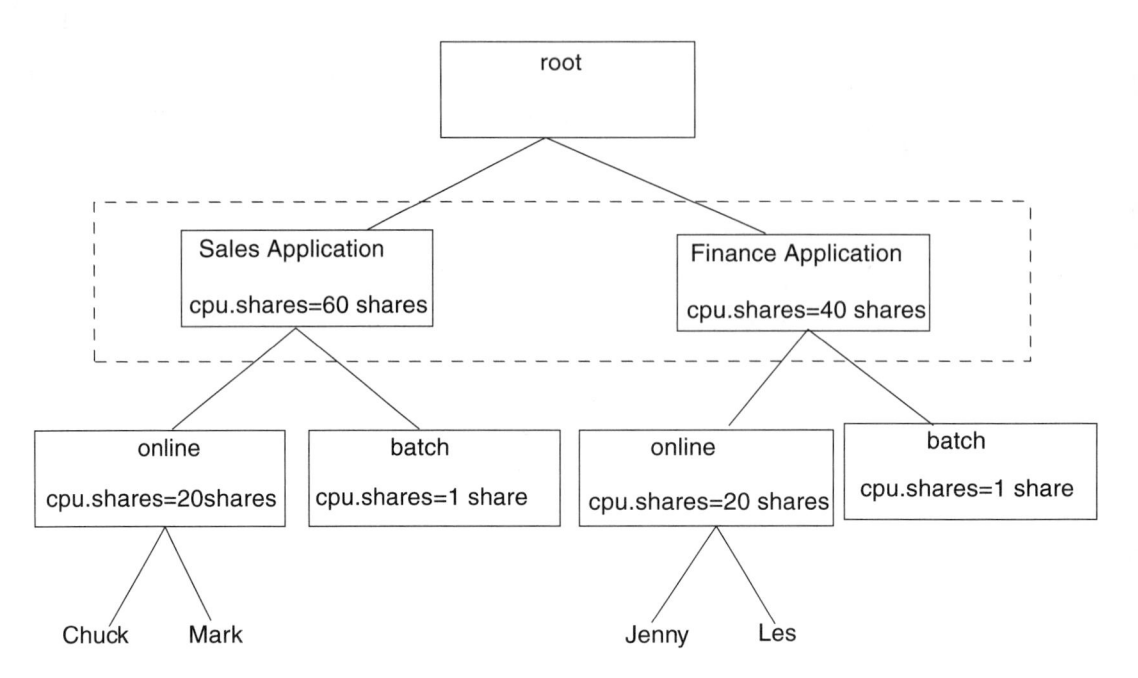

```
                              root
                           /        \
            Sales Application       Finance Application
            cpu.shares=60 shares    cpu.shares=40 shares
              /        \              /         \
         online       batch        online       batch
     cpu.shares=     cpu.shares=  cpu.shares=  cpu.shares=
     20shares        1 share      20 shares    1 share
       /    \                      /    \
    Chuck  Mark                  Jenny  Les
```

FIGURE 7-26 A Sample Hierarchy

The `limreport` and `liminfo` Commands

A common requirement might be to generate billing information for all users in the online group. We can do this with the `limreport` command:

```
# limreport 'flag.real==set && sgroup=online' '%f' cpu.accrue
```

At a global level we may want to know the usage information for the two departments, sales and finance. This can be obtained by looking at the lnodes for finance and sales since the usage information is accrued up the hierarchy.

188 Resource Management

You can use the `liminfo` command to display the resource usage information for both lnodes and to print a list of lnodes matching a certain criteria.

```
# liminfo -c sales
Login name:              sales         Uid (Real,Eff):        5000 (-,-)
Sgroup (uid):         root (0)         Gid (Real,Eff):         200 (-,-)

Shares:                     60         Myshares:                  0
Share:                    41 %         E-share:                 0 %
Usage:                  880425         Accrued usage:    3.28954e+09

Mem usage:     890.0859 / 484.2266 MB  Term usage:          2d9h8m41s
Mem limit:                   0 B       Term accrue:         2d9h8m41s
Proc mem limit:              0 B       Term limit:                 0s
Mem accrue:     3.247672902309 PB.s

Processes:              110 / 56       Current logins:             0
Process limit:               0

Last used: Tue Oct 4 15:04:20 1998
Directory: /
Name:      Sales node in hierarchy
Shell:     /bin/false

Flags:
```

You can also use the `limreport` to view the group level information with selective formatting.

```
# limreport 'flag.real==set && uid==5000' - lname cpu.accrue

# limreport 'flag.real==set && uid==5000' '%-20s %20.0f' lname cpu.accrue
```

The `limreport` command is a flexible report generator that can produce reports using the fields from the lnodes. It does this by doing a linear scan though the `passwd` database and looking up the lnode for each entry. Notice that in our example the match criteria includes the `flag.real==set`, this is to prevent `limreport` from trying to get data from lnodes that don't yet exist, which is likely if the user has never logged in. The complete list of fields available to `limreport` are shown in TABLE 7-3.

TABLE 7-3 Identifiers to the `limreport` Command

Identifier	Description
lname	string; login name
uid	integer; userid
gid	integer; initial groupid
pword	string; encrypted password
dirpath	string; initial (home) directory
shellpath	string; initial shell
comment	string; the comment, or gecos field
gecos	string; a synonym for comment
sgroupname	string; the login name of the user's scheduling group parent
now	integer; the current time
level	integer; the depth of the lnode in the scheduling tree; root is 0. For orphan lnodes, this is the depth within the disjoint tree
orphan	integer; is non-zero if the lnode is an orphan
preserve	string; a list of attribute value assignments using the syntax of `limadm` (1MSRM). Read-only attributes are omitted from the list. The command: `limreport 'flag.real' - lname preserve` will generate output which, if passed to limadm using the `-f` option, will completely reconstruct the state of all users' lnodes at the time of execution of the limreport command
myuid	integer; the userid of the lnode to which `limreport` is attached
mylname	string; the login name corresponding to myuid
clear	flag; a constant
set	flag; a constant
group	flag; a constant
inherit	flag; a constant
shellpath	string; initial shell

The full list of identifiers can be obtained with the `limreport -?` command.

The operators to the `limreport` command are summarized in TABLE 7-4.

TABLE 7-4 Operators to the `limreport` Command

Op	Description	Op	Description
*/	Multiply/divide	%	Integer modulo
:+ -	Add/subtract	& | ^	Bitwise and/or/exclusive-or
~	Bitwise complement	:	Is a member of scheduling group
== !=	Equal/not equal to	> <	Greater/less than
>= <=	Greater/less than or equal to	&& ||	Logical and/or
{...}	A date and time		
!	Unary logical not	(expr)	A sub-expression

On systems with large password databases using name servers, the `limreport` command can take a very long time to execute. This can be resolved by setting the `/etc/nsswitch.conf` to files if absolutely necessary.

CHAPTER **8**

Dynamic System Domains and Dynamic Reconfiguration

In the Resource Management framework, the Sun Enterprise 10000 (Starfire) Server's Dynamic System Domains (DSDs) provide the unique capability of dynamically relocating CPU, memory, and I/O resources within the same machine to accomplish expected service levels. DSDs provide a coarse-grained management of resources since the technology is restricted to relocating system boards with all of the allocated components (all or nothing CPU, memory and I/O resources hosted by a system board).

DSDs are logical, hardware-isolated server entities that can add (attach) or remove (detach) hardware resources through the use of Dynamic Reconfiguration (DR) software, without incurring any down time on their operating system instances. DSD's electrical isolation provides a fault-fencing mechanism which allows applications to run independently of each other within the same machine. In addition, DSDs can increase their Reliability, Availability, and Serviceability (RAS) service levels by making use of the Sun™ Cluster software.

Dynamic System Domains

DSDs are Starfire's independent hardware entities formed by the logical association of system boards. DSD is the preferred term when referring to Starfire domains because the generic term "domain" is overused by the industry to reflect different applications (for example, mail servers, name servers, and Microsoft Windows NT have distinct representations of "domains").

The current second generation Starfire DSD technology was originally introduced in 1995 with the Cray CS6400 machine (it later became the Sun CS6400 server). DSDs were originally inspired by the Multiple Domain Feature™ (MDF™) hardware capability introduced by Amdahl® Corporation in 1985, which allowed CPU and I/O resources on their mainframes to be allocated to logical entities and concurrently run multiple operating system instances on the same machine.

Mainframe companies have enjoyed plenty of time to develop robustness in their operating systems and hardware. High mainframe prices have appropriately funded engineering developments and materials cost. However, the Starfire platform implements some of the best mainframe attributes at a fraction of the cost, while still providing a larger memory capability and improved I/O capacity and performance.

DSDs are separate Solaris servers in their own right. Each has a separate boot disk (to execute a private instance of the Solaris operating environment) as well as separate disk storage, network interfaces, and I/O interfaces. In addition, system board resources can be relocated between DSDs within the same machine to accommodate workload needs without having to stop running applications or reboot the machine.

Theoretically, the Starfire server can support 16 DSDs, but 8 is the currently supported maximum. The granularity of floating resources allocated to DSDs is the system board. The Starfire platform supports a maximum of 16 system boards with each system board configured to contain a maximum of:

- 4 CPUs
- 4 Gbytes of memory, 32*128 Mbyte DIMMs (dual in-line memory modules)
- 4 SBUS I/O interfaces or 2 PCI I/O interfaces

When to Use Dynamic System Domains

DSDs alleviate the need to over-configure hardware to handle peak loads and eliminate idle or under-utilized resources because they can be dynamically re-allocated without the need for a reboot. Currently, there are no mechanisms to manage the automatic transfer of system boards between DSDs based on workload needs. Such process currently requires manual operator intervention.

DSDs are well suited to commercial applications because of their manageability, flexible processing, I/O capacity, as well as their fault and resource isolation features. Because DSDs are virtual independent machines, *all* Solaris applications and available resource management tools that apply to the entire Sun Enterprise 3000-6500 Server line are available.

Relationship to Other Solaris Resource Management Products

The `psrset` utility can create processor sets to address individual processing needs of different workloads within the same DSD. The Solaris Resource Manager (SRM) product enables an enhanced workload resource control over `psrset` by managing CPU, Virtual Memory, number of processes, number of logins and connect time to achieve a guaranteed service level for each application.

The SyMON product can currently be used to monitor each individual DSD and to perform limited control functions; however, the System Service Processor (SSP) is still the primary administrative interface for DSDs. The Solaris Bandwidth Manager product can be used to address the individual network bandwidth requirements of separate workloads within the same DSD.

Server Consolidation Workload

DSDs provide the simplest approach to customers entertaining server consolidation, which is an attempt to relocate applications running on smaller servers into a single physical footprint, thereby reducing data center space. DSDs provide a guarantee that a misbehaving workload will not affect the rest of the consolidated applications because each instance is restricted by hardware to its own Solaris operating environment.

The maximum number of DSDs supported by a single Starfire platform represents the hard limit on the number of distinct workloads to be consolidated. Having numerous DSDs restricts the amount of shared resources, while it increases administrative overhead.

SRM can take advantage of the large size, scalability, and performance of a single Starfire DSD by enabling a higher granularity of resource management. SRM does not currently control physical memory and DSDs are still the best way to consolidate memory-intensive workloads.

Database Workload

Dynamic Reconfiguration (DR) is a software mechanism that allows resources to be attached (logically added) or detached (logically removed) from the Solaris operating environment control and without incurring any system downtime.

Commercial Relational Database Management Systems (RDBMS) vendors such as Oracle®, IBM® DB2, Informix®, and Sybase®, attempt to guarantee a service level by reserving system resources and controlling how and when such resources are utilized.

Because each RDBMS vendor has its own proprietary architecture, each is affected differently by the dynamic resource increments or decrements introduced by DR. A table of database resource management compatibility can be found in TABLE 4-2.

Dynamic CPU Resources

Oracle™ 7.x and 8.0 are process-based products that can tolerate the increment and decrement of CPU resources introduced by DR. However there are some performance implications when changing the number or processors for a running instance. (See Oracle8*i* "Databases in a Resource Managed Environment" on page 77). The Oracle Resource Manager must know exactly how many processors are available, and currently must be restarted after a DR event that chages the number of processors.

DB2 Universal Database™ (UDB) is a process-based product that can easily adapt to the increment and decrement of CPU resources introduced by DR. DB2 UDB uses shadow processes that uneventfully get queued to run across an expanded or reduced CPU pool through the Solaris kernel scheduler. A reduction of CPUs available to the Solaris kernel scheduler will have a negative impact on performance by having the same number of processes allocated to fewer CPUs.

Sybase Adaptive Server Enterprise™ (ASE) is engine-based and each configured engine is typically assigned to an available CPU. A Database Administrator (DBA) can dynamically register a CPU resource increment by bringing up more engines, but engines are not allowed to be dynamically removed. Sybase ASE will be adding the capability to bring down engines in version 12.0, which is expected to be available by the end of 1999.

Informix OnLine Dynamic Server™ (ODS) allows a number of CPUs to be added to a specific processing class (CPU, AIO, PIO, LIO, SHM, STR, TLI, and SOC) using the `onmode` command. Informix ODS only allows CPUs to be removed from the CPU class provided polling threads are not executed (poll threads can be assigned to run in a degraded mode in the SHM, TLI or TLI classes instead).

Dynamic Memory Resources

Many databases make use of the Intimate Shared Memory (ISM) capability in the Solaris operating environment where shared memory can be exclusively reserved and locked into RAM to prevent paging. ISM makes use of the shared page table, to make more efficient use of the page translation lookaside buffers (TLBs). Informix Online Dynamic Server™ is the only RDBMS that currently allows dynamic addition or removal of its shared memory allocation.

During a DR-detach process, the ISM associated with the system board being removed is considered non-pageable memory and needs to be relocated to memory available on the remaining boards (the DR operation will fail if there is insufficient memory available in the remaining system boards).

During a DR-attach process, the allocated shared-memory size for the database will not change since it is statically registered in the database configuration. The only way to increase the shared-memory footprint increasing system memory through a DR-attach process is by shutting down the database instance, changing the database shared-memory parameters in the configuration file, and then restarting the database.

DSD Implementation Examples

To get a better idea about the resource management role of DSDs in the data center, we'll consider three different Starfire setups represented in FIGURE 8-1. Keep in mind that every scenario introduces the opportunity to relocate resources between DSDs in anticipation of the variable workload demands perceived on a real-time, daily, weekly or a monthly basis. When relocating a system board to a DSD, some of the components can be ruled out of the configuration for security purposes or simply to speed up the DR-attach process through use of the `blacklist(4)` file.

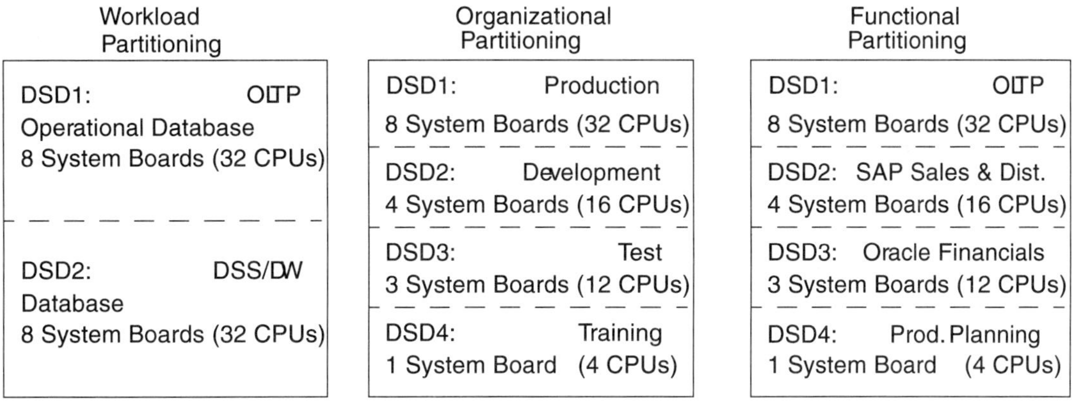

Workload Partitioning	Organizational Partitioning	Functional Partitioning
DSD1: OLTP Operational Database 8 System Boards (32 CPUs)	DSD1: Production 8 System Boards (32 CPUs)	DSD1: OLTP 8 System Boards (32 CPUs)
	DSD2: Development 4 System Boards (16 CPUs)	DSD2: SAP Sales & Dist. 4 System Boards (16 CPUs)
DSD2: DSS/DW Database 8 System Boards (32 CPUs)	DSD3: Test 3 System Boards (12 CPUs)	DSD3: Oracle Financials 3 System Boards (12 CPUs)
	DSD4: Training 1 System Board (4 CPUs)	DSD4: Prod. Planning 1 System Board (4 CPUs)

FIGURE 8-1 DSDs Implementation Examples

Workload Partitioning: OLTP and DSS/DW

The Decision Support System/Data Warehousing (DSS/DW) workload involves the movement of large amounts of continuous disk data into the server for analysis. Such operation will normally consume all available I/O bandwidth and available CPU capacity.

Online Transaction Processing (OLTP), in contrast with DSS/DW, involves massive registration of small asynchronous transactions, each requiring minimal CPU capacity and real-time random access to small portions of disk data.

OLTP and DSS/DW applications do not provide a good working solution when placed on the same server because OLTP transactions might get delayed whenever outstanding DSS/DW queries consume all available server resources. A single Starfire can easily support these two conflicting workloads by providing two separate DSD instances, which establish the required hardware isolation and appropriate separation of the operating system instances.

In this example, the OLTP DSD has the ability to relocate system boards from the DSS DSD to meet the high volume of OLTP transactions during peak hours. The DSS DSD can also have resource-demanding queries postponed to a time when the OLTP transactions are minimal and system boards can be safely relocated from the OLTP DSD.

In addition, DSDs introduce the possibility of instantly migrating OLTP data resident on disk devices and making it immediately available to the DSS/DW DSD without resorting to time-consuming network transfers.

Organizational Partitioning: Production, Development, Test, Training

DSDs can produce separate processing nodes in support of software development, training and testing or simply to allow organizations that share ownership of the Starfire platform to have their own private piece of the machine. The Test DSD in this example can take resources from the Training and Development DSD whenever new software or operating system releases need testing before getting rolled out into production.

Customers can easily create and remove DSDs outside of their production environments to help support functions that are important but not critical in the data center environment.

Functional Partitioning: OLTP, Sales, Financials, Planning

DSDs allow partitioning of a Starfire platform in support of different processing functions within the same company. The importance of processing functions within a company varies with time, and DSD resources can be re-allocated to serve those varying needs. As an example, the sales and distribution function becomes more important than the production planning function during a quarter-end cycle. System boards from the production planning DSD can be migrated to the sales and distribution DSD to help meet the anticipated seasonal surge in the workload.

Resource Management Controls

DR was an exclusive feature of the Starfire platform, but it now supports the entire Sun Enterprise 3000-6500 Server line. The Starfire DR allows the relocation of resources within a single system (a Starfire chassis), while the Sun Enterprise 3000-6500 DR allows the relocation of resources between separate systems.

DR works in conjunction with the hot-swap hardware capability to allow the physical insertion or removal of system boards. Additionally, DR increases the level of availability and serviceability by providing a way to execute on-line hardware upgrades and maintenance.

The Starfire DR provides full functionality (CPU, memory, and I/O interfaces) starting with the Solaris 2.5.1 release. In contrast, the Sun Enterprise 3000-6500 DR provides full functionality after the Solaris 7 (5/99) release and support for I/O interfaces only in the Solaris 2.6. 5/98 release (see TABLE 8-1).

TABLE 8-1 Dynamic Reconfiguration Functionality Matrix

Solaris Version	Starfire	Sun Enterprise 3000-6500
Solaris 2.5.1	Yes	No
Solaris 2.6	Yes	Support for I/O interfaces only in 5/98 release
Solaris 7	Yes, in 5/99 release	Yes, in 5/99 release

If required, Alternate Pathing (AP) software provides an additional mechanism in support of DR to provide redundant disk and network controllers (and their respective physical links) to sustain continuous network and disk I/O when resources are removed (detached) from a DSD. While AP is supported on both the Starfire and the Sun Enterprise 3000-6500 servers, it is *not* a prerequisite for DR.

Managing Resources with Starfire DR

The Starfire DR has an extended resource management functionality over the Sun Enterprise 3000-6500 DR since it enables system resource sharing between DSDs. The Starfire DR allows the logical detachment of a system board from a *provider DSD* (DSD from which resources are borrowed) and the logical attachment of the same system board to a *receptor DSD* (DSD where loaned resources are applied). The Sun Enterprise 3000-6500 DR is also equipped to handle logical sharing, but it would require idle resources within the same server be activated only when they are needed.

To provide a mental picture of all resource management issues involved when using DSDs we'll next present a hypothethical HPC (High Performance Computing) workload in need of more CPU power, a larger memory footprint, and an increased disk I/O bandwidth. Each of the HPC workload resource needs is addressed as a separate instance in the following paragraphs and each instance is assumed to have fulfilled appropriate DR pre-requisites.

Managing CPU Resources

If the hypothetical HPC workload running on a Starfire DSD had access to a system board populated with just CPUs, then the detach sequence executed in the *provider DSD* followed by the attach sequence in the *receptor DSD* would take the same amount of time every single time (approximately one minute for the detach process and approximately six minutes for the attach process).

Managing Memory Resources

If the hypothetical HPC workload running on a Starfire DSD had access to a system board populated with just memory, then the detach time would be variable, depending on how much of that memory is being used by the *provider DSD*. There is no such thing as a Starfire system board populated with just memory since at least one on-board CPU is required to enable Power-On Self-Test (POST) execution.

All dirty memory pages resident on the board to be detached get immediately flushed to the swap area (either memory or disk), while all non-pageable memory gets copied to the available memory remaining in the *provider DSD* system. The time required for the attach process is determined by the execution of POST (approximately six minutes with default POST level 16).

The kernel cage is a special data structure (normally contained by a single system board) which controls the dynamic growth of all non-relocatable memory, including the OpenBoot™ PROM (OBP) and kernel memory. When detaching a system board containing the kernel cage, you must quiesce the operating system to ensure that no I/O or kernel activity exists while the kernel cage is being relocated. The operating system quiescence involves the suspension of *all* device driver activity and user/kernel threads to avoid corruption of such critical memory.

During a DR-detach process, the ISM associated with the system board being removed is locked down and cannot be paged out to disk. ISM will always be relocated to memory available on the remaining system boards. If a system is already experiencing memory pressure (paging and swapping), the removal of existing system memory to make room for the ISM footprint will impact the performance of running applications and delay the DR-detach operation.

Note – After the release of the Solaris 7 software, the kernel cage is confined to the highest physical address which translates to the highest numbered system board in the DSD. There is a patch to the SSP software which introduces the appropriate modifications to `hpost(1M)` to override the Starfire's physical memory address change introduced with the Solaris 7 software and preserve the kernel cage in the lowest numbered system board. The Sun Enterprise 3000-6500 DR *does not* allow the relocation of the kernel cage.

Managing I/O Resources

If the hypothetical HPC workload running on a Starfire DSD had access to a system board populated with just disk I/O interfaces then the detach time will be dependent on the number of disk devices and the queued pending transfers because they need to be serviced before the I/O interfaces are quiesced. Again, there is no such thing as a Starfire system board populated with just I/O interfaces because at least one on-board CPU is required to enable POST execution.

Starfire DR-Detach and DR-Attach Timing Reference

To provide a sense of timing for the DR-detach and DR-attach operations, we refer to a lab exercise, executed under the Solaris 2.6 operating environment and using System Service Processor software version 3.1, where we relocated a system board populated with the following:

- Four 250 Mhz UltraSPARC-II CPUs with 4Mbytes of external cache
- One Gigabyte of memory

- Four SBus FWDIFF-SCSI controllers attached to seven tape drives (contained by a single Sun StorEdge™ L3500 tape library

The recorded times for the DR-detaching operations involved in releasing the system board from the provider DSD were as follows:

- The drain of the 1 Gigabyte resident memory took approximately two minutes
- DR-detach completion process took approximately one minute.

The times for the DR-attaching operations involved in introducing the system board to the receptor DSD were as follows:

- The POST execution against the newly attached system board (with default POST level 16) took approximately six minutes.
- DR-attach completion process: approximately one minute

Note – The timing references introduced in this section reflect the lower end of the spectrum since they were extracted from an idle system. The detach and attach times in a production environment will depend on the system load. The DR-detach operations described in this section reflect the installation of the appropriate collection of patches required for DR as well as ensuring that any non-DR-compliant driver instances contained by the system board were appropriately unloaded.

DR with and without DSDs

In the interest of resource management and to have DR best serve your application needs, you must understand the differences between the DR capabilities applicable to the Starfire and those applicable to the Sun Enterprise 3000-6500 servers.

The Sun Enterprise 3000-6500 DR is simpler in nature because it doesn't support DSDs, and its functionality is limited to bringing brand new system board resources into the Solaris instance or detaching system boards to be serviced or shared with other Sun Enterprise 3000-6500 servers.

In contrast, the Starfire DR is more complex in nature because it includes all of the Sun Enterprise 3000-6500 DR functionality as well as DSD support to allow resource sharing within the same platform.

Resource Sharing

In the Resource Management framework, the Sun Enterprise 3000-6500 platforms are limited to physically sharing system board resources with other Sun Enterprise 3000-6500 platforms. Physical sharing involves the powering down and physical removal of a system board from a system (after having it removed from Solaris operating environment control). After the system board has been removed from the original system, it can then be inserted into an alternate system, powered up, and registered with the active Solaris operating environment instance.

Both the Starfire and Sun Enterprise 3000-6500 platforms share the risk of having bent pins damage the backplane interface and bring down the whole Solaris operating environment instance when exercising physical sharing. The Starfire DR eliminates the danger of having bent pins or worn out connectors by allowing the logical relocation of system boards between DSDs.

Note – Physical removal or installation of system boards might invalidate service contracts if attempted by non-qualified service personnel.

Memory Interleaving

The Starfire and Sun Enterprise 3000-6500 platforms *require* that memory interleaving be disabled in order to support DR. Memory interleaving helps increase memory subsystem performance by reducing the probability of hot spots or contention in a few memory banks by spreading access to multiple memory banks.

The active Gigaplane-XB™ interconnect on the Starfire provides main memory access through a point-to-point data router, which isolates data traffic between system boards and minimizes any performance degradation when memory interleaving is disabled. The passive Gigaplane bus interconnect on the Sun Enterprise 3000-6500 platforms is shared by all system boards and may introduce performance degradation with memory intensive workloads when memory interleaving is disabled.

System Board Diagnostics

The Sun Enterprise 3000-6500 DR executes POST as soon as the system board is attached to the system. The Sun Enterprise 3000-6500 system boards do not have hardware isolation applicable to DSDs and will expose the server to the possibility of bringing down its active Solaris operating environment instance by registering faulty on-board components. The Starfire DR, in contrast, controls the POST operation from the SSP over the JTAG (Joint Test Action Group, IEEE Std. 1149.1) interface and does not activate a newly attached system board until its full functionality is guaranteed.

Note – The Starfire DR allows an increased test coverage on all system board components by temporarily increasing the POST level through modification of the SSP's `postrc(4)` file.

User Interfaces

Both the Sun Enterprise 3000-6500 DR and Starfire DR functions have their own private user interfaces that require manual intervention from a system administrator. The Sun Enterprise 3000-6500 DR uses the SyMON framework and the `cfgadm(1M)` command interface to invoke the required DR functions.

The `cfgadm(1M)` command provides an interface to build automated DR scripts. Script building for unattended DR operations must be handled with caution when detaching a system board because removing system resources may have a negative impact on applications executing in the machine.

The SSP manages all the resources that are allocated to DSDs and keeps track of their boundaries; thus, it has to initiate all DR operations. The Starfire DR is performed through the following SSP applications:

- The `drview(1M)` command, which produces a GUI to be invoked only through the `hostview(1M)` interface, see FIGURE 8-2.

- The `dr(1M)` command, a Tool Command Language (TCL) application that produces a command line interface monitor that supports a set of commands that integrate all DR functionality, see FIGURE 8-3.

Currently, the Starfire DR user interface does not provide mechanisms to automate DR operations. The current user interfaces are exclusively interactive.

FIGURE 8-2 The SSP Hostview `drview` Application

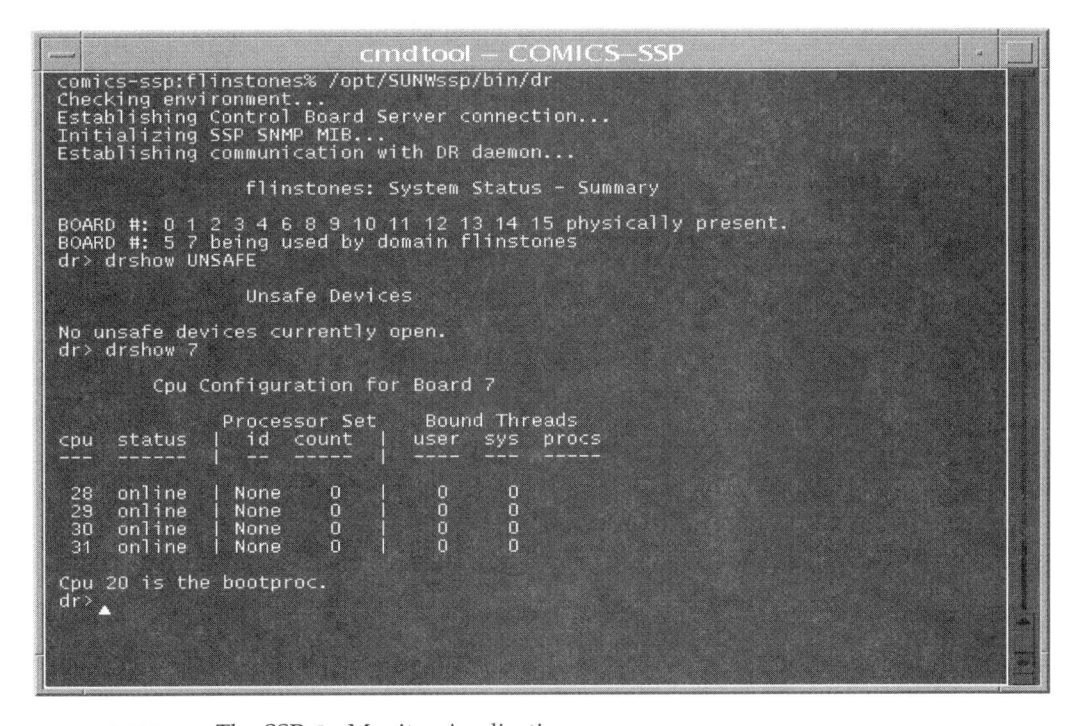

FIGURE 8-3 The SSP `dr` Monitor Application

Chapter 8   Dynamic System Domains and Dynamic Reconfiguration   205

Clustered DSDs

In the clustering world, DSDs qualify as independent servers and can be clustered to enhance hardware availability for mission-critical applications. The following are four recommended failover permutations of DSD clustering through use of the Sun Cluster 2.2 software ranging from the highest to the lowest availability level (see FIGURE 8-4):

- Clustering of two DSDs in two separate Starfire cabinets each with many DSDs. This configuration is applicable to servers handling customer orders and money transactions that are intolerant of system down time
- Clustering of two DSDs in two separate Starfire cabinets, each with a single DSD which is applicable to read-only databases with backed-up source data
- Clustering of a DSD and a non-Starfire external system, which is applicable to file and print servers handling non-critical data
- Clustering of two DSDs within the same Starfire cabinet, which is applicable to development servers that are tolerant of system downtime

Currently, clustered DSD nodes do not support DR because of the amount of time involved quiescing (suspending) the operating system whenever the *kernel cage* needs to be relocated. The time that the operating system spends in the suspended state is dependent upon system resource availability during the DR-detach operation. A really busy system might stay in the suspended state for a long time and trigger a non-responsive node alarm in the cluster management software.

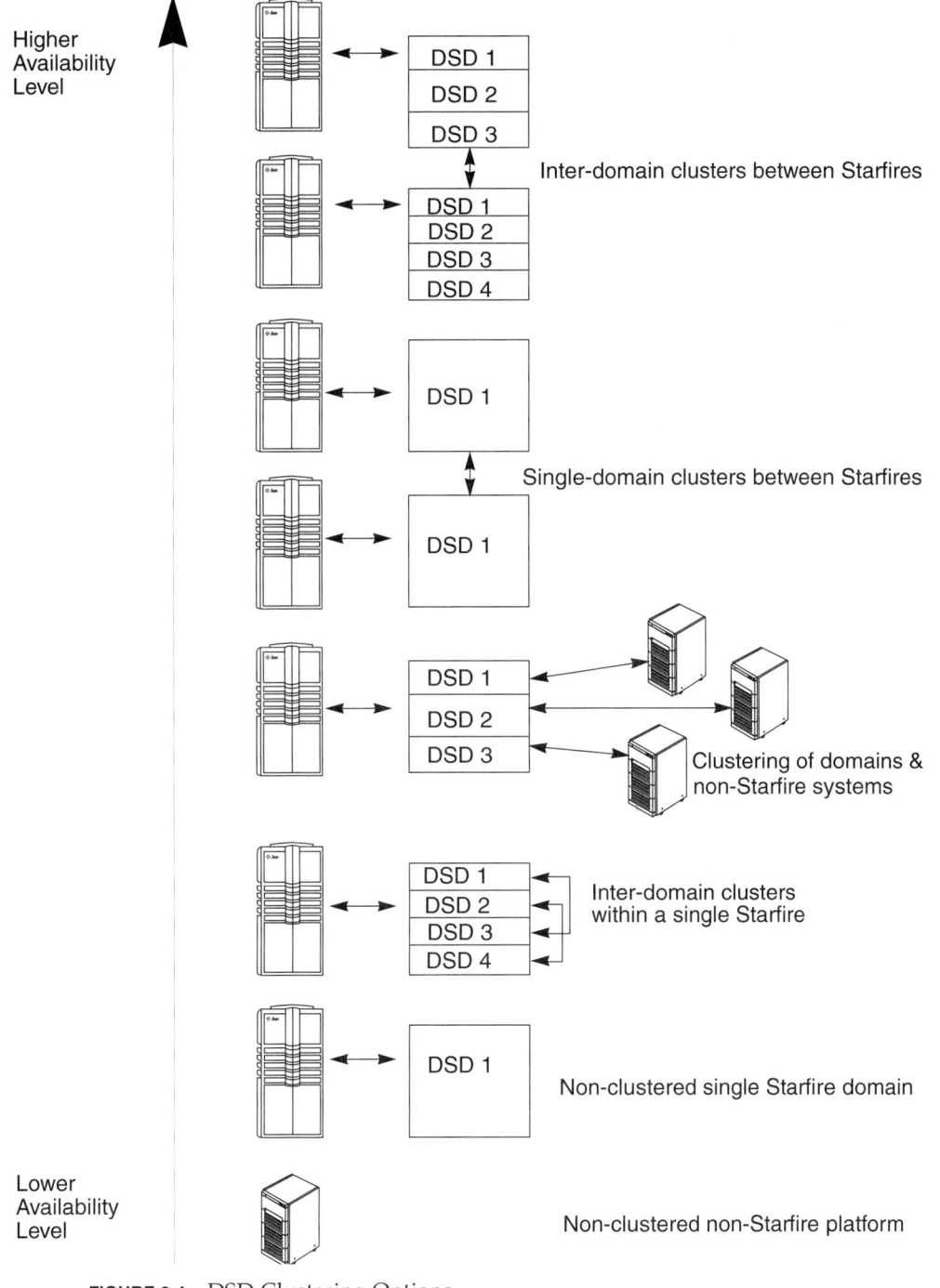

FIGURE 8-4 DSD Clustering Options

Chapter 8 Dynamic System Domains and Dynamic Reconfiguration 207

Starfire Architecture

Each DSD is centrally managed by the SSP. The SSP is an independent workstation loaded with the Solaris operating environment and additional SUNWsspxxx software packages, which manages the Starfire hardware and DSD resource allocation (see FIGURE 8-5). The SSP manipulates system board hardware registers through an Ethernet link attached to the control board to reflect DSD boundaries. The control board converts TCP/IP traffic from the SSP to the JTAG protocol.

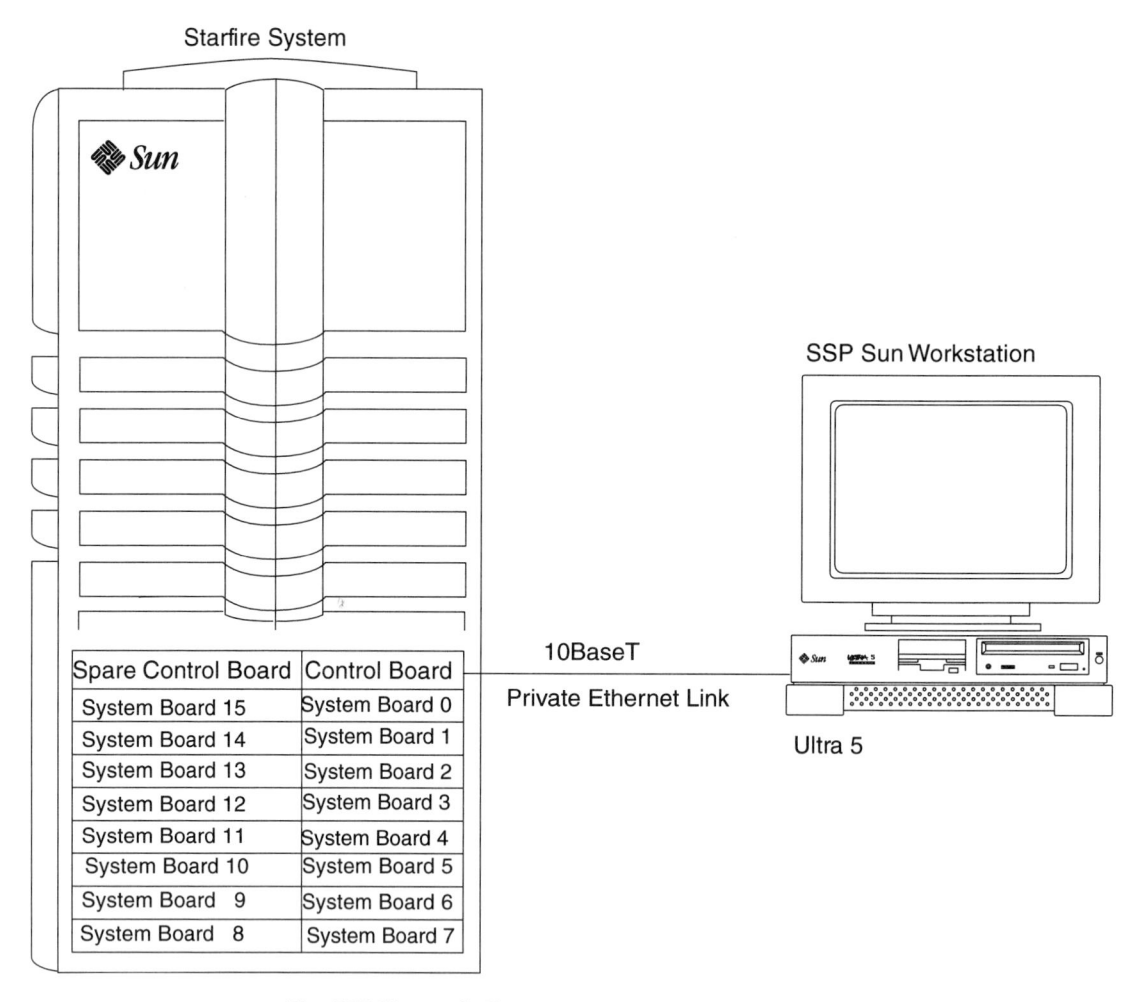

FIGURE 8-5 The SSP Network Connection

The Gigaplane-XB interconnect is at the heart of the Starfire's high performance, availability, and scalability. It uses four interleaved address buses, a 16x16 interboard data crossbar, and point-to-point routing for all of the interconnect data, arbitration, and address busses. The implementation of point-to-point routing provides the electrical isolation that enforces hardware and software independence between DSDs by filtering all address requests.

There is always at least one DSD in the machine, each containing a minimum of one system board (4 CPUs) and a maximum of 16 system boards (64 CPUs on a fully configured machine).

A primary DSD for the Starfire system is created at the factory using a DSD key, which is a special string of alphanumeric characters required by the SSP to create the required DSD data structures. Each DSD has a unique hostid, a machine identity used by software licensing schemes, which is extracted from the DSD key.

Note – Each DSD qualifies as an independent machine and is normally separately licensed by software vendors. Some software vendors are already providing DSD licensing discounts.

Each DSD is allocated its own directory structure on the SSP, which contains an OBP image as well as hardware logs that are being extracted on a continuous basis. Each DSD forwards system logs to the SSP through the `syslog.conf(4)` file, which builds a centralized error message repository in the SSP's `/var/adm/messages` log file.

Note – The `/var/adm/SUNWssp/adm/messages` file produces a general log of the SSP and all DSDs interaction. The `/var/adm/SUNWssp/adm/`*domainname*`/messages` log file produces a detailed log of the SSP and each DSD (*domainname*) interaction.

FIGURE 8-6 shows the Hostview GUI, the system administration application on the SSP, which provides a visual representation of DSDs and the Starfire platform. All system boards and active/standby control boards plug into the centerplane (eight system boards plus a control board in the front and eight system boards plus a spare control board in the back). The active centerplane has four address buses and two paths to each half of the data crossbar. When viewed on the screen, each system board icon has a color border representing the DSD to which it belongs.

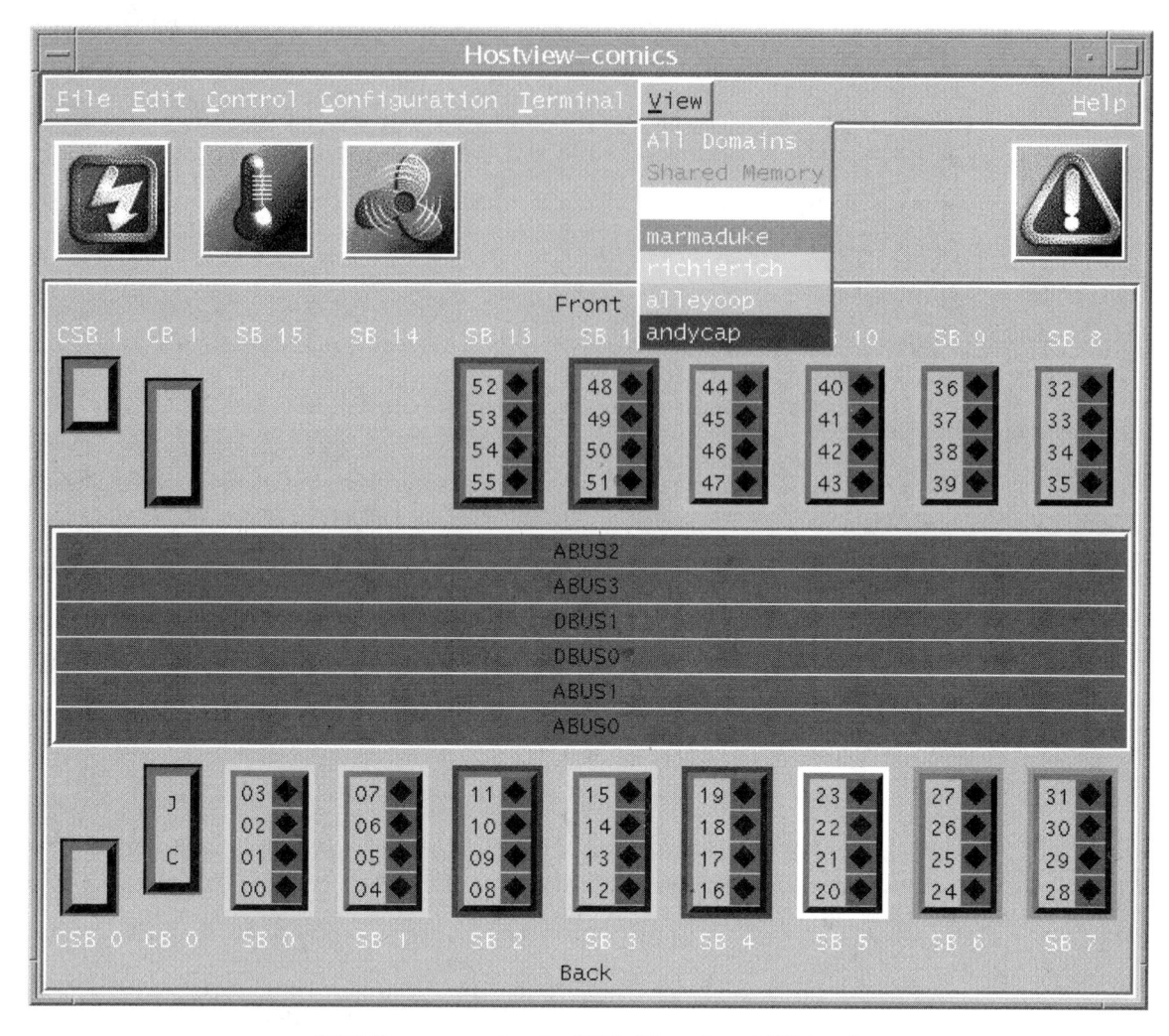

FIGURE 8-6 DSD Representation by SSP's Hostview GUI Application

Starfire DR Architecture

The DR framework was merged in Solaris 7 to provide some module commonality between the Starfire and the Sun Enterprise 3000-6500 platforms. FIGURE 8-7 shows all software modules involved in the Solaris 7 Starfire DR for both the SSP and DSD sides.

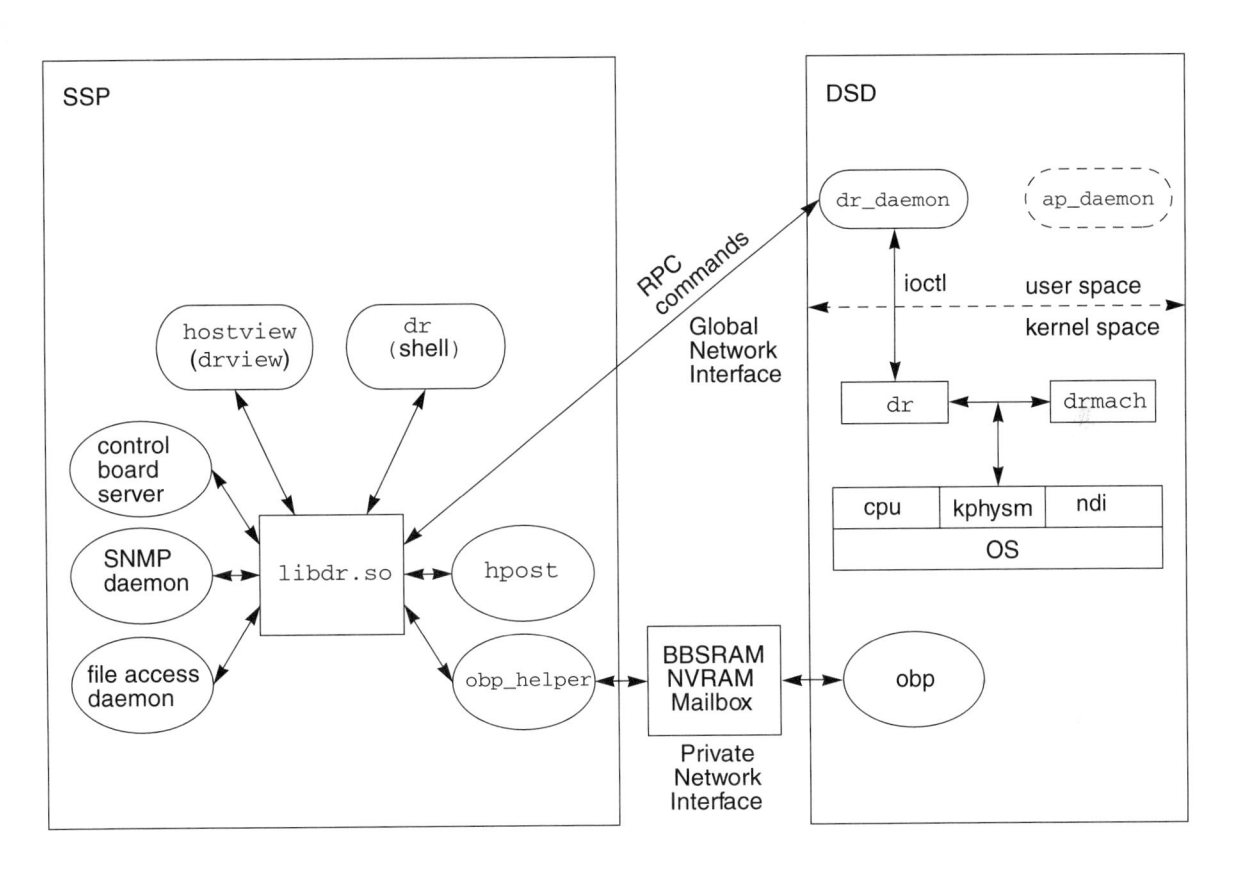

FIGURE 8-7 Solaris 7 5/99 Starfire DR Software Architecture

On the Starfire platform, all DR operations are initiated by the SSP, and only one outstanding operation is allowed at a time. Both the SSP and the DSD manage their own states to synchronize and guarantee the integrity of the DR operations.

The hostview(1M) and dr(1M) applications on the SSP provide user interfaces for executing DR operations. Both applications are dynamically linked to the libdr.so shared-object library, which provides access to the dr_daemon process on the DSD side through TCP/IP Remote Procedure Calls (rpc(3N)). The DR daemon process acts as a translator and intermediary between the SSP and the DSD.

The `libdr.so` library invokes both the `hpost(1M)` and `obp_helper(1M)` processes to register resource changes in the OBP kernel device tree and to execute POST on added system boards.

If the `ap_daemon` were present on the server, the `dr_daemon` process would communicate appropriate device information to invoke the rerouting of I/O calls through registered alternate devices. The `dr_daemon` invokes the `dr` driver module, which is a common, platform-independent module currently used by the Starfire platform only. The `dr` driver communicates with the loadable `drmach` platform-specific module to invoke hardware-specific functions. Currently, there is only one `drmach` module applicable to the Starfire platform.

The `ndi` (nexus device interface) layer provides the framework to manipulate the I/O device tree in support of the DR-attach and DR-detach operations. The `dr` module will register the addition or removal of CPU, memory and I/O resources using the generic Solaris kernel interfaces.

Starfire DR-Detach Details

The software mechanism by which Dynamic Reconfiguration reduces resources available to the operating system is called detaching (see FIGURE 8-8).

The DR-Detach process requires you to do strategic planning because it reduces the overall CPU and memory resources available to the DSD, and it may involve removing I/O interfaces that are critical to the operation of the machine. Before removing a system board, it is critical that all on-board I/O devices be closed since I/O drivers will fail to detach when an application has open device instances.

Note that removing CPU and memory resources from an already busy system (a system running short of memory and using excessive amounts of CPU) will significantly delay the DR-Detach process because the removed memory will have to be transferred to the swap disk.

DR-Detach Prerequisites and Actions

To guarantee a successful DR-detach process the following rerequisites must be fulfilled:

Pre-Boot Requirements

The following prerequisites require a system reboot to take effect:

- All system memory must not be interleaved between system boards.
- In the Solaris 2.5.1 and Solaris 2.6 5/98 operating environments, the dr_max_mem OBP environment variable must be set to a value equal to or greater than 512 Mbytes. The dr_max_mem OBP environment variable is not required after Solaris 7 5/99 because the required VM structures are dynamically allocated.
- The soc driver requires the following entry in the /etc/system file to enable the suspend-resume/detach-attach features:
  - set soc:soc_enable_detach_suspend=1
- In the Solaris 2.6 5/98 operating environment, the socal driver requires the following entry in the /etc/system file to enable the suspend-resume features:
  - set socal:socal_enable_suspend=1
- The pln driver requires the following entry in the /etc/system file to enable the suspend-resume/detach-attach features:
  - set pln:pln_enable_detach_suspend=1
- Activation of the *kernel cage* requires the following entry in the /etc/system file:
  - set kernel_cage_enable=1

System Requirements

The following prerequisites need to be fulfilled immediately before the DR-Detach operation takes place:

- All on-board non-DR-compliant drivers need to be unloaded using the modunload(1M) utility.
- Real-time processes are *not* allowed whene the kernel cage is being relocated because their behavior becomes unpredictable with the operating system quiescence. All real-time processes must be reassigned an alternate scheduling class using the priocntl(1) command or killed using the kill(1) command. The hostview(1M) interface provides the force option to override this requirement.
- Processor sets or processes bound to CPUs hosted by the system board to be removed are *not* allowed. Processor sets must be torn down using the psrset(1M) command and processes bound to on-board processors must be unbounded using the pbind(1M) command.

- All swap devices contained by the system board must be deleted using the `swap(1M)` command and removed from the `/etc/vfstab` file.
- All on-board non-network I/O interfaces must be brought down.
- All file systems hosted by the system board to be detached must be unmounted.
- If AP is not used, disks hosted by the system board to be detached must be removed from Veritas VxVM control using the `vxdiskadm(1M)` command with the `replace` option.
- Tape drives hosted by the system board that is to be detached must be empty or have a loaded tape sitting at `BOT`.

DR-Detach Actions

The following steps are automatically executed on both the SSP and DSD sides during the DR-Detach operation:

1. All free pages associated with the system board to be detached are locked to avoid further use by applications. All dirty pages are flushed to swap (swap could be either memory or disk).

2. ISM *must* be relocated to memory available on the remaining system. If there isn't available memory, dirty pages from the remaining system are flushed to disk to make room for the ISM footprint.

3. If the kernel cage is located on the system board to be detached, the `dr` driver invokes the `DDI_SUSPEND` driver function on all I/O devices in the system and the operating system is quiesced (suspended) to allow the safe relocation of the entire address range associated with the system board to be detached.

Note – When the kernel cage is relocated, a target system board is selected (out of the remaining system) to absorb the entire memory address range assigned to the board being detached. The relocation process involves releasing the memory content from the *target system board* as defined in steps 1-2 above. Once the memory content is evacuated out of the target system board, the entire memory range for the board to be detached is transferred to the target system board through the copy-rename routine (running out of a single CPU cache). When the copy-rename routine completes, the memory controller on the target system board is updated to reflect the physical address range of the copied memory and the whole system is then *resumed*.

4. If the board to be detached *does not* contain the kernel cage, its associated address range is removed from the system. If the kernel cage is located on the system board to be detached, the address range associated with the *target system board* is removed from the system.

5. The memory controller on the detached board is disabled and the removed memory is taken out of the kernel memory pool.

6. All processors resident on the system board to be detached are offlined and removed from the kernel configuration. The Boot processor is reassigned if needed.

7. The `dr_daemon` automatically downs and unplumbs all network devices resident on the system board.

8. The `dr` driver invokes the `DDI_DETACH` function on all onboard I/O devices. The kernel updates the operating system device tree (`devinfo`) to reflect the removed I/O devices.

9. The SSP reprograms the detached system board and centerplane hardware registers to remove any DSD association. The `domain_config(4)` is executed to remove the detached board from the DSD configuration.

Pre-Boot Requirements:

-System memory must not be interleaved.
-The `dr_max_mem` OBP variable must be set (not needed after Solaris 7).
-The `/etc/system` entries for `soc/socal/pln` drivers must be in place.
-The `/etc/system` entry to enable the kernel cage must be in place.

System Requirements:

-On-board non DR-compliant drivers must be unloaded.
-All Real Time processes must be deactivated if kernel cage is relocated.
-On-board CPU binding to processes must be removed.
-On-board processor sets must be removed.
-On-board swap devices must be deleted.
-On-board non-network I/O interfaces must be brought down.
-On-board file systems must be unmounted.
-On-board disks must be removed from VxVM control.
-On-board tape drives should be empty or sitting at BOT.

DR-Detach System Board D →

DR-Detach Actions:

1. Free pages are locked and pageable memory is flushed to swap (memory or disk).
2. If kernel cage is relocated system is quiesced (DDI_SUSPEND invoked on all drivers), a target system board is selected to transfer memory range from detached board.
3. Detached memory is removed from kernel pool.
4. On-board processors are offlined and removed from kernel pool (boot proc. reassigned).
5. On-board network interfaces are automatically unplumbed.
6. If kernel cage is not relocated `dr` driver invokes DDI_DETACH on onboard drivers.
7. SSP executes `domain_config()` to remove detached system board from DSD.
8. SSP reprograms system board and centerplane hardware registers.
9. OBP updates the OBP device tree and kernel updates the OS device tree.
10. If device links need updated: drvconfig;devlinks;disks;ports;tapes sequence.

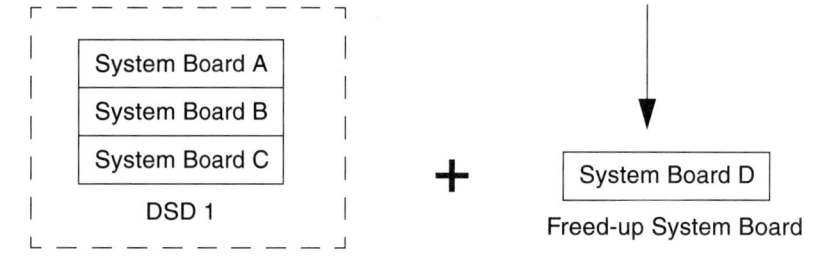

FIGURE 8-8 DR-Detaching a Single System Board from a DSD

Starfire DR-Attach Details

The software mechanism by which Dynamic Reconfiguration increases resources available to the operating system is called attaching (see FIGURE 8-9).

The DR-attach mechanism provides a way for the operating system to logically integrate new cpu, memory and I/O resources into its resource pool and make them immediately available to applications requiring the increased capacity. The

DR-attach process creates the appropriate device file links and loads the appropriate drivers to support the newly introduced I/O interfaces contained by the system board.

If there's a non-DR-compliant driver associated with the system board to be attached, the DR operation will not fail, but it will not load the appropriate drivers either. A workaround for detaching system boards with non-DR-compliant drivers is to load the driver manually using the `modload(1M)` command.

Note – The `modinfo(1M)` command must be used to verify an existing driver instance for the non-DR-compliant driver (i.e. `modinfo |grep sg`). The `modunload(1M)` command must be executed before the `modload(1M)` command if there is an existing instance of a non-DR-compliant driver associated with the system board that is to be attached.

DR-Attach Prerequisites and Actions

To guarantee a successful DR-attach process the following prerequisites must be fulfilled:

Pre-Boot Requirements

The following prerequisites require a system reboot to take effect:

- All system memory should not be interleaved between system boards.
- In the Solaris 2.5.1 and Solaris 2.6 5/98 operating environments, the `dr_max_mem` OBP environment variable has to be set to a value equal to or greater than 512 Mbytes. The `dr_max_mem` OBP environment variable is not required after Solaris 7 5/99 because the required VM structures are dynamically allocated.
- The `soc` driver requires the following entry in the `/etc/system` file to enable the suspend-resume/detach-attach features:
  - `set soc:soc_enable_detach_suspend=1`
- In the Solaris 2.6 5/98 operating environment the `socal` driver requires the following entry in the `/etc/system` file to enable the suspend-resume features:
  - `set socal:socal_enable_suspend=1`
- The `pln` driver requires the following entry in the `/etc/system` file to enable the suspend-resume/detach-attach features:
  - `set pln:pln_enable_detach_suspend=1`
- Activation of the kernel cage requires the following entry in the `/etc/system` file:
  - `set kernel_cage_enable=1`

System Requirements

The only prerequisites to be fulfilled before the DR-Attach process are as follows:

- The system board to be attached must be powered up and not be a part of any domain.
- The system board to be attached must host at least one CPU to enable POST execution.

DR-Attach Actions

The following steps are automatically executed on both the SSP and DSD sides during the DR-Attach operation:

- The `domain_config(4)` is executed to add the new system board to the DSD.
- `hpost` (POST through the JTAG interface) is executed against the newly attached system board to guarantee full functionality before configuring components.
- CPU code is downloaded to the `BBSRAM` (Boot Bus Static Random Access Memory) `NVRAM` (Non-Volatile Random Access Memory) `mailbox` to handle the newly attached processors. CPUs are taken out of reset and start executing downloaded code.
- The SSP reprograms the attached system board and centerplane hardware registers to create the DSD association.
- OBP probes newly attached board devices and updates the OBP (`dnode`) device tree. The Solaris kernel updates the corresponding operating system (`devinfo`) device tree.
- The Solaris kernel starts the newly attached processors and adds the newly attached memory to the memory pool.
- The `dr` driver invokes the `DDI_ATTACH` function on all device drivers associated with the newly attached system board.

Pre-Boot Requirements:

- System memory must not be interleaved.
- The `dr_max_mem` OBP variable must be set (not needed after Solaris 7).
- The `/etc/system` entries for `soc/socal/pln` drivers must be in place.
- The `/etc/system` entry to enable the kernel cage must be in place.

System Requirements:

- Make sure system board is powered on and it's not part of any existing DSD.
- System board must host at least one CPU to execute POST.

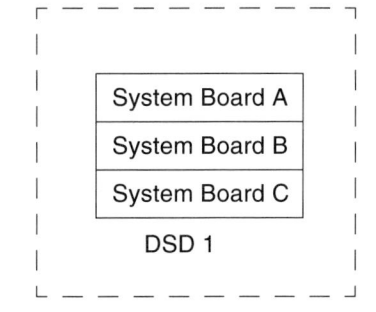

```
┌─ ─ ─ ─ ─ ─ ─ ─ ─ ┐
│ ┌─────────────┐ │
│ │System Board A│ │          DR-Attach System Board D     ┌──────────────┐
│ ├─────────────┤ │  ◄──────────────────────────────       │System Board D│
│ │System Board B│ │                                        └──────────────┘
│ ├─────────────┤ │
│ │System Board C│ │
│ └─────────────┘ │
│       DSD 1     │
└─ ─ ─ ─ ─ ─ ─ ─ ─ ┘
```

SSP Actions:

1. Board added to Target DSD (`domain_config`).
2. Diagnostics (`hpost`) executed and system board configured.
3. Code downloaded to BBSRAM and new processors taken out of reset.
4. System Board merged with Target DSD (system board/centerplane HW registers).

Operating System Actions:

5. OBP Probes Board Devices and builds OBP (dnode) device tree
6. Kernel builds Corresponding OS (`devinfo`) device tree
7. Kernel starts new processors
8. New memory added to page pool
9. Invoke `DDI_ATTACH` on all I/O devices
10. If required execute the drvconfig;devlinks;disks;ports;tapes sequence

```
┌─ ─ ─ ─ ─ ─ ─ ─ ─ ┐
│ ┌─────────────┐ │
│ │System Board A│ │
│ ├─────────────┤ │
│ │System Board B│ │
│ ├─────────────┤ │
│ │System Board C│ │
│ ├─────────────┤ │
│ │System Board D│ │
│ └─────────────┘ │
│       DSD 1     │
└─ ─ ─ ─ ─ ─ ─ ─ ─ ┘
```

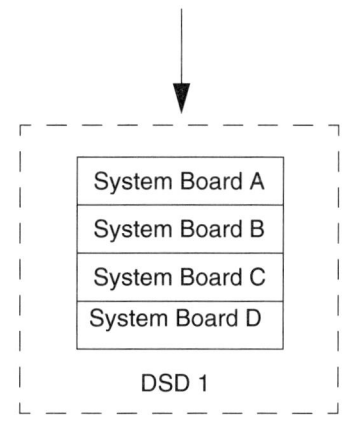

FIGURE 8-9   DR-Attaching a System Board to a DSD

DR I/O Device Driver Requirements

To support DR operations, all I/O device drivers associated with the system board that is to be attached or detached must be able to build (attach) and tear down (detach) all device instances spanning from its root.

This section covers the specific device driver functions required to support DR, but it does not provide enough detail for software developers to create their own device drivers. I/O drivers intended to be supported by the DR framework must fully implement the following Solaris DDI/DKI (Device Driver Interface/Device Kernel Interface) entry points as specified in the *Writing Device Drivers* section of the *Driver Developer Site 1.0 AnswerBook*[TM] (http://docs.sun.com):

- DDI_ATTACH (attach(9E))
- DDI_DETACH (detach(9E))
- DDI_SUSPEND
- DDI_RESUME

An additional requirement to support DR is that drivers which allocate memory directly through the page_create(), page_create_va() or through some other kernel routines must not hold the memory pages locked for extended periods of time.

The specific lock in question is the p_selock of the page_t structure typically acquired through the page_lock() routine. The p_selock is intended as a transient lock and holding the lock interferes with the memory drain required when a system board is detached. The page_create(), page_create_va() and page_lock() routines are not DDI/DKI compliant interfaces and their use is strongly discouraged.

Note – In the Solaris 2.5.1 and Solaris 2.6 releases, the Starfire DR requires newly created DR-compliant drivers to register with the dr driver by introducing the following line in the /etc/system file: set dr:detach_safe_list1="driver1 driver2... driver n". In the Solaris 7 release, newly-created DR-compliant drivers are required to set the D_HOTPLUG bit in the cb_ops data structure.

FIGURE 8-10 provides an abstraction of the I/O devices file path to better explain the DR attach and detach functions. For example, the Starfire /devices/sbus@54,0/ SUNW,fas@0,8800000/sd@2,0:a device file represents a SCSI disk registered with a fast/wide SCSI controller located on SBus0 of System board 5.

When detaching a system board, the dr driver locates the device tree associated with the system board and traverses it from the bottom up to invoke the detach function on every leaf of the tree.

A full configuration of the system peripherals device tree can be obtained through execution of the prtconf(1M) utility. In addition, the dr(1M) command on the SSP, supports the drshow(1M) function (with the I/O option) to display all devices associated with each system board, their physical location, associated drivers, device file and open instances.

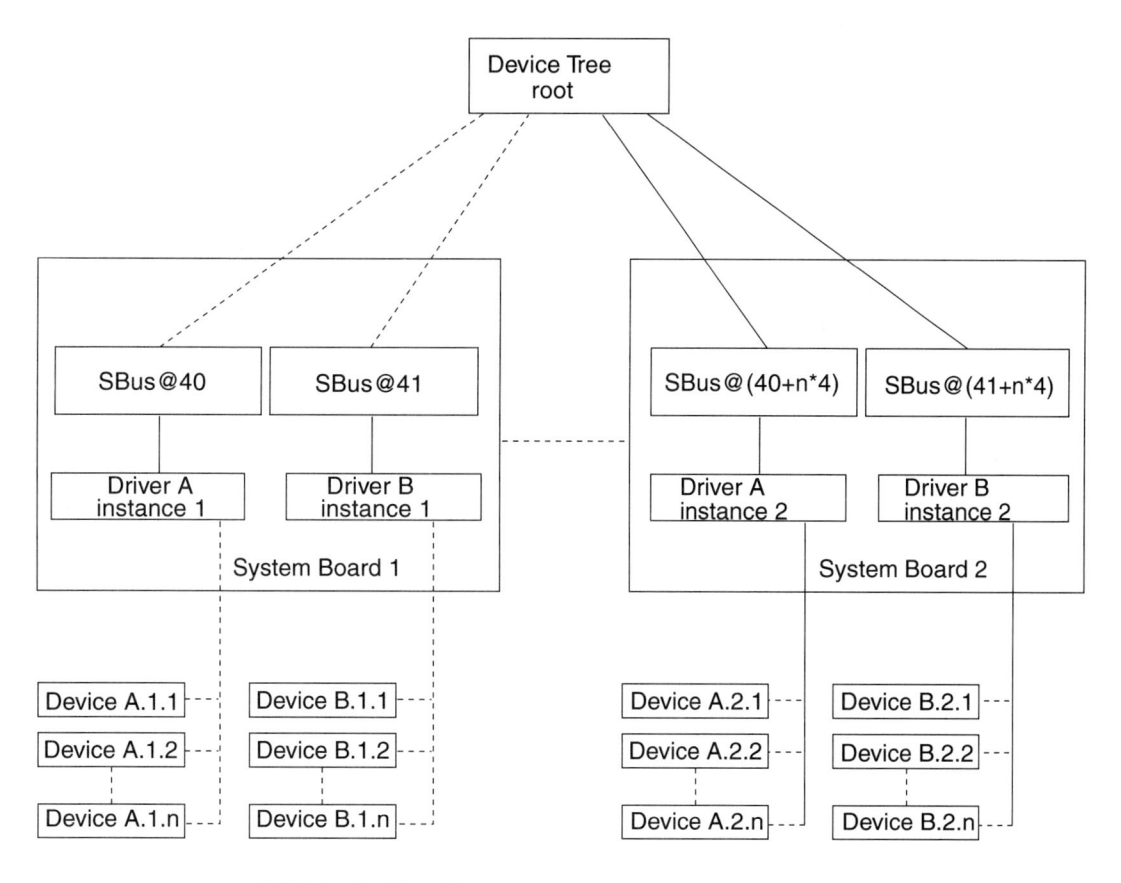

FIGURE 8-10 I/O Device Tree Representation

Device Driver DR Functions:

For a driver to be compliant with DR operations, it must support the `DDI_DETACH`, `DDI_ATTACH`, `DDI_SUSPEND` and `DDI_RESUME` functions.

`DDI_ATTACH` and `DDI_DETACH`:

The `DDI_ATTACH AND DDI_DETACH` functions provide the ability to attach or detach a particular instance of a driver without impacting other instances that are servicing separate devices. For example, if System board 1 in FIGURE 8-10 were to be attached or detached, the `dr_driver` would invoke the `DDI_ATTACH` or the `DDI_DETACH` function on each device under both Driver A's first instance and Driver B's first instance without affecting other driver instances.

If there's a non DR-compliant driver associated with the system board to be *attached*, the DR operation will not fail, but it will not load the appropriate drivers either. A workaround for attaching system boards with non DR-compliant drivers is to manually load the driver using the `modload(1M)` command. If there are already driver instances of the non DR-compliant driver, the `modunload(1M)` must be executed previous to the `modload(1M)` command execution.

If there is a non DR-compliant driver associated with the system board to be *detached*, the DR operation will fail. A workaround for detaching system boards with non DR-compliant drivers is to use the "big hammer approach" by manually unloading the driver using the `modunload(1M)` command. The `modunload(1M)` command requires that all open device instances be closed, and its application will remove all driver instances throughout the entire system.

`DDI_SUSPEND` and `DDI_RESUME`:

The `DDI_SUSPEND` and `DDI_RESUME` functions enable the ability to detach a board that contains the kernel cage (OBP, kernel and non-pageable memory). The kernel cage can only be relocated after all of the drivers throughout the entire DSD (not just on the board being detached) are quiesced to guarantee the data integrity of the kernel cage relocation.

CHAPTER **9**

Solaris Bandwidth Manager Software

The Solaris Bandwidth Manager software allows you to manage your network resources to provide quality of service (QoS) to network users. It allows network traffic to be allocated to separate classes of service (CoS), so that urgent traffic gets higher priority than less important traffic. Different classes of service can be guaranteed a portion of the network bandwidth, leading to more predictable network loads and overall system behavior. Service level agreements can be defined and translated into Solaris Bandwidth Manager controls and policies. Tools and APIs provide the interface for monitoring, billing, and accounting options.

This chapter explains how to use the Solaris Bandwidth Manager software as part of a resource control framework.

The Need for Bandwidth Management

Since almost all network links are shared by multiple users and applications, the available bandwidth must be shared. Bandwidth management tools enable you to manage how the bandwidth is shared.

If a network link is continuously congested, the link must be upgraded to provide greater capacity. In many cases, however, the average load on a link is within the link capacity, and the link is only congested temporarily. Temporary congestion is sometimes predictable; for example, there are typically peaks in network use at particular time of the day or following a particular event. Other causes of temporary congestion, such as the transferring a large file, are not predictable.

The Solaris Bandwidth Manager software enables you to manage the bandwidth used by IP traffic. It does this by:

- Allocating traffic to a class based on the application type, source and destination IP address, URL group, or a combination
- Assigning individual limits for each class. For example:

- Traffic to engineering must have at least 50 percent of the link.
- HTTP traffic cannot exceed 10 percent of the link.
■ Prioritizing traffic. Some types of traffic, for example interactive traffic generated when using `telnet` or `rlogin`, need a quick response time. Solaris Bandwidth Manager lets you assign a higher priority to that traffic. Traffic that does not require a quick response time, such as a file transfer using FTP, can be assigned a lower priority.

By balancing the bandwidth allocated to different types of network traffic and the relative priorities, you can optimize your network performance. Solaris Bandwidth Manager also allows you to monitor the achieved performance of your network, and has interfaces for third party billing applications.

The current version of the product as of this writing is Solaris Bandwidth Manager 1.5; the previous version of the product was known as Sun Bandwidth Allocator 1.0.

Examples of When to Use Bandwidth Management

You are the owner of a LAN, leasing a network connection from a service provider. You can use the Solaris Bandwidth Manager software to make sure you make the most efficient use of the capacity you lease. Bandwidth allocation ensures that your higher-priority traffic is sent first and that you always get the maximum use of the capacity you are paying for. It will no longer be necessary to over-specify your requirements just to guarantee that priority traffic can be sent. You might even be able to reduce the capacity you lease.

You are the owner of a WAN, providing network services to many clients. The Solaris Bandwidth Manager software enables you to regulate the traffic in your network. You can provide a guaranteed minimum bandwidth to a client, and as a bonus, provide additional bandwidth from time to time when it is not required by other clients. Since you know the level of guaranteed bandwidth, capacity planning will be both easier and more accurate.

You are a web service provider, hosting several web sites on behalf of commercial companies. The Solaris Bandwidth Manager software enables you to guarantee your client companies that a given bandwidth is available to the customers visiting their web sites. Today, many web providers charge based on either disk space used or on the number of times a site is visited. Disk space used is not a good indication of the cost to a provider, since a small site that is visited frequently can be as expensive to provide as a large site that is visited less frequently. Using the number of visits to a site is a better indicator of the cost to a provider, but is potentially an unbounded cost for the client. With Solaris Bandwidth Manager you can charge clients for a guaranteed bandwidth for their web site. Additionally, you can provide extra functionality such as providing a higher priority to network traffic originating from web site visitors who are paying for online shopping goods as opposed to visitors who are just looking around.

You are an ISP providing services to many customers. The Solaris Bandwidth Manager software enables you to provide different classes of service to different customers. For example, you could offer Premium and Standard services, with different guaranteed minimum access levels, to suit the needs and budgets of your customers. This will also allow you to start consolidating many services from many small machines onto fewer larger servers. Optional Resource Management products such as Solaris Resource Manager (covered in Chapter 7) can be used on these servers to guarantee processing power as well as networking bandwidth to your customers, while at the same time reducing the total cost of administration and cost of ownership.

End-to-End Quality of Service

To manage network resources, it is not sufficient to manage and control only the network segment close to the computer systems that supply the services in question. Clients can be anywhere on the network, and the whole network path from client to server needs to be considered. This is what is meant by end-to-end QoS, and in general, it can be very difficult to achieve. If congestion takes place anywhere on the network, it will affect the overall QoS. Therefore, routers need to help supply QoS. In the Internet Engineering Task Force (IETF), several working groups have been working on this problem, notably the Integrated Services working group (Int-Serv) and the Differentiated Services working group (Diff-Serv).

Integrated Services

In recent years, several developments in the IETF have attempted to make end-to-end QoS to the Enterprise and the Internet a reality. To guarantee a certain bandwidth to an application, each hop in the network from client to server must guarantee the resources that are required.

The Internet Integrated Services framework (Int-Serv) was developed by the IETF to provide applications the ability to have multiple levels of QoS to deliver data across the network. It consists of two components:

- Network components along the path must support multiple levels of service.
- Applications must have a way to communicate their desired level of service to the network components.

The RSVP protocol was developed for the latter. It requires each hop from end to end be RSVP-enabled, including the application itself (through an API). Bandwidth will be reserved at each hop along the way before transmitting begins, guaranteeing that enough resources will be available for the duration of this connection.

For the internet backbone, RSVP never received widespread acceptance. One reason is that backbone routers handle the forwarding and routing of very large amounts of concurrent *flows* (connections). Deploying RSVP means that routers need to keep state on each connection. This puts a very high load on these routers, which leads inevitably to performance, scalability, and management problems.

Still, RSVP could be the right solution for certain applications, especially on better contained networks (such as corporate). The Solaris Bandwidth Manager software does not use RSVP to manage bandwidth. However, Sun offers a separate product called Solstice™ Bandwidth Reservation Protocol 1.0 that does exactly that. It can be downloaded from `http://www.sun.com/solstice/telecom/bandwidth`.

Differentiated Services

More recent developments in the IETF's *Diff-Serv* working group are attempting to resolve the concern of overloaded backbone routers. Instead of requiring per-flow resource reservation at each hop, it moves the complexity of this to the network edge, to keep the packet-forwarding mechanisms in the network core relatively simple.

The IPv4 packet header includes a field called ToS (Type of Service) which can be used to mark a packet for different levels of quality. In the Diff-Serv context, this IP header is renamed the *DS header byte*. The IPv6 header has a similar field. At the edge of the network, packets and flows are classified and shaped (scheduled). The DS field in the IP header is marked for a corresponding level of service, and the network core routers inspect the DS field and give the type of service that was requested. In the Diff-Serv specification, care was taken to supply as much backwards compatibility with the original meaning of the Type of Service header, as defined in RFC 791 (the original IP specification) and RFC 1349 which refines these definitions.

For more information regarding Diff-Serv, see RFC 2474 and RFC 2475.

The Solaris Bandwidth Manager software is Diff-Serv compliant. The software can classify, filter and mark network packets based on the DS field contents. This allows the software to be deployed in a Diff-Serv environment together with networking equipment (such as routers and switches) from other vendors that are Diff-Serv compliant.

How Bandwidth Allocation Works

Bandwidth is allocated to a class of network traffic. The class of a packet is defined by some or all of the following factors:

- IP source address
- IP destination address
- IP protocol (TCP, UDP, or other)
- Source ports for TCP and UDP
- Destination ports for TCP and UDP
- Type of Service (ToS) value in the IP header
- URL or URL group

Class definitions are hierarchical and every class has a parent. For example, if you define a class for FTP traffic and a class for FTP traffic to a host called *pear*, the classes are connected in a hierarchy as shown in FIGURE 9-1.

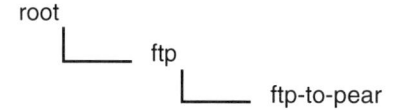

```
root
   └── ftp
          └── ftp-to-pear
```

FIGURE 9-1 Hierarchical Class Definitions

In this example, the ftp class is a child of the root class and is the parent of the ftp-to-pear class.

The configuration of Bandwidth Manager specifies the set of known classes for a node, defined in terms of the values of some or all of these factors. It also allocates a percentage of bandwidth and a priority to each class. The priority of a class is an integer from 1 (highest priority) to 7 (lowest priority).

When a packet arrives, the classifier analyzes the packet protocol, ToS value, URL information, source information, destination information and allocates the packet to a class queue where it waits to be processed. If the queue to which a packet is allocated is full, the packet is dropped. Normal retransmission ensures that the packet is resent. Normal TCP/IP behavior such as slow start and congestion avoidance assures that traffic flows adapt to the bandwidth that is made available to each flow.

The scheduler uses the percentage of bandwidth that is configured and the priority for each class to decide the order in which class queues are processed. Within a class queue, the packets are processed on a first-in, first-out basis. When the network traffic reaches the maximum allocated for a class, packets from the next class in priority order are processed, as illustrated in FIGURE 9-2.

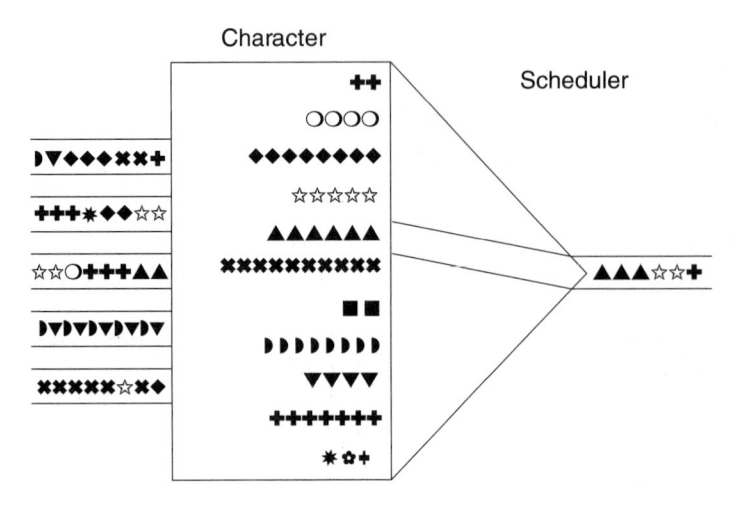

FIGURE 9-2 Bandwidth Allocation

Borrowing Bandwidth

Each class is guaranteed a percentage of the available bandwidth, and when that limit is reached, normally no more traffic from that class can be forwarded. However, if the network link is not fully used, a class can borrow bandwidth from its parent's class, and send traffic at a percentage that exceeds its allocation.

Similarly, if not all the bandwidth allocated to a child's class is being used, the parent of that class can use it. The amount of spare bandwidth allocated to a class depends on the percentage of bandwidth that the class can borrow. This is called the *maximum bandwidth*.

When there is spare bandwidth, it will be allocated among the highest priority classes first, until there is no more spare bandwidth, or until all those classes reach their maximum bandwidth. If the latter happens, the remainder of the spare bandwidth will be divided among the next highest priority, and so on.

Example of Borrowing Bandwidth

In this example, 15 percent of the bandwidth is spare, and there are three classes with packets queued (`http`, `ftp` and `smtp`). See table 9-1. The spare bandwidth will be divided between `http` and `ftp` traffic, since they have the highest priority. The `http` class will get 15 percent * 50 / (50 + 20) = 11 percent and the `ftp` class will get 15 percent * 20 / (50 + 20) = 4 percent. The `smtp` class will get nothing extra.

TABLE 9-1 Example of Borrowing Bandwidth

Class Name	Priority	Guaranteed Bandwidth (percentage)
http	1	50
ftp	1	20
smtp	3	10

If `http` has been allocated a maximum bandwidth of 55 percent, and `ftp` has a maximum of 22 percent, then `smtp` can borrow 8 percent. Of course, if no `http` traffic or `ftp` traffic is scheduled at all, `smtp` can borrow the full 15 percent of the spare bandwidth.

It is possible to define a class that has 0 percent bandwidth guaranteed but may borrow bandwidth from its parent class. A packet allocated to such a class is only forwarded if there is no other traffic of higher priority waiting. Allocating 0 percent and no borrowing to a class means that the class is blocked.

Flows

A flow is a complete exchange of information between a sender and a recipient, as seen from the user's point of view. Examples of flows include sending a mail message or downloading a web page.

A flow is defined by:

- The interface used
- The source and destination IP address
- The IP protocol (TCP, UDP or other)
- The source and destination ports (TCP and UDP)
- The IP ToS value
- The URL

Since the ToS value can change during the lifetime of a flow, a flow can move from one class to another.

Information about all current flows is stored in a cache. When a packet arrives, its flow characteristics are compared with the cache information to see whether it is part of an existing flow or whether a new flow has started. The cache record includes the flow identification information and the following statistics:

- The number of packets sent
- The number of octets sent
- The system uptime when the first packet arrived
- The system uptime when the last packet arrived

A flow is terminated 60 seconds after the last packet in the flow was detected.

Monitoring flows rather than classes gives a more accurate picture of network usage, at finer granularity. This enables you to predict future network needs more accurately, and gives you information that can be used in accounting. See "Monitoring, Accounting, and Billing" on page 243 for more details.

Type of Service Packet Marking

An IP packet contains a ToS header field. Its purpose is to convey information about how the packet should be routed. The Solaris Bandwidth Manager software can use this information when classifying a packet. It can also change the information, to influence how the packet is routed.

IP Specification of ToS

The IP specification includes a definition of a ToS field in the IP packet header. This is used by upper-layer protocols to pass information to the Internet layer about how to optimize routing for the packet. The topology of the Internet is such that there are often a number of available routes between the source and destination of a packet. Some routes are more reliable than others. Some are expensive, with high call setup or usage charges, while some are low-cost but slow. The most suitable route for a packet depends on the application and user, and might even vary with other factors such as the time of day. For example, if you are a system administrator monitoring a remote system, you need to receive alarm traffic as rapidly as possible regardless of the cost, because the cost of routing the alarm is significantly lower than the cost incurred by a system problem. However, if you start to get a document by ftp from the same system at the end of your working day, intending to use it the following day, a low-cost slow route is sufficient.

The Internet has no direct knowledge of how to optimize a route for a given application or user. The ToS facility was intended to provide hints about how best to route a packet, influencing both queueing algorithms and routing.

```
 0     1     2     3     4     5     6     7
|     |     |     |     |     |     |     |     |
|     Precedence     |        TOS        |    MBZ    |
|     |     |     |     |     |     |     |     |
```

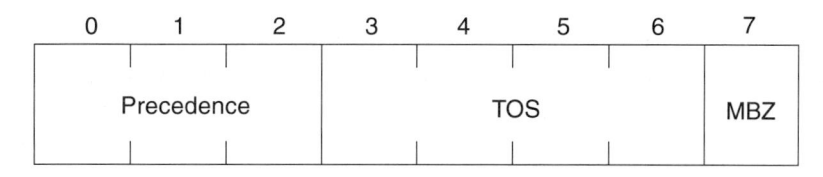

FIGURE 9-3 IP Type of Service Byte

The *Precedence* bits are used to denote the importance or priority of the packet. The *ToS* field denotes how the network should make trade-offs between throughput, delay, cost, and reliability when routing this packet. The last bit, MBZ (which stands for "Must Be Zero"), is as the name implies currently unused.

Differentiated Services

The ToS facility has not been extensively used in the past, and the Differentiated Services working group within the IETF has been working to extend the use of ToS to encourage its use to achieve end-to-end QoS. In this context, the ToS header field has been renamed the DS header field. Currently, only the first six bits of the DS field are being used, as shown in FIGURE 9-4.

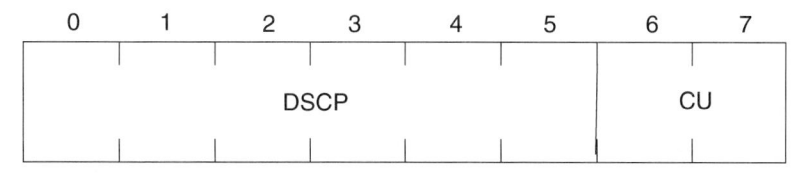

```
 0     1     2     3     4     5     6     7
|     |     |     |     |     |     |     |     |
|              DSCP              |      CU      |
|     |     |     |     |     |     |     |     |
```

DSCP: differentiated services codepoint
CU: currently unused

FIGURE 9-4 DS Header Field

The way that the DSCP bits are set in a packet is called its *codepoint*, and network devices translate DSCP codepoints to device configurations. For example, a DS compliant router that has two priority queues (one for regular priority traffic and one for high priority traffic) could be configured to have several codepoints map to the high priority queue, and several others to the regular priority queue. An attempt was made to provide some sort of backwards compatibility, by having the first three bits of the DSCP field map to behaviors similar to the definitions of the three precedence bits of the ToS byte that existed before Diff-Serv came along.

Solaris Bandwidth Manager Software and Type of Service

To be completely flexible with ToS and Diff-Serv for current and future to be defined queuing behaviors, the Solaris Bandwidth Manager software can be configured to filter a packet for any possible value in the ToS field as the classification criteria, and packets can be marked and remarked in any possible way. It is up to the Solaris Bandwidth Manager administrator to give meaning to this in the context of the network where the Solaris Bandwidth Manager software is deployed, and the administrator is responsible for keeping the configuration compliant to the standards (for example, with the Solaris Bandwidth Manager software, you can filter on the last two bits of the DS header, even though they are currently defined to be unused.

HTTP Support

The popularity of the World Wide Web is one of the main reasons that network traffic has sky-rocketed so much over the last 5 years. Information now is easily accessible at everybody's fingertips. For a large part, HTTP traffic is bound to destinations on the internet, and many corporations have had to upgrade their internet connection's bandwidth or their network backbone as a result of this.

Unfortunately, it is not easy to distinguish important business-critical HTTP traffic from less important traffic such as live sports scores or stock tickers. Because firewalls often block ports of protocols such as real-audio, vendors now start tunneling these protocols over port 80 (HTTP), and it is increasingly hard for network administrators to manage the network strain resulting from this. One option is to use Proxy Cache systems that filter unwanted traffic by refusing access to certain classes of web destinations, but it still doesn't address the need to prioritize the remaining web traffic on the network. For example, you could allow real-audio on the network as long as nobody else has a need for the required bandwidth.

ISPs could give higher priority to URLs from customers who are willing to pay more.

Web Hosting Providers could use HTTP prioritization to give higher priority to the web pages of visitors who are in the process of buying a product, rather than web pages for the customers who are merely browsing the online product catalog.

When to Use Solaris Bandwidth Manager

Without any form of bandwidth management, it is difficult to maintain a network that has predictable performance characteristics. Nevertheless, this is how most networks are run today. Network usage is estimated or modeled, and then enough bandwidth is configured to achieve respectable latencies. Enough is a relative term, it could mean that there will always be sufficient bandwidth for all applications that would possibly need it, or it could mean that the network is oversubscribed, knowing that on average only a certain percentage of users is actually using the network. When new applications are deployed, or existing applications become more popular, links become congested and users start complaining about slow application performance, until the network gets upgraded. For many customer environments, this is a completely acceptable way to maintain network resources. New technologies such as switched networking equipment and gigabit ethernet have rapidly become available at continuously decreasing prices.

Deploying any type of QoS solution is no magical fix to a bandwidth shortage on the network, and the term Quality in Quality of Service is subjective. When the network is overloaded, bandwidth management software can help determine which network traffic to penalize more in respect to other (more important) traffic. If the network is not oversubscribed, then deploying bandwidth management might be a futile exercise, since there is no network bandwidth shortage to begin with.

However, many networks *are* oversubscribed, and critical network services might be affected during peak loads on the network. The Solaris Bandwidth Manager software can help define which network services are more important than others, and set priorities and bandwidth percentages to enforce them so these services are not negatively impacted by other, less important traffic on the network.

In addition, the Solaris Bandwidth Manager software can be used for billing based on network usage. Clients who pay more can be offered a larger piece of the network bandwidth.

Relationship to Other Resource Management Products

The Solaris Bandwidth Manager software can be used along other resource management products to offer additional control over the available resources. Examples are:

- **Solaris Resource Manager** software for managing system resources such as CPU and memory. The Solaris Bandwidth Manager software can offer control over resources which are hard for SRM to manage, such as NFS.
- **Sun Enterprise SyMON** software as an encapsulating managing platform. The Solaris Bandwidth Manager software has SNMP support, and the Bandwidth Manager SNMP MIB can be loaded into SyMON, where monitoring rules and alarms can be configured.

Where to Deploy Solaris Bandwidth Manager

Typically, the Solaris Bandwidth Manager software is deployed at the edge of the network. There are two ways to configure the Solaris Bandwidth Manager software in the network: on a host which originates network traffic (server mode), or in front of a router at a network choke point (IP-transparent mode).

Server Mode

In Server Mode, bandwidth originating from a given server can be managed. The Solaris Bandwidth Manager software sits as a STREAMS module directly in the path of incoming and outgoing network traffic, between TCP/IP and the network card device driver.

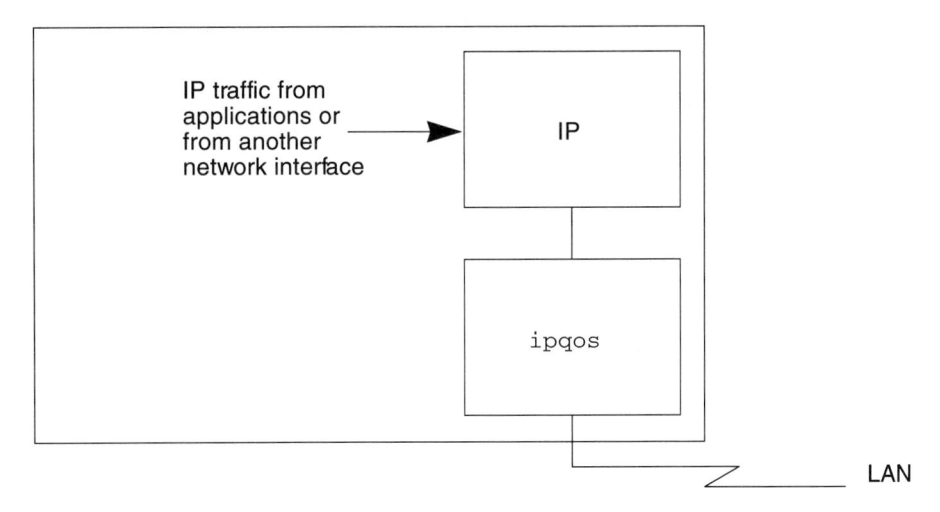

```
                    ┌──────────┐
IP traffic from     │          │
applications or ───▶│    IP    │
from another        │          │
network interface   └────┬─────┘
                         │
                    ┌────┴─────┐
                    │          │
                    │  ipqos   │
                    │          │
                    └────┬─────┘
                         │
                         └──────── LAN
```

FIGURE 9-5 Server Mode

When the network interface is initialized (usually at system boot time), the Solaris Bandwidth Manager policy agent reads the configuration file and loads the configuration information into the `ipqos` module. The `ipqos` module then processes all traffic according to the configured definitions.

The advantage of running in Server Mode is that by being on the same machine as the traffic generating application, the Solaris Bandwidth Manager software can take better advantage of application specific requirements for allocating network bandwidth.

IP-Transparent Mode

This mode is called IP-transparent because the host running the Solaris Bandwidth Manager software is completely transparent to the IP network and is perceived as just another machine connected to the LAN. The LAN and the WAN behave as though they are directly connected through the router only. It is not necessary to modify the routing tables.

```
                    ┌─────────────────┐
                    │ Host running    │
                    │ Bandwidth Manager│
                    │                 │
                    │ le 0    qe 1_out│
                    └──┬─────────┬────┘
                       │         │      ┌────────┐
                       │         └──────│ Router │──→
                       │                └────────┘
                    LAN
```

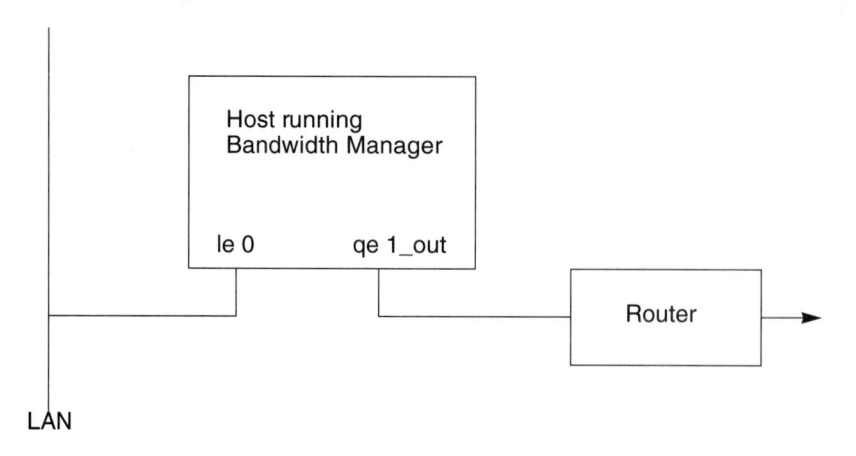

FIGURE 9-6 IP-Transparent Mode

The advantage of running in this mode is that bandwidth can be managed completely transparently, usually at locations in the network topology where there is a network choke point. This is often the connection from a LAN to a WAN.

Other alternatives are to run the Solaris Bandwidth Manager software on the same host as the firewall. Packets can be classified before encryption takes place (after which it is much harder to do packet classification).

Solaris Bandwidth Manager Architecture

Solaris Bandwidth Manager consists of the following major components:

- The *administration tool*, `batool`, provides a graphical interface for configuring the Solaris Bandwidth Manager software. This can be run as an applet or an application from any machine in your network that has a Java Virtual Machine.
- The *policy agent* implements the configuration and handles communication with the kernel module. See "The Policy Agent" on page 240 for details of how the policy agent works.
- The *kernel module* is viewed as a STREAMS driver, `/dev/ipqos`, by the tools in user space, and is viewed as a STREAMS module, `ipqos`, by the IP stack. It contains the classifier and the scheduler.
    - The *classifier* allocates packets to a class queue.
    - The *scheduler* determines the order in which queued packets are forwarded across the network and applies the bandwidth limits and priorities configured for each type of traffic. Class Based Queuing (CBQ) is the underlying queuing technology used in Solaris Bandwidth Manager.
- *Commands*, *utilities* and *API's* for managing the Solaris Bandwidth Manager software and for monitoring your network.

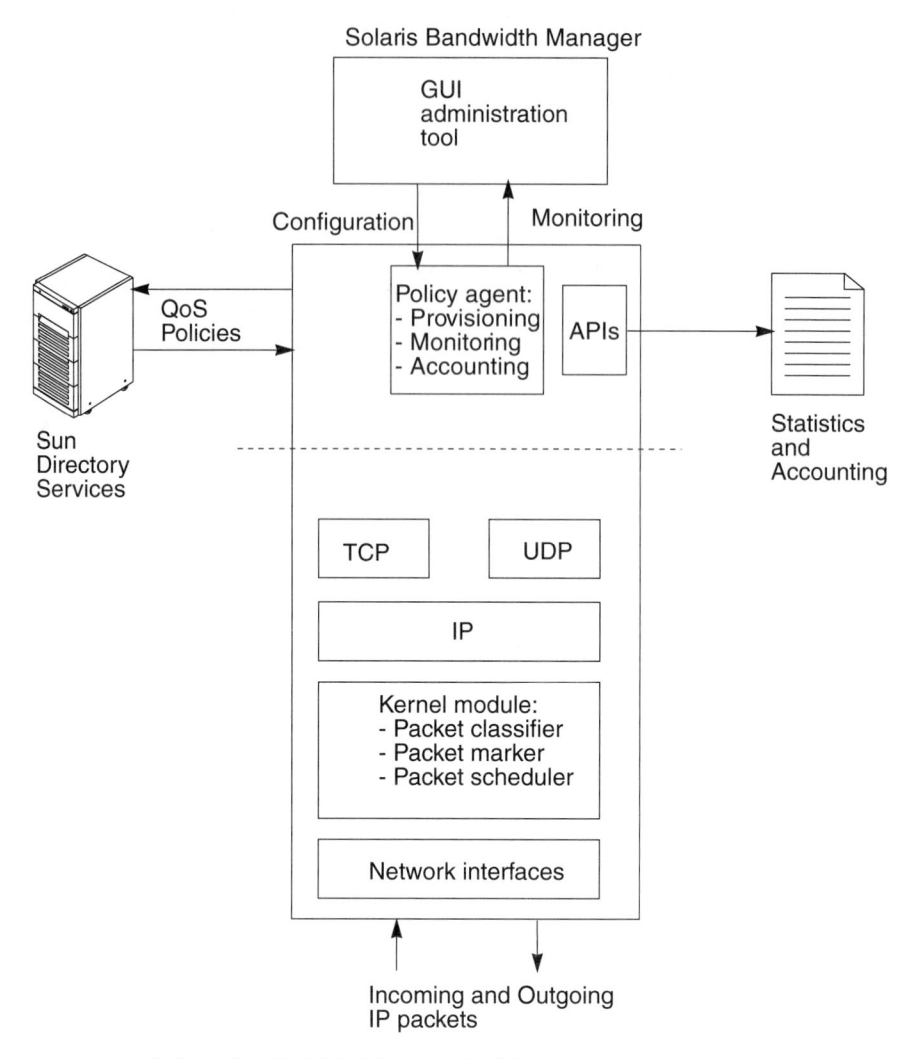

FIGURE 9-7 Solaris Bandwidth Manager Architecture

Java Dynamic Management Kit

The administration tool and the policy agent are implemented using the Java Dynamic Management™ Kit.

The Java Dynamic Development Kit is a JavaBeans based framework for developing and deploying dynamic management based applications. Autonomous agents can be deployed in real-time to perform management tasks for devices on the network.

A Java Dynamic Management Kit agent consists of a lightweight framework that runtime JavaBeans components can be plugged in to. These management beans (or *m-beans*) can be dynamically pushed to the agent with push and pull technology built into the Java Dynamic Management Kit. Management applications operate on the methods of the instantiated m-beans.

Communication services between the Java Dynamic Management Kit agent and the management application are implemented through *protocol adapters* which are also JavaBeans-based.

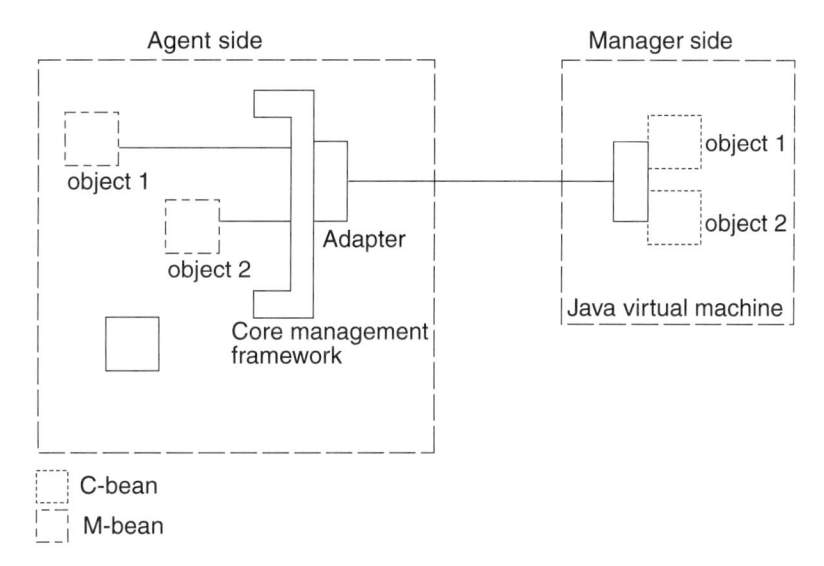

Bundled protocol adapters exist for RMI, HTTP and SNMP. A Java MIB compiler can integrate existing SNMP device management directly in the Java Dynamic Management Kit agent, and agents can be managed by traditional SNMP applications, as well as Java and web based applications.

For more information regarding Java Dynamic Management Kit, see `http://www.sun.com/software/java-dynamic`.

The Administration Tool

The Solaris Bandwidth Manager administration tool (`batool`) is a Java application that can be run on client platforms such as Windows or Solaris. It communicates with the Policy Agent (see below) over the HTTP protocol, which makes it easy to run remotely, even when firewalls are configured between the management client and the Bandwidth Manager station running the Policy Agent. Use the GUI to control the m-beans running in the Policy. The m-beans in turn control the Solaris Bandwidth Manager application configuration.

The Policy Agent

The Policy Agent is an instance of the Java Dynamic Management Kit framework, in which several management JavaBeans (m-beans) are configured. The Policy Agent runs on the same machine as the Solaris Bandwidth Manager software.

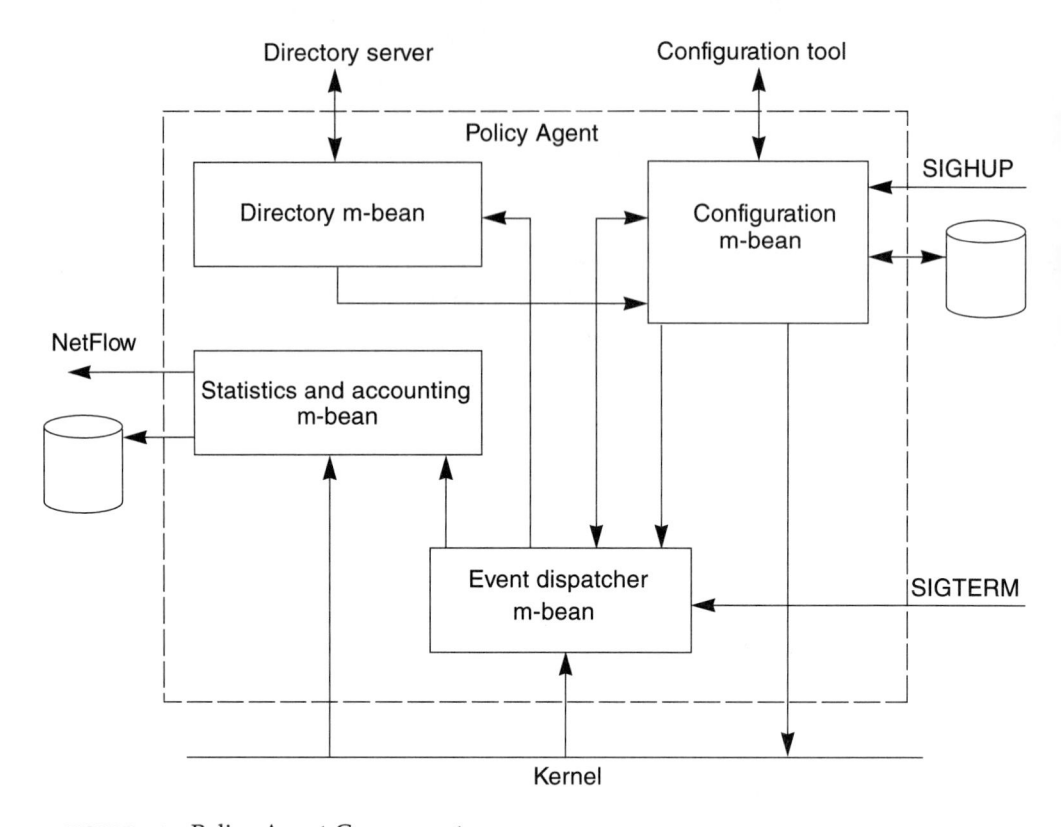

FIGURE 9-8 Policy Agent Components

The m-bean interfaces are documented in the Solaris Bandwidth Manager documentation set, and you can develop custom management applications and GUI's using them.

Configuration m-bean

The configuration m-bean handles configuration issues such as reading the configuration file, or updating the Solaris Bandwidth Manager configuration dynamically when a directory event happens (such as a new user logging in to the network). The event-driven model of the m-bean allows the Solaris Bandwidth Manager software to adapt to changing network behavior in real-time, which is powerful concept.

Directory m-bean

The directory m-bean contains information used when interacting with a directory service. Listeners can be configured to wait for certain directory events and react appropriately.

When configured with a directory server such as the Sun Directory Server 3.1 software, the Policy Agent is configured as a replica of the Directory Server. When the Directory gets updated, for example when a new user dial in through the RADIUS server, then the directory replication mechanism can immediately update the Solaris Bandwidth Manager configuration.

Statistics and Accounting m-bean

This m-bean uses the JDBC interface to write flow statistics to a text file, after each 30 seconds of flow activity.

Configuration Interface

Communicates the configuration interface between the Policy Agent and the kernel. Also used by SNMP monitoring.

Accounting Interface

Communicates statistics and accounting information between the Policy Agent and the kernel. Also used by SNMP monitoring, and by the C statistics API.

LDAP Directory Integration

Solaris Bandwidth Manager configuration and policy information can be stored in a directory service such as the Sun Directory Services 3.1 software. The advantage of storing configuration and policy information in a directory instead of a configuration file is that the configuration can be dynamically updated upon detection of user connections or traffic flows. It also makes it possible to update the configuration of multiple instances of the Solaris Bandwidth Manager software from a single point: the directory.

When a remote user connects to the network through a remote access server or network access server (NAS) using the RADIUS protocol, the IP address of the user's point of presence can be dynamically recorded in the user's directory entry. The policy agent detects this information and triggers a change to the dynamic configuration, to add the required policies for traffic associated with this user.

You can also write an application to detect the start of a flow, or the presence of traffic in a new flow and update the configuration to take account of that flow. To support this dynamic configuration, you need a way to store information about the policies to be applied to traffic in a new flow. A directory service, such as the Sun Directory Services 3.1 software, can be used to hold the policy rules and to relate them to a new flow.

When you want to ensure consistency in configuration for multiple instances of the Solaris Bandwidth Manager software, a directory is the ideal location for storing and modifying the configuration. Using standard directory replication processes, the configuration can be loaded into the policy agents, rather than configuring each one individually.

Directory Enabled Networks

Computer networks are becoming increasingly more complex to manage. Currently, most network devices are independently, and mostly statically configured. Effective resource management is not feasible using this model. Ideally, higher level SLAs and *policies* would be automatically translated in dynamic network configuration changes. To achieve this, some kind of centralized view of the network is needed, and directories (such as LDAP based ones) are an ideal match for this.

Currently, directories store mostly user and application information. The goal of the Directory Enabled Networks working group (DEN) is to offer a standard information model and directory schemas to tie users and applications with network elements, protocols, and services through specific relationships. By complying with this information model and the DEN schemas, different network equipment and application vendors should be able to build interoperable network elements around a central directory.

Instead of duplicating work that already has been done, the DEN working group is using work done by the Desktop Management Task Force (DMTF), which already has an information model called CIM (Common Information Model) for managing computer systems. DEN is using the CIM schema as much as possible, and has been extending it to add network specific information. Because of the close relationship between the DEN information model and CIM, the DEN draft recently has been transferred to the DMTF group for review and approval.

The Solaris Bandwidth Manager software is DEN compliant. The LDAP schema used is based on DEN schemas, and the schema extensions that were defined for the Solaris Bandwidth Manager software are documented in the product manuals.

Monitoring, Accounting, and Billing

The Solaris Bandwidth Manager software provides real-time statistics on resource usage as well as SLA commitment level information (when combined with the right applications). This information can be used for monitoring network usage or as input to accounting and billing systems.

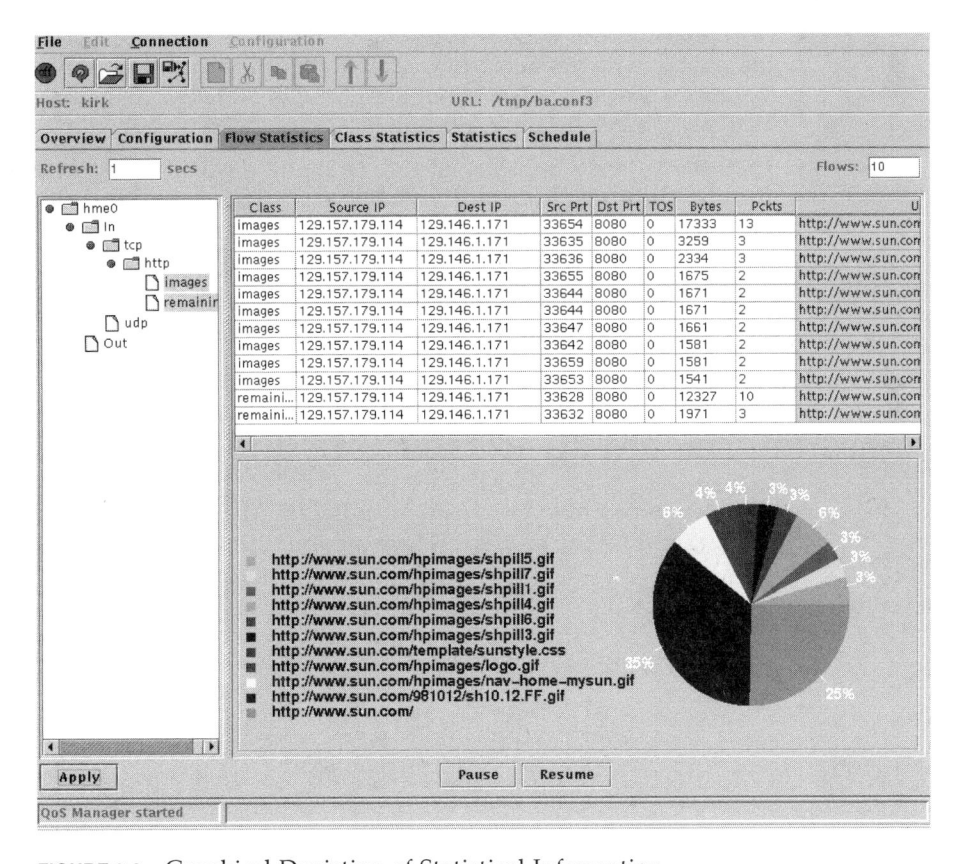

FIGURE 9-9 Graphical Depiction of Statistical Information

Statistics

Statistics information includes per class and per flow statistics:

- number of bytes and number of packets sent
- number of bytes and number of packets dropped
- average throughput
- number of borrows from a class to its parent

Monitoring Statistics

Statistics and accounting information can be extracted from the Solaris Bandwidth Manager software in several ways:

- Statistics can be accessed directly and displayed graphically through the Java administration tool or manually through a command line utility.
- Flow statistics can be viewed from any billing or accounting package that is compatible with version 5 of Cisco's NetFlow protocol. The Solaris Bandwidth Manager software can be configured to send NetFlow diagrams directly to a NetFlow FlowCollector application.
- The Solaris Bandwidth Manager software has Java and C APIs for building stand-alone monitoring utilities or for integrating the Solaris Bandwidth Manager software statistics with existing monitoring systems.
- A Solaris Bandwidth Manager-specific SNMP MIB is included with the Solaris Bandwidth Manager software. The MIB data can be extracted, processed, and viewed using an appropriate tool.

Interface with Accounting and Billing

Statistics extracted from the Solaris Bandwidth Manager software can be input into accounting and billing systems. There are four output options:

- ASCII format
- NetFlow datagrams
- Java and C APIs
- SNMP

ASCII Format

An accounting agent collects accounting information, and outputs it in ASCII format which can be accepted by a billing system.

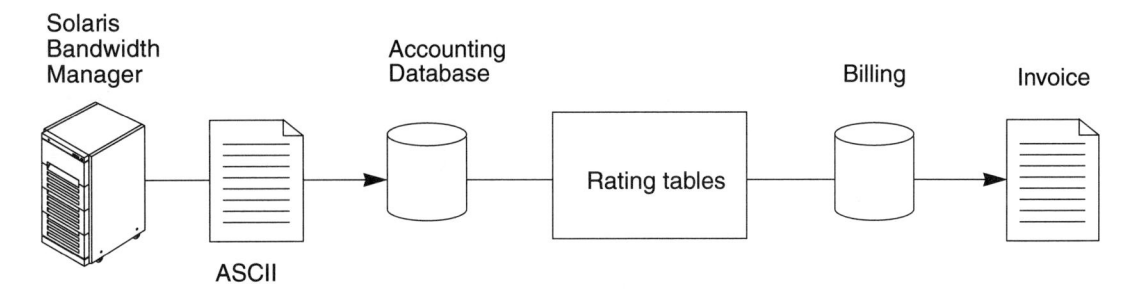

FIGURE 9-10 Solaris Bandwidth Manager Converts Accounting Information to ASCII

Accounting data includes details such as sender and receiver IP addresses, packet and byte counts, time-stamps, and application port numbers. Thus both Internet service providers and enterprise customers can choose from a variety of charging parameters including time-of-day, bandwidth usage, application usage, traffic class, and so on. Accounting data also provides the base for billing for advanced QoS-enabled IP services such as premium charging for premium CoS.

NetFlow

NetFlow support is built into the Solaris Bandwidth Manager software. NetFlow technology, developed by Cisco Systems, allows the collecting and processing of information for accounting and billing, network planning and network monitoring. The Solaris Bandwidth Manager software can be configured to send NetFlow V5 datagrams directly to Cisco NetFlow FlowCollector software.

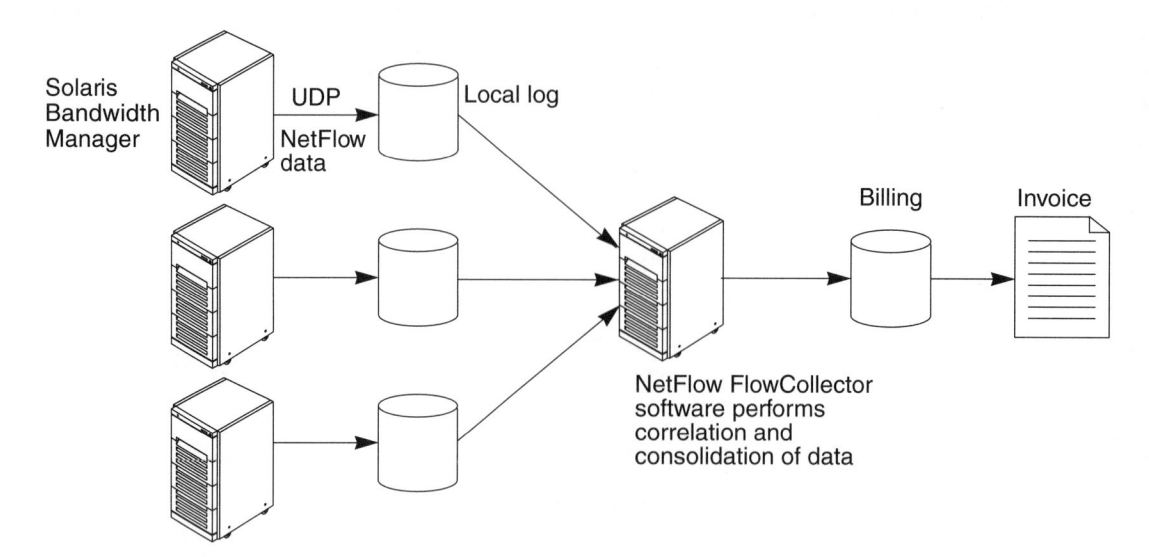

FIGURE 9-11 Solaris Bandwidth Manager Working with NetFlow FlowCollector

Java and C APIs

The inclusion of Java and C APIs with the Solaris Bandwidth Manager software allows for development of custom applications for real-time, usage-based billing. For example, you can build your own proprietary applications for local collection of accounting data and aggregation into a centralized billing application.

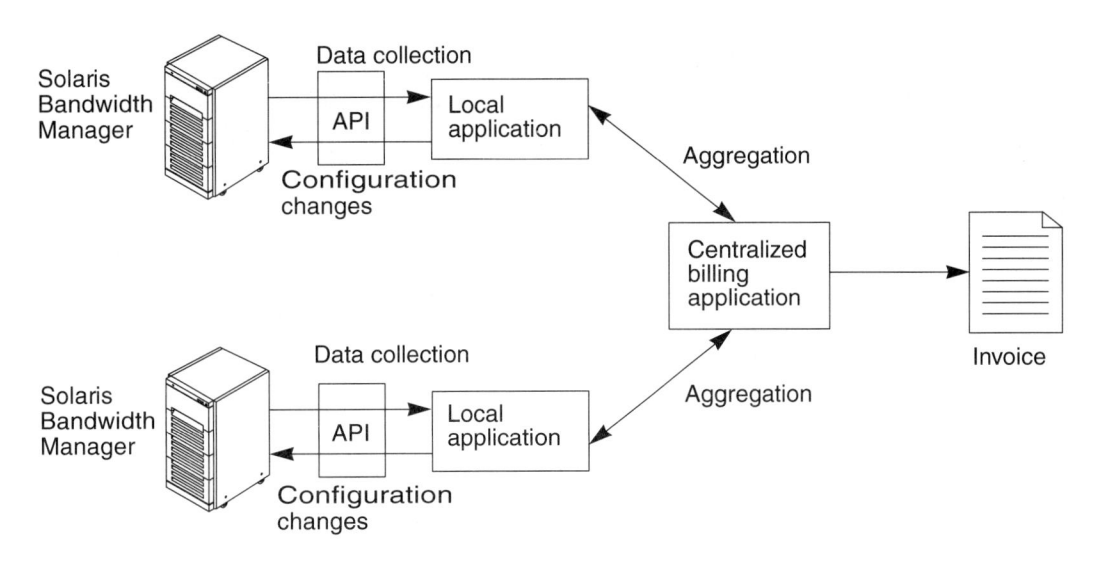

FIGURE 9-12 Solaris Bandwidth Manager Using Local Application

The local application collects local accounting information, and local events (such as new flow, end of flow, and so on). It reacts to traffic thresholds and events, either managing these locally, or escalating events to the central billing application.

SNMP

Traffic statistics and configuration information can be read by any standard network management application, such as SunNet Manager, or Solaris Enterprise Manager via the SNMP interface included in the Solaris Bandwidth Manager software.

Customizing and Extending Solaris Bandwidth Manager Software

The Java and C APIs included with the Solaris Bandwidth Manager software enable you to develop your own JavaBeans plug-ins or applications.

The Java plug-ins are placed directly in the Solaris Bandwidth Manager policy agent. The applications either access the Solaris Bandwidth Manager software remotely, or exist on the same local machine.

Plug-ins

Java plug-ins can be developed to implement network usage policies. For instance, a plug-in can be developed to perform internal statistics monitoring and react to statistics events by instigating an action. The action could be to generate an alert, or to dynamically change the configuration of the Solaris Bandwidth Manager software.

A concrete example is a plug-in that checks traffic statistics. If it detects that Premium Class traffic is reaching capacity, it can dynamically reconfigure the Solaris Bandwidth Manager software. As a result, Standard Class is disconnected to ensure that Premium Class traffic has guaranteed access.

Plug-ins are implemented using the Java Dynamic Management Kit. The plug-ins are m-beans, instantiated in the Java Dynamic Management Kit management framework in the policy agent. They can be pushed to or pulled from the policy agent dynamically, without having to restart the application.

Applications

The Solaris Bandwidth Manager APIs can be used to develop self-contained management applications or interfaces to existing management applications. For example, an application could be developed that provides a GUI to integrate the Solaris Bandwidth Manager software into a proprietary network management solution.

CHAPTER **10**

Load Sharing Facility Software

The Load Sharing Facility (LSF) software enables you to execute batch and interactive jobs on a pool of networked computers. The Sun Microsystems High Performance Computing (HPC) package includes LSF as a vehicle for launching parallel applications on an HPC cluster. Besides starting batch jobs, LSF also provides load balancing by determining which computer possesses the optimum resources on which to run the jobs.

This chapter explains how to deploy LSF as a resource management tool and how it interoperates with other Solaris resource management controls.

When to Use LSF

LSF is part of the Sun HPC software foundation package and is required as a job starter to launch parallel applications within an HPC cluster environment. In most cases, an HPC cluster is composed of computers dedicated to running complex tasks that require supercomputer speeds. In these instances, all the resource management of the cluster is performed through LSF and other HPC tools. However, there may be environments, such as universities, where not all the CPU cycles in an HPC cluster are always dedicated to run highly compute intensive parallel applications. In these environments, resource management controls besides LSF can be deployed, such as the SRM software and Solaris processor sets.

LSF software may also be obtained directly from Platform Computing Corporation (www.platform.com) and run independent of Sun's HPC software. In this environment, the LSF software creates its own *cluster* of computers independent of the Sun HPC software. LSF clusters are created so batch jobs can be launched on the least busy computers in the cluster that contains sufficient resources to run them. The LSF cluster can consist of a collection of both servers and workstations.

Workstations are typically used by interactive users who usually do not keep the CPU busy 100 percent of the time. This results in a lot of CPU cycles going to waste. By deploying an LSF cluster, the unused CPU cycles in a network of high performance workstations and servers can be harnessed to do productive work. The LSF software can also be used in conjunction with other Solaris resource management controls such as the SRM software and processor sets to create an environment that can provide a predictable level of service to both interactive and batch users.

Good Workload Candidates for LSF Software

A typical environment where the LSF software is useful is where numerous compute-intensive jobs must be run on a limited number of computers with some jobs having higher priority than others. In this environment, a compute server farm is constructed of high end Sun Enterprise servers to which batch jobs are dispatched. Additonally, engineering workstations can be added to the server farm during non-working hours to take advantage of unused CPU cycles.

An example would be regression tests run during the ASIC microprocessor design process. In this scenario, there is the activity of building a model of the ASIC, adding new functionality to the model, and performing functional tests against the model. Once new functionality is added to the ASIC model a slew of regression tests need to be run to assure existing functions continue to work properly. Because of the complexity of ASICs, regression tests can number in the thousands. Since testing new functionality is more important than running regression tests, these batch jobs must be granted a higher priority.

Another type of workload where the LSF software is applicable is running complex analysis applications, where the application has been parallelized using the industry standard Message Passing Interface (MPI) library. An example would be the design of an airframe where complex structural analysis must be performed. Techniques such as Finite Element Analysis (FEA) are typically employed to create a model of the airframe, then stress forces are applied to the model. Since the analysis can be broken up into smaller pieces which can run in parallel on different computers, creating a cluster of compute servers by deploying the Sun HPC software that includes the LSF software, makes sense.

LSF-Aware Applications

Workloads that use applications that are LSF aware can also benefit by deploying the LSF software. Platform Computing provides some applications that are LSF aware. These applications contact the LSF software to locate the best host to run on. Two examples are: lsmake and lsnamed.

The `lsmake` application is a version of GNU `make` that performs parallel makes. This application is useful in reducing the total build time of software projects by distributing compilations to multiple computers.

The `lsnamed` application can be used to load balance DNS lookup requests. The DNS lookup will be dispatched to the least busy DNS server, thus reducing the chance that one server will become overloaded with lookup requests.

For applications other than those Platform Computing provides, you can write a *wrapper* that makes calls to the LSF software. An example of where a wrapper could be beneficial is the execution of a CGI script used on a web server. Instead of having the CGI script always run on the same server, the wrapper would call LSF and execute the script on the least busy server that contains the appropriate resources.

Commercial Applications

Many batch jobs that run on mainframes require that processing be performed in a well defined sequence. The output from one part of the process is used as the input for the next. An example of this is a program that extracts data from a database and then sorts it. A subsequent program takes the sorted data and performs an analysis on it. In this case, it is important that the second program doesn't start until the first process is complete. While LSF can track job dependencies, many customers choose another batch management system to run their commercial applications such as Platinum's AutoSys, which provides a GUI for designing complex job flows.

Many companies deploy mission critical ERP packages such as SAP R/3 to help run their business. These ERP packages typically have their own scheduler to run batch jobs. These schedulers do not interoperate with the LSF software, so those batch jobs would run outside the LSF software control. Likewise, a single Sun Enterprise server primarily used to run Oracle applications, would use the Oracle application's batch job facility and not the LSF software. Customers who desire to run all their batch jobs under the control of a single scheduler, might choose to deploy Platinum's AutoSys. Alternatively, Platform can provide specific integrations, where needed.

Relationship to Other Solaris Resource Control Features

This section discusses the relationship between the LSF software and other Solaris resource control features.

Base Solaris Software

Batch jobs that are launched by LSF run as user level processes in the timesharing scheduling class. As such, the priority that these jobs run at can be adjusted using the Solaris nice(1) command. However, it is not necessary to assign different nice levels to different batch jobs, since batch jobs can be placed in different priority batch queues. The LSF software launches the batch job based on its batch queue priority and can suspend a running job if a higher priority job is waiting or if the batch job is using more than its allotted resources. The LSF software does not implement its own scheduling class like the SRM software does. The scheduling of LSF batch jobs is performed at a level higher than the operating system schedulers.

The LSF software deploys its own process monitoring agents that track the resources being used by the running batch jobs. This agent is a separate process that collects performance data over time, such as that given by the Solaris ps and vmstat commands. Thresholds on CPU and memory usage are set in the LSF software for each batch job. If the thresholds are exceeded or the system activity is too high, than the running batch job will be suspended. The job is restarted when there are sufficient system resources or another batch job has reached its resource usage threshold.

Solaris processor sets may be used in conjunction with the LSF software, but care must be taken to avoid unwanted side effects. The LSF software provides a facility for running a script before and after a batch job is run. The batch job can be confined to run on a particular processor set by specifying the psrset command in the start up script. However, this is a manual process since the current version of the LSF software has no awareness that processor sets are being used on a particular host. Likewise, the LSF monitoring process has no knowledge of processor sets, so it will assume all the CPU cycles on the host are available for running batch jobs. This could cause a batch job to be started on a less than optimum host. Platform Computing is currently working on processor set aware features for the next release of the LSF software.

The Solaris oftware provides a batch scheduler called *cron*, which can be invoked using the at command. In a limited fashion, some of the LSF features can be duplicated using a combination of cron and shell scripts. You can write a script that checks the CPU load on hosts in a network, then launches jobs on the least busy hosts. However, trying to monitor running jobs and prioritizing jobs would be very difficult. Unlike the LSF software, which maintains multiple batch queues for jobs of different priorities, cron only provides a single batch queue. Since the LSF software has no way to manage the cron batch queue, it is not advisable to launch batch jobs with both the LSF software and cron on the same computer.

Solaris Resource Manager Software

The SRM software provides the capability of limiting resource consumption of processes based on the user running that process. Since batch jobs launched by the LSF software can be run as specific users, the LSF software batch jobs can be controlled by the SRM software . In this scenario, the jobs launched by the LSF software would be run as a particular user, for example, one called *batch*. The user *batch* would then be granted a certain number of SRM shares. Using this method, batch jobs are not allowed to consume all the resources of a host. Therefore, interactive users are not be penalized, by having batch jobs run on the same computer, since they are always guaranteed a certain level of resources.

Unlike processor sets, which do not allow consumption of unused CPU cycles by processes not bound to a particular processor set, the SRM software allows batch jobs to use whatever unused CPU cycles are available. If interactive users are active on the computer, they can reclaim their share of resources. The result is that the batch jobs take longer to complete. However, since batch jobs are guaranteed a certain share of the computer's resources, a predictable *maximum* time to complete can be established and be part of a SLA. The upside here s that based on interactive usage, the batch jobs can run *faster* than the time specified in the SLA.

There is one caveat with running the LSF software on computers under SRM control. The monitor process of the LSF software cannot predict the level of resources that will later be available on a host. If there are two hosts to choose from, the LSF software will normally choose the least busy one to launch a batch job on. If, while the batch job is running, interactive usage picks up substantially on the host and drops on a host that was not chosen to run the batch job, optimum results will not be achieved. the LSF software has the ability to terminate a job on one host, then restart it on another one, but this is not always desirable. Even though the optimum host was not chosen, the batch job will still get its percentage of the computer's resources as determined by its SRM shares.

Dynamic System Domains

Each Sun Enterprise 10000 *domain* looks like a separate host to the LSF software. Therefore, the LSF software treats *domains* as separate hosts and applies whatever LSF policies are established for them.

Dynamic Reconfiguration

The LSF software maintains both static and dynamic information about hosts in an LSF cluster. If a Sun Enterprise 10000 is dynamically reconfigured, the static parameters that the LSF software uses must be manually updated.

Other Third-Party Batch Management Systems

Some applications like SAP have a facility for scheduling and running batch jobs. Running end of month ERP reports, for example, can be scheduled and controlled by SAP software. While the LSF software can coexist with other batch management systems, avoid scheduling conflicts. For example, if ERP reports are to be run the last day of each month using the SAP batch facility, write the LSF policy for that host so as not to conflict with the anticipated load on that host during that time.

LSF Resource Management Viewpoint

The LSF software has a cluster viewpoint of resource management. It is essentially unaware of other resource controls which may be implemented on the hosts that make up the LSF cluster. The LSF software assumes that all the resources within its cluster are at its disposal. Network bandwidth is not a major concern of the LSF software since the batch jobs it controls do not generate much network traffic and neither does the monitoring or management of jobs running on execution hosts.

In the Sun HPC environment, a high speed interconnect is used for message passing between hosts running parallel applications. Since this is a dedicated channel, resource control of the traffic on the interconnect is not required.

LSF Cluster Viewpoint

The term *cluster* is widely used to describe a configuration of computers in a network that some how share resources. In LSF terminology, a *cluster* is a federation of computers, each running LSF software. There are no special hardware configuration requirements except that the computers be networked together and running TCP/IP.

There are no special software dependencies as long as all the systems in the *cluster* are running one of the supported operating systems. File sharing between the systems is recommended, but not required. Running a directory service such as NIS makes things easier, but again, is not a requirement.

To create an LSF *cluster*, the LSF software must be loaded on each computer and a configuration file modified to reflect the cluster's available resources. The role of the *master host* is determined automatically by the LSF software, so no manual configuration is required.

LSF Functions

The LSF software provides a full range of resource management functions. You can establish policies for where and when batch jobs can be run. Monitoring processes are put in place to control the amount of resources consumed by batch jobs. After batch jobs are run, information about job resource usage, number of jobs run, and so on is recorded for later workload analysis and department charge back.

Establishing Policies

The LSF software provides a number of controls that can be used to establish resource management policies. These controls include: setting job priorities, establishing scheduling policies, setting limits on job slots, and setting user permissions.

Job Priorities

Each LSF batch queue has a priority number. The LSF software tries to start jobs from the highest priority queue first. Within each queue, jobs are dispatched in a first come, first served order, unless a *fairshare* scheduling policy has been established.

Jobs can be dispatched out of turn if pre-execution conditions are not met, specific hosts or resources are busy or unavailable, or a user has reached the user job slot limit. To prevent overloading any host, the LSF software waits for a configured number of dispatching intervals before sending another job to the same host.

Scheduling Policies

The LSF software provides several resource controls to prioritize the order in which batch jobs are run. Batch jobs can be scheduled to run on a first-come-first-served basis, fair sharing between all batch jobs, and preemptive scheduling where a high priority job can bump a lower priority job that is currently running. Other policies include deadline constraint and backfill of resources reserved for large jobs that are not yet ready to run.

Note – The fairshare scheduling the LSF software uses should not be confused with the scheduling class implemented by the Solaris Resource Manager software. The LSF software is implemented on top of the Solaris timesharing scheduling class and only manages jobs submitted to LSF batch queues. The SRM software provides fairshare scheduling for all jobs running on a Solaris system.

Fairshare in Queues

Fairshare scheduling is an alternative to the default first come, first served scheduling. Fairshare scheduling divides the processing power of the LSF cluster among users and groups to provide fair access to resources for all jobs in a queue. The LSF software allows fairshare policies to be defined at the queue level so that different queues can have different sharing policies.

The main purpose of LSF fairshare scheduling is to prevent a single user from using up all the available job slots, thus locking out other users.

Fairshare in Host Partitions

Host partitions provide fairshare policy at the host level. Unlike queue level fairshare, a host partition provides fairshare of resources on a group of hosts, and it applies to all queues that use hosts in the host partition. Fairshare scheduling at the level of queues and host partitions are mutually exclusive.

Hierarchical Fairshare

Hierarchical fairshare allows resources to be allocated to users in a hierarchical manner. Groups of users can collectively be allocated a *share*, and that *share* can be further subdivided and given to subgroups, resulting in a share tree. Note that LSF shares are not related to SRM shares.

Preemptive Scheduling

Preemptive scheduling allows the LSF administrator to configure job queues so that a high priority job can preempt a low priority running job by suspending the low priority job. This is useful to ensure that long running low priority jobs do not hold resources while high priority jobs are waiting for a job slot.

Exclusive Scheduling

Exclusive scheduling makes it possible to run exclusive jobs on a host. A job only runs exclusively if it is submitted to an exclusive queue. An exclusive job runs by itself on a host. The LSF software does not send any other jobs to the host until the exclusive job completes.

Processor Reservation and Backfilling

Processor reservation and backfilling ensure that large parallel jobs are able to run without under-utilizing resources.

There might be delays in the execution of parallel jobs when they are competing with sequential jobs for resources. This is because as job slots become available, they are used in smaller numbers by sequential jobs. This results in the larger number of job slots required by a parallel application never becoming available at any given instant. Processor reservation allows job slots to be reserved for a parallel job until enough are available to start the job. When a job slot is reserved for a job, it is unavailable to other jobs.

Backfilling is the execution of a job that is short enough to fit into the time slot during which the processors are reserved, allowing more efficient use of available resources. Short jobs are said to backfill processors reserved for large jobs.

Job Slot Limits

A job slot is the basic unit of processor allocation in the LSF software. A sequential job uses one slot whereas a parallel job that has N components, uses N job slots, which can span multiple hosts. A job slot can be used by a maximum of one job. A job slot limit restricts the number of job slots that can be used at any one time. Each LSF host, queue, and user can have a slot limit.

Job slot limits are used by queues when deciding whether a particular job belonging to a particular user should be started on a specific host. Depending on whether or not preemptive scheduling policy has been configured for individual queues, each queue can have a different method of counting jobs toward a slot limit.

Resource Controls

Determination of where to run particular jobs is often based on the resources required by the job and the availability of those resources. The following section explains what those resources are.

Resources Based on Location

After an LSF cluster is created, an inventory of all resources in the cluster is taken, so jobs will know the best place to run. Resources can be classified by location into two categories:
- Host-based resources
- Shared resources

Host-Based Resources

Host based resources are resources that are not shared among hosts, but are tied to individual hosts. An application must run on that host to access such resources. Examples are CPU, memory, and swap space. Using up these resources on one host does not affect the operation of another host.

Shared Resources

A shared resource is a resource that is not tied to a specific host, but is associated with the entire cluster, or a specific subset of hosts within the cluster. Examples of shared resources include:
- floating licenses for software packages
- disk space on a file server which is mounted by several machines
- the physical network connecting the hosts

An application may use a shared resource by running on any host from which that resource is accessible. For example, in a cluster in which each host has a local disk, but can also access a disk on a file server, the disk on the file server is a shared resource and the local disk is a host-based resource. There will be one value for the entire cluster that measures the utilization of shared resources, but each host based resource is measured separately.

Resources Based on Type

Resources can also be categorized as dynamic and static.

Dynamic Resources

The availability of dynamic, non-shared resources is measured by load indices. Certain load indices are built into the LSF software and are updated at fixed time intervals. Other indices can be specified and are updated when an external load collection program sends them. The following table summarizes the internal load indices collected by the LSF software.

TABLE 10-1 Internal Load Indices Collected by the LSF Software

Index	Measures	Units	Direction	Averaged Over	Update Interval
status	host status	string	N/A	N/A	15 seconds
rl5s	run queue length	processes	increasing	15 seconds	15 seconds
r1m	run queue length	processes	increasing	1 minute	15 seconds
rl5m	run queue length	processes	increasing	15 minutes	15 seconds
ut	CPU utilization	percent	increasing	1 minute	15 seconds
pg	paging activity	pages in+pages out per second	increasing	1 minute	15 seconds
ls	logins	users	increasing	N/A	30 seconds
it	idle time	minutes	decreasing	N/A	30 seconds
swp	available swap space	megabytes	decreasing	N/A	15 seconds
mem	available memory	megabytes	decreasing	N/A	15 seconds
tmp	available temporary space	megabytes	decreasing	N/A	120 seconds
io	disk I/O	kbytes per second	increasing	1 minute	15 seconds

The `status` index is a string indicating the current status of the host. The possible values are:

- **ok**

    The host can be selected for execution

- **busy**

    A load index exceeds a defined threshold

- **lockU**

    The host is locked by a user

- **lockW**

The host's availability time window is closed

- **unavail**

  The host is not responding

- **unlicensed**

  The host does not have a valid LSF license

The `r15s`, `r1m` and `r15m` load indices have the 15 second, 1 minute, and 15 minute average CPU run queue lengths. This is the average number of processes ready to use the CPU during the given interval.

On multiprocessor systems more than one process can executed at a time. The LSF software scales the run queue value on multiprocessor systems to make the CPU load of uniprocessors and multiprocessors comparable. The scaled value is called the *effective run queue length*.

The LSF software also adjusts the CPU run queue based on the relative speeds of the processors. The *normalized run queue length* is adjusted for both the number of processors and the CPU speed. The host with the lowest normalized run queue length will run a CPU intensive job the fastest.

The `ut` index measures CPU utilization, which is the percentage of time spent running system and user code. A host with no process running has a `ut` value of 0 percent, while a host on which the CPU is completely busy has a `ut` of 100 percent.

The `pg` index gives the virtual memory paging rate in pages per second. This index is closely tied to the amount of available RAM and the total process size. If there is not enough RAM to satisfy all processes, the paging rate will be high.

The paging rate is reported in units of pages rather than kilobytes, because the relationship between interactive response and paging rate is largely independent of the page size.

The `ls` index gives the number of users logged in. Each user is counted once, no matter how many times they have logged into the host.

The `it` index is the interactive idle time of the host, in minutes. Idle time is measured from the last input or output on a directly attached terminal or a network pseudo terminal supporting a login session.

The `tmp` index is the space available on the file system that contains the `/tmp` directory in megabytes.

The `swp` index gives the currently available swap space in megabytes. This represents the largest process that can be started on the host.

The `mem` index is an estimate of the real memory currently available to user processes. This represents the approximate size of the largest process that could be started on a host without causing the host to start paging. This is an approximation because the virtual memory behavior is hard to predict.

The `io` index measures the I/O throughput to disks attached directly to the host in kilobytes per second. It does not include I/O to disks that are mounted from other hosts.

Static Resources

Static resources represent host information that does not change over time such as the maximum RAM available to processes in a machine. Most static resources are determined when the LSF software starts up. The following table lists the static resources reported by the LSF software.

TABLE 10-2 Static Resources Reported by the LSF Software

Index	Measures	Units	Determined by
type	host type	string	configuration
model	host model	string	configuration
hname	host name	string	configuration
cpuf	CPU factor	relative	configuration
server	host can run remote jobs	Boolean	configuration
rexpri	execution priority	nice(2) argument	LSF
ncpus	number of processors	processors	LSF
ndisks	number of local disks	disks	LSF
maxmem	maximum RAM available to users	megabytes	LSF
maxswp	maximum available swap space	megabytes	LSF
maxtmp	maximum space in temporary file system	megabytes	LSF

The `type` and `model` resources are strings specifying the host type and model.

The CPU factor is the speed of the host's CPU relative to other hosts in the cluster. If one processor is twice the speed of another, its CPU factor is twice as large. For multiprocessor hosts, the CPU factor is the speed of a single processor. The LSF software automatically scales the host CPU load to account for additional processors.

The server resource is a Boolean, where its value is 1 if the host is configured to execute tasks from other hosts, and 0 if the host is not an execution host.

Monitoring Resource Usage

Since the amount of available resources on an execution host is constantly changing, some method of monitoring the current state of that host must be deployed to avoid overloading it. Also, some check of the resources consumed by a particular batch job must be performed to assure that the batch job is not consuming more resources than specified in the resource policy for that job. The LSF software uses the Load Information Manager (LIM) as its resource monitoring tool. The LIM process running on each execution host is responsible for collecting load information. The load indices collected by the LIM include:

- Host status
- Length of run queue
- CPU utilization
- Paging activity
- Available swap space
- Available memory
- I/O activity

The load information is gathered at predefined intervals ranging from 15 seconds to one minute.

To modify or add load indices, you can write an Extended Load Information Manager (ELIM). The ELIM can be any executable program, either an interpreted script or compiled code. Only one ELIM per host is allowed; but each ELIM can monitor and report multiple measures.

LSF Scheduler Components

The following diagram shows the components used by the LSF software to schedule jobs. The `mbatchd` daemon runs on the *master host*, which manages the run queues. A job is submitted to these run queues along with the resources the job requires.

The `mbatchd` daemon periodically scans through the jobs ready to run and compares their resource requirements with the host resources contained in the Load Information Manager (LIM). When the appropriate resources become available for the job, the load conditions on the available hosts are checked to find the least loaded host.

Once the most appropriate host is found, `mbatchd` sends the job to the `sbatchd` daemon running on that system. When the job is started, `sbatchd` keeps track of the resource consumption of the job and reports back to `mbatchd`.

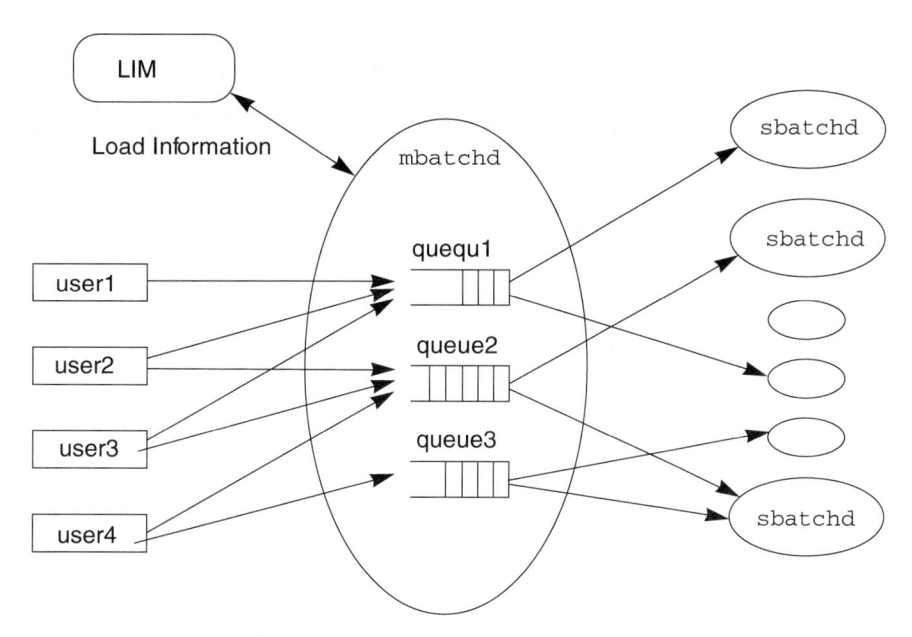

FIGURE 10-1 LSF Scheduler Components

Exceptions and Alarms

When managing critical jobs, it is important to ensure that the jobs run properly. When problems are detected during the processing of the job, it becomes necessary to take some form of corrective action. The LSF software allows the user to associate each job with one or more exception handlers, which tell the system to watch for a particular type of error and take a specified action if it occurs. An exception condition represents a problem processing a job. The LSF software can watch for several types of exception conditions during a job's life cycle.

An alarm specifies how a notification should be sent in the event of an exception.

Events

An event is a change or occurrence in the system (such as the creation of a specific file, a tape drive becoming available, or a prior job completing successfully) that can be used to trigger jobs. The LSF software responds to the following types of events:

- **time events**

    Points of time (defined by calendars and time expressions) that can be used to trigger the scheduling of jobs.

- **job events**

    The starting and completion of other jobs.

- **job group events**

    Changes in the status condition of job groups.

- **file events**

    Changes in a file's status.

- **user events**

    Site specific occurrences, such as a tape mount, defined by the LSF cluster administrator.

- **exception events**

    Conditions raised in response to errors in the scheduling or execution of jobs.

Job Starters

A job starter is a specified command (or set of commands) that executes immediately prior to a submitted batch job or interactive job. This can be useful when submitting or running jobs that require specific set up steps to be performed before execution, or jobs that must be performed in a specific environment. Any situation in which a wrapper would be written around the job you want executed, is a candidate for a job starter.

There are two types of job starters in the LSF software: command level and queue level. A command level job starter is user defined and precedes interactive jobs. A queue level job starter is defined by the LSF administrator and precedes batch jobs submitted to a specific queue.

Job starters can also be used to run a job on a specific processor set, or to start a job inside an application-specific shell.

Analyzing Workloads

The LSF software can process historical workload data to produce reports about a cluster. The workload data includes information about batch jobs, system metrics, load indices and resource usage. The data obtained from the analyzer can be used for chargeback accounting and generating chargeback reports and invoices. It can also be used to plan for additional computing purchases.

The primary features of the LSF software for analyzing workloads are:

- Profiles highlighting the number of jobs processed by the system, job resource usage, system metrics, load indices, and resource usage
- Usage trends for the LSF system hosts, users, queues, applications, and projects
- Information to manage resources by user and project
- Chargeback accounting for users or projects providing reports and invoices
- Data export to comma separated values (.csv) file format compatible with industry standard spreadsheet and data analysis tools
- Built-in and user generated templates to automate analysis

The LSF software collects and analyzes historical data stored in the LSF database to produce statistical reports that are designed to suit your needs. The analysis can be displayed in table, bar, area, and line charts and can be saved as a template, which makes it convenient to repeat the analysis any time.

LSF Workload Configuration

The following diagram depicts an LSF cluster configuration.

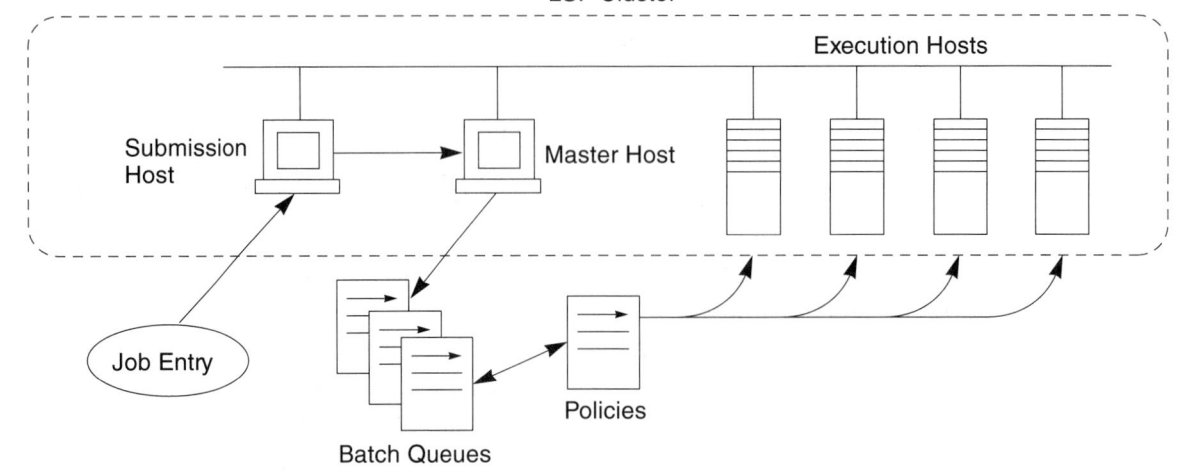

FIGURE 10-2 LSF Cluster Configuration

The *submission host* computer is the node where the user, or operator, submits the task to be performed. Typically, user accounts, established for these computers, grant the user permission to write data files on the *execution host's* storage. There is nothing special about being a submission host, since any node in the cluster can submit jobs. In fact, jobs can be submitted by computers outside the cluster by invoking an *xterm* session on one of the cluster nodes, or by using the Motif based tool provided with the LSF software.

The *master host* is the node where the LSF batch queues reside. When the LSF software initializes, one of the nodes in the cluster is elected to be the master host. This election is based on the order of nodes listed in a configuration file. If the first node listed in the configuration file is inoperative, the next node is chosen, and so forth.

The execution hosts are the nodes where the jobs will be executed. A master host can function as an execution host and usually does. If a node fails while a job is running, the job is lost, but no other nodes are affected. The failed node is then marked as offline in the cluster and no further jobs will be sent to it. All failed jobs are rescheduled on another available host.

Setting up an LSF cluster requires some planning. Besides collecting configuration data on each execution host, care must also be taken to assure that the batch job has access and correct permissions for reading and writing data files. Also to avoid a single point of failure, it is a good idea to implement the LSF software's high availability features.

Setting Correct Permissions

Correct permissions are required to at several levels to run batch jobs.

File Access within a Cluster

At some point, the batch jobs that run in the LSF cluster will need to write data to a file system. Since the batch job runs with the same access rights as the user who submits it, that user must have appropriate permissions to access files that the batch jobs requires. Also, the data files, which are required, must be accessible to the host that is running the job.

The easiest way to assure file accessibility is to NFS mount the file systems containing program data on all systems in the cluster and use NIS for user authentication. Alternatively, the LSF software can be configured to copy the required files to the host running the job, then copy them back when the job is complete.

Note – If the LSF software is used in a mixed environment of Solaris and Windows NT servers, NFS can still be used as long as the NFS client on Windows NT supports the Universal Naming Convention. Since mounting disks on drive letters is not performed until a user logs in, these type of mounts will not work in an LSF cluster.

Host Authentication Considerations

When a batch job or a remote execution request is received, the LSF software first determines the user's identity. Once the user's identity is known, the LSF software decides whether it can trust the host the requests come from.

The LSF software normally allows remote execution by all users except *root*. The reason for this is that by configuring an LSF cluster you are turning a network of machines into a single computer. Users must have valid accounts on all hosts. This allows any user to run a job with their own permission on any host in the cluster. Remote execution requests and batch job submissions are rejected if they come from a host not in the LSF cluster.

User Account Mapping

By default, the LSF software assumes uniform user accounts throughout the cluster. This means that a job will be executed on any host with exactly the same user ID and user login name.

The LSF software has a mechanism to allow user account mapping across dissimilar name spaces. Account mapping can be done at the individual user level or system level.

High Availability Features

The LSF software has several features that assure high availability. The following diagram shows the failover features of the LSF software.

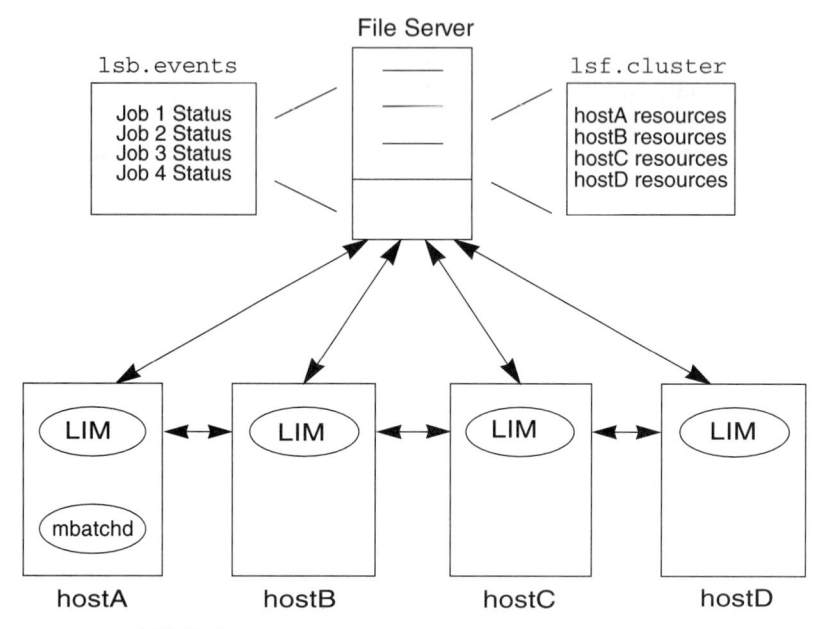

FIGURE 10-3 LSF Failover Features

In the above diagram there are four LSF servers, or hosts, connected to a fileserver. Although only a single fileserver is shown, in actuality, this could be a pair of fileservers in a HA cluster. The fileserver contains two key files: `lsf.cluster` and `lsb.events`.

The file `lsf.cluster` is the main configuration file LSF uses. All the names of the hosts in the LSF cluster are listed in this file along with the resources each has. By default, the host that appears first in `lsf.cluster` becomes the master host. As the master host, this node is responsible for maintaining the batch queues and launching jobs.

The file `lsb.events` is a log of jobs that have run and their current status. This file is updated only by the master host. It is usually kept on a separate file server or replicated if it is kept on a local disk.

In the event of a master host failure, the LIMs on the surviving nodes perform an election to determine which node should become the new master. The rule is to choose the next host listed in the `lsf.cluster` file. Once a new master host is established, the control of the `lsb.events` log is transferred to it. The LSF software also has an option to keep a copy of `lsb.events` on the master host. In the event the fileserver fails, the second copy of `lsb.events` prevents a single point of failure.

Parallel Jobs with Sun HPC

The Sun High Performance Computing (HPC) product suite provides an environment for running compute intensive parallel applications. These applications are written using the Sun MPI libraries and launched using the LSF software. These are typically scientific applications written in scientific programming languages such as FORTRAN.

Parallel Job Support in LSF Software

Applications that are too compute-intensive to run effectively on a single computer, can be broken into smaller pieces that can run simultaneously on several computers. A popular method for creating these parallel applications is to create the application using the Message Passing Interface (MPI).

To execute a parallel application under the LSF software, it must first be compiled with the MPI libraries. The following diagram shows the job execution flow of a parallel application.

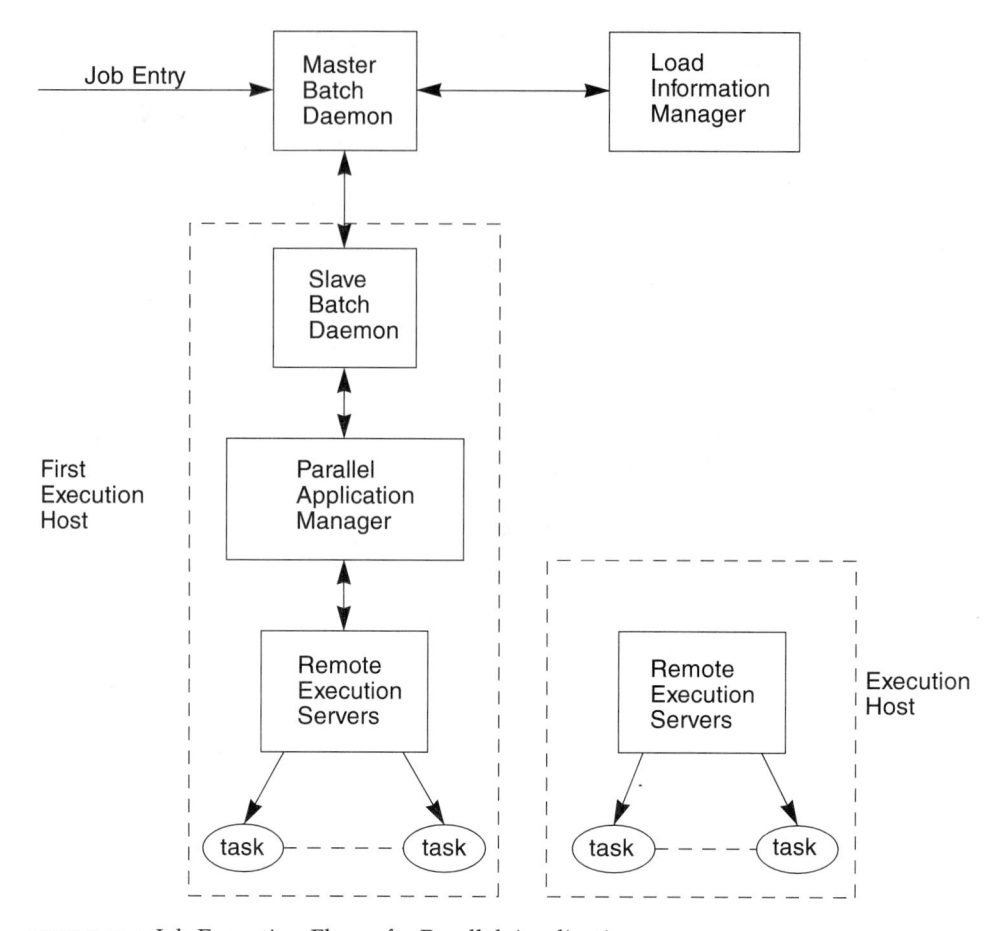

FIGURE 10-4 Job Execution Flow of a Parallel Application

The Master Batch Daemon (MDB) dispatches the job based on data obtained from the Load Information Manager (LIM). The MBD then contacts a Slave Batch Daemon (SBD), which starts the Parallel Application Manager (PAM) on one of the execution hosts. The PAM then dispatches pieces (tasks) of the job to other execution hosts in the LSF cluster.

Other Similar Products

The LSF software is a very complete offering and was chosen by Sun for that reason: but it is not the only batch system product available. Other products are listed below.

Distributed Queuing System

The Distributed Queuing System (DQS), from Florida State University is available in the public domain. The set of system resources it understands includes:

- Host (by name)
- System architecture
- Operating system type
- Amount of memory
- CPU usage

Users can start xterm sessions via interactive queues and some built-in support for PVM jobs is available. Limited high availability features are included since the master scheduler cannot migrate to another host.

Network Queuing System

Network Queuing System (NQS) is public domain software that has been enhanced by many hardware vendors. Sterling Software offers a distributed version of NQS called NQS/Exec that is geared toward a supercomputer environment. Limited load balancing is provided as there is no concept of *demand* queues, utilizing traditional *push* queues instead. There is also no control over interactive batch jobs.

Load Balancer

Load Balancer from Freedman Sharp and Associates, Inc., uses a single master queue for all jobs and only uses CPU usage as the sole metric for load balancing. Like NQS, the master queue scheduler cannot migrate to another host; thus it represents a single point of failure.

LoadLeveler

Loadleveler, from IBM, is a product based on the public domain Condor package developed at the University of Wisconsin. It is supported on AIX, IRIX, and SunOS and is compatible with NQS. Load balancing is based solely on CPU usage.

Task Broker

Task Broker, from Hewlett-Packard, is available on HP, Sun, and RS6000 platforms. It operates by having hosts bid for a job. The integer value of the bid returned from potential target hosts is either hard coded or determined by an affinity script which the system manager can define.

With Task Broker, the resources required by specific tasks are preconfigured by the system manager. Users do not have control over which resources can be used to run a particular task.

CHAPTER **11**

The Jiro Initiative

Jiro is an industry wide initiative sponsored by Sun Microsystems, Inc. that will deliver a standard, open platform for storage software development and management. The initiative is managed through Sun's Java Community Process (JCP), in which the community directs the content and the development of a standard infrastructure for the management of storage resources using the Java (and Jini) technologies.

The Jiro initiative uses the Java Community Process (JCP) in the development of standard specifications. The JCP enables the resulting APIs to be extensions to the Java Platform, while the execution of the Sun Community Source License (SCSL) provides the licensee access to the source code. The result of the community process is a set of specifications that provides guidelines and standards for the development of storage management applications.

The Storage Management Problem

Currently, no end-to-end software development standards for the storage industry are available. As a result, vendors have to develop individual, proprietary interfaces to all the other components in the system, thereby making the management process highly complex. Customers face vendor lock-in with difficult choices between competing systems. For example, Veritas has to develop different interfaces for Sun StorEdge, EMC, and CLARiiON. In addition, storage management is difficult, because each vendor chooses a different user interface, and there is no simple way today to administer all the server and storage resources necessary to ensure optimum performance for the entire system.

With Jiro, Sun takes a leadership position in an industry initiative to develop an open standards based software management platform for the storage industry. The platform applies to any environment that supports Java Virtual Machine (JVM), including both the Solaris operating environment and Microsoft Windows NT.

Storage Solution Requirements

The Jiro Initiative provides an enabling technology designed to facilitate the development of enterprise storage management solutions. This technology enables storage solutions having the following requirements:

- Simple Storage Management—The management of storage must be accomplished through a high level of abstraction.
- High Integrity Management—The integrity of the management operations must be assured.
- Simple Programming Model—The learning curve required for adoption must be minimized.
- Remote/Distributed Management—The solution must be accessible remotely without regard to distance and network topology.
- Centralized View of Management—The solution must be able to access a wide domain from a single location.
- Automated Management—The solution must allow software that minimizes the manual intervention necessary for complex and tedious steps.
- Flexibility for Future Solutions—The solution must allow composition with other solutions into new applications outside the scope of the original design.
- High Availability Management—The solution must be tolerant of the loss of a management server.
- Non-Compounding Management—The solution itself must not itself be a management problem.

The Jiro Solution

The architecture of the solution is three tiered: the management client, the management logic, and the management resources. These are described in more detail below.

The Client Tier

The client locates and communicates with the management logic as a proxy for the human administrator. As solutions are combined, a solution is considered a client when it utilizes the interface designed for client interactions. In this respect, a client is a relative relationship between solutions.

The Management-Logic Tier

The management logic provides simple management components that can be assembled together to provide complete management solutions. Management-logic servers host these components on either shared servers or private servers. Shared servers are available across managed resources provided by different vendors. Private servers are components private to the managed resource. In a domain, groups of shared and private servers are called a federation of management servers and are the deployment target for management components.

The Resources Tier

The resources include both the framework resources, which are used exclusively by the management server framework, and the component resources, which are used exclusively by management components. Framework resources include state and behavior servers. Component resources include managed resources such as storage devices and storage software. Framework resources provide the underlying technology support that is the core of this enabling technology, providing the base services and infrastructure to support the requirements of storage solutions. Component resources for storage management are represented as Managed Objects (MO), with local representation of these objects being Managed Object Proxies (MOP). The MOs themselves are based on the Common Information Model (CIM).

Jiro and Resource Management Possibilities

The Jiro core enables resource management of the capacity, performance, and availability of data storage. Storage can be managed to a Storage Service Level, elevating the view of storage to where users, not the administrators, think about it. Backup and archival policies can be used to automate migration of data to a tape library. Measurements of capacity and performance characteristics are combined with availability policies, and the operator will be alerted of any problems. Ultimately storage subsystems will be reconfigured automatically.

Jiro provides the platform on which SLAs can be established. At present, Jiro does not include a general purpose rule script-based policy engine. Policies are embedded in the Java code for component and configuration management.

Integration between the system viewpoint and the storage viewpoint has some of the same problems as integration of system and network viewpoints. The traffic on the SAN does not contain any indication of which user or process generated the request. Within the Solaris software it is possible to trace storage accesses on a per-process per-device basis, but the overhead of collecting and analyzing this data is quite high. There may be a need for a Jiro-based Bandwidth Manager that bridges multiple management viewpoints.

Jiro Architecture

The core of Jiro is based on Java and Jini technology. It also includes a distributed object model (DOM). A set of base services, such as scheduler, logging, notification, and persistence, is offered to enable components to be built based on the Jiro platform. These fundamental services are required by most applications, so the developer does not need to implement these base services and can add more value in their core competency.

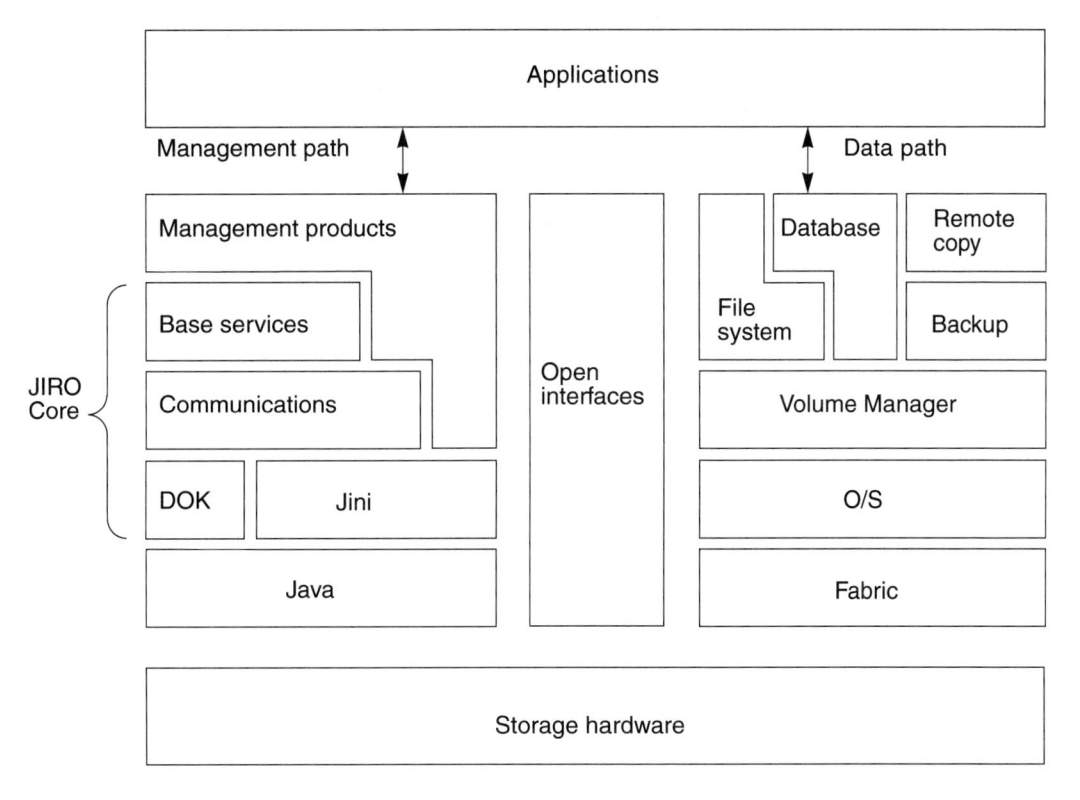

FIGURE 11-1 Jiro Architecture

Object Model

The object model extends the Java technology-based object model to add distributed operations. This extension provides a simple mechanism to communicate with remote objects. The framework used to extend the Java technology-based object model is referred to as the Distributed Object Kernel (DOK). A summary of the major enhancements to achieve the distributed operations follows:

- Proxies—The distributed equivalent of an object reference. A proxy to an object supplies a handle to a remote object in the system. The proxy concept allows the distributed operations conducted on classes and objects to function similarly to those on a local class or object.

- Logical Threads—The distributed implementation of a thread or flow of control for a local operation. The use of logical threads allows the distributed framework to be able to understand and handle concurrency control in the system.

- Composite Exception—This provides a familiar way of generating exceptions in the distributed framework that is intuitive to the programmer of the Java programming language. It provides the convenience of allowing multiple exceptions to be composited and gathered from distributed points in a uniform manner.
- Internationalization—The framework contains all of the necessary support for internationalization of management applications. It does this in a non-intrusive and uniform manner to promote clear and concise localizations.
- Security—Due to the distributed additions to the Java technology based object model, security becomes a high concern. The framework provides a security solution that restricts management applications to authorized usage and protects vital storage systems from intrusion.

Component Model

The component model provides support for the construction of applications from components. Thus, it primarily is concerned with how components are deployed and assembled. The framework provides an environment that enables the components to be deployed and assembled by providing the following:

- ORB—The management server is a specialized object request broker that has been decorated for storage management.
- Execution Environment—Provides the core platform supports the solution object software.
- Logging—Provides the ability to track operations and instantiations of components in the system.
- Notification—Provides the ability for a uniform manner of event passing between components in the system and the user.
- Scheduling—Allows time-based operations of the components in the system.

The Java Community Process

The JCP is a formal process for developing high-quality Java technology specifications in "Internet-time" using an inclusive, consensus building process that not only delivers the specification, but also the reference implementation and its associated suite of compatibility tests.

JCP suggests that the best way to develop a specification is to start with a handful of industry experts who have a deep understanding of the technology in question and then have a strong technical lead work with them to create a first draft. Consensus is then built using an iterative review process that allows an ever-widening audience to participate and to see their comments and suggestions incorporated into successive draft versions of the specification prior to its final release.

The expert groups established under the JCP, such as the Jiro Core Expert Group, will be responsible for individual specifications, proof-of-concept Reference Implementations (RI), and Compatibility Test Suites (CTS) within the Jiro initiative.

Momentum Behind Jiro

Jiro has obtained endorsements from many key vendors in the industry, who plan to use the Jiro Open Standard to simplify their developments and provide greater choice and ease of use to their customers.

As this book goes to print in, Exabyte, Fujitsu, Hitachi Data Systems, Hitachi Computer Products, Legato, StorageTek, Sun, and VERITAS form the initial Jiro Core Expert Group. This group will define the core specifications and corresponding reference implementation. In the following months, other expert groups may be formed in areas such as console, volume management, and backup.

The benefits of the initiative will be substantial for end users, developers, and systems integrators. Jiro frees developers from tedious tasks such as porting multiple applications and interfaces to multiple platforms; thus, enabling resource vendors to concentrate on adding value for their customers. Jiro helps ISVs by enabling them to focus on creating new, high-value storage services and by broadening the market for storage services. Jiro also enables customers to save money on storage appliances by increasing the functionality and manageability of existing storage systems.

More information on Jiro can be obtained from:

```
http://www.sun.com/jiro/
```

CHAPTER **12**

Sun Enterprise SyMON 2.0 Software

The Sun Enterprise SyMON 2.0 (SyMON) software was developed by Sun to act as a user interface to hardware features. It is a powerful and extensible system and network monitoring platform that is used to manage other products. The Solstice SyMON 1.x software was a Motif based system monitor for a single machine. The Sun Enterprise SyMON 2.0 software is a Java based monitor with multiple user consoles that can monitor multiple systems using the secure extensions to SNMPv2 to communicate over the network.

When to Use SyMON Software

The SyMON software is good at monitoring many systems and large and complex hardware configurations. It has knowledge about possible hardware error conditions embedded in it, and can be used to browse details of the configuration.

SyMON Software Availability and Support

Solstice SyMON 1.x was included for free with the Solaris operating environment as part of the Sun Computer Systems server bundle. The SyMON software will also be free when it is used to monitor and control a single server. To unlock its capability to manage more than one server at a time, an extra license must be purchased. SyMON software can also be used to manage any number of generic SNMP devices without additional licensing. SyMON software supports Solaris 2.5.1, Solaris 2.6, and Solaris 7 operating environments running on the sun4d and sun4u architectures. This includes the SPARCcenter™ 2000 and SPARCserver™ 1000, and most UltraSPARC™ based systems. It will not monitor sun4m based SPARCstation™ 5, 10 or 20 systems. It is not currently supported on the Sun Enterprise 10000, as the hardware configuration is far more complex and requires special support that is currently being developed for shipment later in 1999.

SyMON software can be downloaded from the Sun web site at
`http://www.sun.com/symon`

SyMON Software Architecture

The overall architecture is shown in FIGURE 12-1. Multiple Java-based GUIs can be installed that allow several administrators to use the system at the same time. The GUIs, which can be installed on a Solaris system or a Microsoft Windows or Windows NT system, can communicate using Java RMI calls to a central server process that is partly written in Java, but includes other native Solaris processes to perform some functions, so must run on a Solaris system. The SyMON server process talks to SyMON agent processes and other generic devices using the Simple Network Management Protocol (SNMP). When talking to a system that is managed by a SyMON agent, the enhanced SNMPv2 protocol is used with secure authentication from the GUI to the system being managed. Other tools can obtain data from a SyMON agent via SNMP.

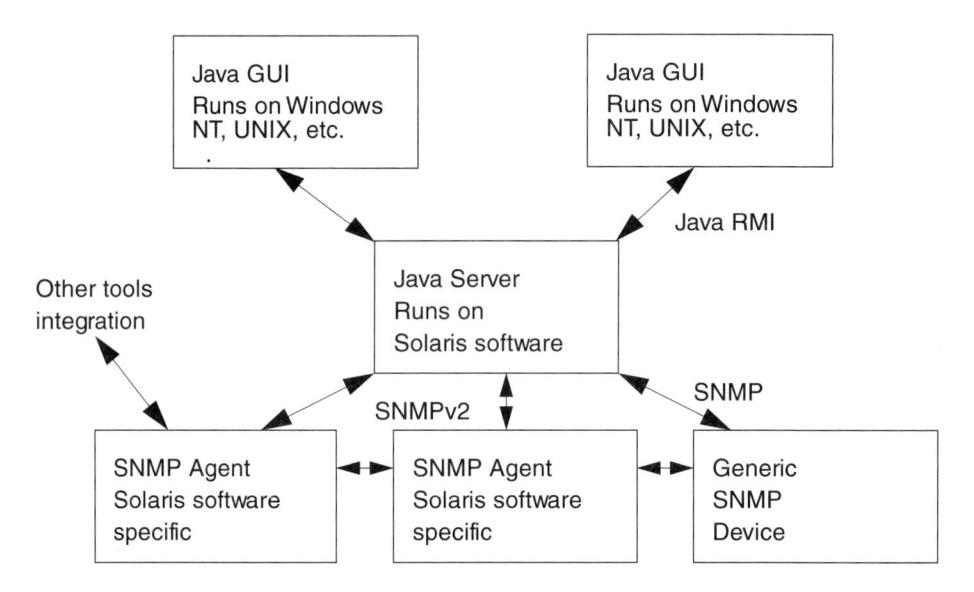

FIGURE 12-1 SyMON Software Architecture

The initial SyMON software screen is a login authorization process. When the authorization is completed, the network-wide view is displayed. Multiple administrative domains containing hundreds of nodes can be configured, but it is a powerful and useful tool even using the free single system license.

SyMON software has a dynamically extensible agent. At run time, you can request it to load a new module, and this module will be automatically loaded the next time the SyMON agent starts up.

Resource Monitoring with SyMON Software

The SyMON software can be used in several ways to monitor the resource usage of systems, this can be useful in both manual and automatically managed resource control environments. This section illustrates how to configure and use the SyMON software to perform basic monitoring operations and to discover the resources that are available in a system. The system used in the examples is an Ultra Enterprise 4000 configured with two 167MHz CPUs and about 300 disks.

The SyMON Health Monitor

The SyMON software includes a system health monitoring module that you can use in a resource management scenario to see if a system has enough resources to run comfortably. For example, if the CPU state is reported as red, that system probably needs either less work or more CPU power. Similarly, if the memory rule reports red, then the system may need more memory.

The health monitor is based on a set of complex rules developed over several years by Adrian Cockcroft, one of the authors of this book. The rules have become known as the "virtual adrian" rules as this is the name of the SE Toolkit script that first implemented them. The health monitor is not enabled by default when you first install the SyMON software because only the basic modules are loaded into the agent.

To load the health monitor module, start the SyMON program with the default administrative domain. Select the system and popup a menu. Then, select the Load Module option from the menu. In the example shown in FIGURE 12-2, a single red alert is present because one of the file systems on this machine is 98 percent full.

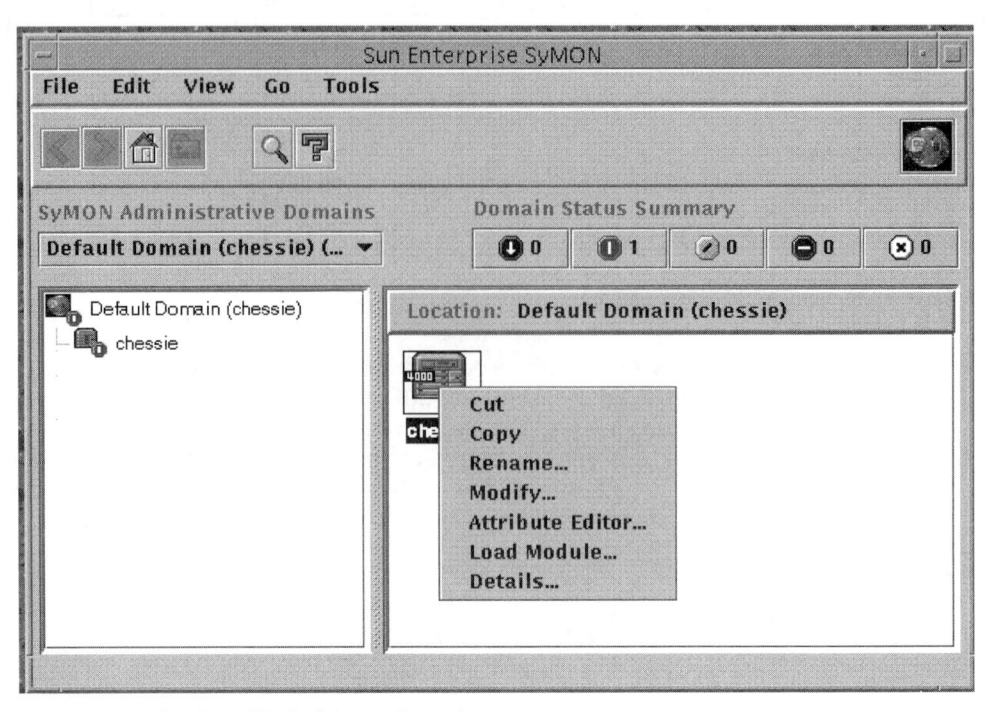

FIGURE 12-2 The SyMON Software Console

Next, scroll down and choose the Health Monitor module. It may already be loaded if the SyMON software has been pre-configured. Otherwise, select it and press the OK button.

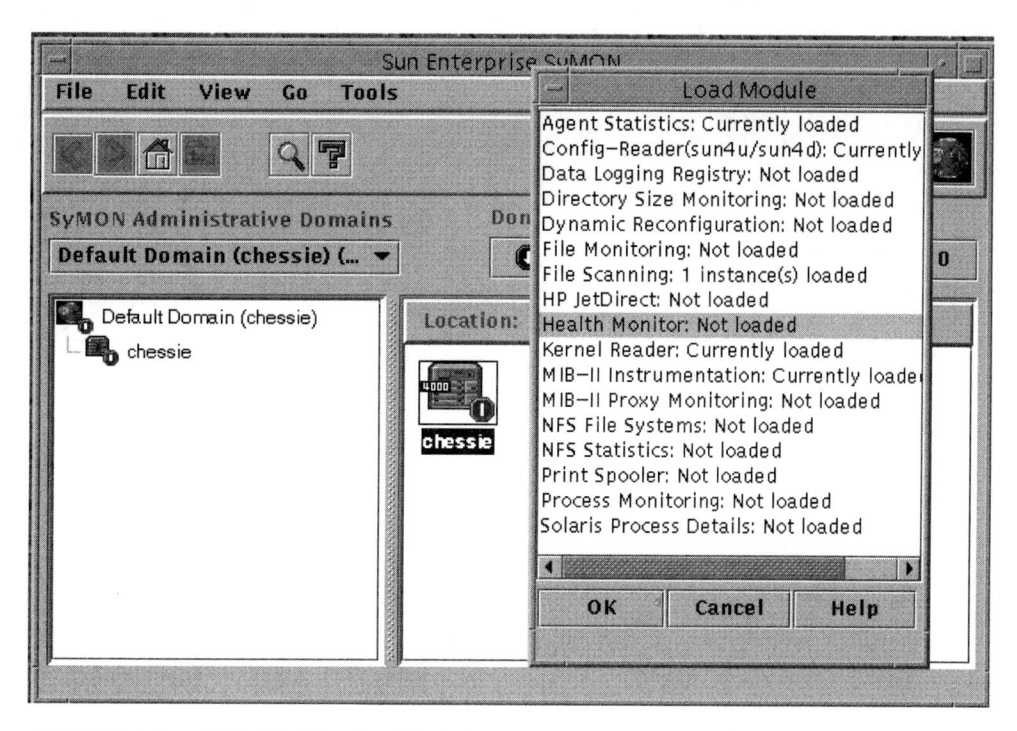

FIGURE 12-3 Load Health Monitor Module

Now any Health Monitor alerts will be logged for this system. We could drill down to the subsystem that caused the alert, but we don't expect any Health Monitor alerts yet. Since there is already an unrelated disk space alert on this system, we will select the system and bring up the detailed view. The Details menu option was shown in FIGURE 12-2. When you select the Details option, a second window opens that is specific to the system being monitored.

Chapter 12   Sun Enterprise SyMON 2.0 Software   285

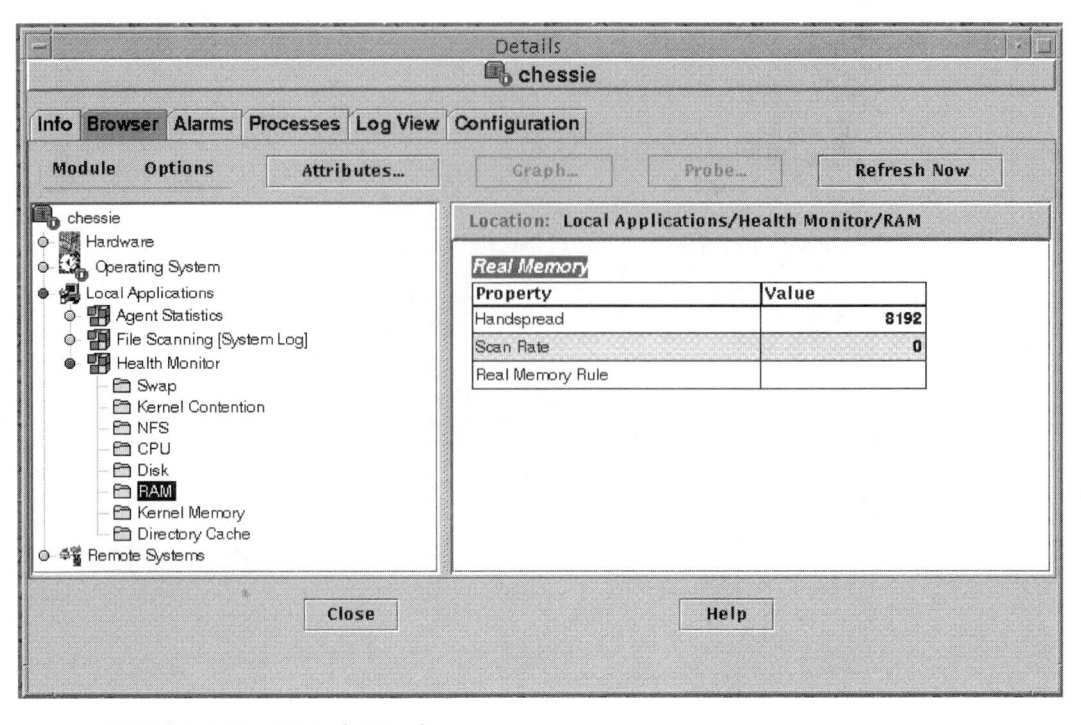

FIGURE 12-4 Host Details Window

The Browser tab of the host Details window shows the modules that are loaded. Under local applications (which opens up if you click on the bullet next to it) you will find the Health Monitor module. Inside it, you find the eight rules that are implemented based on `virtual adrian`. Each rule shows a few variables. The RAM rule that is displayed in FIGURE 12-4 shows that the current scan rate is zero so the rule value is a white box. If the ratio of scan rate to handspread went too high and the page residence time dropped below the pre-set threshold, this box would turn red and the red state would propagate up the hierarchy. To view and edit the rule attributes and thresholds, pop up a menu over the rule value.

The best way to use these rules is to increase the thresholds on a system that is performing well until in normal use there are no warnings. Then as the load increases, you will get warnings that indicate which subsystem is likely to be the bottleneck. If you have a system that is not performing well to start with, then these rules can help you eliminate some problem areas and indicate which subsystems to concentrate on.

This browser mode can be used to explore all the operating system measurements supplied by the kernel reader for this system, including CPU usage, paging rates, and disk utilization.

Handling Alarms in SyMON Software

When a simple rule or one of the more complex health monitoring rules generates an alarm, it is logged by SyMON software. At the domain level console, the worst alarm state for each system being monitored is counted. This means that with only one system being monitored only one alarm will be indicated. In this case, it is in the red state.

If you click on the red indicator, shown in FIGURE 12-5 with a '1' next to it, a new window opens that shows all the alarms for all the systems in this domain.

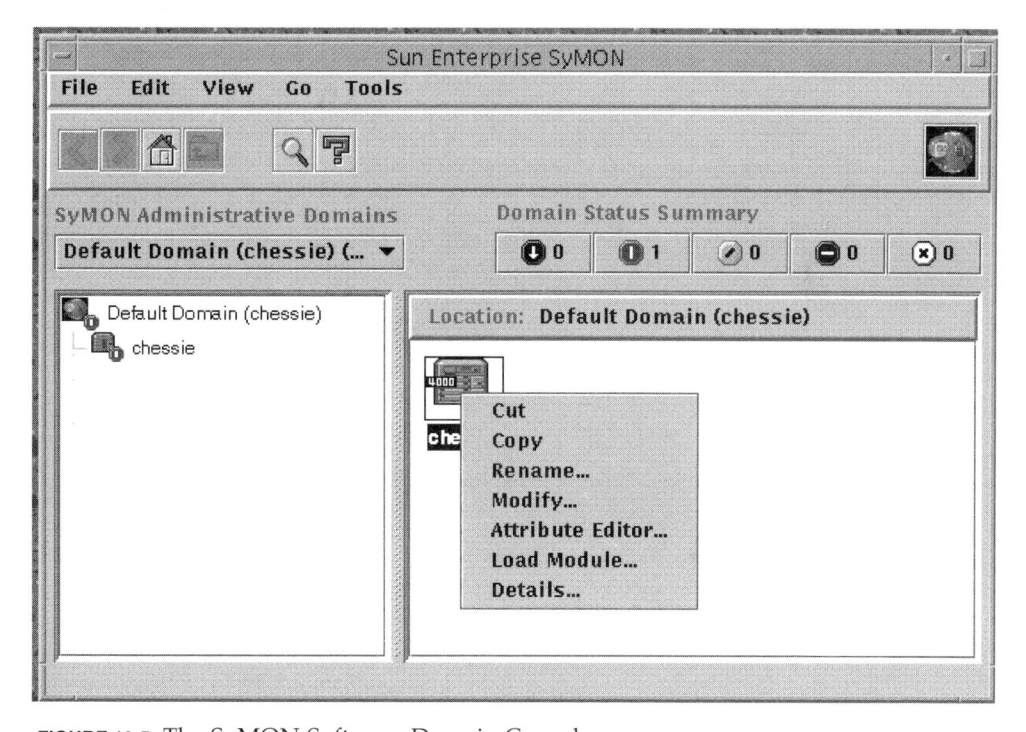

FIGURE 12-5 The SyMON Software Domain Console

FIGURE 12-6 displays only systems or other network components that are in the red (critical) state. In this case, one of the file system contains too many small files, so it is almost out of capacity.

Chapter 12   Sun Enterprise SyMON 2.0 Software   287

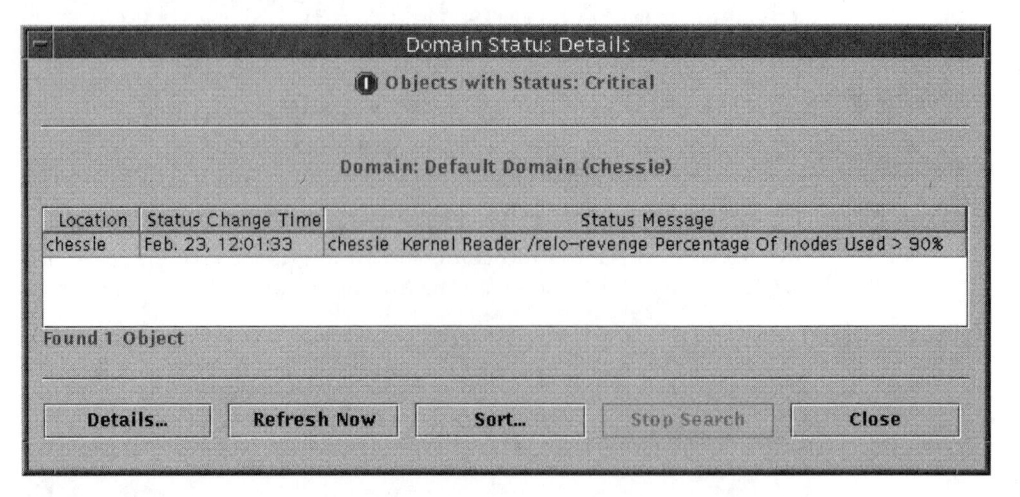

FIGURE 12-6 Domain Status Details Window

If you either double-click on the alarm or select the alarm and press the Details... button the Details window for that system opens with its alarm display tab selected as shown in FIGURE 12-7. This shows that in fact there are three alarms on this system, with only the most important one (red) being shown at the domain level.

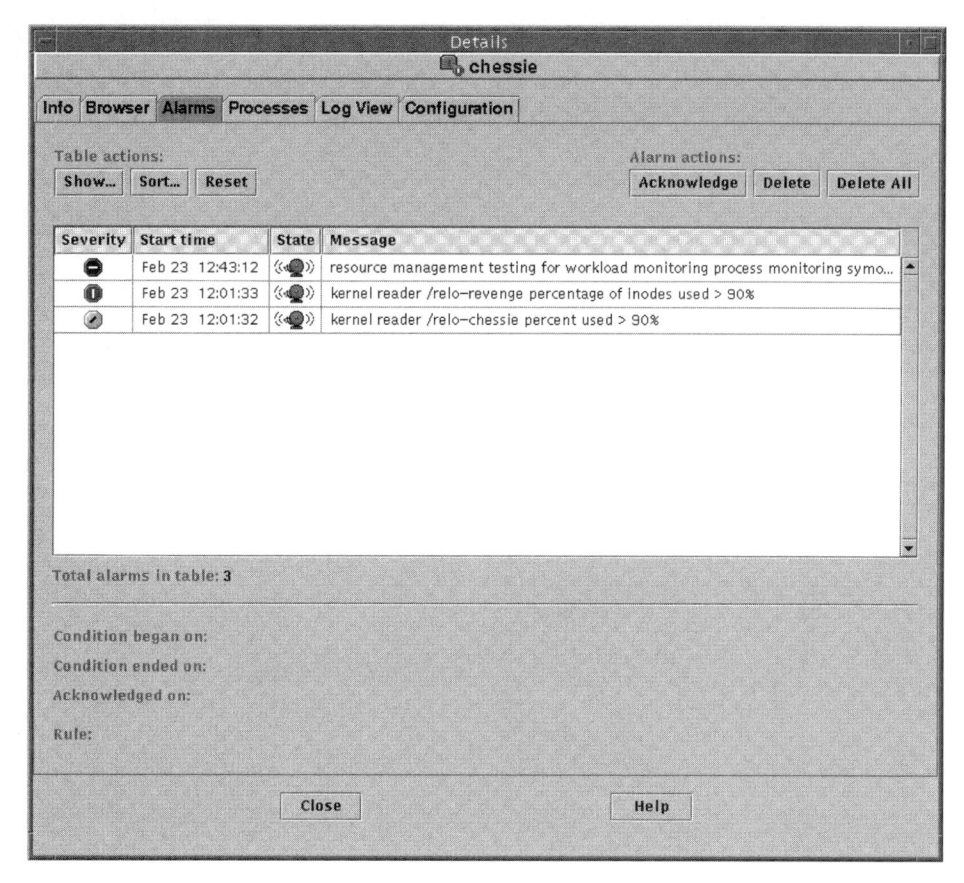

FIGURE 12-7 Alarm Details Window

Next, select one or all of the alarms and acknowledge them by pressing the Acknowledge button. It is best to select all the alarms by clicking on the first one and sliding the cursor down, then acknowledge them all at once. It takes some time to perform the acknowledgment because it involves communicating all the way back to the agent on the server being monitored. Once an alarm is acknowledged, a tick mark appears by it as shown in FIGURE 12-8

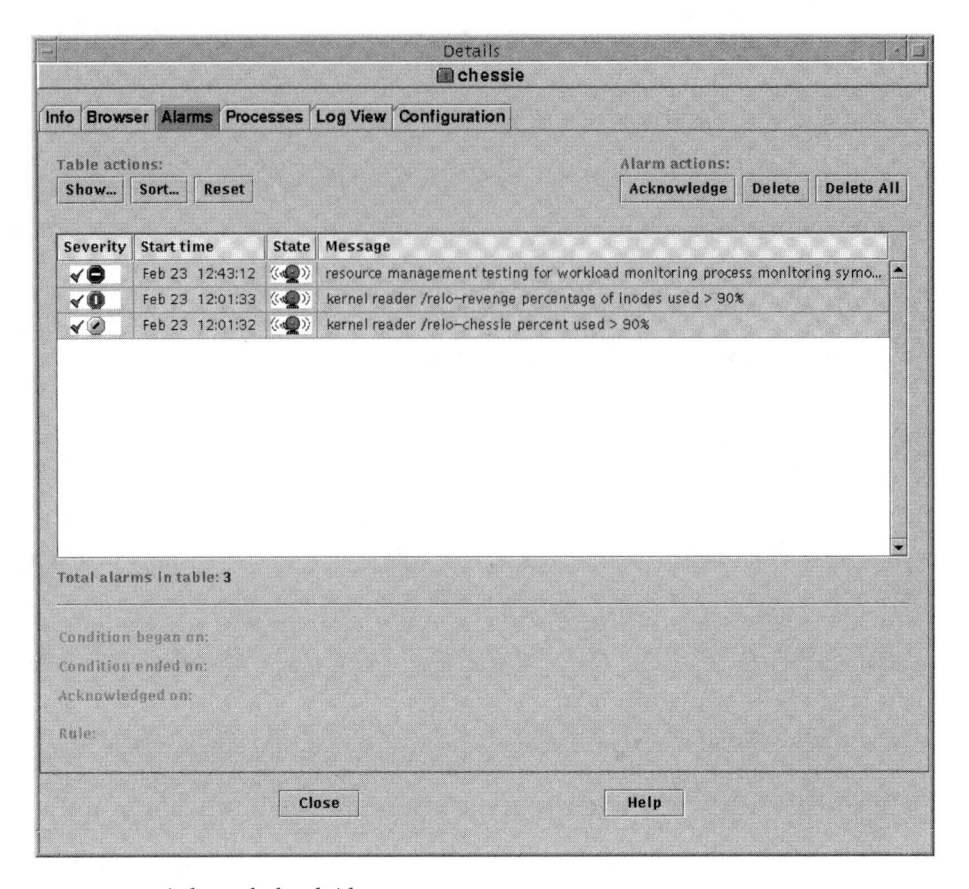

FIGURE 12-8 Acknowledged Alarms

If you close the Details window and return to the Domain Status window, it may not have changed. Press the Refresh Now button, and the alarm entry will go away as shown. You can now close the Domain Status window as well. Looking back at the Domain Console as shown in FIGURE 12-9, you will see that the server no longer has a red marker on it, and the Domain Status summary is all zeroes.

FIGURE 12-9 Refreshed Domain Status Details Window

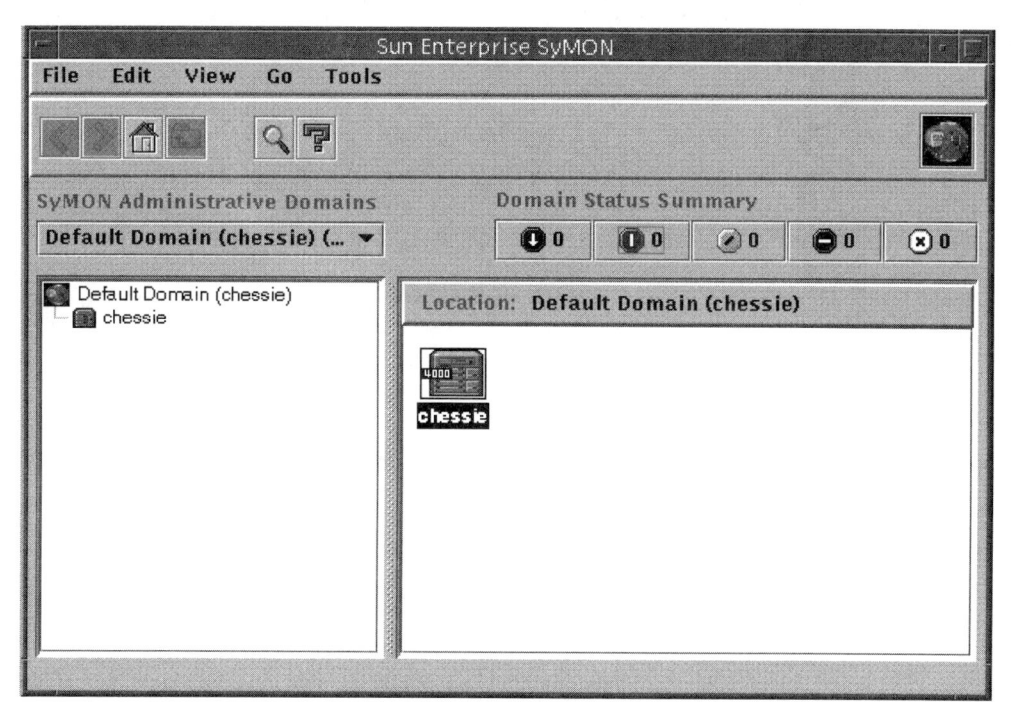

FIGURE 12-10 The SyMON Software Domain Console with No Alarms

Process Monitoring with SyMON Software

You can use the SyMON software to monitor processes and groups of processes that form workloads. This is described in detail in Chapter 5.

Browsing Configuration Information

The SyMON software includes detailed knowledge of the configuration of Sun hardware. This includes color pictures of components, so you can look inside a large server system to see exactly how the system boards are configured. This is a useful availability feature because you do not have to turn off a system and take it apart to find out what components are present. Any failed components are clearly indicated and the errors are logged to assist in problem diagnosis, which saves time and reduces the chance of accidentally changing the wrong component.

From the host details window, select the configuration tab. The initial view, FIGURE 12-11, shows a list of the main hardware resources in this Enterprise Server system.

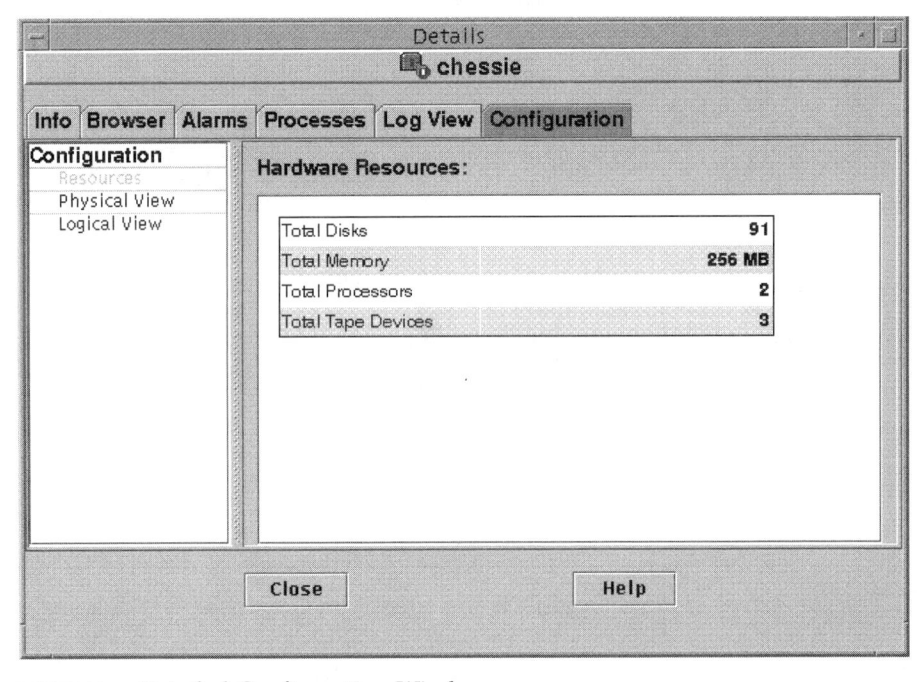

FIGURE 12-11 Detailed Configuration Window

On the left, there are three options: Resources, Physical View and Logical View. Select the Logical View and wait while the configuration information is loaded. This takes longer on larger and more complex systems.

The right pane changes to show the device hierarchy as shown in FIGURE 12-12. If you press the Show Details button, a second pane appears to show details of the properties of each device. A portion of the device tree shows a slot containing an IO board, that has an SBus with a fiberchannel serial optical controller (soc) plugged into it, and a SPARCstorage™ Array (SUNW,pln) containing 18 drives. The first drive is selected and the property shows that this is device ssd96, which is also known as controller two, target zero, device zero, c2t0d0.

FIGURE 12-12 Logical View of Hardware Configuration Tree

You can also view the physical layout of the system. Selecting Physical View on the left changes the pane on the right to show a picture of the front view of the system cabinet. A menu option allows you to change to the rear view of the system. Pressing the Show Details button displays level of details shown in FIGURE 12-13.

Chapter 12   Sun Enterprise SyMON 2.0 Software   293

Move the cursor over a component to highlight it. Its properties are displayed in the right pane. In FIGURE 12-13, one of the SBus card slots is highlighted to show that it is the soc card we saw in the Logical View.

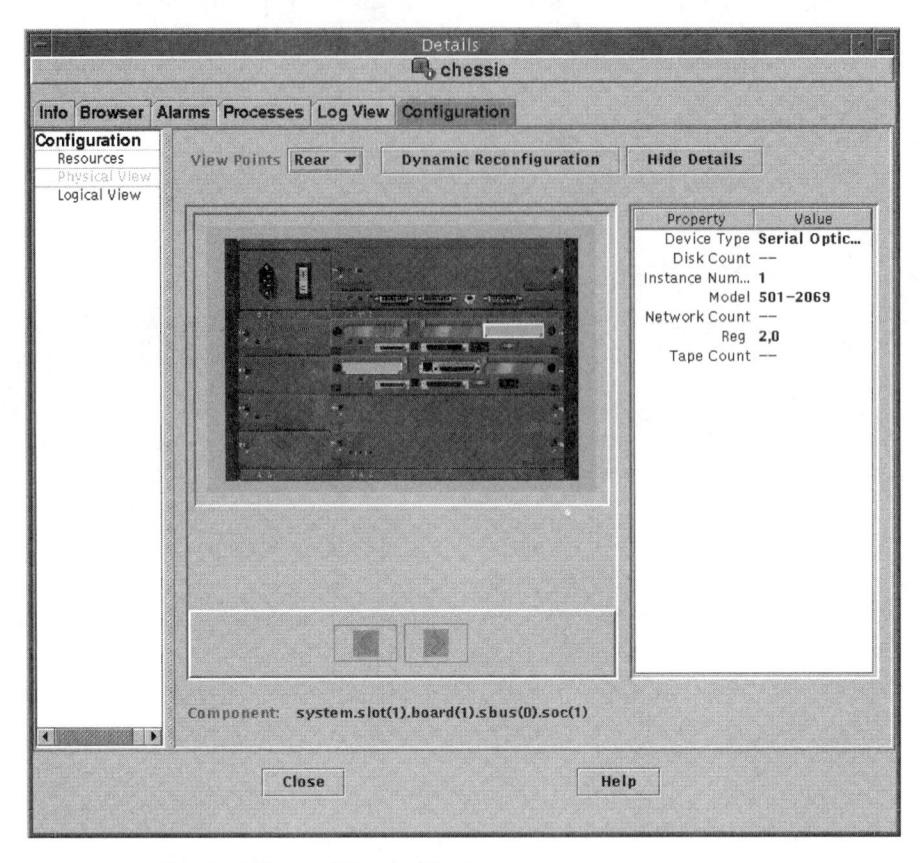

FIGURE 12-13 Physical View of Rear of System

Note the Dynamic Reconfiguration button. Dynamic Reconfiguration makes it possible to unconfigure an I/O board, so that it can be unplugged from a running system without a reboot. Conversely, an additional I/O board can be added. With the Solaris 7 software, it is also possible to add and remove CPU or memory boards on these midrange Enterprise Servers. The high end Sun Enterprise 10000 server also uses Dynamic Reconfiguration, which is described in Chapter 8.

Click on the I/O board end plate itself to see a view of the board and the components that are plugged into it as shown in FIGURE 12-14. Unfortunately, the SyMON software does not yet have explicit support for all the possible storage options, so the physical view stops here. If a Sun StorEdge A5000 enclosure were connected instead of the SPARCstorage Array, then its physical configuration would have been shown.

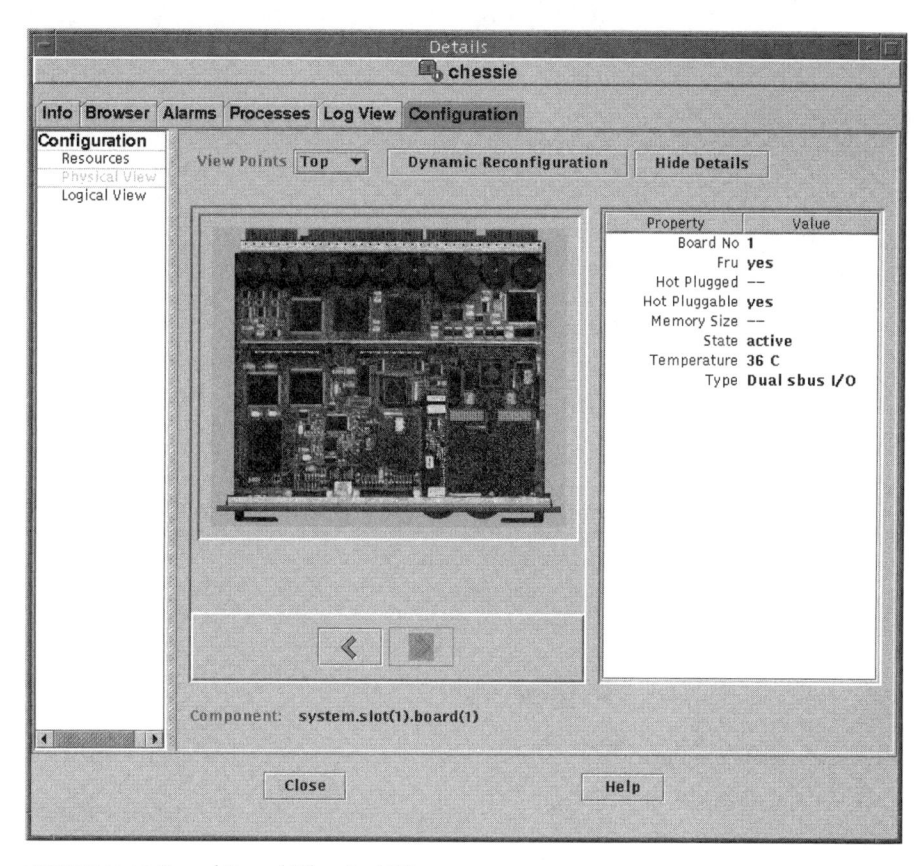

FIGURE 12-14 Board Level Physical View

CHAPTER **13**

IBM Workload Manager for OS/390

This chapter provides an overview the possibities available with extensive use of resource management and serves as a guide to help design long-term resource management goals for application developers. The relatively proprietary nature of the mainframe environment has afforded IBM the opportunity to manage resources effectively because of their ownership of most of the components: computer hardware, operating system, middleware, and applications. This is not the case in open systems, or specifically UNIX, environments. However, as we move forward we will see a great deal of collaboration between the major computer system component vendors to provide an environment with resource management interoperability. Initial evidence of this is the CPU and Network resource management work being done by Sun and bandwidth management with companies like Cisco.

Mainframe Data Center Resource Management

Mainframe administrators and system programmers are familiar with the resource and workload management facilities provided by IBM Workload Manager (WLM). WLM is a comprehensive tool set that provides an automated resource management environment, driven by high-level business goals, and that, in many cases, is self tuning. Tools are provided to define the business goals or objectives, to control system resources, and to feed metrics concerning these resources back to the resource controller, which attempts to ensure that the goals are met. This is an implementation of the measure/policy/control loop described in "Resource Management Control Loop" on page 7.

Historically, IBM has been driven by the same needs that drive Sun: making computer systems easier to manage and making better or more efficient use of their capacity. WLM is key to IBM's future in reinforcing its position within the data center by lowering the cost of managing their large mainframe systems.

The Solaris resource management components together with the measurement techniques under development form the building blocks for the long term future of Solaris resource management and the foundation on which automated, business-level, goal-driven resource management will be built.

Workload Manager Overview

WLM, with the ability to run in goal mode, was first released with MVS/ESA version 5 in 1995. It is tightly integrated into the core of the operating system and available on all OS/390 implementations, including Sysplex configurations. IBM is strongly encouraging existing users to migrate to the the OS/390 environment so that they can take advantage of this product. The functionality of WLM is described only in very general terms within this book. IBM-specific terminology has been avoided wherever possible and replaced with terms that are familiar to the open systems literate reader. As a consequence, some detail has been sacrificed to aid readability and understanding. The notable exception is the terminology associated with goals, which is both descriptive and generic.

WLM Modes of Operation

WLM allows an OS/390 or Sysplex environment to run in two, mutually exclusive modes:

- Compatibility mode
- Goal mode

Dynamic switching between these modes is supported.

Compatibility Mode

This mode allows the Sysplex system resources to be managed in a traditional fashion, that is, manual tuning and defining rigid boundaries of resource limits and guarantees. It assumes that performance metrics are gathered and analyzed by skilled engineers who then tune the appropriate system parameters. These parameters can be changed and are usually set following an extended period of metrics gathering.

Goal Mode

The key feature within WLM is the ability to run in goal mode. In this mode, the system is driven by simple business goals, for example:

- Provide a given response time for a specific transaction type.
- Ensure that a certain percentage of transactions complete within the specified per transaction time.
- Ensure that a certain batch run is completed within a given time frame.

In goal mode, no manual configuration or performance tuning is required. Indeed it is not permitted. Tuning and resource management are carried out automatically, with system parameters changed on the fly. Something that cannot be carried out manually. All of this is performed by WLM and its components to ensure that the specified goals are met. Performance groups and performance domains, the traditional resource management tools of the system tuner, are not supported by WLM when running in goal mode. However, most of the components or tools used to manually control resource consumption are integrated and used in some form within WLM. WLM is tightly coupled with the underlying operating system and with system services, especially transaction based environments such as CICS and IMS. Thus it can measure consumption and control key, low level, resources such as processor, memory and disk storage I/O while integration with CICS and IMS allows performance to be measured at the level the business perceives, transaction response time.

Defining Service Policies within WLM

When running in goal mode, WLM manages resources based upon a service policy. The service policy is a complete set of policies, including goals, that drive the entire OS/390 or Sysplex entity. Within a Sysplex, an instance of WLM is present on each node, or under each MVS, but all act in concert, with all nodes using the same policy. A number of these service policies can be defined, but only one can be in force at any given time. However, the enforced policy can be changed dynamically.

The service policy consists of the following major components:

- Resource groups
- Service classes
- Periods
- Duration
- Importance
- Goals

Resource Groups

Resource groups allow maximum and minimum processor service levels to be defined and then shared between one or more member service classes. Processor service level is not as simple as PRM percentages or SRM(IBM) shares. Assignment and measurement of processor resource uses standardized values, which take into account the relative performance of different processors.

Service Classes

A service class defines a set of goals, together with periods, duration, and importance. A number of individual processes and CICS/IMS transactions can be assigned membership of a service class. They will then become subject to the specified goals and constraints, including those imposed by any resource group subscribed to by the class. In essence, this is analalous to the Solaris Resource Manager lnode, which effectively defines a resource management policy that can be subscribed to.

Periods and Duration

Up to eight periods can be defined for each service class, each of which except the last has a duration (expressed in another standardized IBM form). These are used to vary goals and their relative importance with time. Thus each service class and period combination, usually referred to as the service class period in IBM documentation and here also, has a duration, an importance, and a goal. For example, if a process does not complete within the first period, subject to the first period's goal, then it becomes subject to the goal and importance associated with the second period. Periods can not be defined for CICS or IMS transactions.

Importance

Importance defines the relative priority of the goal and is represented by a number between one and five, one being most important. This allows goals to be prioritized and resources redistributed in cases where multiple goals are not being met. It does not affect scheduling or any other form of priority unless goals are not being met and there is contention between service class periods.

Goals

Goals are defined for a given service class period. Four types of goal are recognized:

- Average response time—The average response time, including queuing, to be provided within the period.
- Response time with percentile—The percentage of transactions that should complete within a specified time. For example:
  - CICS—90 percent of transactions complete within 0.7 seconds
  - Batch—Turnaround time of < 5 minutes
  - TSO—99 percent of jobs complete within 4 seconds
- Execution velocity—This is a goal for controlling application execution through access to processor resource. It effectively defines priorities based on ensuring that a process is run a given percentage of the time that it is runnable. Thus, velocity is given by velocity = (ticks process was run x 100) /(ticks process was run + ticks process was runnable but not running) This is considered especially useful for long running and nontransaction orientated jobs. It is intended to ensure that processes don't get just the appropriate amount of processor resource during a given time span, but that they get the processor resources when they need them. If a velocity goal is assigned to a service that handles transactions on behalf of others, who may have service classes with transaction throughput goals, WLM will ignore the velocity goal after start-up and only use the specified transaction goals.
- Discretionary—This is defined by WLM as work without a specific service class. No importance is attached to discretionary goals, and they will always lose resource when a service class period with another type of goal requires resources.

WLM Components

WLM consists of a number of major software components including:

- WLM—Workload Manager.
- SRM—System Resource Manager, referred to as SRM(IBM) in this document to differentiate it from the Solaris Resource Manager software. This component provides the algorithms for managing resources and caters to dynamic switching between compatibility and goal modes.
- RMF—Resource Measurement Facility. Tracks metrics including progress against goals.
- XCF—Cross-System Coupling Facility (Sysplex interconnect communications infrastructure). Communicates policies, metrics, and control data between Sysplex nodes.

- ISPF—Interactive System Productivity Facility, a generic MVS interface that can be used to define, activate, and deactivate policies.
- CP/SM—CICSPlex/System Manager—Acts as a Sysplex TPM by dynamically routing CICS queries to appropriate MVS nodes for both capability and response in line with goals.

These are all products that work together to dynamically manage performance and resources for components of IBM Sysplex systems. WLM is based on hierarchical control of resources. Thus each node within the Sysplex is responsible for managing its assigned share of the workload and communicates with the WLM to ensure that it is appropriately co-ordinated and meets the Sysplex wide goals. Also some sub-systems, specifically CP/SM effectively have delegated responsibility for managing the resources they are capable of controlling, in such a way as to ensure that goals are met.

WLM Control Architecture

Control within WLM is centered around the SRM(IBM) component which is responsible for:

- Resource adjustment
- Policy adjustment—this does not refer to the service policy but to the way resources are distributed and how this is adjusted and balanced. SRM(IBM) is capable of doing this because of the ability of WLM components to appropriately gather and assign metrics and then to control the requisite resources. When in goal mode it effectively controls the following resources:
    - Processor
    - Virtual memory system (MVS)
    - Disk I/O

Once a series of goals have been assigned, in the form of service class periods, WLM ensures that all of the appropriate measurements are taken during the process or transaction. Periodically, it compares observed performance with that required to meet the specified goal and then modifies its internal policies, that is detailed policies that determine individual resource consumption requirements and constraints. Finally, it applies the appropriate controls for the next period or interval.

Gathering Metrics

Because of the tightly integrated architecture of the MVS environment and its subsystems, especially with IMS and CICS, a wide variety of metrics can be gathered and attributed appropriately. In particular, transactional components can be easily identified and their resource consumption traced. Tools are present which allow the gathering of very fine grained statistics for each component of a transaction, no matter where it is being executed, and for those components to be recognized as being from a particular transaction or transaction type. This allows it to dynamically determine the routes of the transactions, aiding resource management and control.

A number of control interfaces, some similar to ARM, are provided to the various components of WLM, to allow them to communicate each other as well as with applications and transaction processors. These allow you to set transaction boundaries that collect and share metrics, and allow applications to determine their own service classes and goals. These tools are used by standard IBM resource measurement utilities so that the metrics gathered can be viewed and manually analyzed or automatically processed by WLM. The WLM analysis engine can determine both the attribute resource consumption and locate performance bottlenecks. This is possible because of the type of statistics gathered, especially delay metrics. These can indicate how often a desired resource was demanded but was not available.

The Performance Index

All of the WLM algorithms are run by SRM(IBM), are based on meeting the Sysplex wide goals and are driven by a metric referred to as the performance index. This is the ratio of work completed versus the amount of work that should have been completed to meet the goal.

For example, if the goal was for an average response time, then the performance index would be

Performance Index = Actual Average Response Time / Goal Average Response Time

An index of less than one indicates that the workload is not on target, one indicates that it is on target and more than one shows that it is overachieving. This is the prime mechanism used by the WLM to measure performance against goal and to redistribute or limit resources as required.

Most of the performance index calculations are very simple. However, the calculation for response time with percentile is based on a distribution. That calculation has been simplified, without sacrificing too much accuracy, to provide rapid processing.

Component and Server Topology

As mentioned earlier, WLM can independently determine the routes taken by transactions and can thus determine the overall transaction server topology. This is possible because it understands the different applications, the different TP services, and their location, possibly on different nodes within the Sysplex. A service can process the transactions from a number of different clients, who may belong to different service classes. WLM can track what serves whom and control each of the elements. This is key to its ability to manage transactions effectively.

Also, because WLM is capable of this, it ignores velocity goals for underlying TP servers if it recognizes that they service transactions from different clients. It will enforce their transaction goals instead.

All of this is used by WLM to automatically and dynamically tune CICS, and manage the resources supporting CICS and IMS to meet the goals. This includes ensuring that all transactions that belong to the same service class period use the same components of the service provider, that is CICS regions. WLM then creates dynamic internal service classes (DISC) to allow it to manage the transactions. Each DISC is associated with one or more normal service classes and a given server component. The number of transactions using each route then allow the DISCs to be weighted. Thus if the external or standard service class goal is not being met, the associated DISCs can be managed (if that is where the bottleneck lies).

Policy Adjustment

Because WLM can effectively monitor and control resource consumption at the appropriate level of attributability, it can vary resource control policies to ensure that service class period goals are met. A resource control policy effectively defines the type and quantity of resources that should be provided to service classes to ensure this.

The mechanism used by WLM to balance all of these needs is based on a simple principle: sharing resources among the service class periods to keep each of their performance indices at one. This must be done while still adhering to any limitation imposed on a service class on account of its resource group membership.

Note that policy adjustments are almost always carried out at the service class period level and not at the process or transaction type level.

Policy adjustment is cyclic and by default occurs every 10 seconds. The balance is achieved or maintained by adjusting the policy to benefit a class that is not on track to meet its goal, the receiver, and by penalizing one, or more, that is, the donor(s). During each cycle the aim is to modify one receiver appropriately.

Receivers are defined as service classes where the goal is being missed and where WLM has the requisite control of resources to provide help. Thus, service classes with a performance index well below one but which are I/O or lock bound will not be made a receiver and granted help. WLM cannot control the specific resource.

As stated previously, WLM's ability to understand bottlenecks is key. Once a receiver and its bottlenecks have been identified, one or more donors of the required resources can be sought. Donors can only donate processor or memory resources.

The policy adjustment cycle is as follows:

1. Select a potential receiver class.

2. Determine if the bottleneck is a WLM controlled resource. If not return to 1.

3. Determine if there is a donor available using the opposite criteria

4. Adjust policy. And return to 1, 2, or 3

5. Enforce resource group limitations if present.

6. End

Selecting a Potential Resource Receiver

Selection of a potential receiver service class is based on the following criteria, in decreasing order of importance:

- Whether the goal is being met. Is the performance index less than 1?
- Whether its resource group minimum service level is being utilized.
- How far below its minimum resource group service level the service class is. Most is preferred.
- Its importance. Most importance (lowest number) preferred.
- How high its performance index is. Highest is preferred.

These are only the basic criteria.

IBM's policy with respect to performance index is to allocate receivership to processes nearest their goal. This is not particularly intuitive at first sight However, this is based on the premise that resource donation must make a difference. If a single large resource sink is identified, and other potential receivers are identified, these would be brought on track prior to dealing with the resource sink. Thus only one service class would be in difficulty. If the reverse where the case, that is lowest performance index was used as the differentiator, then resources would be donated onlyto the resource sink. All the other service classes would risk becoming sinks or lagging behind their targets themselves. The aim is to keep as many service classes as possible on target.

Determining the Receiver Bottleneck

Before a receiver candidate can be confirmed, WLM ensures that its poor performance is caused by the lack of a resource which WLM can manage. It checks the delays associated with processor and memory usage for the service class period and for any transaction services derived DISCs.

If the bottleneck is not associated with processor or memory, for example, it could be due to database locks or I/O constraints, then another receiver candidate is sought. If the bottleneck is associated with a WLM controlled resource, then a receiver is assigned. This will be the original service class in the case of nontransaction-based service classes or maybe a DISC in the case of transaction-based service classes.

Following this, one or more candidates for resource donation are sought.

Selecting a Resource Donor

Resource donation is focused on donation of the resource needed by the designated receiver. Donor service classes are selected for each resource bottleneck. Their selection criteria are based on the following, in decreasing order of importance:

- Whether their goal is being met. Is the performance index greater than or equal to 1?
- Discretionary goals. These are considered as universal donors.
- Whether resource group minimum service level is being utilized.
- How far below the resource group minimum service level the service class is. Least is preferred.
- Its importance. Least important preferred.
- How low its performance index is. Lowest is preferred.

Again these are the basic criteria.

The value of the donation to the receiver is tested to ensure that it will have a good net effect. This is to ensure that potential resource sinks are avoided and that resources are not donated to service classes where they will make little difference. WLM would rather donate them to slightly below target service classes where their effect can be greater proportionally. If there is value, then the trade off between the loss of resource to the donor and the benefit to the receiver is checked. All aspects of the resource groups, service class periods, importance and goals are checked, as are projected performance indices. Only if the net value favors the receiver will the donation occur. Otherwise, the cycle is begun again with a new receiver being identified.

If one donor cannot provide all the appropriate resource or if there is more than one bottleneck, a number of donors can be selected by repeating the selection process.

Some resources can also be donated, or rather scavenged, if they are considered to have little effect on the system's ability to meet its goals. For example an analogy would be the virtual memory system choosing to donate pages from processes if paging is not considered overly detrimental to the system.

Carrying Out the Donation

Once the receiver and donor(s) have been identified, together with their associated resources, the policies are modified. This includes any capping of the receiving service class required by resource group membership. Finally the policy adjustment algorithm hibernates until the next cycle is due.

Typical Uses for WLM

WLM is typically used in the following way:

- Long running batch jobs and non transactional jobs are run in velocity mode and presumably within resource groups. This attempts to guarantee resource capacity and responsiveness.
- User transactions or transaction based applications are run in either average or percentile response time mode.

When appropriate planning has been undertaken, WLM implementations seem to be very successful. The main keys to success seem to be

- Correctly identifying the business goals to be met and the applications which will provide the services.
- Understanding how these services are delivered, i.e. how the applications work.
- Not being to ambitious in terms of granularity of goals. Twenty goals for business critical applications is far better than one for every user and application/service combination. The cost of having too many goals can impose an unacceptably high overhead in terms of capacity.

Finally, the area that is key to WLM's success is the proprietary nature of the environment which it manages—specifically tightly coupled hardware, operating environment, and middleware—and IBM's ownership of these components. The very high cost associated with this type of environment is why better resource utilization is such a key issue.

In the UNIX, or open systems environment, no one vendor has such ownership or is able to exercise such control. However the presence of massive data center UNIX systems, such as the Sun Enterprise 10000, enable extremely complex and high capacity applications to be deployed and large numbers of smaller services to be consolidated on a single platform. The attraction of access to new applications, combined with the lure of cost reduction through both hardware and software consolidation is inevitably driving customers to do this. This in turn will drive the need to guarantee service levels and improve the utilization of such platforms, maximising the return on ever increasing investment. Partnership between many of the key hardware and software vendors who deliver these service platforms will lead to tools, with capabilities similar to WLM, becoming available

Glossary

access control list	(ACL) A file that specifies which users can access a particular resource, such as a filesystem.
accounting	Keeping track of resource usage on a machine. SRM provides accounting features.
ACL	See *access control list*.
administration Tool	A GUI tool for configuring Solaris Bandwidth Manager.
administrative domain	A collection of network elements under the same administrative control and grouped together for administrative purposes.
ADOP	See *automatic degree of parallelism*.
alarm	The means by which notification is sent when an exception occurs.
attaching	See *DR Attach*.
Alternate Pathing	(AP) A software mechanism which works in conjunction with Dynamic Reconfiguration (DR) to provide redundant disk and network controllers and their respective physical links. The main purpose of Alternate Pathing is to sustain continuous network and disk I/O when system boards are detached from a machine or DSD (in the case of the Starfire) that is running a live copy of the Solaris operating environment.
AP	See *Alternate Pathing*.
application resource measurement	(ARM) A means of measuring the end-to-end response time of a system.
ARM	See *application resource measurement*.
ASE	Sybase Adaptive Server Enterprise.

automatic degree of parallelism	(ADOP) A feature of the Oracle8*i* Database Resource Manager that attempts to optimize system utilization by automatically adjusting the degree of parallelism for parallel query operations.
backfilling	The execution of a job that is short enough to fit into the time slot during which the processors are reserved, allowing for more efficient use of the available resources. Short jobs are said to backfill processors reserved for large jobs.
BBSRAM	Boot Bus Static Random Access Memory.
blacklist	A file that enables you to specify components, such as system boards, that should not be configured into the system. The blacklist file is read and processed at bringup time.
BMC Best/1	BMC Software's BEST/1 products provide tools to address performance management requirements across OS/390, Parallel Sysplex, SAP R/3, Unix, Windows NT, VM and AS/400 environments.
CBQ	See *Class Based Queuing*.
CCMS	A tool that provides information to SAP R/3 allowing it to measure the performance of key user transactions and the response time of the backend database for applications.
CICS	See *Customer Information Control System*.
CIM	See *Common Information Model*.
Class Based Queuing	(CBQ) The underlying queuing technology used in Solaris Bandwidth Manager.
Classes of Service	A feature supported by Solaris Bandwidth Manager that allows network traffic to be organized so that urgent traffic gets higher priority than less important traffic.
classifier	A component of the Solaris Bandwidth Manager that allocates packets to a class queue. When a packet arrives, the classifier analyzes the packet protocol, ToS value, URL information, source information, destination information and allocates the packet to a class queue where it waits to be processed.
CLI	Command Line Interface, as opposed to Graphical User Interface (GUI).
cluster	A collection of computers interconnected via a high-speed interface that allows the environment to behave as a single unified computing resource.
clustered cache	A method of caching web pages where multiple servers use the intercache protocol (ICP) to talk among themselves and form an explicit hierarchy of siblings and parents. If the load would overwhelm a single server or if high availability is important, multiple servers are configured as siblings. Each sibling stores data in its cache but also uses ICP to search the caches of other siblings.

CMIP	A scalable OSI-based network management protocol that is used in situations where SNMP is not powerful enough.
codepoint	A construct used by the ToS facility of the Solaris Bandwidth Manager. The way that the DSCP bits are set in a packet is called its *codepoint*, and network devices translate DSCP codepoints to device configurations. For example, a DS compliant router that has two priority queues (one for regular priority traffic and one for high priority traffic) could be configured to have several codepoints map to the high priority queue, and several others to the regular priority queue.
Common Information Model	(CIM) A metamodel based on the Unified Modeling Language (UML) that supplies a set of classes with properties and associations. The Common Information Model provides a conceptual framework within which it is possible to organize information about a managed environment.
control interval	In control theory, the rate at which measurements are made and corrections are applied.
CoS	See *Classes of Service*.
Cross-System Coupling Facility	A WLM component that communicates policies, metrics, and control data between Sysplex nodes.
Customer Information Control System	(CICS) An interactive transaction processing system from IBM.
DDI_ATTACH	A function, used by DR (called from the `dr_driver`) that provides the ability to attach a particular instance of a driver without affecting other instances that are servicing separate devices.
DDI/DKI	Device Driver Interface/Device Kernel Interface. These are function call entry points that device drivers should implement in order to fully support DR. DDI/DKI is specified in the "Writing Device Drivers" section of the *Driver Developer Site 1.0 AnswerBook* (`http://docs.sun.com`).
DDI_DETACH	A function, used by DR (called from the `dr_driver`), that provides the ability to detach a particular instance of a driver without affecting other instances that are servicing separate devices.
DDI_RESUME	A function, used by DR (called from the `dr_driver`), that provides the ability to detach a board that contains the kernel cage (OBP, kernel, and non-pageable memory). The kernel cage can only be relocated after all of the drivers throughout the entire DSD (not just on the board being detached) are quiesced to guarantee the data integrity of the kernel cage relocation. `DDI_RESUME` resumes the drivers after the quiesce period.
DDI_SUSPEND	A function, used by DR (called from the `dr_driver`), that provides the ability to detach a board that contains the kernel cage (OBP, kernel, and non-pageable memory). The kernel cage can only be relocated after all of the drivers

throughout the entire DSD (not just on the board being detached) are quiesced to guarantee the data integrity of the kernel cage relocation. DDI_SUSPEND suspends the drivers to begin the quiesce period.

decay The period by which historical usage is discounted.

DEN The Directory Enabled Networks working group. The goal of this group is to offer a standard information model and directory schemas to tie together users and applications with network elements, protocols, and services through specific relationships. By complying to this information model and the DEN schemas, different network equipment and application vendors should be able to build interoperable network elements around a central directory.

detaching See *DR Detach*.

Diff-Serv The Differentiated Services working group of the Internet Engineering Task Force (IETF). Diff-Serv addresses network management issues related to end-to-end Quality of Service (QoS) within diverse and complex networks.

DIMM Dual In-Line memory Module. A memory module with higher capacity and faster performance than SIMMs (Single In-Line Memory Module) It is currently used as the memory source for all Sun Microsystems platforms.

direct control A means of control that operates on the resource you want to control. For example the Solaris Resource Manager software controls CPU usage per user by implementing a scheduling class that decides who should get what share of the CPU.

DISC Dynamic internal service classes created by WLM. These classes enable WLM to manage transactions. Each DISC is associated with one or more normal service classes and a given server component. The number of transactions using each route then allow the DISCs to be weighted. Thus, if the external or standard service class goal is not being met, the associated DISCs can be managed (if that is where a bottleneck lies).

distributed queuing system A batch system product from Florida State University that is available in the public domain. The set of system resources it understands is host (by name), system architecture, operating system type, amount of memory, and CPU usage.

DMTF Desktop Management Task Force.

DQS See *distributed queuing system*.

DR See *Dynamic Reconfiguration*.

DR Attach The process of bringing a system board under the control of the Solaris operating environment through use of the DR mechanism.

DR Detach The process of removing a system board from Solaris operating system control through use of the DR mechanism.

DSD	See *Dynamic System Domains*.
DSS	Decision Support System.
DSS/DW	Decision Support System / Data Warehousing.
Dynamic Reconfiguration	(DR) A Sun Microsystems technology supported on the Starfire and other Sun Enterprise servers which allows system boards to be added (attached) or removed (detached) from a single server or domain.
Dynamic System Domains	(DSD) Starfire independent hardware entities formed by the logical association of its system boards. Each domain on the Starfire enjoys complete hardware isolation from other domains, executes its own private version of the Solaris operating system, and is centrally managed by the SSP.
ELIM	See *Extended Load Information Manager*.
Enterprise 10000	See *Sun Enterprise 10000*.
ERP	Enterprise Resource Planning
error event	A discrete on/off event, as opposed to a continuous variable to be compared against a limit.
exception	A condition that represents a problem in processing a job. LSF can watch for several types of exception conditions during a job's life cycle.
exclusive scheduling	A type of scheduling used by LSF that makes it possible to run exclusive jobs on a host. A job only runs exclusively if it is submitted to an exclusive queue. An exclusive job runs by itself on a host. LSF does not send any other jobs to the host until the exclusive job completes.
Extended Load Information Manager	(ELIM) LSF uses the Load Information Manager (LIM) as its resource monitoring tool. To modify or add load indices, an Extended Load Information Manager can be written.
fairshare	A form of scheduling used by LSF to prevent a single user from using up all the available job slots, thus locking out other users. Fairshare scheduling is an alternative to the default first come, first served scheduling. Fairshare scheduling divides the processing power of the LSF cluster among users and groups to provide fair access to resources for all jobs in a queue. LSF allows fairshare policies to be defined at the queue level so that different queues can have different sharing policies.
FlowAnalyzer (NetFlow)	An application that uses the output from NetFlow FlowCollector. It provides very elaborate processing, graphing, and reporting options that can be used for network analysis, planning, trouble shooting, and more

FlowCollector (NetFlow) — A NetFlow datagram consumer for one or more NetFlow devices. These devices simply point to the host and port number on which the FlowCollector software is running. The FlowCollector aggregates this data, does preprocessing and filtering, and provides several options to save this data to disk (such as flat files). Other applications such as network analyzing, planning, and billing can use these files as input.

Gigaplane-XB — The interconnect on the Starfire that provides main memory access through a point-to-point data router which isolates data traffic between system boards and minimizes any performance degradation when memory interleaving is disabled.

goal — Goal-based policies are prescriptitive rather than reactive. A goal can be translated into a mixture of limits, priorities, and relative importance levels. Goals can include actions to be performed when the goal cannot be met.

Health Monitor — See *SyMON Health Monitor*.

heavily damped — A system is heavily damped if you feed back a small proportion of an error over a longer control interval. A heavily damped system tends to be sluggish and unresponsive when a large time constant is used.

hierarchical fairshare — A method of sharing resources, supported by LSF. Hierarchical fairshare enables resources to be allocated to users in a hierarchical manner. Groups of users can collectively be allocated a share, and that share can be further subdivided and given to subgroups, resulting in a share tree.

host based resources — Resources that are not shared among hosts, but are tied to individual hosts. An application must run on that host to access such resources. Examples are CPU, memory, and swap space. Using up these resources on one host does not affect the operation of another host.

Hostview — A GUI program that runs on the SSP machine (which is a component of an Enterprise 10000 system). Hostview enables you to monitor and control the Enterprise 10000. For example, Hostview can display continuous readouts of power and temperature levels at various locations within the Enterprise 10000 server.

HPC — High Performance Computing

HP OpenView — Computer-oriented local and wide area networks are normally managed using SNMP protocols, with Solstice SunNet Manager or HP OpenView products collecting and displaying the data. Both products provide some visibility into what is happening in the computer systems on the network, but they are focused on network topology. Resource management is done on a per-network basis, often by controlling the priority of data flows through intelligent routers and switches.

HTTP — Hypertext Transfer Protocol. HTTP is used by Web servers to host content and respond to HTTP requests from Web browsers.

IBM Workload Manager A comprehensive tool set for MVS that provides an automated resource management environment, driven by high level business goals, and that, in many cases, is self tuning. Tools are provided to define the business goals or objectives, to control system resources, and to feed metrics concerning these resources back to the resource controller, which attempts to ensure that the goals are met.

IETF Internet Engineering Task Force.

indirect control A means of control that works via resources that are dependent upon the resource that is being controlled. For example, to limit the I/O throughput of a process, it is sufficient to be able to measure the I/O throughput and limit the CPU resources for that process.

intercache protocol (ICP) A protocol used to implement clustered caches. (See *clustered cache*.)

interleaving See *memory interleaving*.

intimate shared memory (ISM) A way of allocating memory so that it can't be paged. The shared memory area is often the largest component of a database's memory requirements, and is the easiest to insulate between database instances. Because intimate shared memory is wired down, the memory allocated to each database instance stays allocated and one instance cannot steal memory from another.

Int-Serv The Integrated Services working group of the Engineering Task Force (IETF).

IP Internet Protocol. IP is the foundation of the TCP/IP architecture. It operates on the network layer and supports addressing. IP enables data packets to be routed.

ISM See *intimate shared memory*.

ISP Internet Service Provider, a company that provides Point-of-Presence access to the Internet.

ISPF Interactive System Productivity Facility, a generic MVS interface that can be used by the operator/administrator to define, activate, and deactivate policies.

Java Dynamic Management Kit A JavaBeans based framework for developing and deploying dynamic management based applications. Autonomous agents can be deployed in real-time to perform management tasks for devices on the network.

JTAG Joint Test Action Group, IEEE Std. 1149.1. JTAG is an alternate communications interface between the SSP machine and the Enterprise 10000 server, and is used when the standard network connection between the SSP and the Enterprise 10000 is unavailable.

Jiro	A technology being developed at Sun to address modern storage issues. Storage is now open for access in a heterogeneous multivendor environment, where multiple server and storage vendors can all be connected over the Storage Area Network (SAN). This is an emerging technology, and tools to manage a SAN are still being developed. Jiro is based on a distributed pure Java framework that can run on servers from any vendor, interface to other storage management software, and manage any kind of attached storage.
Java Virtual Machine	The machine image, implemented in software, upon which Java code runs.
JVM	See *Java Virtual Machine*.
kernel cage	A special data structure (normally contained within a single system board) that controls the dynamic growth of all non-relocatable memory, including the OpenBoot PROM (OBP) and kernel memory. When Dynamic Reconfiguration (DR) is used to detach a system board containing the kernel cage, it is necessary to quiesce the operating system to ensure that no I/O or kernel activity occurs while the kernel cage is being relocated.
kernel memory	Memory that is used to run the operating system.
kernel module	A Solaris Bandwidth Manager module that contains the *classifier* and the *scheduler*.
LAN	See *local area network*.
lightly damped	If you feed back a large proportion of an error with a short control interval, the system is said to be lightly damped. A lightly damped system is very responsive to sudden changes but will probably oscillate back and forth.
LIM	See *Load Information Manager*.
limit	A simple rule with a single input measurement. It is also common to have several thresholds with a warning level action and a critical problem level action for the same measure.
lnode	Limit node, a node in a special resource tree used by Solaris Resource Manager (SRM). SRM is built around lnodes which are a fundamental addition to the Solaris kernel. Lnodes correspond to UNIX UIDs, and may represent individual users, groups of users, applications, and special requirements. The lnodes are indexed by UID and are used to record resource allocations policies and accrued resource usage data by processes at the user, group of users, and application level.
Load Information Manager	(LIM) The resource monitoring tool used by LSF. The Load Information Manager process running on each execution host is responsible for collecting load information. The load indices that are collected include: host status, length of run queue, CPU utilization, paging activity, available swap space, available memory, and I/O activity.

Load Share Facility	(LSF) A software facility that provides the capability of executing batch and interactive jobs on a pool of networked computers. The Sun Microsystems High Performance Computing (HPC) package includes the Load Share Facility as a vehicle for launching parallel applications on an HPC cluster. In addition to starting batch jobs, the Load Share Facility also provides load balancing.
local area network	A set of computer systems in relatively close proximity that can communicate by means of networking hardware and software.
LPAR	Logical Partitions, an IBM S/390™ logical entity which runs its own operating system instance and it's allocated resources and managed by PR/SM.
LSF	See *Load Share Facility*.
LWP	Lightweight Process
Management Information Base	A database that contains network management variables and can be accessed via SNMP.
master host	The node where the LSF batch queues reside. When the LSF software initializes, one of the nodes in the cluster is elected to be the master host. This election is based on the order of nodes listed in a configuration file. If the first node listed in the configuration file is inoperative, the next node is chosen, and so forth.
maximum bandwidth	The amount of spare bandwidth allocated to a class by the Solaris Bandwidth Manager. The maximum bandwidth is dependent upon the percentage of bandwidth the class can borrow.
MDF	Multiple Domain Facility, an Amdahl Corporation™ technology which provides logical partitioning for its mainframes. By integrating special hardware for each logical partition or domain, Amdahl processor complexes could run multiple operating systems at close to native performance.
memory interleaving	A method of using computer memory that helps increase memory subsystem performance by reducing the probability of hot spots or contention in a few memory banks. This is accomplished by spreading access to multiple memory banks.
Message Passing Interface	(MPI) An industry standard interface used to parallelize applications.
MIB	See *Management Information Base*.
microstate accounting	A method of accounting for resource usage where a high-resolution timestamp is taken on every state change, every system call, every page fault, and every scheduler change. Microstate accounting provides much greater accuracy than sampled measurements.
MPI	See *Message Passing Interface*.
MTS	See *Multi-Threaded Mode*.

Multi-threaded mode	A database topology where a single process serves many users.
negative feedback	A method of applying feedback to a system where you take the error difference between what you wanted and what you got, and apply the inverse of the error to the system to reduce the error in the future.
NetFlow	A product from Cisco that is supported by Solaris Bandwidth Manager. NetFlow allows for detailed network measurements that can be sent to other software packages which can process and analyze the data.
Network File System	An application that utilizes TCP/IP to provide distributed file services.
network queuing system	(NQS) A public domain software product that has been enhanced by many hardware vendors. Sterling Software offers a distributed version of NQS called NQS/Exec which is geared toward a supercomputer environment. Limited load balancing is provided as there is no concept of demand queues, since it uses traditional push queues instead. There is also no control over interactive batch jobs.
NFS	See *Network File System*.
NQS	See *Network Queuing System*.
NVRAM	Non-Volatile Random Access Memory
OBP	OpenBoot PROM
ODS	Informix OnLine Dynamic Server
OLTP	Online Transaction Processing
operational policy	A policy that is implemented manually as part of operations management. For example, an availability policy can include a goal for uptime and an automatic way to measure and report the uptime over a period. There is no direct control in the system that affects uptime. It is handled by operations staff.
Oracle8*i* Database Resource Manager	An Oracle facility that ensures system resources are applied to the most important tasks of the enterprise at the levels required to meet enterprise goals.
PC NetLink	A product from Sun Microsystems that is based on the AT&T Advanced Server for UNIX. PC NetLink adds functionality that was not previously available on Solaris servers with products such Samba and SunLink™ PC™ (a.k.a. Syntax TotalNET Advanced Server). PC NetLink adds file and print services, and enables Solaris servers to act as Microsoft® Windows NT™ Primary Domain Controllers (PDC) or Backup Domain Controllers (BDC). For enterprises with mixed NT and Solaris servers and desktops, PC NetLink 1.0 offers many new options for utilizing hardware resources and minimizing system administration overhead.
Platform Computing Load Share Facility	See *Load Share Facility*.

PDP	See *policy decision point*.
PEP	See *policy enforcement point*.
performance index	The ratio of work completed versus the amount of work which should have been completed in order to meet the goal.
PIN	See *policy ignorant node*.
policy agent	A component of the Solaris Bandwidth Manager that implements the configuration and handles communication with the *kernel module*.
policy control	The application of rules to determine whether or not access to a particular resource should be granted.
policy decision point	In policy administration, the point where policy decisions are made.
policy element	A subdivision of policy objects. A policy element contains single units of information necessary for the evaluation of policy rules. Examples of policy elements include the identity of the requesting user or application, user or application credentials, and so forth. The policy elements themselves are expected to be independent of which Quality of Service signaling protocol is used.
policy enforcement point	In policy administration, the point where policy decisions are enforced.
policy ignorant node	A network element that does not explicitly support policy control using the mechanisms defined in the applicable standard policy.
policy object	An object that contains policy-related information, such as *policy elements*, and is carried in a request or response related to resource allocation decisions.
policy protocol	A protocol for communication between the policy decision point and policy enforcement point. The policy protocol can be any combination of COPS, SNMP, and Telnet/CLI.
POST	Power-ON self tests, a suite of hardware diagnostic tests which ensure full functionality of a system board.
preemptive scheduling	A method of scheduling where a high priority job can bump a lower priority job that is currently running. LSF provides several resource controls to prioritize the order in which batch jobs are run. Batch jobs can be scheduled to run on a first come first served basis, fair sharing between all batch jobs, and preemptive scheduling.
priority	A relative importance level that can be given to the work done by a system as part of a policy that prioritizes some activities over others.
priority decay	See *process priority decay*.

priority paging	A method of implementing a memory policy with different importance factors for different memory types. Application memory is allocated at a higher priority than file system memory, which prevents the file system from stealing memory from other applications. Priority paging is implemented in the Solaris 7 operating environment.
process measurements	Measurements that show the activity of each user and each application.
process memory	Memory allocated to processes and applications.
Process Monitor	An optional module within Sun Enterprise SyMON that can be used to view all the processes on a system. The Process Monitor can also be configured to pattern match and accumulate all the processes that make up a workload.
process priority decay	A process decay method used by SRM, where each processes priority is decayed according to a fixed decay factor at regular intervals (each second).
processor reservation	A method that allows job slots to be reserved for a parallel job until enough are available to start the job. When a job slot is reserved for a job, it is unavailable to other jobs. Processor reservation helps to ensure that large parallel jobs are able to run without under utilizing resources.
processor set	The set of processors available to a system.
provider DSD	Dynamic Reconfiguration (DR) on the Starfire allows the logical detachment of a system board from a provider DSD (the DSD from which resources are borrowed) and the logical attachment of the same system board to a receptor DSD (the DSD where loaned resources are applied).
provider domain	When relocating resources between DSDs, a "provider domain" is the domain where a system board gets logically detached from to then have it attached to a "receptor domain".
proxy cache	A method of caching Web pages. A proxy caching Web server sits between a large number of users and the Internet, funneling all activity through the cache. Proxy caches are used in corporate intranets and at ISPs. When all the users are active at once, regardless of where they are connecting to, the proxy cache server will get very busy
PR/SM	Processor Resource/Systems Manager), an IBM S/390 hardware feature which allows customers to statically allocate processor and I/O resources to LPARs to concurrently run multiple operating system instances on the same machine.
QoS	See *Quality of Service*.
Quality of Service	A measure of the speed and reliability of a service. Solaris Bandwidth Manager provides the means to manage your network resources to provide Quality of Service to network users. QoS is a network-wide issue; if congestion takes place anywhere on the network, it affects the overall quality of service.
RAS	Reliability, Accessibility and Serviceability

receptor DSD	Dynamic Reconfiguration (DR) on the Starfire allows the logical detachment of a system board from a provider DSD (the DSD from which resources are borrowed) and the logical attachment of the same system board to a receptor DSD (the DSD where loaned resources are applied).
receptor domain	When relocating resources between DSDs, a "receptor domain" is the domain which receives a system board after having it logically detached from a "provider domain."
repository access protocol	The protocol used to communicate between a policy repository and the repository client. LDAP is one example of a repository access protocol.
Resource Management Facility	A component of WLM that tracks metrics including progress against goals.
RMF	See *Resource Management Facility*.
RSVP	A protocol (part of the Int-Serv framework), that provides applications the ability to have multiple levels of Quality of Service (QoS) when delivering data across the network. RSVP provides a way for an application to communicate its desired level of service to the network components. It requires each hop from end-to-end be RSVP-enabled, including the application itself (through an API). Bandwidth is reserved at each hop along the way before transmitting begins, guaranteeing that enough resources will be available for the duration of the connection.
SAN	See *Storage Area Network*.
scheduler	A component of the Solaris Resource Manager (SRM) that schedules users and applications.
scheduler term	The period of time during which the Solaris Resource Manager (SRM) ensures that a particular user or application receives its fair share of resources.
security policy	A type of policy that aims at preventing access to certain resources or allowing designated users to manage subsystems. For example, Sun Enterprise SyMON 2.0 software includes access control lists for operations that change the state of a system, and multiple network domain views to give different administrative roles their own view of the resources being managed.
SE Toolkit	A toolkit that can be used to develop customized process monitors. The Solaris software can provide a great deal of per-process information that is not collected and displayed by the ps command or Sun Enterprise SyMON 2.0 software. The data can be viewed and processed by a custom written process monitor. You could write one from scratch or use the experimental scripts provided as part of the SE Toolkit. The SE Toolkit is a freely available but unsupported product for Solaris systems. It can be downloaded from the http://www.sun.com/sun-on-net/performance/se3.

server consolidation A current trend by data centers to reduce cost of server ownership by reducing physical footprint and reducing number and management cost of multivendor platforms. The basis of server consolidation is to combine applications and data contained in several smaller servers into a single larger server.

service class A class that defines a set of goals, together with periods, duration, and importance. A number of individual processes and CICS/IMS transactions can be assigned membership of a service class. They will then become subject to the specified goals and constraints, including those imposed by any resource group subscribed to by the class. In essence, this is analogous to the SRM lnode, which effectively defines a resource management policy that can be subscribed to.

Service Level Agreement A written agreement between system managers and end users that captures the expectations and interactions between end users, system managers, vendors, and computer systems. Often, many additional interactions and assumptions are not captured formally.

Service Level Management The process by which information technology (IT) infrastructure is planned, designed, and implemented to provide the levels of functionality, performance, and availability required to meet business or organizational demands.

service provider In a network policy, the service provider controls the network infrastructure and may be responsible for the charging and accounting of services.

service time The time it takes for an I/O device to service a request. This can be complex to measure. For example, with today's disk storage systems, the device driver issues a request, that request is queued internally by the RAID controller and the disk drive, and several more requests can be sent before the first one comes back. The service time, as measured by the device driver, varies according to the load level and queue length and is not directly comparable to the old-style service time of a simple disk drive.

SEVM Sun Enterprise Volume Manager, technically equivalent to Veritas Volume Manager.

ShareII A resource management product from product from Softway. The Solaris Resource Manager (SRM) is based on ShareII.

shared resources A resource that is not tied to a specific host, but is associated with the entire cluster, or a specific subset of hosts within the cluster. Examples of shared resources include: floating licenses for software packages, disk space on a file server which is mounted by several machines, and the physical network connecting the hosts.

SHR Scheduler A component of the Solaris Resource Manager (SRM) that controls the CPU resources. Users are dynamically allocated CPU time in proportion to the number of shares they possess (analogous to shares in a company), and in inverse proportion to their recent usage. The important feature of the SHR scheduler is that while it manages the scheduling of individual threads, it also portions CPU resources between users.

Simple Network Management Protocol (SNMP) An open network protocol used by network management systems that are based on TCP/IP.

SLA See *Service Level Agreement*.

SNIA Storage Network Industry Association.

SNMP See *Simple Network Management Protocol*.

Solaris Bandwidth Manager A product from Sun that provides the means to manage your network resources to provide Quality of Service (QoS) to network users. It allows network traffic to be allocated to separate Classes of Service (CoS), so that urgent traffic gets higher priority than less important traffic. Different classes of service can be guaranteed a portion of the network bandwidth, leading to more predictable network loads and overall system behavior. Service Level Agreements can be defined and translated into Solaris Bandwidth Manager controls and policies. Tools and APIs provide an interface for monitoring, billing, and accounting options.

Solaris Management Console An application that provides a generic framework for gathering together operating system administration tools and interfacing to industry standard initiatives such as the Web-based management initiative (WebM) and the Common Information Model (CIM).

Solaris Resource Manager (SRM) A software tool for enabling resource availability for users, groups, and applications. The Solaris Resource Manager provides the ability to allocate and control major system resources such as CPU, virtual memory, and number of processes. The Solaris Resource Manager software is the key enabler for server consolidation and increased system resource utilization.

Solstice SunNet Manager Computer-oriented local and wide area networks are normally managed using SNMP protocols, with Solstice SunNet Manager or HP OpenView products collecting and displaying the data. Both products provide some visibility into what is happening in the computer systems on the network, but they are focused on network topology. Resource management is done on a per-network basis, often by controlling the priority of data flows through intelligent routers and switches.

SPARCcluster A highly integrated product line that is focused on improved availability in commercial environments. Its management tools will eventually become an integrated extension to the Sun Enterprise SyMON2.0 software. For High

	Performance Computing, Sun HPC Servers use the Platform Computing Load Share Facility (LSF) to perform load balancing on much larger and more loosely coupled clusters.
SRM	See *Solaris Resource Manager*.
SRM(IBM)	The System Resource Manager of WLM. The term SRM(IBM) is used in this book to differentiate it from Solaris Resource Manager. SRM(IBM) provides the algorithms for managing resources and caters for dynamic switching between compatibility and goal modes.
SSP	System Service Processor. Starfire's system administrator & system monitoring interface. The SSP configures the Starfire hardware, through a private ethernet link, to create domains. The SSP collects hardware logs, provides boot functions, and produces consoles for each domain.
Starfire	See *Sun Enterprise 10000*.
static resources	Host information that does not change over time, such as the maximum RAM available to processes running on the host.
Storage Area Network	(SAN) A complex managed storage system, where networked storage using fiber channel makes up an interconnection layer between multiple servers or clusters and multiple storage subsystems. A storage area network can contain switches and routers just like local or wide area networks, but the protocol in common use is SCSI over fiber channel rather than IP over ethernet. A storage area network may also span multiple sites, for example where remote mirroring is being used for disaster recovery.
submission host	In a typical LSF workload configuration, the submission host is the node where the user or operator submits the task to be performed.
Sun Enterprise 10000	A highly scalable 64-processor (UltraSparc II) SMP server with up to 64 Gbytes of memory and over 20 Tbytes of disk space.
Sun Enterprise SyMON 2.0	A product developed by Sun to act as a user interface to hardware features. It is a powerful and extensible system and network monitoring platform that is used to manage other products. Sun Enterprise SyMON 2.0 is a Java-based monitor with multiple user consoles that can monitor multiple systems using the secure extensions to SNMPv2 to communicate over the network.
SunNet Manager	See *Solstice SunNet Manager*.
SyMON	See *Sun Enterprise SyMON 2.0*.

SyMON Health Monitor	A SyMON module that can be used in a resource management scenario to determine if a system has enough resources to run comfortably. For example, if the CPU state is reported as "red", then either less work or more CPU power may be needed on that system. Similarly, if the memory rule reports "red" then the system may need more memory
system level measurements	A type of measurement. System level measurements show the basic activity and utilization of the memory system and CPUs. Some network measurements such as TCP/IP throughput are also available on a per system basis. Per process activity can be aggregated at a per system level then combined with network measurements to measure distributed applications.
Teamquest	A workload analysis product. See www.teamquest.com.
time constant	In control theory, the rate at which a system responds to changes.
TNF	See *trace normal form*.
ToS	See *Type of Service*.
trace normal form	(TNF) A format used to implement tracing (which makes it possible to trace the execution steps of user and kernel processes). Trace normal form, which is supported by the Solaris operating environment, provides a self-describing trace output format. Trace normal form allows data structures to be embedded in the trace file without the need for an external definition of their types and contents.
Type of Service	(ToS) A header field contained in IP packets. Its purpose is to convey information about how the packet should be routed. The Solaris Bandwidth Manager can use this information when classifying a packet. It can also change the information, to influence how the packet is routed.
UDB	DB2 Universal Database.
usage decay	A form of decay used by SRM. The user scheduler is the most important and visible portion of SRM and it implements usage decays which control long term CPU allocation responsiveness.
virtual memory	A type of memory that is allocated from a central resource pool and is consumed by an application when it requests memory from the operating system. Virtual memory is not directly related to physical memory usage because virtual memory is not always associated with physical memory. For example, if an application requests 16 Mbytes from the operating system, the operating system will create 16 Mbytes of memory within that application's address space but will not allocate physical memory to it until that memory is read from or written to.

virtual Web hosting	A web server configuration where a single server is configured to respond to hundreds or thousands of Internet addresses. Virtual web hosting is often used in situations where web sites receive little or no activity most of the time. In these situations, it is usually too expensive to dedicate a single computer system to each web site.
WAN	See *wide area network*.
WebM	Web-based management initiative
wide area network	A network that provides connectivity across a large geographical area.
WLM	See *IBM Workload Manager*.
Workload Manager	See *IBM Workload Manager*.
XCF	See *Cross-System Coupling Facility*.

Index

SYMBOLS
/etc/passwd, 138
/etc/system, 33

A
access control lists (ACLs), 27
Accounting, 100, 243
   and Chargeback, 7
   data structure, 102
   extracting data, 187
   information, 186
   system resource, 186
Accrued, 149
Alarms in Sun Enterprise SyMON, 287
Alternate Pathing, 199
AP, 199
ap_daemon, 212
Application Resource Measurement Standard, 89
Application specific measurements, 88
application-centric viewpoint, 15
attach(9E), 220

B
backfilling, 257
Bandwidth Allocator, 224
Bandwidth Manager, 137
batch jobs, 255

batch management, simple, 151
batch queue, 255
Batch Workloads, 85
batool, 237, 239
BBSRAM, 218
Billing, 243
billing issues, 186
blacklist(4), 197
BMC Best/1, 49, 89
Business workloads, 88

C
Capacity Planning and Exception Reporting, 6
CCMS, 89
cfgadm(1M), 204
cgi-bin, 73
CIM, 242
Cisco, 103
Class Based Queuing, 237
Classes of Service, 223
Cluster, 193
cluster, 206, 254
cluster-centric viewpoint, 11
Clustered Proxy Cache Architectures, 59
clustering, 206
Commercial Workloads, 65
Common Information Model, 242
complex rules and hierarchies, 20

Configuration Information, 292
Consolidation, 152
consolidation process, 17
control, 22
control interval, 9
control limits, 22
Controls Available with Solaris Resource Manager, 140
CoS, 223
CPU percentage, 52
CPU Power, 26
CPU time measurements, 97
CPU usage, 74
cpu.accrue, 149
cpu.myshares, 148
cpu.shares, 148
cpu.usage, 149
cron, 252
CS6400, 193

D

damping, 9
Data Warehousing, 198
Database
    consolidation, 74
Database Listener, 73
Database Server, 73
Databases, 153
    in a resource managed environment, 77
databases, 35
DB2, 79, 195
DDI/DKI, 220
DDI_ATTACH, 218, 220, 222
DDI_DETACH, 220, 222
DDI_RESUME, 220, 222
DDI_SUSPEND, 220, 222
deadline goals, 21
decay, 140, 141
    algorithms, 165
    factors, 164
    usage, 166
Decision Support System, 198

default memory allocation policy, 31
Delegated Administration of Policies, 139
delta, 176
DEN, 242
Desktop Management Task Force, 242
detach(9E), 220
detach_safe_list1, 220
detaching, 212
devinfo, 215, 218
Differentiated Services, 226
Diff-Serv, 226, 232
direct, 22
Directory Enabled Networks, 242
Disk
    bandwidth, 66
    I/O Policies, 27
    space, 66
Disks
    how to decide a disk is overloaded, 109
dispadmin, 164, 184
Distributed Queuing System (DQS), 271
DMTF, 242
dnode, 218
domain_config(4), 215, 218
DR, 193, 195
dr(1M), 211
dr_daemon, 215
dr_daemon, 212
dr_max_mem, 217
dr_max_mem, 213
drshow(1M), 221
drview(1M), 204
DS header, 226, 231, 232
DSDs, 193
DSS, 198
DW, 198
Dynamic Reconfiguration, 137, 193, 195, 294
Dynamic System Domains, 136, 193

E

email, 35
E-Share, 148

execution host, 266

F
fair share, 141
file service, 35
file system paging, 75
firewall, 236
Flags, 150
flags, 140
Flows, 229
Foglight Software, 87

G
GID, 147
Gigaplane, 203
Gigaplane-XB, 203, 209
goal-based policies, 20

H
half-life, 141
hierarchical limits, 139
Hierarchical Structure, 138
hierarchy, flat, 145
Hostview, 209
`hostview(1M)`, 204, 211
HPC, 200, 201, 249
hpost(1M), 212
hpost(1M), 201
HTTP, 232

I
I/O, 76
IBM Workload Manager, 86
indirect, 22
information technology (IT), 3
Informix, 79, 195
Integrated Services, 225
Internet Engineering Task Force, 231

Internet Service Provider, 35
Internet Service Provider Workloads, 55
Intimate Shared Memory, 196
Int-Serv, 225
iostat command, 105
IP-Transparent Mode, 235
irtual address space size, 52
ISM, 196, 201

J
Java Dynamic Management Kit, 238, 248
JavaBeans, 247
JTAG, 203, 208, 218

K
kernel cage, 201, 206, 222
Kernel Memory, 185
`kill(1)`, 213

L
Landmark Predictor, 49
lastused, 150
LDAP, 241
`libdr.so`, 212
LIM, 262
limadm, 138
`limadm`, 146, 147
`liminfo`, 146, 147
limits, 140
limits and error event rules, 19
limreport, 188
limshare, 177
lnodes, 138
login limits, 25
Login name, 147
logins, 150
lsb.events, 268
LSF, 250
lsf.cluster, 268

Index **329**

lsmake, 250
lsnamed, 250
`lwps`, 52

M

Mail servers, 65
master host, 266
maxusage, 176
maxushare, 177, 180
mbatchd daemon, 262
m-beans, 239
MDFTM, 193
Measurements, 5
measurements to collect per workload, 18
memory interleaving, 203
memory policy by importance, 33
Memory Usage, 75
memory.limit, 149
memory.myusage, 149
memory.plimit, 149
memory.usage, 149
Message Passing Interface (MPI), 269
Metron Athene, 49
microstate accounting, 52, 97
Microstate Process Data, 97
modinfo(1M), 217
modload(1M), 217, 222
modunload(1M), 222
`modunload(1M)`, 213
Monitoring Workloads, 39
MPI, 250
Multiple Disks On One Controller Disks, 109
Multiple Domain Feature, 193
Myshares, 148

N

negative feedback, 9
NetFlow, 244, 245
Netscape Proxy Cache, 90

network access server, 242
Network Accounting, 103
Network bandwidth, 66
Network latency, 72
Network Queuing System (NQS), 271
network-based policies, 21
network-centric viewpoint, 12
nexus device interface, 212
NFS, 35, 155
    CPU usage, 67
    disk storage management, 69
    metrics, 67
    physical memory usage, 68
    swap space, 69
nice, 136
nice(1) command, 252
Number of Processes, 142

O

OBP, 201, 209, 213
obp_helper(1M), 212
OLTP, 198
Online Transaction Processing, 198
OpenBoot PROM, 201
Oracle, 78, 195
Oracle 8i Preemption Control, 154
Oracle8i Resource Manager, 80

P

p_selock, 220
`pbind(1M)`, 213
`pea.se`, 51
percollator.se, 90
Per-user Resource Usage, 143
physical memory, 30, 66
Physical sharing, 202
Physical View, 295
pln, 217
Plug-ins, 248
Policies and Controls, 6
Policies by Executable Name, 139

policy, 241
policy agent, 247
Policy on Executable Name, 159
policy types, 19
POST, 200, 201, 202, 203, 212, 218
`postrc(4)`, 203
pridecay, 177
`priocntl(1)`, 213
Priority, 20
Priority paging, 33
proc(4) manual page, 94
Process Information, 94
Process limit, 150
Process measurements, 88
process monitoring, 98
Process Priority Decay, 166
Process Rule, 55
Process time percentage, 52
process.limit, 150
process.myusage, 150
process.usage, 150
Processes, 143
Processor Sets, 84, 136, 160
protocol adapter, 239
provider DSD, 200
Proxy Web Cache, 56
prtconf(1M), 221
ps command, 94
`psrset(1M)`, 195, 213
`pw.se`, 53

Q

QoS, 223
Quality of Service, 223
Quantum, 183
queue length, 87
quiescing, 206

R

R,Euid and R,Egid, 147

RADIUS, 242
RAS, 193
RDBMS, 195
Real User Experiences, 5
receptor DSD, 200
relationship between virtual memory and swap space, 29
Reliability, Accessibility, and Serviceability, 193
Remote Procedure Calls, 211
resource management control loop, 7
response time, 87
response time goals, 21
RMI, 239
RSVP, 226

S

SAP R/3, 89
sbatchd, 262
scheduler, 141
Scheduler Parameters, 176
schema, 243
SE, 50
SE Toolkit, 87
security policy, 21
server consolidation, 195
Server Mode, 234
Service Level Agreement, 3, 5, 223, 243
Service Level Definitions and Interactions, 3
Service Level Management, 3
service level requirements, 4
Setting Decay, 176
Sgroup, 147
Share, 148
shared memory area, 75
ShareII, 135
Shares, 148
Shell, 150
SHR, 140
SHR class, 164
shr_quantum, 184
Sizing Estimates, 4
SNMP, 239, 244, 247

Index   **331**

SNMP protocol, 12
soc, 217
Solaris 7, 211
Solaris Bandwidth Manager, 103
Solaris Resource Manager, 225
Solaris Resource Manager Accounting, 102
Solaris Resource Manager Policies, 138
Solaris revisions, 17
Solstice Bandwidth Reservation Protocol, 226
SPECweb96, 90
Squid proxy cache, 90
SRM, 195
srmstat, 186
SSP, 195, 208
Starfire, 193, 194
storage area network, 13
Storage Measurements, 104
STREAMS, 237
submission host, 266
subsystem policies and controls, 25
Sun Directory Services, 241
Sun Enterprise SyMON 2.0, 281
Sun Performance and Tuning, 88
Sun StorEdge L3500, 202
SunNet Manager, 12
superuser, 136
Sybase, 79, 195
SyMON 2.0, 10, 87, 195
SyMON Health Monitor, 283
syslog.conf(4), 209
System Resource Accounting Information, 144
System Service Processor, 195
system-centric viewpoint, 10

T

TCL, 204
Teamquest, 49
Terminals and Login Connect-Time, 142
throughput, 87
throughput goals, 21
time constant, 9
TNF tracing system, 104

ToS field, 232
Tree Depth, 185
TS scheduler, 165
Tuning
    Filesystems, 109
Type of Service, 230

U

Uid, 147
Usage, 149
usagedecay, 176
userid, 139, 147
user-level controls, 25
utilization, 87

V

views of resource usage information, 143
Virtual Memory, 27, 142
Virtual Memory and Databases, 74
Virtual Memory and Swap space, 66
vxdiskadm(1M), 214
VxVM, 214

W

Web Server, 73
Web Server cgi-bin script, 73
Web Servers, 61, 155
Workload Analysis Tools, 35
Workload Based Summarization, 52
Workload Configuration, 145
Workload Consolidation, 65
workload definition, 4
Workload View of Resource Usage, 143
wrapper, 251
wrapper script, 139

X

xterm session, 266

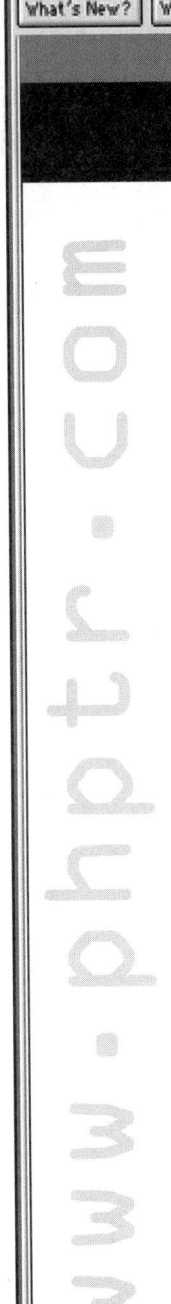

PRENTICE HALL
Professional Technical Reference
Tomorrow's Solutions for Today's Professionals.

Keep Up-to-Date with
PH PTR Online!

We strive to stay on the cutting-edge of what's happening in professional computer science and engineering. Here's a bit of what you'll find when you stop by **www.phptr.com**:

- **@ Special interest areas** offering our latest books, book series, software, features of the month, related links and other useful information to help you get the job done.

- **Deals, deals, deals!** Come to our promotions section for the latest bargains offered to you exclusively from our retailers.

- **Need to find a bookstore?** Chances are, there's a bookseller near you that carries a broad selection of PTR titles. Locate a Magnet bookstore near you at www.phptr.com.

- **What's New at PH PTR?** We don't just publish books for the professional community, we're a part of it. Check out our convention schedule, join an author chat, get the latest reviews and press releases on topics of interest to you.

- **Subscribe Today!** **Join PH PTR's monthly email newsletter!**

    Want to be kept up-to-date on your area of interest? Choose a targeted category on our website, and we'll keep you informed of the latest PH PTR products, author events, reviews and conferences in your interest area.

    Visit our mailroom to subscribe today! **http://www.phptr.com/mail_lists**